T0040401

Books by Mick Foley

FOLEY IS GOOD

HAVE A NICE DAY!

MICK FOLEY'S CHRISTMAS CHAOS

MICK FOLEY'S HALLOWEEN HIJINX

FOLEY IS GOOD

AND THE REAL WORLD IS *FAKER* THAN WRESTLING

MICK FOLEY

HARPER

An Imprint of HarperCollins*Publishers*

HARPER

An Imprint of HarperCollins*Publishers*
195 Broadway
New York, NY 10007.

First Harper paperback printing: December 2007
First HarperTorch paperback printing: June 2002
First HarperCollins hardcover printing: May 2001

11

For Colette, my wife and best friend.
Your love has made these pages possible.

Contents

Introduction

THROUGHOUT THE PAGES OF THIS BOOK, I frequently mention a screenplay I wrote based on *Have a Nice Day!*, my towering *New York Times* number one bestseller. I wrote the screenplay in just over two days, feverishly working with pen and notebook as the images of a new American movie classic poured forth onto the pages. Not only did I think it was good, I knew it was good. So good, in fact, that I flew to WWE headquarters to meet with WWE head honcho Vince McMahon to ask him to consider making the film a WWE project. Unfortunately, my screenplay was still being typed up at the time of our meeting but I convinced Vince of its greatness and he seemed genuinely interested.

A few weeks later, I received my masterpiece in its typed form. I resisted the urge to devour it instantly and instead went to bed comforted with the knowledge that it would be there waiting for me in the morning. Indeed it was, and I cradled that screenplay like it was a newborn pup until I was comfortably seated on Delta flight number 1212 from Pensacola to Atlanta, which would then connect with Delta flight number 1999 to Los Angeles. I had a long day of flying ahead of me and was looking forward to every minute of it. Why? Because I had a friend with me. A friend that would catapult my life story onto the big screen where it belonged. A friend that would soon entertain millions of theatergoers.

A friend that would make me rich. As the plane departed Pensacola, I began to read.

After twenty minutes, I was confronted with an uncomfortable realization. *Wow, this really isn't very good.* I put the screenplay down for a while and con-

sidered the possibility that maybe the early wake-up time that the early morning flight required had left my brain incapable of absorbing my witty dialogue and hard-hitting action sequences.

So I waited until the Los Angeles leg to read some more, at which time I was forced to consider the possibility that my dialogue wasn't all that witty and that my action sequences didn't hit all that hard. I was forced to consider the possibility that I hadn't written a new American movie classic, and forced to admit that as a screenwriter, I more or less sucked. I had boarded that plane in Pensacola looking forward to spending time with my friend. Now I find myself hating him.

That afternoon in Los Angeles, Jamie, one of the writers for that evening's *Raw* television show, asked me about the script. Jamie had written several scripts, and so I had been enthusiastically talking shop with him during the weeks in which my screenplay was being typed. "Well, Jamie, it's not quite as good as I thought it was," I felt forced to admit. "As a matter of fact, it sucks." Jamie's reaction caught me completely by surprise.

"Mick, you've got a gift that most writers will never have—the ability to be objective about your own work."

"Really?" Wow, I had a gift.

"Yeah, Mick, I'm telling you, most writers are convinced that everything they write is great. You're miles ahead of them."

"So what you're saying is that it takes a good writer to know their writing sucks?"

"Exactly."

A few weeks later, on a trip to Southeast Asia, I began writing *Foley Is Good*. I had planned on learning how to use a computer for this task and had actually gone so far as to buy one a month before leaving. Unfortunately, I had not gone so far as to actually open it, let alone learn to use it, so as I departed for Asia, it was with two notebooks, and a collection of Pilot fine-point precise rollerball pens to keep me company.

Seven weeks and 129,000 words later, I had a book (or, more accurately, about 600 pages of barely legible notebook paper) in my hands. While the typing process was underway I began working on an additional section, which is my thoroughly researched answer to an often reckless media's criticism of the world of sports entertainment. These 30,000 words took me an additional seven months to complete and I sincerely hope that it will shed some much-needed light on the proverbial "other side of the story."

During the course of corrections, editing and rewriting, I have read *Foley Is Good* many times. And guess what . . . I like it . . . I really like it. Equally as important, I had a tremendous time writing it, and look forward to future literary endeavors.

I guess it is inevitable that people will compare this book to *Have a Nice Day!* I'm sure many will favor the first book because it has more pages, wrestling, foul language, and blood. A whole lot more blood. I think others (including me) will like this one better, partially because it has less pages, wrestling, foul language, and blood. A whole lot less blood. As for how this book will fare, critically and financially, I can't really say with any degree of certainty.

There is one thing I can say, however, with a great deal of certainty. This book does not suck. If it did, I would know. It's a gift I have.

Sincerely,
Mick Foley
THE HOTEL HERSHEY
HERSHEY, PENNSYLVANIA
FEBRUARY 20, 2001

1: *Night of the Champion*

THE WORCESTER FANS were on their feet, and I was on the shoulders of D-Generation X as they paraded me around the ring. Several pictures later showed the members of DX smiling broadly, and I know that the smiles were too bright to not be real. Much like the early Dude, Mankind—or more accurately, Mick Foley—had made the people feel good about themselves. A chant of "Foley, Foley," began, but unlike my traumatic night at *King of the Ring*, these chants were loud and growing louder. I was let down from the shoulders of the DX and grabbed the house mike. I first addressed Vince, who was yelling and fussing his way offstage, although secretly I suspect he was beaming. I then got down on my knees and spoke from my heart.

"At the risk of not sounding cool," I began, "I want to dedicate this belt to my two little people at home, Dewey and Noelle—Daddy-O did it!"

I know, I know, that's how *Rocky II* started, with the end of the first *Rocky* being shown over again. But hey, *Rocky* is my favorite movie of all time, and I even wrote a screenplay for *Have a Nice Day!* that borrows a couple of lines from *Rocky II*, so why not "borrow" the start of my sequel from it as well. Just for the record, I never liked the title *Have a Nice Day!*—I always wanted *Blood and Sweatsocks*. So if my life story makes it onto the big screen, or even goes straight to video or the History Channel, then by golly, *Blood and Sweatsocks* it's going to be. Unless of course they pay me a lot of money. Then they can call it *The Adventures of a Fat Guy in Tights Pretending to Fight* for all I care.

I had always tried to downplay the importance of the World Wrestling Entertainment title in my career. That is, of course, until I won it. Then it became the most important thing in the world—besides my family and the log flume at Santa's Village. I was definitely feeling good when I got to the backstage area. Handshakes and hugs all around, except for Rodney of the Mean Street Posse, who I refused to let touch me. Actually, Rodney hadn't even started with the World Wrestling Entertainment yet, but I need someone new to pick on in this book, and I have a feeling that the Posse is going to take the brunt of it. Now, don't get the feeling that I'm tired of blasting Al Snow, because I'm not—it's just that all my jokes about him somehow ended up actually helping his career, and I don't ever want to be responsible for something like that again.

A team of psychologists recently determined that up to 28 percent of all children under the age of twelve suffer from some type of attention deficit disorder, or ADD. They also determined that during an Al Snow match, that percentage can jump to as high as 90. Yess! Yess! All right, I lied—of course I'm going to tear Al a new Snow in this book. I just won't do it as often.

Actually, I traveled with Al back to Boston after the match—in a full stretch limo, no less. When I walked into Worcester that afternoon, I had no idea that I was going to leave as the champ, and during the day I had agreed to do a personal appearance in Everett, Massachusetts, as a replacement for Kane. The money wasn't good, but the owner of the store, Phil Castinetti, was a friend of mine, so I said, "What the hell." This guy Phil knew everybody; a few days ago I went to Yankee Stadium with him (my first game there in twelve years), and through his connections, ended up having my picture taken with Mayor Giuliani and eating hot dogs in Yankee owner George Steinbrenner's office. No, George wasn't present at the time, but yes, I did pretend to be George Costanza while I was there.

As much as I liked Phil, I still contemplated holding him up for more money once I won the belt, but

in the end, I realized that a deal is a deal and did it for the original amount. Besides, what could be better than a long dark limo, soft snow flurries on a crisp winter's eve, and the company of Al Snow and the Blue Meanie. Wait a second, did I just say "the company of the Blue Meanie"? With bright blue hair and a belly that made my abs look like Jack La Lanne's, the Meanie was quite a character in the ring. He also had a ring outfit of tight "Daisy Duke" shorts, and a half shirt that exposed stretch marks that, when viewed sideways, looked like a road map of upstate New York. (The Meanie has since lost over a hundred pounds and looks a lot better than me.)

The soft flurries turned into a blizzard, the one-hour trip to Boston turned into three, and by the time we finally rolled into our Holiday Inn, I was more than ready for my post-big-match ritual of a big fattening meal and a Pay-Per-View movie. The meal, which Phil had arranged to have picked up, was supplied courtesy of Kowloon's Chinese Restaurant, and I was just about to dig in when I realized that a frosty beverage had not been provided with my feast. So it was on my way to the soda machine that I saw him. The Meanie, looking forlorn in the lobby of the hotel. "Meanie, what's the matter?" I asked the rotund grappler. (Actually "rotund grappler" is one of the ways, along with "pear-shaped brawler," that the National Enquirer once described me, but for some reason I like the term better when it's applied to someone else.) The Meanie looked up at me with a sad expression in his eyes. "They don't have any more rooms," he said. Ooh, this was a tough decision for me. On one hand, the rotund grappler looked miserable in the lobby. On the other hand, I had just won the World Wrestling Entertainment title and was really looking forward to my solitary ritual. "What time is your flight?" I asked. "Eight o'clock," came the sad reply. Damn! If he had said "six," I could have justified leaving him there under my "don't ever get a room if you're going to be there less than four hours" rule. This was too long to sit in a lobby. Yeah, I deserved to be rewarded, but I couldn't leave the poor guy hanging. "Wanna stay with me?" I mumbled with the same enthusiasm I usually reserve for "let me pay for your dinner."

So it came to pass that I marked my championship night with about seven pounds of Chinese food and the Blue Meanie in my bed.

2: *I Hate That Guy*

"DADDY WON THE BELT! Daddy won the belt!"
At the end of 1998, the World Wrestling Entertainment had television tapings on Monday and Tuesday every other week. On Mondays, they taped matches for various shows until 9 P.M. Eastern, at which time *Raw Is War*, the company's flagship show, aired live. The following week's *Raw* would be taped on Tuesday, to be aired at nine, six days later. So when I came home from Boston, I hid the belt and didn't tell my children, Dewey and Noelle, about winning the title. When they saw it, they went crazy. "Let me see, let me see," they yelled, and then my wife Colette and I proceeded to shoot an entire roll of film as the kids posed, cut promos (interviews), and ran all over with the belt around their tiny waists. Dewey even fell asleep with it on while I read him a bedtime story.

For anyone who didn't read the first book and has picked this one up only because it is tearing up the bestseller charts, I'll answer your question, or at least confirm your thoughts for you. Yes, wrestling is entertainment, and no, I didn't actually "win" the belt in the way that World Series or Super Bowls are won. Instead, the World Wrestling Entertainment title, which is without question the premier title in the business, is more like winning an Academy Award. Usually, it is given to the wrestler that the company thinks can "carry the ball" for them, in terms of drawing crowds in arenas and buy rates on Pay-Per-View. In my case, the belt was more like a lifetime achievement award. I knew I probably wouldn't have it long, but I was sure going to enjoy it while it lasted.

Later that evening, I tuned in to the show of our competition, *World Championship Wrestling*, which I had worked for from 1991 to 1994. They had a Monday night show named *Nitro* that they ran in direct competition to ours, which they also rebroadcast a few hours later. I wanted to watch the program, because it was thought to be pivotal in the Monday night ratings wars, which had been raging since September of 1995, when *Nitro* made its debut opposite *Raw*. In all fairness to WCW, they had been able to capture the public's imagination with a hot angle in July of 1996, and had at one point won the ratings battle for eighty-three straight weeks. With the genius of World Wrestling Entertainment owner Vince McMahon, creative writing of our show, superior production values, the solidification of "Stone Cold" Steve Austin as a media sensation, the emergence of new stars such as The Rock, and the continued evolution of mainstays such as the Undertaker and myself, the World Wrestling Entertainment had forged ahead—but the race was close.

WCW felt that they had momentum on their side. On their previous night's Pay-Per-View, Kevin Nash had ended rookie phenomenon Bill Goldberg's long win streak, and a rematch was set for the next evening's *Nitro*. In addition, Hulk Hogan, who spearheaded the wrestling resurgence in the 1980s and was still a big drawing card, was making a much-publicized return on *Nitro*. Furthermore, whereas our program was taped six days earlier in the relatively small Worcester Centrum, WCW was coming live from the immense Georgia Dome in their home city of Atlanta. So it was with great interest that I tuned in to *Nitro* on January 4, 1999.

Actually my interest wasn't that great, because their show at that point was getting difficult to watch, and they kept going back to a ridiculous scenario that had Bill Goldberg arrested for stalking one of the WCW ladies. After about the fourth poorly executed Goldberg vignette, I turned to my newspaper, until the unlikely mention of my name on the WCW show jolted my attention back to the screen. The words that spewed forth from announcer Tony Schiavone's mouth simultaneously shocked, hurt, and angered me. "We've been informed," Schiavone began, "that Mick Foley, who used to wrestle here in WCW as Cactus Jack, and now wrestles as Mankind, is going to win the World Wrestling Entertainment title tonight on their program, which is a taped show." I couldn't believe it. Then Schiavone continued with the biggest insult of my career, when he sarcastically said, "Wow, now that's gonna put a lot of asses in the seats."

I was so hot that I immediately wanted to call and blister him on his answering machine. Instead, I decided to wait. I watched in disgust as he made several other insulting comments about me during their show, and then tried to go to sleep while I hoped that the Nielsen ratings would vindicate me.

The next afternoon, I called the World Wrestling Entertainment offices and not only did my anger and pain disappear—they were replaced with an unbelievable rush of joy . . . and a thirst for vengeance. The ratings showed that almost 100,000 households switched over to the World Wrestling Entertainment show IMMEDIATELY following Schiavone's comment. IMMEDIATELY! So, not only did their company come across like scumbags for insulting someone whom the fans held in some measure of respect, but they also cost themselves a hell of a lot of viewers.

The World Wrestling Entertainment continued to gain viewers throughout their program, and on a night that many felt would turn the tide back to WCW—we ended up blowing them away. WCW did win the five-minute time period following my title victory, which was actually even worse news for them. It meant that people were, in fact, interested in their title rematch, but had been driven away by their own announcer's foolish remarks.

So now, with the ratings on my side, I decided to give Mr. Schiavone a call. I had known Tony for quite a while and had always gotten along with him, and even though I didn't think he was in Jim Ross's league, I always respected him as an announcer. During my time in WCW, I had physically sacrificed a great deal, always put the company's interests ahead of my own, and had been about as productive as a person can be when he is constantly having the rug pulled out from under him by some of the WCW people who are more concerned with retaining their top spots with the company than making that company successful. Deep down, I sensed that Tony's words were not derived from feelings of his own, but were probably ordered upon him by one of his superiors.

I got Tony's answering machine and resisted the urge to yell. Instead, I very calmly said, "Tony, this is Mick Foley, and I just wanted to say that I heard your comments and they made me sick. Why you would insult someone who worked so hard for your company is beyond me. I have a feeling that the words you were saying weren't your own; but either way, I felt that it was low class and uncalled for, and in truth, it just caused more people to watch our show." Then I left my number and hung up.

A few hours later the phone rang. Colette came to me and said, "Mick, it's Tony Schiavone—he sounds so sad." "Hello, Tony, this is Cactus." When Tony spoke, he did indeed sound sad. As I had thought, the feelings were not his own, but had been forced on him by his superior. Right, Eric? Schiavone's words not only haunted him that night, but for weeks, months, and even years after. Signs started popping up in every arena we went to that disproved WCW's theory. MICK FOLEY PUT MY ASS IN THIS SEAT.

I hate Bill Goldberg. Yeah, I said it. I don't know him, but I hate him. I've heard nice things about him, but I hate him. This isn't blind hate, however; it's deserved for one very good reason.

I was with my family at Santa's Village in New Hampshire in the summer of 1999. I am an amusement park junkie, and as a card-carrying member of American Coaster Enthusiasts, there is nothing I like better than high-powered thrill rides. Except big rides mean lots of teenagers, which means I get besieged by wrestling fans all day long. Which is why I prefer smaller parks like Santa's Village. People still recognize me, but it's a family atmosphere, so they are much more polite about it. On this June afternoon, I was watching Dewey and Noelle on Santa's Red Hot Racers water ride, when a man tapped me on the shoulder. "Hey, aren't you Mankind?" he asked. I told him I was. "We're big Goldberg fans," the man informed me. He then spoke to his son, who appeared to be about six years old. "Joey, show him your Goldberg imitation." I really wanted to see my kids on the ride, but I squatted down anyway so I could see what this little tyke had up his sleeve. *Boom.* The kid punched me in the nose. Now, I don't care how tough you are, or even if you are a hardcore legend like myself. When a six-year-old punches you in the nose—it hurts. I expected the adults to reprimand him just a little, but instead they gave him hugs and said things like "attaboy" and "you showed him, Joey." Man, I hate Goldberg.

3: *I Quit*

EVEN THOUGH I WAS THE CHAMPION, I felt like I knew my role in the company. Steve Austin was the number one good guy in the World Wrestling Entertainment, and The Rock was the number one heel. The two of them needed to be separated until *WrestleMania*—the World Wrestling Entertainment's premier event. That's where I came in. While Austin was tied up with the Undertaker, I would occupy The Rock's time. As a matter of professional pride, I considered it my duty to do more than just occupy his time—I wanted to "get him ready" for Austin. I considered one of my strengths as a performer to be getting my opponent "over," or in The Rock's case, even further over, as the guy was already receiving a tremendous reaction from the crowd. His level of reaction was so strong and he was so entertaining that it was hard to keep him a heel. The Rock was a third-generation star, and his combination of movie-star looks, Herculean physique, and interactive promos made him hard to boo. I felt like the people needed to hate him, and I felt that he needed to show a genuine mean streak. In a decision that would create more turmoil and controversy than anything I have ever done, I suggested an "I Quit" match to Vince McMahon.

The idea behind an "I Quit" match is really very simple—two guys beat the hell out of each other until one yells the two magic words. It is a tremendous premise, and when done properly, as Terry Funk and Ric Flair did it in 1989, the intensity can be incredible. When done improperly, it is embarrassing. One such match ended when the referee asked a wrestler if he quit, and when he replied, "No, you quit it," the match was over. I guess that was the "*You* Quit" match. Even worse was the time that the referee asked Buddy Landell, "Do you quit?" in the Smoky Mountains territory in 1995. When Landell said yes, the match was over. Landell then protested the decision by claiming he thought the referee asked if he thought he was handsome. Pretty pathetic. Actually, it's pretty much par for the course when you consider wrestling's past history of "country whippin' " matches where no one got whipped, a hair-vs.-hair match between a guy with a crew cut and a guy who was bald, hardcore matches featuring Rodney, and retirement matches where no one retires. I'll get back to that last one later.

I wanted this to be a real "I Quit" match. I wanted there to be a definite winner and a definite loser, and I wanted the fans to see a side of The Rock that they could truly despise. I also wanted to explore the devastating effects, not so much physical, but mental, that such a match would have on a guy who had built his reputation and career on never giving up. Even as the loser of this proposed match, I had no doubt that, if it was done right, I could eventually emerge from the scenario more over with the crowd than ever.

The story line I proposed would be heart-wrenching. I would be bludgeoned, I would be helpless, and my wife would be watching from the front row. To be helpless, I would need to be handcuffed. I had come up with this idea years earlier, and used to get major adrenaline rushes while I roared down the highway at 4 A.M. thinking of my emotional scenario. If I happened to have the *Bruce Springsteen Live* cassette, forget about it. I would play "Candy's Room" a dozen times and get goose bumps over and over while the scene ran through my head. I had actually used the handcuff trick in Philadelphia-based Extreme Championship Wrestling three years earlier while facing my old DeNucci School of Wrestling friend Shane Douglas, but that one had never gone that extra emotional mile. To go that mile, I would need Colette.

"Are you sure that you would be willing to do this?" Vince asked. I was sure. "Vince, if we can make the fans actually feel the dilemma I'm going through, it will be the heaviest angle we've ever done." I then told him how I thought it should go, starting slow, and then culminating with a series of chairshots to my unprotected skull. Vince became very concerned. Ever since the infamous "Hell in a Cell" match in June of 1998, which had left me with a concussion, one and a half missing teeth, a dislocated jaw, fourteen stitches in my mouth, a dislocated shoulder, and a bruised kidney, Vince had forced me to take it a little easier. He voiced his objections to the idea, but I was insistent. "Vince, he only has to use the chair a few times. The anticipation of what he's going to do will be much worse than the actual shots. I mean Rock can take two minutes in between each shot. When that camera shows Colette crying, and then cuts back to me watching her cry, the fans will be begging me to quit. We can build up the drama so that the damage seems much worse than it actually is." I think the part about not doing too much actual damage sold him on the idea, and I had the match I had been dreaming about for years.

"I want to go too, Dad." "Me too, big Daddy-O." My kids wanted no part of being left out of a trip to California, which is where the 1999 *Royal Rumble* would take place. I told the kids that it would just be a few days, but there's something about Noelle's prolonged, five-year-old *"pweease, puhweeze"* that was almost impossible to say no to. So I said what all take-charge dads say: "Let me talk to your mother."

"Colette, maybe they can come but not watch the match," I said. She knew the kids would never buy it. If Colette had any idea how bad things were going to turn out, she never would have said her next words. "Mick, the kids have grown up with you getting hurt. You said it wouldn't be that many chairshots, right? So why not let them watch?" I sat both kids down and had one of my serious father-son-daughter talks. "Dew, Noelle, if you go to this match, it will look like Daddy's going to be hurt. Will you get scared?" They both vehemently denied that there would be any fear. "Now, you know that The Rock is Daddy's friend?" They nodded. "And The Rock would never really hurt Daddy, right?" Again they nodded while Noelle chimed in, "I want to go so bad, Dad. You have no idea how bad."

I thought it over. I had been involved in some extremely intense matches over the past year, and my body had been screaming for a break. After the *Rumble* match, I was going to "disappear" for a few weeks, during which time the announcers would speculate about my physical and mental well-being. I intended to spend a lot of time with the kids, and their wanting to be at the match caused an idea to flash into my mind. "Kids, if you go to California, after the match would you like to go to Disneyland?"

For some reason, that postmatch Disney vacation comforted me whenever I thought of my kids watching their dad get beat up. Every day I would talk to them about the match, either at home or on the phone, and every time they would assure me that they wouldn't be scared. "And where are we going to go after the match?" I would ask. "Disney!" they would yell. "And it's gonna beee?" "Great." I wish it had been.

I somehow was able to convince Vince that my children would be fine and then approached him about another subject. "Vince, I'm going to be coming to California as the champ, and leaving as an ex-champ, and it would really mean a lot to me if my family could fly first class." Vince didn't even think about it. "Mick, I would love to fly your family first class." Hey, this was going to be great—first-class treatment, a few weeks off, a Disney vacation. At least that's what I thought.

At this point in my career, I had been wrestling for fourteen years. I had been flying in first class for two weeks. I never asked to be flown in first—I just one day saw an *F* on my ticket. I didn't know what the hell it meant. At first I thought it was a mistake, but those *F*s just kept coming. Kind of like my friend Scott Darragh's college transcript.

A call from head writer Vince Russo two weeks before the *Rumble* threw a wrench into the works. "Mick, we're going to put a match on during half-time of the Super Bowl, and we want you to be in it." Bye-bye, vacation; bye-bye, Disney. I couldn't do this to the kids. I had once taken them to Disney World in Florida on a Jewish holiday, and the place had been so crowded that we left after forty-five minutes. Even now, four years later, I can still hear them crying in my mind. I wasn't going to let them down again. I decided that I would simply take them out of school for a few days and go to Disney before the show. Unfortunately, I had lost the important advantage of being able to walk up after the match and say, "We're going to Disney!" Almost like one of those commercials. "Mick Foley, you've just had the crap beaten out of you in front of your children. You've terrified them, and they'll grow up to be serial killers—what are you going to do now?" "I'm going to Disneyland!" I tried putting myself in my kids' shoes. If my dad had walked up to me when I was five and said, "Okay, I'm going to get the crap beaten out of me and then we'll go to Disney for four days—do you want to do it?" I would have screamed, "Hell, yeah!" But if he'd said, "Okay, kids, we're going to go to Disney for four days, but then you have to watch me get the crap beaten out of me," I'm not sure I would have taken the deal.

Barry Blaustein then called, and my life would never be the same. Barry was a well-known screen-writer who had been instrumental in the early success of Eddie Murphy on *Saturday Night Live*. Indeed, many of Eddie's best-known bits had been written by Barry, including "The Shooting of Buckwheat," "Mr. Robinson's Neighborhood," "Gumby," and "James Brown's Hot Tub Party." After *SNL*, Barry had written several successful movies, including the Murphy hits *Coming to America*, *The Nutty Professor*, and its sequel, *The Klumps*.

Barry had been a wrestling fan since childhood, a fact that he'd been hiding for several years, as, until recently, a love for wrestling was something that was better left unsaid. I guess in Hollywood until recently wrestling fans adopted Bill Clinton's "don't ask, don't tell" policy. But Barry loved wrestling, and even more, he was intrigued by the actual guys behind the characters. Because of his success with Universal Pictures, he had been able to get the studio to finance his idea for a documentary on the lives of professional wrestlers. That was in 1994. I met him in 1995 when I was in Las Vegas for an independent show. I heard a knock on my hotel door, and when I opened it I saw a man named Barry Bloom. With Bloom was another man, who was introduced as Blaustein. I had met Bloom when I worked for WCW, when he was Jesse Ventura's agent. (Hey, I try not to drop names too often, but when I do, I make sure it's a good one.) Blaustein explained that he was going to be making a documentary and asked if I would be interested in participating.

At the time Barry was considering me for the "former-star-now-wrestling-in-small-towns" role. As fate would have it, Vince McMahon, the benevolent genius, plucked me out of small buildings and Japanese "death" matches and made me a "World

Wrestling Entertainment Superstar." Personally, I hate the term "superstar," but that is our given moniker. I mean that the term is inclusive of all World Wrestling Entertainment wrestlers. So, technically, Al Snow is a "superstar." Somehow it doesn't seem right. This term was responsible for one great moment on an airplane, when after a short conversation with me, the flight attendant got on the public-address system and cheerfully stated, "Ladies and gentlemen, American Airlines would like to welcome *all* of the World Wrestling Entertainment Superstars . . . and Al Snow." Al refused to admit that I had scored a verbal knockout by proxy, but did admit that watching me laugh until tears came out of my eyes was somewhat amusing.

The World Wrestling Entertainment had agreed to give Barry access to all of the guys, and as a result, I was used to his camera being around sporadically. I had told him earlier that I had reason to believe I would be leaving California without the belt, and when he found out my kids were coming, he decided to be at the show with his crew. I told him I was planning something memorable, but didn't go into details. I had no idea just how memorable it would be.

When I left for Los Angeles—in first F'n class—I actually had the fear that the camera would show my kids in the audience, and they wouldn't look concerned at all about their dear old dad. Worse yet, I feared they would be laughing. In retrospect, I wish they had been.

We had a great time at Disneyland, which the kids decided they loved even more than Disney World, but even as they were yelling "let's go again" after a ride on Space Mountain, I couldn't shake the feeling that the *Royal Rumble* was a big mistake.

The night before the *Rumble*, I received a call from Vince Russo at approximately eleven o'clock. "Cactus, we've got to change the finish," Russo said, using the name that I had used for the first eleven years of my career. I was hot. "Change the finish! Why?" Well, it turned out that Vince had just come from a meeting of the Television Critics Association at which the head of USA (the network that, at the time, aired *Raw*) had taken a lot of heat for the controversial content of the show. He told his detractors that he had no problem with the content, and in fact, he was taking his nine-year-old son to sit ringside. "Mick, if we do that finish, we're going to bury the guy after he went to bat for us." Russo had a point, but, damn, this could have been brought up to me a little earlier. "Vince," I said, "if we don't do the finish, I'll be the one who gets buried." Russo quickly offered an alternative. "What if you take a big bump, and Colette pleads with you to quit—that would make sense." Yeah, it would make sense if I wanted my wife to receive hate mail and have my kids beat up at school. "We can't do that," I told Russo. "Everyone remembers the 'Hell in a Cell'— they saw what I went through. If I take a bump that can't even come close to those two, and then quit because my wife asks me to, the fans will fart on it. I don't know who would be the bigger heel—Colette for whining, or me for listening to her."

On and on it went, until I told him I would try to think of a Plan B, which I eventually did. As far as Plan Bs went, this one was pretty good, and in retro-

spect, with the way things got carried away, it's a good thing that my children weren't on television.

I found it hard to sleep, as I often do the night before a big match. Dewey and Noelle woke up early, and I took them back over to the park for a few prematch rides. Then on to the building. When I got to the Arrowhead Pond venue, Barry's crew was already there. The camera stayed on me most of the day. I don't know if it was the camera, or the pressure of the match, but I had never been as nervous as I was that night. To make things worse, I had two other problems to contend with. First, I had a cut on my head from a previous match that hadn't healed yet, and was afraid it was going to open at any time. Instead of going to an emergency room after that match for a quick three or four stitches, I opted to try the macho wrestling method of gluing the cut together. Mr. Gargulia, my old elementary school art teacher would have failed me for sure if he'd seen my botched art/first-aid project.

Compounding my problems was a meaningless television match with 450-pound wrestler Viscera that was designed to let The Rock get heat on me before we went to the Pay-Per-View. Actually, we had done a wonderful job of promoting the match, and The Rock had plenty of heat already. Instead of trying to have a good match, I spent most of my time hoping I wouldn't bleed during this fiasco.

When I got back through the curtain, it was time for Colette and the kids to take their seats. Colette looked beautiful, Dewey looked so gosh-darn handsome, and Noelle looked like a precious little present in her little red dress. The Rock came over and spoke to the kids before they went outside. He asked them all about Disney and assured them that he would never do anything to hurt their dad. Even with things getting out of hand later that night, what The Rock ended up hurting most was my feelings.

The Rock and I had great chemistry inside the ring. On this night, we didn't talk much about what we were going to do, but decided to improvise most of it. We did decide on the number of chairshots that would be given—five—and that the last one, the knockout blow, would be to the back of the head.

I stretched out and tried to get rid of the strange feeling that something was wrong. Then Rock's music played, and I knew I had about a minute until showtime. I feel like I vaguely know how a death-row inmate feels when his number is finally called. Sometimes, I can't wait to get through that curtain, but on this particular night, I was hoping that his ring music would go on forever.

Then I heard the shrieking of brakes, the shatter of glass, and a catchy three-chord guitar riff. My time was at hand. I crossed myself for safety and stepped through the curtain. I didn't feel much like the World Wrestling Entertainment champion, and after seeing the tape, I don't think I looked much like one either. Instead I looked like someone pretending to be the World Wrestling Entertainment champion. I walked by the ring and I saw Noelle. I leaned over and gently kissed her on the cheek. I looked for my little buddy, but couldn't see him—maybe he was hiding behind Colette. Then I stepped into the ring, and moments later the bell rang.

It's strange. Without the aid of a videotape, I remember almost nothing about the first half of the match, and almost everything about the last. After about ten minutes of intense back-and-forth action, highlighted by good microphone work, where we each attempted to make the other say the magic words, we headed up the aisle. There was a ladder lying on the ground by the back of the arena, so I put it to use by slamming Rock on top of it. I attempted to drop an elbow on him, but he moved out of harm's way, and the sound of my body hitting the steel elicited a groan from the crowd.

Rock then took the ladder, after admonishing me that "only The Rock can drop a true People's Elbow," and propped it up against the wall so that the top of the apparatus reached the next level of the audience. Once the ladder was in place, he began to climb. I should point out now that the People's Elbow is one of The Rock's patented moves, and is possibly the most foolish thing seen in any form of entertainment. He doesn't like when I say that, but actually it's a compliment. With Rock halfway up the "People's Ladder," I began to give chase.

I was looking for the illusion of Rock luring me up the ladder, and then knocking me off, but we probably overdid it by fighting in the crowd for several seconds before I took the big punch that knocked me off the balcony and onto a set of lighting equipment a legitimate eight to ten feet below. I say "legitimate" because wrestling does have a tendency to exaggerate heights a little bit. We've all heard it. "He was just thrown fifteen feet off of that ramp," and then the EMTs run in to help and their heads come within inches of the ramp. So either these EMTs are fourteen and a half feet tall or someone's stretching the truth a little. But this fall really was a long way and it hurt for a long time. Upon impact, sparks flew out of the system, which then tipped over on me (which also hurt), and half the houselights in the building went off. To answer the doubters who automatically assumed that the speakers were gimmicked, here's the truth: lighting equipment, real; sparks and blackout, gimmicked. In any event, it was a cool effect, and the *ooh*ing and *aah*ing went on for several seconds.

This was where Russo had suggested that Colette come out and call the whole thing off, at which point The Rock would no longer have been the company's top heel—my wife would have been. Instead, we took the opportunity to show off The Rock's new mean streak.

Shane McMahon (the boss's son and an excellent talent in his own right) came out, and as one of the leaders of The Rock's heel faction, "the Corporation," actually told Rock to end the beating. "Come on, Rock, he's done, that's enough," Shane said, to which The Rock reacted violently. "He's not done, not until he says the words." (Author's Note: I don't know the exact words. I'm sitting in my hotel in Jakarta, Indonesia, and don't have access to a tape. Don't worry, though, with the exception of the quotes, everything else is burned into my memory.) With that, The Rock picked me up, and we began a long stumble/beating/walk up the aisle and into the ring.

I sincerely believe that professional wrestling is at its best when the performers lose their own sense of disbelief and begin to actually "feel it." In a sense, the match becomes real, or at least real in that they actually "become" their character, and actually "feel" what the story line is attempting to make the audience feel. As I took the beating up the aisle, I lost that sense of disbelief and began to actually "feel" that I was the wounded Mankind, so beat-up that I could hardly stand. Now, if you're Robert De Niro on the set of *Raging Bull* and you "feel" like Jake LaMotta, it's probably a positive. If you're Mick Foley, and you're about to be handcuffed and bludgeoned in front of your children, it's probably not.

The Rock rolled me into the ring, and while I was down and "feeling it," produced a pair of handcuffs. The audience began to understand. While I was on my belly, The Rock cuffed my wrists behind my back and began to taunt me. "Come on, say it, or The Rock's gonna kick your fat ass." He put the mike in front of my mouth. "Up yours." *Boom*— The Rock sent me down with a punch. Somehow I managed to make a comeback while handcuffed, and even managed to drop a headbutt on the "People's Jewels." But while I was recuperating, The Rock got to his feet and met me with a devastating clothesline when I got to mine. Upon impact, I could feel my jaw dislocate.

A jaw that dislocates easily has always been one of my Achilles' heels. I trace the origin of this to the second match of my career, when the Dynamite Kid tore a ligament in my jaw with a clubbing clothesline to the point of my chin. In theory, these clotheslines are supposed to be delivered just under the neck, but in practice, well, sometimes the aim is a little off. I used to ice the jaw for days and wait for the swelling to go down. In the last few years, I have relied on the unique skills of Frenchman François Petit, to move it back into place with a "Meek, Meek, I can fix it . . ." *snap!*

As I lay on the ground, I heard a definite *ooh* of anticipation from the crowd. Rock had the chair. He rolled me onto my back and placed the chair over my face. I instinctively turned my head to the side so that the coming impact wouldn't damage my nose or teeth. Rock signaled for the People's Elbow, and when he landed, and the steel of the chair smashed into my skull, the move certainly didn't feel all that silly. Upon viewing *Beyond the Mat*, I could see my family scream at this impact. I wish I could say that my mind was on them at this point, but I was thinking only of the match, and the first of the five chairshots to my head which I knew was coming next.

Slowly I got to my feet, with my back to The Rock, who had the chair high overhead. I knew that I wouldn't go down on the first one because in my entire career one shot had very rarely been enough to do the trick. I turned to face him, and *crash*, I was wrong. I went down to my knees. The shot had legitimately knocked me down, and it had hurt worse than any chairshot that I had ever taken. I hadn't taken into account how the cuffs would alter my body's ability to give with the blow and thereby cushion the impact. Every chairshot hurts, but this one had been extraordinary. I resigned myself to the fact that I would have to take four more and comforted myself with the knowledge that I had about a minute of Rock's mike work and taunting before having to take another one.

Crash! I was wrong. That one minute had suddenly shrunk to about three seconds, and the impact had been violent. The blow knocked me off my knees and onto the ground, but I was up quickly and begging for more.

Over the past eighteen months I have tried many times to rationalize my behavior after this and I'm still not sure how to do it. The best I have come up with is that by not allowing me time to recuperate, and by legitimately hurting me, The Rock had triggered a great deal of anger within me. That anger, combined with my lost sense of disbelief in the match, caused me to become defiant, and with my children among the 20,000 in attendance at the Arrowhead Pond in Anaheim, California, I looked The Rock in the eye and dared him to knock me down.

Boom. The first one was hard, but I shrugged it off and dared him to give me another. *Boom.* He was up to it, and I wasn't quite as feisty, but still on my feet. *Crash!* The third one was perhaps the hardest shot I've ever received, and sent me straight down on my back. It also not only opened the cut that I had

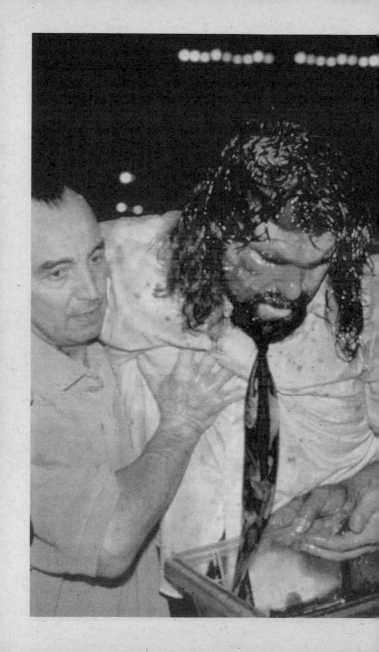

suffered days earlier, but tripled it in length and depth. As I lay there, I felt the blood start to flow. At this point both Colette and the kids were devastated. Noelle had her head buried in Colette's shoulder, and Dewey's crying was causing him to shake. Once again, I wish I could say that my mind was on them, but I was oblivious to everything but the match. It would be five months before I saw Barry's footage of my family. The impact the video had on me made those chairshots seem weak in comparison.

Five shots. That's all it was supposed to be. Five had already been given, but I was still in the ring and not up the aisle, where the finish was supposed to transpire so as not to make the head of the USA Network look bad. It would take six more to get me up the aisle as my children screamed and the blood poured down my face. My theory of "the anticipation being worse than the actual shots" had been trampled—the shots were much worse than the anticipation. In reality, the shots came quickly, with a minimum of buildup and mike work between them. After eight shots, I turned my back to The Rock and began stumbling up the aisle. This was my nonverbal cue for The Rock to hit me in the back of the head, "knock me out," and end this massacre. By this point my defiance was gone, as was my sense of disbelief. I knew exactly what was going on. I was in a match that had gotten carried away—I was suffering a great deal—and I wanted it to end. Unfortunately, The Rock didn't pick up on my nonverbal cue, as he ran a circle around me and smashed me another time on the top of the head. On the bright side, it seemed that my goal of showing his mean streak was being achieved.

After another shot, I turned my back again and started stumbling up the aisle. This time The Rock was right on the money and caught me with a crushing blow to the back of the head for the "knockout." Then, with Mankind lying still and on his stomach, The Rock again demanded the word, and when the microphone was placed in the general vicinity of Mankind's mouth, a loud "I Quit! I Quit! I Quit!" resounded throughout the arena. Plan B had gone into effect. I was knocked out, and then, as was revealed the following night on *Raw*, Shane played a tape of me promising to make The Rock yell out "I Quit! I Quit! I Quit!" Of course the part about The Rock was left out, and a great percentage of people left the arena that night thinking the impossible: *Mankind had quit*. As I mentioned earlier, it wasn't bad for a backup plan, but in the end, it was still a rip-off.

I was disoriented from the blows and had to be helped to the back, but once I was there, my focus returned to where it should have been all along. "Where are my kids?" I was pointed to them, and as I reached them, the other wrestlers saw me and gave me a standing ovation. "I'm okay, I'm okay," I assured Colette, although I probably should have been asking them if they were okay as well. In my own defense, I must say that they all looked okay, and I had no idea that they had been that upset, until I saw the footage months later. Colette had taken them away from the ring after the fifth shot, and they had calmed down greatly over the next several minutes.

"Are you okay?" Noelle asked me sweetly as we walked to the dressing room, where I had been told

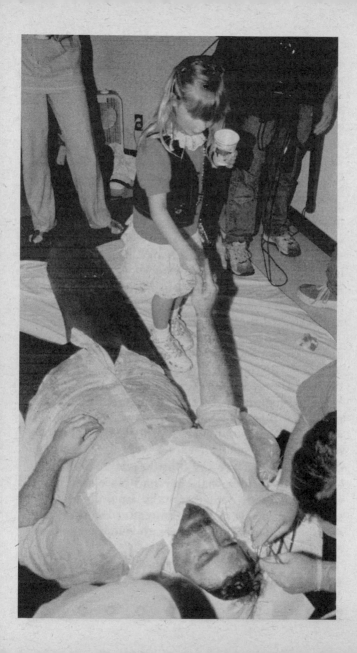

a doctor was waiting. "It's just a little boo-boo," I assured her, before adding, "You can't hurt Daddy." Noelle surveyed the bloody situation before offering her medical opinion, which turned out to be right on the money. "Daddy, that looks like a big boo-boo." It surely was. I looked in the mirror and was not met with the same small gash I had tried to repair. This thing was a four-inch gully in the hairline of the right side of my head. Sadly, I turned, and lay down on the floor to be tended to, while Barry's camera captured the whole gruesome scenario. I guess most children don't have the opportunity to watch their dad get stitched, after getting the opportunity to see him get the crap beaten out of him. At this point the Disney trade-off probably didn't seem like such a great deal.

Dewey stayed very quiet while Noelle made another astute observation as she watched the doctor wrap gauze around my stitched-up head. "Daddy looks kind of cute," she said sweetly, to which Colette agreed. I agreed as well. "Daddy *is* cute . . . in a rugged type of way." Noelle then told me she wanted to wrestle me, to which I said, "Sure, honey, you and Daddy will wrestle when I get home next week." Apparently one week was too long to wait for my tiny angel, as she yelled, "I want to wrestle you right now!" With those few words, she made me feel so much better, for, until viewing the film, I really didn't feel all that bad about what I had done to them. Then it was Dewey's turn to speak up and ease my mind. "Dad, can I go watch the end of the *Rumble*?"

I had many visitors while I lay in that room, all of them asking how I was. Billy Gunn, who I usually shared only a joking relationship with, was very kind, as was Darren Drozdov, who offered up this sentiment: "You are the fucking man." Droz was paralyzed in a match ten months later and remains in a wheelchair. Whenever I think of him, I think of that visit to the dressing room.

When I left the arena, I was troubled by the fact that one wrestler had not come in and checked on me. This would bother me for a long time, and in truth it is something that I have still not forgotten, nor entirely forgiven. Of all the visitors who came into that room, The Rock was not among them.

4: *The Violent Truth*

I CAME UP WITH A tremendous scenario for a rematch. I pride myself on being creative, but when I came up with this bad boy, I knew that I had set new standards for myself. Okay, here it is.

The Rock, fresh from his "I Quit" victory, would find himself somehow unsatisfied with the brutal California skull crushing. No, he would want more—he would want my death. But instead of doing the deed himself, he would send an assistant or a flunky to do his dirty work. Someone like Al Snow. I knew that Al would take great pleasure in killing me, even if it was a fictional scenario. But The Rock wouldn't be satisfied with just a simple death. No, he would want the act to be brutal and he would want a souvenir; like, say, maybe . . . a body part. Yeah, that's it—Al Snow would cut out part of my body and bring it back to The Rock.

There was one thing The Rock wouldn't count on, however. Either through a hidden warm spot in his own heart, or the hope that I would one day maybe team up with him and drag his career out of the toilet, Al Snow would not be able to turn the trick. Instead, he would stooge off The Rock's despicable plan and urge me to flee.

I would then break into a small house and sleep there until the inhabitants came back. Even though I had criminally broken into their home, I would force these innocent people, who suffered from such afflictions as narcolepsy and mental retardation, to completely change their way of life to fit my standards of what was acceptable. If they could not do this, I would not allow them to eat.

Meanwhile, The Rock, having learned of Al's failure, and having punished Al by making him wrestle in poorly received opening matches (or pretty much letting him resume his normal duties), would swear revenge. The Rock would take matters into his own hands by finding the house that I had broken into and killing me.

What The Rock wouldn't count on, however, was my newfound dysfunctional family. Spurred on by love, this group of weirdos would hunt The Rock down and brutally murder him by pushing him off the edge of a cliff.

As I mentioned, however, this group was a little strange, and they wouldn't be content to just bury me and let me rest in peace. No, these people would realize that they had a former World Wrestling Entertainment champion and a *New York Times* number one bestselling author on their hands, and they would put me on display. That's right, this band of bearded bastards would put the hardcore legend on display so they could ogle his twisted physique and one-eared cranium.

Yeah, these guys would be sick, but not as sick as the pampered, pretty-boy necrophiliac who would plant a big kiss on my corpulent corpse before carrying me away, to make me his love slave.

I came up with this idea on a Friday morning and immediately called Vince at World Wrestling Entertainment headquarters. "Vince is in a meeting," I was told. I understood that Vince was the owner of a billion-dollar company, but I also knew that I held in my hand (I had written the idea down and had it copyrighted) the key to making the World Wrestling Entertainment a *multi*billion-dollar company—it was that good. "Tell Vince it's important," I told the woman on the other line. She was back moments later. "Vince said to call back tomorrow."

Tomorrow? Tomorrow? Call back tomorrow? Isn't that what the Emerald City guard told Dorothy in *The Wizard of Oz*? There was a big difference. I wasn't asking him for anything. I didn't need a brain. No, dammit, I was already a number one bestselling author. I didn't need courage either, because I had that too, only nobody refers to it as courage anymore—it's called "testicular fortitude"—and if there's any word that accurately describes what my testicles are full of, it's "fortitude." Hell, the World Wrestling Entertainment even had a special "testicular fortitude" T-shirt made for me, even if I did feel a little foolish wearing it. A heart? No, I had one of those too. And Kansas? No, I didn't need to go there either. I'd already been, and to tell you the truth, with the exception of Harley Race's barbecues, it was kind of boring. (Readers of the first book will fondly recall Harley as the gruff but lovable wrestling legend who never got to bust open my eyebrow.) No, I wasn't asking Vince for a gift. I was giving him one. "Tell Vince that I'm getting on a plane and coming to Stamford," I yelled at the lady. "And tell him I'm pissed."

I stormed into Vince's office seven hours later and

threw my masterwork on his desk. Vince is a man of principle, and doesn't enjoy being bullied. He looked at me with contempt in his eyes and spoke. "I'm a man of principle," he said, "and I don't enjoy being bullied." He may have been my boss, and he may, with exception of the "big gulp of fear," have the best facial expressions in wrestling, but I wasn't about to be deterred. The company, I knew, was planning on going public, and I knew that after reading it, Vince would want this baby on his asset sheet to lure potential investors.

Vince looked it over as I waited for the big smile and bear hug that I knew would be coming my way. Instead, his face contorted in disgust, as if he'd just swallowed sour milk or watched a *Nitro* broadcast. He looked up at me, and noticing the excitement in my eyes, his expression changed to one of sympathy. Slowly, he broke the news. "Mick, I can tell you worked very hard on this, but as the owner of the World Wrestling Entertainment, I cannot, in good conscience, allow your idea to air in any way, shape, or form." I was crushed. After all, Vince had a reputation as a genius, and it was a reputation that, with the exception of the Harvey Wippleman vs. Miss Kitty "Snowbunny" match and the decision to allow Howard Finkel to be seen on national television in his underwear, I felt was deserved. "Vince," I moaned, sensing that my quest for creative nirvana was slipping away faster than spectators to the popcorn stand during a Posse match, "why not?"

Despite his on-air persona as a bigmouthed jerk, Vince can actually be quite a gentleman, and sensing that I was about to cry like a thirteen-year-old at a *Titanic* screening, he broke the news as gently as he could. "Mick, to tell you the truth, despite my reputation for pushing the envelope, I find the whole thing morally reprehensible." Man, it was hard to get happy after that one, especially when Vince continued: "Mick, what you've come up with does sound moderately entertaining, but your story has vile and morbid elements, including, but not limited to, contract killing, murder, sexual harassment, breaking and entering, trespassing, necrophilia, and making fun of the handicapped."

I was devastated, but after reflecting on it, I realized that Vince was right. Still, I wanted to make one last dying grasp. "What if we soften the story, put the idea through animation, and market it to families," I said, hoping that Vince would see the logic in such an idea. Instead, he looked at me as if I was an idiot. "Mick, Walt Disney did something like that over sixty years ago, and called it *Snow White and the Seven Dwarfs*!"

All right, so maybe that conversation never actually took place, but I'm trying to make a point. Wrestling is under a microscope by everyone from the PTC (Parents Television Council) to Muslim leaders I just spoke to in Singapore for being too violent. No need for a microscope, guys—just open up your eyes and look around you. Violence is everywhere. Wrestling is, and always has been, a mirror of the times we live in, and to my eyes at least, it's a fairly innocent reflection. From the "evil" Germans of Karl Von Hess and Fritz Von Erich, to "evil" Russians like Ivan Koloff and Nikolai Volkoff, to Iranian villains like the Iron Shiek, to Iraqi sympathizers like Sgt. Slaughter, wrestling has always been a simplified and somewhat inaccurate "textbook" of modern history. Then again, my text-books in school were simplified and somewhat inac-curate versions of modern history—where else can you learn about the four-hundred-year-long institu-tion of slavery in one easy paragraph?

These days, with no clear-cut bad guys (Kosovo and Rwanda wouldn't sell any tickets anyway) and with some special-interest group crying out over every little stereotype, wrestling has had no other alternative than to create its own bad guys, who the fans, in turn, then love, giving rise to the antihero, such as "Stone Cold" Steve Austin.

But, hey, once again, we're just mirroring society and, in doing so, giving fans what they want. Look at Hollywood—it's filled with heroes that, decades ago, fans would have found offensive. Although the body counts may be on the rise in hit films, it's not as if violence hasn't always been a staple of the view-ing diet. I mean, let's look at some typical family favorites and see what innocent and educational atrocities lie within.

(Keep in mind that the stories I write of are the traditional stories, and not the better-known film versions.)

The Little Mermaid—amputation of tongue, suicide, impaling.

Jack and the Beanstalk—trespassing, robbery, canni-balism, murder by fall from Beanstalk.

Hansel and Gretel—child abuse, child abandon-ment, destruction of property, imprisonment, starva-tion, attempted cannibalism, murder by oven.

The Wizard of Oz—decapitation, chopping off of both arms and both legs (read the book), kidnapping, imprisonment, attempted murder, death by falling house, contract killing, murder by melting.

Sleeping Beauty—rape, adultery, attempted cannibalism.

Little Red Riding Hood—attempted double homicide by eating, murder by drowning.

The Emperor's New Clothes—full male nudity.

Yes, I made a big mistake by letting my kids sit in the front row at the *Royal Rumble*, and I have had a hard time dealing with my decision. But I know that as an avid "read me a story" dad, I often have to substitute the words "sleep" or "hurt" for "die" or "kill," and find a lot of classic children's books, including fairy tales by the Brothers Grimm, to be a little, well, grim.

Last night, in Kuala Lumpur, Malaysia (which is the coolest name of a major city I've ever heard of, even if its literal translation is "city of mud"), I watched the family classic *Seven Brides for Seven Brothers*. Without exaggeration, I was mortified, and not just because Howard Keel and his six brothers broke into song at the drop of a hat. No, I got that way by watching the lovesick brothers get their seven brides by riding into town and kidnapping them while leaving a trail of the girls' beaten boyfriends behind. Then they took off for their mountain home while physically restraining the screaming women. And guess what? The girls all fell for the brothers, and they all lived happily ever after. These days, if you even try to compliment a woman on the beauty and fantasy-inducing properties of her breasts, you'd be slapped with a lawsuit faster than a Vanilla Ice CD flying into the discount bin at Kmart. But these guys not only got the girls—they got a G rating.

Hey, I don't mind violence in the cinema. Some of our greatest movies have also been among the bloodiest. *Saving Private Ryan* is an example. It's a great story, but without the graphic depiction of the Normandy Invasion, it's just not the same. *Platoon* was an Oscar winner, and I had to close my eyes when the American GI played by Kevin Dillon caved in a Vietnamese boy's skull with the butt of his gun. The graphic decapitations in *Gladiator*, the slow-motion brutality of Sam Peckinpah's classic westerns, the blood-streaked face of Dallas Page in *Ready to Rumble*—well, maybe that example was a little off, but you get the idea.

Robert De Niro is probably my favorite actor of all time—next to John C. Reilly, of course. *Rocky* is my all-time favorite movie, but it's hard for me to give Sly Stallone my favorite-actor nod when he's got *Stop! or My Mom Will Shoot* on his résumé. Of course, De Niro didn't do himself any favors with his *Adventures of Rocky & Bullwinkle* turn, but that's beside the point. De Niro's collaborations with director Martin Scorsese in films such as *Taxi Driver*, *Raging Bull*, and *Goodfellas* are widely regarded as tremendous movies, as well as being among my personal favorites. Another De Niro film, *The Deer Hunter*, won an Academy Award for Best Picture in 1978. All of the films were extremely violent and all were filled with language that makes our World Wrestling Entertainment television offerings look like *Barney and Friends*.

I didn't happen to pack a Webster's dictionary on my trip to Southeast Asia, but I believe that true violence has to include a connotation of bad intentions. In wrestling, we now readily admit that the fate of the match is predetermined, the action is often choreographed, and the participants are, for the most part, friends. (Why is it that when we portrayed wrestling as "real," critics called it fake, and now that it is more accurately portrayed as "sports-entertainment," our critics deem it "too violent"?) There are no bad intentions in wrestling—with the possible exception of pushing Billy Gunn as a singles star, the intentions of which probably weren't all that good.

In this respect, we are far less violent than other popular forms of sports-entertainment, which, realistically speaking, all sports are. I mean, as soon as the basic rules of a contest are changed to make the game more enjoyable to watch, it becomes "entertainment." Holler if you hear me, "three-point shot" and "mid-thigh-to-belly-button strike zone."

I recently saw a baseball game where Roger Clemens "beaned" Mike Piazza. For those not familiar with the term "beaned," it means he hit him in the head with a ninety-six-mile-per-hour fastball possibly on purpose. Clemens said no, but Piazza disagreed, as did a lot of other people. But wait, let's not be too hard on Clemens, because, after all, this is a time-honored and accepted tradition—throwing hard objects at people's heads in front of impressionable kids. Besides, I hear that Clemens is a big Foley fan, and I might be able to get good seats to a game

sometime. The next inning, the Mets pitcher hit a Yankee batter with another ninety-something heater, in the somewhat less dangerous area of the spine, and guess what—no one was surprised. In fact, it was expected, even looked forward to. "Oh, the next Yankee up is definitely going to get it" was a common comment heard in between the innings. Okay, let's get this straight. If I were to hit an unsuspecting person with a hard object thrown at high velocity, I would fully expect to be arrested and possibly even sentenced to prison. Do it in front of 60,000, while millions watch on television, however, and my goodness, you're talking about our national pastime.

Speaking of time-honored baseball traditions that could use a little rethinking, don't you think it's about time we took the baseball managers out of their uniforms? For crying out loud, for the most part, you're talking about thick-waisted, middle-aged men, who are wearing ridiculously tight uniforms that were obviously meant for young men to wear. Wait, am I talking about baseball managers or WCW main eventers here? Think about the ramifications if this curious tradition were to carry over to other sports. Phil Jackson's white, hairy, skinny legs while reading *Zen and the Art of Motorcycle Maintenance*. Bill Parcells calling the shots from the sidelines with a set of shoulder pads and a helmet on, while hoping that his jersey hides his expanding gut so he doesn't lose his Slim-Fast deal. Angelo Dundee cheering on his latest boxing protégé with a pair of satin trunks pulled up to within a whisper of his nipples. Or how about a wrestling manager with a gaudy pair of sunglasses, a tacky jacket, and a cane, or a tennis racket . . . oops, we do that already, don't we?

Hockey? Now, there's a good one. What other sport encourages groups of kids, who actually like each other, to fight for real so as to emulate their heroes. I will never forget an episode of street hockey that took place in 1977 between Chris Anderson and Chuck Cheeseman. In the same way that the *Christmas Story* fight between young Ralphie and the bullying Scott Farcus came to be known as "The Farcus Affair," this episode still lasts in my mind as "The Cheeseman Incident." Even though I wasn't officially a part of Anderson's neighborhood, my ability to walk up a big hill and then through a hundred-yard section of woods to get to his house made me a neighbor by proxy. We played a game of street hockey on our home (or Anderson's home) street against the visiting Cheeseman's band of thugs. Actually, all of these guys were my friends, which made Martin Moeckler's reading of the rules even more auspicious. "Okay, here are the rules. We play three fifteen-minute periods." (He had an actual alarm clock in his hand.) "The clock stops during a fight." Hold on a second. This might sound strange coming from a guy with 325 stitches in his body, but I found the whole concept of friends planning on fighting to be more ridiculous than a Joey Abs title shot. And I said so. "What do you mean, fight? Why are we going to fight?" They looked at me as if I had two heads. "Yeah," Bobby Christman said, "when we start fighting, we stop the clock."

This was actually my first official street hockey "game," even though I'd been playing around in the street with my "flow-through" stick since jumping on the Islanders' Stanley Cup–winning bandwagon a few months earlier. Still, I was hoping for some sense of reason here, and as we lined up for the face-off, I approached Christman for a little friendly reassurance. "Bob, these fights don't happen very often, do they?" I asked hopefully. "Sure they do," Bob said. "Every game."

Sure enough, at about three minutes in, or when Mickey Mouse's arms were at the seven and the two, the official street-hockey alarm clock had reason to stop.

After being scolded about a rough body check (which, for the record, I have no problem with), Anderson told the Cheester, "Stop acting like a pussy." Cheeseman walked away. Until, that is, Scott Burgoine appealed to his sense of manhood, or at least to his twelve-year-old boyhood, and said, "Chuck, did you hear that? Anderson called you a pussy." It didn't matter that Burgoine was wrong. Technically "acting like" a pussy and "being" a pussy are two different things. In the heat of a meaningless street-hockey game played by kids who'd just begun to sprout hairs on their sacks, this fact was overlooked. Down went the gloves, off went the clock, and on went the fight.

I don't remember who won the fight, or who else got involved, or even who won the game, but I do remember thinking it was the stupidest thing I'd ever seen. Until of course I got to Memphis in 1988, where my willingness to throw myself onto concrete floors for $25 a night just may have eclipsed the "Cheeseman Incident" on the stupid scale.

I do know, however, that it was the last time I played an organized game of street hockey that involved an official fight clock, and that it was a long time before I watched a game of ice hockey on television again.

Now, I know that hockey is a phenomenally popular sport, and that it is, when played properly, a wonderful game played by tremendous athletes. In fact, I had high hopes when I took Colette and the kids to see a Pensacola Ice Pilots game near our home in the Florida panhandle. Instead, I saw a potpourri of dirty tactics, including the stick between the legs, a check to the testes that even one of our World Wrestling Entertainment referees wouldn't have allowed, and three honest-to-goodness fights. To further enhance my viewing pleasure, the team mascot spent most of the game singling me out by giving me big fake elbows in the crowd. Unlike wrestling, I couldn't tell my kids that these guys were "just playing" or that they were all friends who would hug each other afterward—especially when Dewey and Noelle met the players afterward and saw their bruises and cuts. The Ice Pilots wanted to talk to me about "Hell in a Cell" and I wanted to find out why such a great sport had to be ruined by such bush-league stuff. Their answer was sad. "We're encouraged to fight," one bruised player, who will probably never have Janet Jones for a wife or his own fictional doughnut shop, told me. "If we don't fight, attendance will drop, and the league might fold."

Hey, guys, if the fights are part of the job, let me give you a few words of advice. Fix the damn things! Start using Asiatic thrusts to the throat and a Three Stooges eye rake or two. Who knows, throw in something like a People's Elbow and you might start selling out the place. It works for us.

Lacrosse has tried to take a page out of hockey's book. I played lacrosse for five years, as a surprisingly quick-reflexed goalie who specialized in wearing a bull's-eye on his balls and combat boots on the field and eating worms to "psych out" opponents before games. At least that's what my reputation was. In reality, I wore the bull's-eye during one camper-vs.-staff game at lacrosse camp, wore combat boots one time when I forgot my cleats, and ate one worm during warm-ups at junior-varsity football practice. But you know how reputations are.

In my five years as a lacrosse player, I saw exactly two fights. Years later I saw a thirty-second commercial for a professional indoor lacrosse league. During those thirty seconds, I saw three. And, I'll tell you, there's nothing like watching Ivy League graduates fight to make you appreciate a Pete Gas match. Being that my high school alma mater, Ward Melville, is something of a lacrosse factory, I've known quite a few of these professionals, and they too admit that they are encouraged by the league to fight to ensure the league's existence. And these fights are real too; they just look like they're fake. But I understand their plight, and I get a tear in my eye when I think of those poor players, who would have to slave away at their real jobs as doctors and lawyers should the league fold.

I used to read a lot of "autobiographies" of football stars when I was a kid, and many of the players "wrote" of their propensity for knocking people unconscious—hell, most of them bragged about it. In his book, *They Call Me Assassin*, Jack Tatum, who is best known as the man who paralyzed New England patriot Darryl Stingley, even talked about the rush he received after nearly decapitating an opponent. Of course, knowing now what I've learned about ghostwriters and their permission to use "creative license" on quotes and facts, I'll give the "Assassin" the benefit of the doubt, and hope he never actually felt that way.

In fifteen years as a professional wrestler, I've been knocked legitimately unconscious once—in the June 1998 "Hell in a Cell." My opponent in that match, the Undertaker, didn't feel a rush when it happened, he felt only concern. I've knocked out a few guys as well, and likewise felt no pride in doing so—only an emptiness in my gut as I waited for them to regain consciousness.

The 1985 quarterback sack of Joe Theismann by Lawrence Taylor on *Monday Night Football*, which resulted in a compound fracture of Theismann's leg and the subsequent end of his career, may have been the most nauseating moment in professional sports

history. Granted, it was accidental, and Taylor's immediate reaction to the sack was to plead for help when he heard Theismann's leg crack like the sound of my hand on Al Snow's buttocks. It wasn't cool to watch either. I mean, I doubt that teenage computer geeks who have never touched a female breast were watching that incident over and over on their VCR, like they do now with my first trip off the aforementioned cell. The Theismann incident did, however, offer me an opportunity to compensate for many years of frustration suffered at the hands of ignorant borderline wrestling fans—none of whom I imagine are reading this book.

I saw Joe Theismann on the National Car Rental courtesy van in November 1997 in Charlotte, North Carolina. It turned out he knew who I was, but at the time was keeping his excitement well hidden. I respected Joe for his notable football career, expert commentary on the game, but most of all, for having nailed Cathy Lee Crosby for many years. I decided to break the ice. "Excuse me, Mr. Theismann," I began, thinking of some of the morons who had approached me over the years, "you didn't REALLY break your leg in '85, did you?" Joe laughed a genuine Harvey Korman watching Tim Conway on *The Carol Burnett Show* laugh, and then shared stories about Cathy Lee with me that kept me awake for a week. Not really, but he did do that Harvey Korman thing.

Boxing—now, there's a great one. Not only do boxers try to turn their opponents' brains into unflavored gelatin, they then immediately thank God for having the ability to do so.

A year ago I had to tell a father that I could no longer let his two sons train at the small gym I own when I found out that the boys were actually eleven, and not fourteen, as their dad had told me. The father was very upset, because the boys, he informed me, were boxers, and needed to train so they "could have that one-punch knockout power." All of a sudden I felt so guilty; after all, who was I to deny these kids access to equipment that would help them knock other eleven-year-old boys unconscious?

What about the riots, death, and mayhem in a soccer game? Oh, I'm sorry, we're talking about the sports themselves and not the spectators.

Professional wrestling is a very physical form of entertainment. We entertain fans around the world by presenting a reasonable facsimile of a real fight while adding athletic elements that could not plausibly happen in the real world. Have you ever seen a "reversal of an Irish whip" in a real fight? Or in the Olympics? How about a moonsault or a Hurricanrana? Or the worm? Highly unlikely. We do however, as seen in the "I Quit" match, use chairs, and the chairs do hurt, and I do believe that a scaling down on the number of head shots would be advisable. Shots to the back? Go ahead—they're part of what makes the business fun, and only hurt a minute anyway.

Yeah, shots to the head with a steel chair hurt, unless of course you use the popular "fake chair" that many fans know so much about. Personally, I don't know where to find one, and if such a thing is a reality, I wish someone would have told me a long time ago. I don't, however, see wrestlers using chairs for purposes other than sitting leading to the decay of Western civilization. I've never turned on the news and heard Dan Rather say, "Four men were killed in a failed robbery attempt this afternoon. The assailants, all armed with folding chairs . . ." I don't see militant extremists walking out of "chair shows" with enough steel to overthrow a small country. And as far as I know, there is no such thing as a drive-by chairing in the 'hood, even if the East Coast/West Coast rapper rivalry was rumored to have been kicked off by a chairshot delivered on the Vegas strip following a Butterbean bout.

I just recalled an interview I did several years ago that was deemed "too graphic" even for ECW television. Because it never aired, this, or my recollection of it, is being revealed for the first time. Keep in mind that this interview is being shot in extreme close-up fashion—with only my pained facial expression on the television screen of your imagination.

You used to be mine, didn't you? Mine and mine alone. I could use you, and that was fine, because no one else could. Now when I lie awake in bed, with you in my arms, I do so with the knowledge that you've been held by other men. Used by them. Four or five in a single night. And I've had to watch it all, you cheap whore, and pretend to like it when I see you go up and down, up and down, again and again, on their swollen throbbing heads. And you expect me not to care. When Tommy Dreamer spreads your legs and lowers himself on top of you for the whole dressing room to see? Well, I do care, because I love you, and I always will, and I will always return to the one I love.

Now zoom the camera out to reveal me cradling a steel chair, which I will then passionately make out with until the camera in your mind fades out or until your erection goes away, you little pervert!

Not bad, huh? Maybe now that I've conquered the *New York Times* bestseller list, I will attempt that last bastion of true creative writing—letters to *Penthouse*.

5: *Backyard Wrestling*

WRESTLING HAS ALSO COME under fire recently for the proliferation of backyard wrestling leagues. This hits especially close to home for me, for indeed it was the leap off Danny Zucker's roof in my terrible home movie *The Loved One* that helped get my foot in the door to professional wrestling.

For anyone who thinks that diving off a roof or any similar action is going to get them noticed— forget it. When I did it, it was something new, and all it really did was put me in a position where I could drive a couple hundred miles to drag thousands of pounds of steel and wood out of an eight-story storage space in Brooklyn, load it into an elevator, unload it into a truck, drive the truck, set up the ring, work security, sell hot dogs, take the ring down, drive it back to Brooklyn, unload it into an elevator, then load it back into storage before driving another couple hundred miles back to school. Yes, my roof dive did help me get my start, but its importance, much like stories of my sexual prowess, has been exaggerated. The real keys to my success came from driving 800 miles round-trip to Dominic DeNucci's wrestling school in Pittsburgh every weekend for a year and a half. It came from sleeping in the backseat of my '78 Ford Fairmont on many of those trips, and from a steady diet of peanut-butter-and-jelly sandwiches to save money. It also came from proper teaching, an emphasis on the basics, and a respect for my fellow wrestlers' bodies; not on wild, reckless moves, done without any appreciation for what truly is dangerous, just so some moron holding a camcorder can yell out "Oh my God" while he watches his two buddies risk permanent paralysis.

A few years ago fans started bringing signs to the arenas that proclaimed FOLEY IS GOD. On one hand, I appreciate the sentiment, but as I have always maintained, there should be an extra O in there to state FOLEY IS GOOD, which would be a whole lot more accurate. But let's just for a second assume that I am God, and that all backyard wrestlers must do my bidding. Here are my Ten Commandments of backyard wrestling:

1. Thou shalt not use moves that can compress the vertebrae. I trust the Undertaker more than anybody I have ever been in the ring with, but I was legitimately scared *every* single time I was upside down for a tombstone piledriver. The repercussions of this move, as well as a regular piledriver, a pedigree, a brainbuster, a DDT, a double-arm DDT, a snowplow, a German suplex, a regular suplex, a backdrop, a body slam, a powerbomb, and many others, when done improperly, could be devastating or even fatal. Don't do them.

2. Thou shalt not hit each other with chairs. Please hold on to those brain cells. The real

world is a competitive place—you'll need every one of them.

3. Thou shalt not jump off roofs, or any other surface higher than Mini-me's pelvis. And if you feel like you have to, for God's sake, and for mine (in this case they are the same), don't leave your buddy on the ground to absorb your awkward ass impact.

4. Thou shalt not use fire as a prop. I may not have volunteered this information in the lawsuit I was just a defendant in, but there have been a whole lot of people burned badly while using fire in a pro wrestling match. Terry Funk, Abdullah the Butcher, the Sheik, Wing Kanemoura, and I have all been burned while doing such a thing. I saw a nineteen-year-old girl get burned in Yokohama, Japan, while wearing a spandex singlet. The heat of the flame melted the fabric right onto her skin, and if it had not been for the quick action of the referee, who used his own body to put her out, she might have been engulfed by the flame. I saw her on the stretcher as she was whisked by me backstage. Sometimes I can still hear her screams in my mind.

5. Thou shalt not use extreme props such as barbed wire, thumbtacks, beds of nails, cheese graters, lightbulbs, and a variety of household objects never meant to be used as weapons by teenage boys. It's stupid.

6. Thou shalt not purposely cut thine own self with the intent to draw blood. This act is questionable when done in front of huge crowds.

It was dumb when I did it for $25 in front of seventy-eight people in Evansville, Indiana, in the fall of '88. It is downright asinine when done in your mom and dad's backyard. Hey, I'm the hardcore legend, and in my backyard matches, I used a mixture of food coloring and corn syrup poured out of a Jif jar.

7. Thou shalt not throw real punches or kicks. There is a way to throw real punches and kicks and be somewhat safe about it. Until you attend a respectable wrestling school, forget about learning it. Instead, throw ridiculous punches, or do what pro wrestlers who never can learn the art do—use Asiatic thrusts, and tell your buddy to pretend it hurts.

8. Thou shalt not use the *F* word in wrestling-style interviews, or let your camcorder-holder announcer use it in his commentary. With apologies to Diamond Dallas Page, there are only three situations where I find the *F* word acceptable or enjoyable to use or hear: in traffic, in the bedroom, or on a telecast of *The Sopranos*.

9. Thou shalt not ruin your parents' backyard. It seems that every backyard wrestling tape I'm given (and I am given a lot, being the guru of sorts for these guys) involves "Cactus Jaque" or "Rock Hard Rick Austin" laying waste to Mom's prizewinning petunias or Dad's fence. Next time, guys, tape the ass-kicking that your dad gives you when he gets home—it will be more entertaining.

10. Thou shalt not (and this one could possibly be the most important of all) under absolutely any circumstances, when attempting to imitate your World Wrestling Entertainment heroes, pretend to be Test.

I have spoken. If you really want to be a pro wrestler, there are ways to go about it. I understand that with the phenomenal popularity of the World Wrestling Entertainment there are probably more kids dreaming about main eventing at *WrestleMania* than are dreaming about playing in the Super Bowl, and I happen to think that dream is a great one. If you are intent on getting involved in the world of sports-entertainment, I wish you luck. It can be the greatest job in the world, as well as the most frustrating. This isn't God talking anymore, just Mick, and here are a few helpful hints in your quest.

1. Participate in amateur wrestling. A higher and higher percentage of wrestlers being groomed by the World Wrestling Entertainment, WCW, and ECW have extensive amateur backgrounds. You might not become an Olympic champion like Kurt Angle, but you learn discipline, get in shape, and find out a hell of a lot about being a man.

2. Stay out of trouble. There are enough boneheads in the world without you adding to the list. Wrestling has enough problems with "holier than thou, I know what's best for everyone else" groups, without giving them something or somebody to pinpoint.

3. Go to college. Don't just go there—stay there. Graduate from there. Get an education. The odds of making it in wrestling are low and the odds of getting hurt along the way are high. I don't feel bad for broken-down wrestlers. I do feel bad for broken-down uneducated ones. I started going to DeNucci's school while I was a junior in college, but did so after Dominic laid down his one law: "Stay in school, or I won't train you."

4. Be realistic. There are thousands of wrestlers out there and about a hundred who make a good living doing it. The odds don't favor you, especially with Olympic champions, ultimate fighters, and professional football players as your competition. I'm not saying that wrestling in a high school gym or an armory can't be fun or rewarding. It is. It's just not profitable. Search the wrestling magazines for stories on reputable wrestling schools. Anybody can take three grand from you to teach you a couple of moves. Stay away from them. Look for schools with a proven track record for turning out quality guys. Study tapes of wrestlers who are good. Have fun, but be safe.

ABC's *20/20* ran a story on backyard wrestling a couple of years ago. While preparing for the piece, they found that a majority of these teenagers listed me as an influence, so *20/20* decided to interview me. I showed up at the Nassau Coliseum, hours early, for a *Raw* show, and only minutes after Vince McMahon had finished a very tense and confrontational interview of his own with correspondent Deborah Roberts for the same program, I was pulled into a private room by Jim Ross, where an attorney and a very angry Vince urgently waited to speak to me. Vince spoke first. "They blindsided us, Mick," he said. "The questions weren't fair, and if you don't want to talk to them, you don't have to. As a matter of fact, I'd be happy if you didn't." I had never seen Vince this mad, and thought about his suggestion to forget the whole thing. Then I got a rush of confidence, and a feeling that I wasn't afraid of Deborah Roberts or her questions, even if her husband *was* Al Roker. I told Vince I wanted to do it, and he replied that he trusted my judgment.

The attorney then spoke up. "Mick, in a worst-case scenario, we're afraid they're going to show you a tape of a paralyzed boy who says that you were his inspiration." I felt a chill in my blood, and in all honesty, felt that I needed a secret weapon. I had one in my bag. Slowly I left that office and went down the hall and into the same dressing room that Bubbles (as in "the Nets would have troubles if it wasn't for Bubbles") Hawkins had changed in when I was a kid. Off went the "Job Squad" shirt featuring the newborn giving the middle finger with the slogan ON OUR BACKS SINCE BIRTH on it. In its place was my secret weapon. Slowly, I pulled it over the head, and let the cotton fibers expand to accommodate the grotesque development of my biceps. The secret weapon was intact. The Winnie-the-Pooh/Mick Foley tag team was about to make its mainstream media debut.

I have a theory about Pooh; people will subconsciously be nicer to you if you have him on your per-

son. This theory has never been scientifically proven, but in truth, it's more about common sense than science anyway. Think about it; who could be confrontational or abusive when they see "that chubby little cub all stuffed with fluff"? Even if he and the gang at the Hundred Acre Wood are the ultimate dysfunctional family. Really, these guys would keep a team of therapists rolling in money for years. There is Rabbit, an anal-retentive rodent who once kept poor Pooh stuck halfway in his rabbit hole for four days because he was too damn selfish and concerned about his spotless home to dig him out. Then, there's Owl, a stuffy intellectual prick with a serious superiority complex. Piglet, a paranoid hypochondriac. Tigger, a hyperactive narcissist with a speech impediment. And Eeyore, a textbook example of depression, with a possible touch of homosexuality. Oh, come on, don't act so surprised—look at how he puts his tail on. The guy gets nailed in the butt in every episode. (Just Kidding.) Speaking of which, Christopher Robin always did appear to be walking a little light in those "socks pulled up to his kneecap" loafers, didn't he? Which brings us to Pooh, the poor guy. I don't fault him for his food obsession because I can relate, but after all this time you would think he would have put some pants on him. I also have to feel that deep down he must harbor some resentment toward his parents for naming him after a piece of shit. Finally, there's Roo, Kanga's boisterous little boy. I love that guy, he's adorable.

I'm not kidding about the Pooh shirt, however. I wore it on every mainstream show that I was interviewed for. Check out the A&E *Biography* on me—

you better believe I was sporting that bad boy. Needless to say, Deborah Roberts was no match for the Foley/Pooh tandem. She asked the questions very nicely, and I believe I handled them very well. Things were going very well—I even told an Al Snow joke that elicited a genuine laugh from Ms. Roberts, although it never made the show. Then came the words that I had been dreading: "We'd like you to look at a videotape and get your comments."

"Sure," I said, as cheerily as I could, while bracing myself for the worst. The tape rolled, and . . . it wasn't bad at all. With the exception of a kid being hit with a fluorescent lightbulb, the stuff was downright tame. Just a bunch of kids jumping around, dropping elbows and legs on each other. Actually, it was too tame. I'd seen what these lunatics do to each other, and if ABC was actually doing a story on the rather obscure cult of backyard wrestling (although I'm sure the coverage they gave to it ensured its growth), I was sure they had seen it too. When the minute or so was finished, Ms. Roberts spoke again. "So, Mr. Foley, having seen that footage, what do you think?" I sensed a trap. It was almost as if I was Spider-Man with love handles, and my Spidey senses were tingling.

I looked to my left and saw that the World Wrestling Entertainment had its own camera crew filming the entire interview so as not to have one of its guys misquoted. Still, I knew that news magazines had a tendency to hunt down sound bites that would "fit" into the story they planned, so I thought about my words and spoke them deliberately. "I've seen kids do things a lot worse than that," I began. "And I have a feeling that you're going to show me a tape of that next . . . aren't you?" Roberts nodded. "I wasn't so crazy about that lightbulb over the head, but other than that, that stuff looks like fun. It looks like a bunch of friends having a lot of fun together."

Ms. Roberts nodded, then spoke again. "Mr. Foley, we're now going to show you another videotape." Sure enough, she rolled the tape, and the nonsensical backyard bloodletting began. Barbed wire was featured, as was a cheese grater, and a lightbulb that caused a massive head wound. I felt like George C. Scott watching his daughter earn a buck the hard way in *Hardcore*, but before I could holler "stop the tape" she stopped the tape. "What did you think of that, Mr. Foley?" she said for the second time. This time I had to neither think about my words nor say them deliberately. I just calmly said that it was ridiculous behavior, and even made a plea for the kids to stop.

Three nights later I watched the show. The piece came on, and after a few minutes I was happy with its progress, despite the network's decision not to go with the Al Snow joke, which would have been huge and forever cemented my reputation as Sergeant Hulka to Al's John Winger. Then she said the magic words—"we'd like you to look at a videotape"— and I felt my body tense. Then the screw job went into effect. They showed a tape, all right, but it was the excessively violent tape, complete with barbed wire, cheese graters, and large head wounds. They showed my response as well, but guess what? If you said, "They showed your response to tape number one," you are correct, sir. They sure did, and not only did they show it, but through the magic of editing they erased the "I wasn't so crazy about the lightbulb over the head, but other than that," and kept the "that looks like fun" part. Yes, indeed, there I was on national television, looking like I had a brain the size of a pea, and conscience to match.

I was livid. How could they do this? Obviously, there has to be some law that prevents a huge media conglomerate like ABC from blatantly taking quotes out of context and making innocent people look like uncaring scumbags by doing so. The next day I called the World Wrestling Entertainment and voiced my concern. We had our own videotape—surely we could use it to get an apology. "Sorry," I was told, "there's nothing we can do. That is an acceptable form of reporting."

Acceptable, my ass. If you break down the word "acceptable" it literally means "able" to "accept," and that is one thing I refuse to do. I am not "able" to "accept" the fact that incorrect and misleading statements are passed off as news. I am not "able" to "accept" the reality that if it was done to me, a guy who knew to look for traps, it has undoubtedly been done many times before. And, above all else, I am not able to accept the fact that network newsmagazines (or at least *20/20*), long considered a reliable source of news gathering, are in truth faker than professional wrestling.

6: *Just Blame Vince*

PEOPLE DO GET HURT imitating professional wrestling. That is a fact. Critics of wrestling would jump at the chance to show you that. The number of people hurt is somewhat minimal, especially when the huge popularity of wrestling is considered, but you don't hear the critics offering that information. In no program that I know of has a doctor come forward to claim that there has been a proliferation of wrestling-related injuries. Certainly, if there was that kind of evidence, my friends at *20/20* would have been glad to serve it up to the public. Does the number of children suffering from wrestling-related injuries compare to that of baseball? No way. Does it compare to basketball? No. Does it even approach the number of football-related injuries, which research resoundingly shows is far and away the number one sport, year in and year out, for serious injury to its participants? Not even close. Nothing approaches football for broken bones, head and neck injury, paralysis, and even death. Hell, deaths used to be caused by sadistic coaches, who refused to give water breaks to fully uniformed, out-of-shape students, in the scorching heat of summer afternoons. Death by stupidity. High school and college wrestlers used to die while trying to "suck" weight, because until recently, there were no restrictions on the weight-sucking process.

My children are six and eight years old. I let them watch the World Wrestling Entertainment on television. Not only the Saturday and Sunday morning shows, which are edited specifically for a younger audience, but the Monday *Raw* program and Thursday's *SmackDown!* as well. *Raw* comes with a TV-14 rating, which means it may not be suitable for children under fourteen, and *SmackDown!* carries a TV-PG. I'm not sure if I would let them watch the evening shows if I weren't involved, because there are some slightly risqué moments that are a little much for little kids. (More on that later.)

My kids love to wrestle, and I let them. I have sat down with them and explained that several of the moves hurt, and that many are extremely dangerous. They have a decent understanding of the spinal cord, and which moves pose a threat to it. They know that they can never use these moves on each other or anyone else. If they do so, they know that they will not be permitted to watch the shows or wrestle anymore. Watching the two of them wrestle, complete with "uh-oh, both these guys are hurt" commentary by Dewey, is a thing of beauty. He is extremely gentle with his little sister. With the exception of an occasional bumped head or banged knee, they can wrestle without incident for hours at a time.

Granted, I have an intimate knowledge of wrestling moves, but anyone with even the most basic knowledge of the human anatomy (and this would include anyone with a ninth-grade education) can watch the program with their child and establish similar guidelines. Therein lies the problem. Many parents don't have a clue as to what their kids are watching. They are content to have them occupied. So whether it's Triple H giving Cactus Jack a pedigree, or a twelve-year-old watching porno on the Internet, many parents neither know nor care what the children are watching. That is ignorance, with a little dose of apathy thrown in as well.

In addition to ignorance, wrestling suffers from another stigma that actually is fed by ignorance: the decades-old proclamation that "it's all fake." I would like to think that most parents are responsible and intelligent enough to sit down with their kids, watch the show, and accept it for what it is. "These guys don't really hate each other, Joey, but they do some really athletic things that can be very dangerous. Please don't do them, okay?" Unfortunately, I can almost hear other parents around the world saying, "I don't know why you watch that crap anyway—don't you know it's all fake?" I can see fifteen-year-old Billy trying to correct his mom. "Mom, come and watch, they do some really cool stuff." For which Mom, who has bills to pay, a casserole in the oven, and a deadbeat ex-husband, has the final word. "Yeah, right, anybody can do that crap." So Billy has his friends come over, builds a homemade ring in his backyard, attempts a move that his mother has assured him "anybody can do," lands on his head, and his mother files a lawsuit because she needs somebody to blame. All due to ignorance. Now if Mom knows it's dangerous, and still lets Billy construct his ring and perform dangerous moves without supervision, she's no longer just ignorant—she's a lousy parent.

The *20/20* piece left a lasting impression on me. (In terms of content, not moral accountability.) These kids build some awfully elaborate rings in their parents' backyards. Don't their parents have a clue as to what the kids are doing out there? I'm sorry, but when Mom can't find the cheese grater and twelve-year-old Junior shows up at the dinner table with a forehead that looks like scabby mozzarella, it doesn't take Sherlock Holmes to realize there's a problem. Nor does it take Sherlock Holmes to know that when Dad realizes the living room is a little dark, and sixteen-year-old Peter stumbles in with a piece of glass embedded in his skull, it's definitely time for a talk.

The ring in the backyard needs to come down, kids. Find a new television show to watch. And Mom and Dad, I want you to take a walk into the bathroom together. Go ahead, Dad, put down beer number five just for a second; this is important. Good. Now walk into that room, look in the mirror, and explore the possibility that your child didn't get hurt because Vince McMahon is a bad man. He didn't get hurt because Mick Foley used a cheese grater on the Sandman in the ECW arena in 1994. Instead, open your minds up to the idea that your child quite possibly was injured because you, as parents, suck. By the way, kids, if you insist on using a cheese grater, I've got two words for you: "Fake it." Is there an optical illusion in the world that's easier to pull off than a cheese grater to the head? One guy makes an ugly face and pretends to grate—the other guy screams. Perfect. That's exactly what the pros do.

As of this writing, no one has died as a result of backyard wrestling. But with media attention actually fueling its rise in popularity, a future death is probably inevitable. What then? Should the World Wrestling Entertainment be blamed? What then? In no way do I want to *trivialize* the death of anybody, but in my opinion, pointing fingers and filing suits oversimplifies the cause. I definitely believe in accountability, and in punishment and imprisonment, when applicable. Do I believe that a murderer should be imprisoned? That's an easy one. Do I believe that a bar that serves a stumbling drunk, who subsequently takes a little girl's life in an automobile accident, is accountable? That's a little tougher, but yes, I do. And do I believe that the author of a book on how to make bombs is accountable for the death of babies killed in a terrorist explosion? You're damn right. I do. Put me on the jury, too.

But that's about the end of it. I don't believe in suing the inventor of the handgun, the maker of the whiskey that was ingested, or the guy who chopped down the tree that made the paper that the bomb book was written on. And I don't believe in suing Vince McMahon because a lot of kids happen to enjoy his show.

Really, where do people think accountability ends? Do we sue the estate of Henry Ford for an automobile accident? Do we sue Orville Wright VII for a plane crash in the Andes Mountains? And does the surviving husband of an electrocuted wife sue Marconi because the husband mistakenly knocked the radio Marconi invented into the bathtub while she was scrubbing her armpit? But, man, people like to sue Vince.

I guess when a ridiculously liberal interpretation of cause and effect is applied, some people could claim that professional wrestling has injured young people. There are others who would go further than that and say that wrestling has caused deaths. So why not just get rid of it? Okay, now it's gone and we can all sleep a lot easier tonight. But wait, why stop there? In order to be fair, we have to apply that liberal interpretation to the other sports as well.

We've already determined that football, baseball, and amateur wrestling have caused death, so they've got to go as well. Hockey too. Several young kids have been killed over the years. Not to mention the youth hockey league father who was killed recently during an ice brawl with another parent. Basketball? Do you have any idea how many people have been killed over arguments during pickup games, not to mention the tragic deaths of Hank Gathers and Reggie Lewis? Auto racing is not only dangerous to the drivers themselves, several of whom have died in recent years, but its influence has cost many more lives on the highway. It's got to go. Running is healthy, right? Not so fast. It killed Jim Fixx, who wrote *The Running Book*, so how damn healthy can it be? Gone. Golf has to be the culprit when talking about beloved golfer Payne Stewart's death. I know, golf didn't kill Payne directly, but we're talking cause and effect here, and if Payne wasn't a golfer, he wouldn't have been in that plane, and if he wasn't in that plane he'd still be alive. It's got to go. Skating? Sergei Grinkou. Can't have it anymore. Just to be safe, let's get rid of them all—even badminton. I mean, who wants their cause of death to be listed as "choked on a red-tipped cock"?

Music would be history as well, for a variety of reasons. First off, we can't have impressionable teenagers go to an Ozzy concert and take "Suicide Solution" literally. Come to think of it, let's ban all live music following the deaths of fans at a recent Pearl Jam concert. I almost forgot, we'd better make that "all music," because after all, music causes young people to take drugs, and we all know that drugs kill.

I'm a little concerned about the movies. After all, if a mother convinces her son that "anyone can do that crap" when talking about stuntmen, the kid might try to dive out of a thirteenth-story window after seeing a Jackie Chan flick. Which leaves us only live plays to enjoy, which we obviously can't because Abraham Lincoln was killed at Ford's Theatre, and we all would have been a lot better off if old Abe had stuck around.

Great. Now we'll all live a lot longer—and without a whole hell of a lot left to live for.

7: January 25, 1999: Two-Time Former Champion

"HON, PLEASE PULL OVER, I'm afraid you're going to kill us." Colette was offended, but she knew the Los Angeles traffic was too much for her. So even with nine stitches in, and eleven lumps on, my head, I piloted our rented car to the Los Angeles airport. As originally planned, I would have been starting my vacation at this point, but we now had our "something big during halftime of the Super Bowl" to tape. So I held Noelle as she slept with my flannel shirt as a blanket while Dewey played with his action figures and Colette warned me never to get hit on the head again. With a kiss, a hug, and an "I love you" for each of them, I watched them board their red-eye flight, where I hoped that the first-class seats would allow them to rest, and put what was one of our worst nights as a family behind us.

As for me, I was off to Phoenix to do a quick one-day buildup for our "something big," which would turn out to be an "Empty Arena" match, with the World Wrestling Entertainment title on the line.

A year earlier MTV had done phenomenal ratings during halftime of the Super Bowl by promoting a *Celebrity Death Match* featuring "Stone Cold" Steve Austin. I guess Vince figured why let MTV do big ratings with our guys when *we* could do big ratings with our guys.

The "Empty Arena" idea was derived from an infamous Terry Funk/Jerry Lawler brawl in an empty Memphis Mid-South Coliseum from the early eighties. Anyone in the business with even the slightest appreciation for wrestling history has either seen or heard of this mat classic that began with the most profane interview of all time by the Funker. I think Terry set the indoor record for most frequent usage of the words "bastard" and "son of a bitch" in a three-minute time period. The end of the match is also warmly remembered for Terry's bungled attempt at maiming Lawler with a spike, which caught Terry in his own eye, leaving him bleeding and moaning mournfully, "My eye, my eye, Lawler, you bastard, my eye!"

What most wrestling fans don't remember is that, with the exception of the beginning and end, the empty-arena thing was atrocious. In much the same way that *Star Wars* geeks convinced themselves that *The Phantom Menace* was a great movie, even though cinematic evidence seemed to prove otherwise, wrestling fans have labeled this fiasco a classic. Hey, I'm the Funker's biggest fan, but even he laughs about how bad it was. Still, this was our agreed-upon stipulation, and what the hell, we might as well do our best.

A one-day story line isn't an easy sell, but we certainly gave it the old college try, even if the story line had a bigger hole in it than Tim Robbins's prison cell in *The Shawshank Redemption*.

Raw started with Vince presenting The Rock, his "corporate champion," with $100,000 for helping him win the *Royal Rumble* in what was Vince's first official World Wrestling Entertainment contest. To Vince's credit, he trained like an Olympian, and looked good in winning it. The hundred grand was stored inside an armored truck and was guarded by two armed "guards" that I somehow managed to dispose of, with minimal effort, during a dastardly sneak attack. With the guards knocked out, I pulled out the huge sack of cash, thereby committing an act of grand larceny and assault on national television. Of course, I was able to keep the money, due to the little-used "finders keepers, losers weepers" clause that was in effect at the time of the crime.

Appearing onstage, cash in hand, while an outraged Rock and Vince sulked in mid-ring, I somehow managed to expose the previous night's taped "I Quit" conspiracy, explain my newfound robbery skills, and challenge The Rock to the "Empty Arena" match, all while throwing wads of real cash to the crowd. It was actually quite a good interview, especially considering that my head was still throbbing like the no-reason boner of a fourteen-year-old boy.

For the rest of the show, I came up with inventive ways of spending The Rock's money, including "renting" horizontally challenged Mexican wrestler Max Mini for my kids to play with for the week, buying beautiful blond valet Debra a sweater to cover her oft-exposed cleavage, and giving giant wrestler Kurrgan enough cash to invest in my expertly researched mutual-fund selections. Oddly, no one ever remarked that my proposed theory of "40 percent large caps, 27 percent mid caps, 18 percent aggressive growth, 13 percent international, and 10 percent money market" added up to slightly more than 100 percent.

What could The Rock do? He had to accept it, which he did, in an interview that saw his voice crack more often in three minutes than Dustin Diamond's Screech character did on an entire season of *Saved by the Bell*. It was hilarious—two guys who supposedly hated each other, one night after one of the most brutal displays in sports-entertainment, openly laughing while the crowd laughed along. At least the match was made, and the stage was set for one of the strangest matches of my career.

The "Empty Arena" match was shot like a movie, in segments, in different rooms throughout the building. We didn't rehearse scenes, or do more than one take for each scene, which would have been difficult, seeing the ass-kicking I took in each one of them, but nonetheless, it was different from anything I'd ever done, and many people involved thought it would revolutionize the business.

It was difficult to get pumped up for the match, as none of the other wrestlers had yet arrived, and I was still feeling the pain of my "I Quit" bludgeoning less than forty-eight hours earlier. I really didn't know what to expect as I laced up my boots.

First, we shot our arrivals to the building: The Rock in an elegant stretch limo and me thanking a guy in a '73 Pinto for the lift, and giving him ten bucks as he drove away. Then it was time for our "Empty Arena" entrance, an experience I will never forget. My music began, and I stepped through the curtain wearing more bandages on my head than Boris Karloff in *The Mummy*. We were already skating on thin ice with USA after the *Rumble* match, and the last thing anyone involved wanted was for my head to spring a leak during what we were hoping would be the most-watched match in wrestling history. With that in mind, we made a conscious effort to make the match a "fun" one to watch, especially for the first-time viewers we were hoping to attract. So even though the "Empty Arena" match/movie would turn out to be a physical one, especially for me, we made sure to throw a lot of humor into the mix.

I could hear Vince doing commentary as I made my way to the ring. When I stepped inside, Howard Finkel began his introduction. "Ladies and Gentlemen . . ." I looked around. "Weighing in at 287 pounds . . ." There was not a soul in the building. "He is a former World Wrestling Entertainment champion . . ." I felt like such a jerk. "Mankind." Now I know how the guys in WCW feel. The Rock's music started, and I felt even stranger. I really wanted to just yell out "cut" and go backstage for a little more motivation. I realized that millions of people would be watching the match, and I tried to let that inspire me. It didn't. Instead, I watched in bewilderment as The Rock climbed the second rope to play to a crowd that wasn't there. After what seemed like an eternity, but what was probably only seconds, the bell rang and we went at it.

Guess what? It was actually pretty good. After a

minute inside the ring, the action spilled out to the floor, where I took out an entire section of the security fencing via a Rock Irish whip. Then it was into the chairs with an upside-down flip that put the domino theory into effect—knocking over about twenty chairs in the process. This used to be one of my patented bumps in the independents, Japan, and even ECW, but this had been my World Wrestling Entertainment first, because, well, people actually pay to be in those chairs.

While I lay on the floor, The Rock began piling chair after chair on top of me—burying me as if my body was Ralph Macchio's acting career. I somehow managed to escape the pile of seating devices and mounted a comeback that sent The Rock scurrying up the arena steps with me in hot pursuit. (Or as my brother would say—doing his best *Dukes of Hazzard* Sheriff Roscoe P. Coltrane imitation, "Hot pursuit, hot pursuit, huh kuh kuh kuh kuh.") My brother has every episode of that stupid show on tape, save one, which was spoiled when I took his designated tape off auto record and opted instead to air the Kay Parker film *Steven into Snowy* for my friends during my parents' college-visit absence.

When I got to the top, The Rock was waiting for me with a dreaded Rubbermaid to the head. The blow and two more like it were enough to send me down to the concrete, where I began a quick, rolling descent down the stairs. I managed to get down about thirty of them, but fell short of my goal of all fifty when my foot became wedged in a chair. Nonetheless, it was a pretty impressive start, considering my mummified state, and the fact that I was still sore as hell from the *Rumble*.

I have received some criticism for "taking too much" and not giving enough in return during my matches with The Rock. When I look back at the tapes, there certainly does seem to be some truth to that, but if there is blame to be assigned, it should be assigned to me. As I mentioned earlier, I felt like my ultimate goal was to get The Rock "ready" for *WrestleMania*. I saw myself kind of like a guard in football whose job it is to protect the quarterback. I didn't see "beating the hell out of him" as part of my job description, although, in retrospect, I may have been a little too giving.

The tumble down the stairs led us into the kitchen, which in turn led us to the catering area, a meeting room, an office, and finally the parking lot, with a prevailing theme throughout. The theme consisted of me getting my ass kicked, and The Rock coming up with funny lines as it was happening. Case in point: after throwing salsa in my eyes, which

caused me to scream out in pain, The Rock replied, "That was mild sauce, you baby."

When the action spilled out into the parking lot, I finally gained my revenge. After knocking The Rock to the floor, I commandeered a forklift that was transporting several kegs of beer. I then drove the vehicle over to where The Rock lay writhing in agony (or at least pretending he was) and I lowered the cargo onto his chest. With The Rock trapped beneath enough alcohol to supply a Kennedy wedding reception, I got out of the lift and covered him for the win. Standing up, I looked into the camera and yelled out, "Yo, Adrian, I did it! . . . Again!" This action seems somehow tarnished over time, especially when realizing that actor (and former WCW world champion) David Arquette later did essentially the same thing on an AT&T commercial. How dare he bastardize my attempt to bastardize *Rocky*.

So now I was the World Wrestling Entertainment Champion for the second time. Somehow this one didn't seem quite as special. Maybe it was the sense of having been there before. Or maybe it was because of my exhausted state. Or maybe it was due to the fact that I had salsa, ketchup, guacamole, and mud all over me, and had won the match with a finish so ridiculous that I could almost see Lou Thesz tearing up his Cauliflower Alley membership card.

The finish made me visualize one of wrestling's classic grumpy old men standing on a street corner, yelling out to no one in particular, "In my day, we didn't use guacamole as a weapon. We didn't fight in kitchens, and we didn't need Steven Spielberg to direct our title matches. We wore black boots, we wore black trunks, and we didn't need beer kegs and forklifts to win titles. We wrestled for real . . . seven days a week . . . 365 days a year . . . and we liked it!" Still, beer kegs or not, it felt good to hold that World Wrestling Entertainment belt again. So good, in fact, that I didn't speak up when I should have. Even though I knew better, I walked away when they said, "Mick, that's great. Rock, we just want to get one more camera shot."

I watched the match from the airport lounge in Charlotte. Not many of the patrons were wrestling fans, and even though they protested when I switched the television station, they seemed to get caught up in our Hollywood production rather quickly. Even one guy's comment—"Come on, a bag of popcorn doesn't hurt when you get hit with it"—couldn't ruin the mood. Until the finish.

They were cheering as I finally leveled The Rock in the parking lot. Rooting me on as I gained control of the forklift with a commanding "Can I please use this?" and laughing as they sensed what was about to happen. And then, in a moment, it was dead. One hokey, completely unrealistic bird's-eye view of a groggy Rock coming to and realizing that he was about to be crushed ruined the whole thing. "Oh, come on, where did that camera come from?" as if he were looking at the dailies of the *Harry Potter* film. "That's not a wrestling match, that's a movie," cried out another. Slowly, I slunk away, knowing that with one ridiculous camera shot, we had completely ruined their suspension of disbelief.

On the whole, I thought the match was fun. And I'm in favor of any match that results in me being the champion. But I'm glad that the match wasn't an

unbelievable success artistically (for a short time it was the most-watched match of all time) and that it didn't revolutionize the business. Good wrestling matches are an art, as is good moviemaking. But they're different arts, and I'm glad that, for the time being at least, they will stay that way.

Preliminary reports on the *Royal Rumble* buy rate looked to be outstanding. Now we just needed one more Pay-Per-View until the big one, *Wrestle-Mania*. Fans had been so into the *Rumble* confrontation between Vince and his nemesis Stone Cold that they had been booked into a steel-cage match at February's *St. Valentine's Day Massacre*. During wrestling's infancy on Pay-Per-View, going back to 1986, the World Wrestling Entertainment had offered five Pay-Per-View shows a year: *Wrestle-Mania*, *SummerSlam*, the *Royal Rumble*, the *Survivor Series*, and *King of the Ring*. WCW soon came up with an equal number. In 1993, WCW decided to run monthly Pay-Per-Views, and World Wrestling Entertainment was forced to follow suit, thereby changing forever the wrestling landscape.

Instead of building up for angles every ten weeks, the World Wrestling Entertainment (and WCW as well) had to create, promote, and execute angles for Pay-Per-View every month, while presenting four hours of new programming every week (not including Saturday and Sunday "wrap-up" shows). With the World Wrestling Entertainment relying on a very small talent pool at the very top of the organization, frequent rematches were inevitable. With *Wrestle-Mania* on the horizon, and the chemistry between me and The Rock still going strong, a decision was made to have a title match between Mankind and

The Rock for the fourth month in a row, in addition to the Super Bowl adventure. This one was billed as a "Last Man Standing" contest, which continued the time-honored tradition of bouts based on Bruce Willis box-office failures. (Actually, I like Bruce, especially in his more understated roles in films like *The Sixth Sense*, *Nobody's Fool*, and *In Country*.)

While getting ready for "Last Man Standing," I got a chance to make my big-screen (or at least straight-to-video) debut. The film was called *Big Money Hustlas*, or as I refer to it, "My chance to get a SAG (Screen Actors Guild) card." Hey, I was willing to do anything to get that card, which would allow me access to the best health insurance plan in the country. For years, I had been paying massive dollars for minimal coverage, and when I really needed my benefits a few years ago, my carrier screwed me like a three-dollar hooker. I would have done anything to get that card—even *Big Money Hustlas*. Actually, the film was pretty cool, even though my one day of shooting involved standing outside in my T-shirt in five-degree weather for hours at a time, with only the borrowed Winnebago of the rock band the Misfits to seek occasional refuge in.

I had never heard the Misfits' music, but knew of their reputation as a hardcore band with a loyal, somewhat weird following. The guys dressed demonically and sang of such subjects as murder and decapitation (no, they don't write the music for Disney films). So it was with some surprise that I was greeted by bass player Jerry with a "I thought you might be hungry, so I had Grandma make you some home-made meatballs." Not only was he a nice guy, but his teenage son, who was with him, actually seemed to like him. Nothing gives me hope for the future like seeing teens who actually like their parents.

I couldn't help but notice that the sleeping accommodations on the vehicle seemed a little cramped. There were little sleeping cubicles built in everywhere. I swear, it reminded me of when Kramer rented out his dresser drawers to Japanese visitors to sleep in on *Seinfeld*. "Jerry," I said, noticing that there was a bed wedged in between two sets of tiny bunk beds, "I'll bet you make sure that you get the bed, right?" "Kind of," he said. "I share it with my brother and the drummer." I couldn't believe it. Eleven guys slept in that Winnebago—eleven! All of a sudden listening to the Blue Meanie's snoring and farts in a Red Roof didn't seem all that bad.

I liked Jerry so much that I was proud to accept his gift package of evil-looking skull T-shirts and CDs. As a matter of fact, I couldn't wait to slide that CD in as soon as I got to my car. And slide it in I did, and waited for Jerry's groovy bass lines to take me away to another place in my mind. Hey—maybe the Misfits would be my new band to inspire me to a whole new level of matches and interviews. Eleven seconds later I pressed eject, and the CD slid out, never to play again. I hope this doesn't hurt Jerry's feelings—he really is a great guy. But I guess that could be somewhat akin to somebody saying, "Hey Mick, I read your book, and you sound like a great guy. But as a wrestler, you suck." But honestly, if I were forced to make a decision at gunpoint between listening to the Misfits and watching a *Best of Test* video, I think I'd watch the video, even if it had the Rodney match on it.

Speaking of music, I usually don't listen to it while I'm writing, but I was forced to do so when writing these last few pages, by a group of obnoxious teenage girls on my flight from New York to Atlanta. So I put on a CD called *Broken Things*, by a woman named Julie Miller, and man, it's a great one. "All My Tears" will give you goose bumps. That is, of course, if you like music that no one else listens to.

"Last Man Standing" was a tricky one to figure out. How do we live up to the concept of the match, which involves two guys trying to knock each other unconscious, while avoiding the over-the-top brutality of "I Quit" that had made the match hard to enjoy? Actually, I have not yet run into, nor do I want to, the guy who says, "Man, that 'I Quit' was the greatest match of all time—I watch it every day."

Having apparently not learned anything from January's mistake, I had again brought Colette and the kids. Actually, the proximity of the show's location in Memphis, and the following two days of television in Alabama and Tennessee, had been the deciding factor in my decision. With four shows a week on the World Wrestling Entertainment schedule, and with my decision to accept outside appearances on off days several times a month, and a whole lot of time spent on airplanes in between, I tried to take the family with me whenever I was remotely close to Florida.

Accepting these outside appearances was a matter of great trouble for me. On one hand, I desperately wanted to be home as often as I could. On the other hand, I was beginning to realize that my time as an active wrestler was coming to an end. I had been going full tilt for a long time, and my body was really slowing down. Financially, the past year had been a good one, but with the possibility of retirement poking its head out at me, I felt like I had to make as much as I could, while I still could. The World Wrestling Entertainment's popularity was soaring, but wrestling fans, historically, have short memories, with the legends of wrestling past being right up there with the guy operating the Ferris wheel at the Johnson Country Fair, in terms of esteem. Maybe this will change—maybe it won't, but nonetheless, I felt the need to make hay while the sun was shining.

I had promised Colette that this match would be different, and had agreed to go on "headshot probation" indefinitely. For months, I would have to preface prematch conversations with opponents with "I'm not allowed to get hit in the head." They would usually laugh and ask me if I was serious, and I would assure them I was. With the exception of one necessary blow to conclude "Last Man Standing," and one tremendous chair to the face that was designed to impress tennis star Monica Seles, I actually went almost a year without a single chair to my head.

In this respect, we've got an advantage over the "real" sports. If former Philadelphia Flyer Eric Lindros had been able to tell opponents, "Watch it, guys, I've taken a few too many whacks lately," he'd be a whole lot better off now. And if San Francisco 49er Steve Young had been able to say, "Hey, I just watched a twenty-four-hour *Gilligan's Island* marathon, so I think I've had too many head injuries," I'm sure he would have been playing a few more years.

I received some strange news when I got to the building that day. The World Wrestling Entertainment aired a show called *Heat* on Sunday evenings, and on the one Sunday a month that we had a Pay-Per-View, *Heat* would air live, as a way of creating interest for the PPV. On this show, I would be surprised to see three old friends, who would train me for the big match. "It will be great," writer Vince Russo assured me, "with these guys training you, it will be hilarious." I saw things a little bit differently. "Vince, even a moron knows that you don't start training two hours before a match." (With the exception of Ken Shamrock—who once actually did train that long in order to look good as guest referee.) Russo was worried about offending the three guys who had been flown in especially for this training session. Indeed the three men, Bob Backlund and the Iron Sheik, who were both former World Wrestling Entertainment champions, and Dominic DeNucci, the man who trained me to wrestle, were all wrestling legends. Which, of course, didn't mean a whole lot to the crowd, anyway.

I thought about it for a second. "Vince, I don't mind if they *attempt* to train me, but why not have some fun with it? Let me be the straight man here, and they can run around like lunatics if they want." And so it came to pass that the Iron Sheik tried to teach me the art of "Persian clubs," Bob Backlund ran up and down several flights of stairs, and a wide-eyed Dominic continually attempted to preach to me on the merits of the dropkick. In his day as a performer, Dominic had a well-deserved reputation as an excellent technical wrestler, as well as a well-deserved reputation as being a not-so-excellent interview. Witness the infamous mid-1960s San Francisco promo where Dominic, who had just arrived in the States and spoke little English, was instructed to promote a steel-cage matchup. In reality, this "steel" cage was made of chicken wire, a fact the promoter urged Dominic not to expose. "I tell you," Dominic said in his promo, "this cage may look like-a chicken wire, but it's not-a chicken wire."

If anyone should have known of my dropkick shortcomings, it would be Dominic, for after all, fourteen years earlier he had witnessed my only attempt at it. After catching Kurt Kaufmann in the mid-left-nut area, it was agreed that I could probably do without having the dropkick in my arsenal. I swear, I think Captain Ahab had more spring in his leg than I did. And that was when I was nineteen! And 230 pounds. In February 1999, at age thirty-three and hovering around the 300-pound mark, I didn't see the dropkick fitting into the evening's itinerary.

But Dominic was insistent. "Mickey, my boy" he began, with eyes flashing widely, "tonight, if you give him the dropkick, then maybe, my boy, you will finally be the champion." His promo wasn't scripted, and neither was my response, a simple, "Dominic, I already am the champion," to which Dominic replied, "Oh."

The Iron Sheik was one of wrestling's great "behind the curtains" characters. A legitimate Olympian for Iran decades earlier, and a real-life bodyguard for the Shah of Iran, the Sheik, whose real name was Kosraw Vasori, had come to the United States as a Spartan athlete. That was a long time ago. He had been the man who dropped the title to Hulk Hogan in 1984, which begat "Hulka-mania," and he had remained a huge draw for years after. Hell, the guy still does independent shots, and the fans *still* hate him when he sings the Iranian national anthem.

He was also the archrival of Sgt. Slaughter during the Sarge's phenomenal run in 1984, with their classic "Boot Camp" match in Madison Square Garden still among my all-time favorites. The in-ring stories pale in comparison, however, to behind-the-scenes Sheik stories. He spoke in a loud boisterous voice, with a strong Iranian accent, and his statements were often hilarious. One time he was bemoaning the fact that he had been forced to do a job (lose) to Vader, the man responsible for tearing off my right ear in 1994. "Can you believe that," the Sheik yelled out, "the Iron Sheik, a former douba-you, douba-you, hef shompion, losing to a fat jehbroni." At that point Vader walked through the curtain, and the Sheik, without missing a beat, stuck out his hand. "Be-a-utiful, bay-beh, the Sheik loved it!"

I saw him a few months ago in the Atlanta airport, and he hadn't changed a whole lot. He was still attempting to pay for drinks with eight-by-ten promo shots of him with the World Wrestling Entertainment belt in 1984, and as usual, he made life interesting, even during so mundane an experience as riding the airport convenience cart through the terminal. Now, usually, the cart makes a tiny little *beep, beep, beep* noise that commands about as much attention as Jiminy Cricket at a Marilyn Manson concert. With the Sheik aboard, however, the people moved out of the way a whole lot quicker. "Vot, are you deaf, brothah?" he yelled out, as if he were a strange Middle Eastern beacon in the night. "Vot the hell is wrong WITH YOU!"

On this night in Memphis, the Sheik was trying to sing the virtues of his "Persian clubs," Iranian training tools that were heavy and legitimately difficult to master. With these clubs, the Sheik was an expert, and he was able to speak to me as he strained mightily. "Tonight, Sheik teach you the Persian clubs. With these, you gain power, balance, stamina." The Sheik then let them drop with a mighty thud. I looked at him curiously and said, "Sheik, maybe I can just hit him in the head with them instead," to which the Sheik exclaimed, "Ex-zackly!"

Backlund was a World Wrestling Entertainment Champion for almost five straight years, before dropping the belt to the Sheik in December 1983, with a young and ruggedly handsome Mick Foley in attendance. Like most wrestlers who watch Bob's matches years later, I look up and say, "How did he get to keep the belt for so long?" He was a former collegiate champion, and an unbelievably well-trained athlete, but he was to "smooth" what Dolly Parton is to flat-chested.

Bob was always known as a nice guy, but he was, like, scary nice. I met him in 1985, and after having had my picture taken with him, I asked him if he would sign an autograph for me. Bob mistakenly thought I asked if he would sign the picture, at which point he whipped out a pen and gave me his home address, which he told me to send the photo to. I did, and guess what? He actually signed it and sent it back.

Bob admitted to me that he had trouble reading as a youngster, and that he'd been given preferential

treatment due to his status as an athlete. So Bob had vowed to teach himself to read, and rare was the time that he was found without a big, thick, overly intelligent tome in his hands. Bob would then take the big words he'd learn and use them in conversation, often in a humorous manner.

Such was the case on this important night, after I told Bob that I didn't feel like running up and down the stairs. "Young man," Bob scolded me, "don't you exacerbate me!" I grew very serious as I told Bob, "I never exacerbate before a big match." I thought for sure he'd laugh, but he didn't. Instead, he paused and replied with a straight face, "Nobody should." When we heard "cut," we all laughed like crazy. Everyone, that is, except Bob, who never cracked a smile. When it comes to Bob, I often wonder if he gets in his car after the show and suddenly goes, "Okay, I'm through fooling the boys—time to act normal again."

Bob kept insisting that I run up and down the damn stairs, and after he replied yes to my, "If I do this, will you leave me alone?" question, I began my slow ascent. While celebrating my inaugural ten-step accomplishment like I was Rocky Balboa at the doors of the Philadelphia Museum of Art, I was blindsided by The Rock, who, in accordance with my earlier suggestion, went after my legitimately sore right knee. At this point in my career, I still believed in the "real is better" philosophy, and felt that faking an injury when I had a perfectly good real injury to exploit would be scandalous.

To make things even better, or worse, depending on how or when I look at it (better at the time, worse after I thought about it), I had The Rock continue the knee assault during the match. The psychology of the match was that instead of trying to knock me senseless to meet the "Last Man Standing" stipulation, The Rock would work on my knee until I was unable to stand.

One of my strengths as a performer is coming up with creative ways to get hurt. The upside to this is that my matches look original, and thereby cool. The downside is that the less painful ones get duplicated by others to the point that only a wrestling historian (a guy without a girlfriend) knows that I was the innovator, and I am left with the genuinely torturous ones to call my very own. In this latter, ridiculously painful group was the gem I came up with for this match, where The Rock lifted the steel ring steps overhead, while standing in the ring, and threw them onto my prone body outside the ring. Ouch!

The Rock, on the other hand, thrived on coming up with creative things that weren't painful in the least. This night's offering was a rendition of "Smackdown Hotel," which seemed appropriate in Elvis Presley's Memphis hometown. With Mankind down on the mat, The Rock grabbed the house microphone and began serenading me. "Well, since Rock's baby left him, he found a new place to dwell, it's down at the end of Jabroni Drive, that's Smackdown Hotel." The crowd went crazy. He may have been the bad guy, but he was pretty damn funny. After a pause he continued. "Rock feels so lonely, baby, Rock feels so lonely, Rock feels so—*oughuff!*" When Rock leaned over, I had caught him in the "Socko Claw."

Socko Claw? What the heck is the socko claw?

Actually, most people know, but seeing as how *Have a Nice Day!* actually was well liked by people who didn't even watch wrestling, I'll give a short background. Upon my entry into the World Wrestling Entertainment in 1996, I began using the "mandible claw," a nerve hold that applied pressure with the fingers to the nerve underneath the tongue. Two and a half years later, in an attempt to cheer up the ailing Vince McMahon, I (at the suggestion of Al Snow) created "Mr. Socko," the world's ugliest sock puppet. Mr. Socko became an immediate hit, and shortly after, in what may have been the most important cultural combination since Marty's chocolate bar fell into John's peanut butter, the "Socko Claw" was born. Thank goodness it was, because especially after this match, I would grow to depend on Socko like a 2 A.M. boob in an infant's mouth.

With The Rock reeling from the Sock, I mounted a big comeback that climaxed with Mankind mounting the second turnbuckle, ready to pounce on The Rock, who was staggered outside the ring. Like a 300-pound, one-eared bird, I took to the sky (I can't jump high, so I jump from high places), and like a 260-pound intelligent man, The Rock moved out of the way. I knew I was hurt the moment my right knee hit the corner of the table. The table collapsed, but did so slowly, unlike my knee, which did so immediately. As a foolish subscriber to the "real is better" philosophy, I refused to have anything to do with "gimmicked" tables, and I had just paid a heavy price for my foolishness. If I had to point to one moment in time that signaled the beginning of the end of my career, it would be this table collision.

After that, Mick Foley and quality matches (with a few notable exceptions) parted company for a long time.

I struggled back into the ring for the finish, which had changed dramatically over the previous few days. I had assumed all along that I would be putting The Rock over in this match, in order to set the stage for *WrestleMania*. Instead, Vince Russo had informed me, *Mania* was going to be a three-way match between Austin, The Rock, and myself. I tried to talk him out of it, believing that Austin vs. The Rock was the way to go, but he was insistent. "Mick, after everything you've done, Vince [McMahon, the "real" Vince] says there's no way we can go to *Mania* without you in the main event." Great, I was in. But now, how do we get through "Last Man

Standing" without beating either me or The Rock? You got it—screw the people. Actually, if anyone felt ripped off after the match we had, they can feel free to screw themselves, but I still felt funny about our inconclusive ending.

This is where my one necessary head shot comes in (the non–Monica Seles one). Do you remember The *Rocky II* finish? Good. Now substitute chairs for boxing gloves, and substitute me for Creed and Rocky for, um, Rocky, and you've got our finish— simultaneous chairshots that knocked us both out. Believe it or not, The *Rocky II* finish had actually been done a few years earlier, in the 1975 movie *Let's Do It Again*, with Jimmie "Dy-No-Mite" Walker playing boxer Bootsey Farnsworth. So I guess I am guilty of ripping off a movie that had ripped off another movie. Still, I was carried out of the arena as the World Wrestling Entertainment Champion. For less than twenty-four hours, as it turned out.

I arrived in Birmingham, Alabama, the next day in terrible pain. When I was a kid, I used to question my dad's decision to leave Yankee Stadium after the sixth inning in order to "beat the traffic." Now I was questioning my own previous night's decision to forgo treatment on a serious knee injury for the same reason. Indeed, I had bolted with Colette and the kids right after my match, and was halfway to Birmingham when I stopped to check on the knee. I took off my tights, and then slid down my knee pad to reveal a massive amount of swelling. I bought some ice at a convenience store to try to reduce the size, but the thing was purple and throbbing (my knee, that is) when I showed up at the arena the next day. François worked diligently on it, and was actually quite helpful, but I was still having difficulty doing even the simplest things—i.e., walking, bending, making fun of Al Snow in front of the boys.

While my knee was being mended in one room, my career was being upended in another, where a decision was made to scrap me from the *Wrestle-Mania* main event. It seems to me that some people thrive on controversy, as well as dissension. Former wrestler Shawn Michaels not only seemed to thrive on it, but seemed to have a genuine talent at creating it, which he did on this day by convincing all parties involved that the *WrestleMania* main event *had* to be a one-on-one contest. Shawn had main-evented several *Manias*, and believed the integrity of the event would be hurt by a three-way match. Ironically, Shawn was actually pushing for me to remain in the match, but was outvoted. Instead, I was asked to drop the belt to The Rock in a ladder match later, on that night's *Raw*, and saw my *WrestleMania* dream disappear.

8: *Limpin'*
Ain't Easy

IT WAS A CLASSIC good-news-bad-news situation. The bad news was that I was broken down, burned out, and had only a few good matches left in my system. The good news was that nobody noticed. In their fourteenth minute, the quality of my matches went downhill faster than Milli Vanilli's career, but the reaction to them actually grew stronger. The Mankind character had benefited greatly several months earlier by upping the comedy quotient. One part hardcore badass and one part lovable dork had proven to be a successful formula. Now, with Mother Nature and Father Time teaming up to kick my ass, I changed the equation once again. Over the course of the next several weeks, Mankind would, as Triple H put it, become a "human Muppet," with half a thimbleful of a badass reputation dusted on top. I began to have the worst matches—and the best time of my career.

In truth, I'm probably being too hard on myself. In retrospect, my performances in October and November of '99, when I truly did suck, made my March and April offerings look like Flair vs. Steamboat by comparison. Also, by being booked primarily in "Fatal Four-Way" matches around the country, I was able to hide my weaknesses and have more fun in the ring than ever before. I was tentatively set to have knee surgery following *Wrestle-Mania*, so for the next several weeks I gutted it out, stunk up the ring, and made audiences laugh, while I looked forward to some time off.

Las Vegas, Nevada, in March of 1999, stands out in my mind as a good time, and not because of gambling. My mother told me about traveling across country after she graduated college, and how she only gambled one quarter in Vegas. I've got her beat, because I've been there well over a dozen times and never wagered once. I mean why give my money to casinos when worthwhile organizations like the IRS need it so much more? Vegas is wonderful because it is this country's only city with world-class roller coasters at its hotels. So, after experiencing the joys, loop-the-loops, corkscrews, and G-force of New York, New York with Al Snow, I headed to the arena.

A small group of teenagers had gained access to the backstage area with cable-access press credentials, and were seeking out interviews with World Wrestling Entertainment performers. I went up in front of the camcorder and was immediately besieged with questions about my hardcore wrestling past. "Mick Foley," began one kid, trying to sound like a pimply-faced, goofy-haired Edward R. Murrow, "you are known as the 'King of the Death Match,' you've been in barbed-wire matches, thumbtack matches, and bed-of-nails matches. Do you have any scars?" Do you have any scars? Oh, this was great. I had been waiting to be fed a line like this since Scott Darragh and I had shown up as freshmen at Cortland State University in upstate New York, with jokes so bad that we were immediately shunned from any and all sexual activity on campus. "What was that last part?" I asked the kid. "I asked if you had any scars," he replied. "I'm sorry," I told the group, "I don't smoke." I then burst out into the biggest fake laugh my body could handle. "Ho, ho, ho, ha, ha, ha—get it? You asked if you had any scars, and I said I don't smoke! Oh, that's good. Owen, come here, listen to this." Owen Hart came forward, and I asked the kid to repeat the question. When he did, I landed the same horrible joke, and Owen, who was no stranger to bad jokes himself, burst out laughing. Together, we spent the next half hour pulling aside every wrestler, crew member, custodian, and Godfather "Ho" we could find, and repeated the ritual. When I was finished, I had fake-laughed myself hoarse, and took a break while I watched the Godfather in action.

The Godfather was the real-life Charles Wright, who at this point was in the opening stages of creating a character for himself that would finally get over. In 1990, I had once split a room in Dallas with Charles, where I spent the night saying sweet nothings over the phone to Colette's expanding belly. Despite that bonding experience, I wasn't especially close with him, but felt I knew him well enough to see that his previous personas—Soultaker, Papa Shango, Kama, and Kama MustaFa—were missing their mark. Good wrestling characters are usually exaggerated slices of a performer's real-life persona, and Wright's dark, brooding characters didn't seem to embody the real person in any way. In real life, Charles was vibrant, outgoing, and happy. In the ring, he had actually become known (never to his face) as "The Black Hole of Charisma," because not only did he have no charisma in the ring, he seemed to suck the charisma out of his opponents as well. After seeing him in action at the hotel lounge in Chicago one night, I wondered why he couldn't channel his natural charisma into his wrestling persona.

Enter The Godfather—neon-bedecked, shade-wearing, spliff-smoking, throwback-to-Huggy-Bear 1970s pimp! That's right—a pimp. In every town, The Godfather would have Ho's (whores) who were tapped from the local gentlemen's clubs, in what I understand is considered a pretty big honor in that particular field of entertainment. One night in New Orleans, World Wrestling Entertainment road agent Jack Lanza (knowing New Orleans was within driving distance of my house) voiced disappointment when he found out my wife hadn't made the trip by saying, "That's too bad, Colette could have been one of the Ho's tonight." To this day, Lanza can't understand why I was offended.

I've got to admit, the first time I saw the act, I had my doubts, but the fans loved it. Hell, they made him a baby face (good guy)! Since then, he had engaged in a legendary feud with Tiger Ali Singh, which had been touched off when Singh referred to the girls as "sluts." Now, those are fighting words—how dare he call those Ho's sluts!

On this night in Vegas, I watched as he launched into his familiar speech. "Once again, it's time for everybody to climb aboard the Hooooo train. Now I want everybody to light a fatty for this pimp daddy, light that mother up, and say it out loud—Pimpin'

Ain't Easy." At that moment I knew deep down in my heart that I would do with that catchphrase what I do with all catchphrases that I like—I would rip it off.

Later I watched as Al Snow and Bob Holly tried to destroy each other for fifteen minutes in a tremendous hardcore matchup. "Hardcore" used to mean using anything at your disposal, in a display of pride and intestinal fortitude. Presently, it means comedy matches with guys running all over the arena using the dreaded cookie sheet. But on this night in Sin City, the curmudgeonly, non-carnival-attending Holly and his opponent, Snow, were letting it all hang out. Tables, chairs, and hard bumps on concrete were all enlisted to make for a very enjoyable, hard-hitting match. Then they went for the popcorn. Gimmick infringement. As any reader of *Have a Nice Day!* will tell you, the big Santa's sackful of popcorn to the head and back belonged to me and Owen Hart, who had stunk up many a sold-out arena with it. Now here was Al bastardizing it for his own personal gain. Now, I don't care if someone wants to borrow or blatantly steal my dangerous stuff—but leave my hokey stuff alone. What next? Was Al going to "borrow" my dumping of 1,000 soft-drink lids, which Owen and I had invented in Los Angeles? Owen had sold the plastic lids like sledgehammer shots, with his knees buckling while the lids floated to the ground. Was nothing sacred? I decided to take the appropriate steps to ensure that this blatant thievery would not happen again. I told Vince's son, Shane McMahon.

Al and Bob looked like hell when they walked through the curtain. Bob hits harder in a pro wrestling match than most people do in a street fight, and Al's face showed the results. His eye was slightly swollen, and a thin trail of blood trickled from his nose. Both men's chests were bruised from the brutal open-hand chops they had both endured. Despite his worn-down condition, Al had about him a look that was unmistakable—a look of pride. Until, that is, Shane asked to speak to him.

I was too far away to hear the conversation, but I could read Al's body language as he nodded meekly, before bowing his head and walking away dejectedly. A moment later Shane called him back, and spoke again, prompting Al to point to me and Owen, who by this point were doing our best not to bust out and yell, "You!" Al came over and told us Shane's talk had gone something like this. "Al, you know, we work real hard to try to protect people's gimmicks around here, right?" Al nods. "Well, using popcorn in a match is Mick's gimmick, and we're trying to protect that. We can't have you stealing it and using it in your matches." Al walks away. "Wait, Al, come back here—you know I'm kidding, don't you?" At this point Al simply says, "Mick," and points to me and Owen. Later Al said, "I should have known that something was up when I saw you and Owen huddled together." I took that as a huge compliment.

Later that evening, before our "Fatal Four-Way" main event with The Rock, Kane, Mankind, and Stone Cold, The Rock grabbed the mike to begin another hilarious monologue. "Finally, The Rock has come back to Las Vegas. You know, The Rock has been around the world, and The Rock can say that beyond a shadow of a doubt, this is the largest gathering of trailer-park trash The Rock has ever seen." The crowd laughed and booed simultaneously and showered "The Great One" with the familiar chorus of "Rocky Sucks." The Rock smiled, and pointed at Kane, who was already in the ring, and continued. "First, The Rock is going to beat your big, red, retarded ass, then he's going to take Mankind's monkey ass and kick it all over the corner of Know Your Role Boulevard and Jabroni Drive, and then finally, The Rock is going to lay the Smacketh down on Steve Austin's candy ass." The crowd booed, but deep down, they were dying to love the guy. Even my angle with Rock was only delaying his inevitable face turn.

I heard my music and stepped through the curtain. I always limped slightly when I walked, but on this night in Vegas, the walk was exaggerated greatly. The roar of the crowd was Hegstardish in its intensity and Laurentiis-like in its duration. It was nice to be loved, even without the World Wrestling Entertainment belt. I grabbed the mike and tried to sound sad as I began to address the crowd. "I guess you can tell that I am in considerable pain by the way I walk." The crowd nodded in agreement. "Indeed, walking with an injury is very difficult, or in other words, 'LIMPIN' AIN'T EASY.'" The remark was met with both laughter and groans from the audience, and great amusement from Kane and The Rock. I had made some mental notes backstage during The Rock's speech, and with my "Limpin'" line out of the way, was eager to share them with the residents of Sin City. "You know, Rock, I couldn't help but overhear you talk about my monkey ass. Then I heard you talk about Steve Austin's candy ass. Hell [pointing to Kane], I even heard him talk about your big, red, retarded ass." The crowd roared, and I could see that The Rock was interested to see where I was going with this impromptu speech. A moment later I showed him. "Now, I could be wrong, but it certainly seems to me that The Rock likes to talk about men's asses a lot." The crowd roared, and The Rock feigned anger while doing his best not to laugh. Especially when I spoke again. "All of this has gotten me to thinking— maybe it's true—maybe The Rock really does suck after all!"

The crowd's response was huge, and they immediately broke into a prolonged chorus of "Rocky Sucks," while The Rock adamantly denied doing any such thing. Please realize that in front of 16,000 screaming fans, a verbal accusation is not enough. To properly reach the top levels of an arena, an elementary knowledge of pantomime must be utilized. I'm not talking about white-faced, Marcel Marceau "trapped in a box" pantomime either. That stuff can get your ass kicked in some parts of the country. I'm talking about "grabbing an imaginary penis in your hand and pretending to gnaw on it" type of pantomime. There's a fine line you don't want to cross here, though. When accusing someone of such an act, you can't seem so proficient at the miming that the crowd can picture you with a real one in your hand. Instead, you just kind of haphazardly hold it while rolling your tongue around your own inner cheek. Granted, I have never, in my own limited experience, seen or heard of this technique being implemented in a real-life sex scenario, but it is nonetheless the time-honored technique for pantomimed fellatio. Now The Rock was livid, or at least his character was.

Suddenly The Rock had an imaginary penis in *his* hand and was using it in the way that I just described, but was shaking his head in disagreement, as if to say, "No, The Rock doesn't do this." I continued my playacting but nodded my head as if to say, "Oh yes you do, Rock." A giant crash signaled Austin's entrance, and as suddenly and mysteriously as the invisible penises had appeared, they vanished into thin air. Austin arrived to the ring with the accompaniment of a pop (crowd reaction) even more Hegstardish and Laurentiis-like than my own. After hitting all four corners with his patented one-finger salute, Stone Cold grabbed the mike and began to speak. Actually, he began to tell a story. Austin is a tremendous promo guy, but in the ten years that I'd known him, I had never actually heard him tell a story. Why would he pick this match to begin? "My uncle was a man of the sea," Steve began. "He provided for his family by fishing for small crustaceans. Then one day a storm came along and sunk my uncle's boat. When he came home, he only had one thing to say . . . Shrimpin' Ain't Easy."

The ring had now turned into a children's play area, where big, bruising thugs looked about as dangerous as a gaggle of baby geese. The Rock tried to gain control with something about Austin's "monkey ass," but I cut him off. "Rock, you're always talking about monkeys, which you know are part of the primate group, as is the chimpanzee. And everyone knows . . . Chimpin' ain't easy." The Rock lost all semblance of being in character and burst out laughing. Austin simply put his face in the corner so no one could see it, but his shaking stomach gave his laughter away. Even Kane, whose entire face was hidden, wasn't safe. I looked at him, and his mask was moving up and down, up and down, with waves of laughter. It truly was a memorable night—quite possibly the funniest of my career. Until we got to Milwaukee the next day.

I hadn't been to Milwaukee since the previous May, when, as Dude Love, I had been in a tremendous match with Stone Cold that was detailed in *Have a Nice Day!* As Dude Love, I had sold out to Vince McMahon's Corporation, and as a result, was combing my hair, wearing sport jackets, speaking like a pompous professor, and of all the rotten things, was wearing false front teeth. As part of the match, Austin had pulled the offensive dental work out of my mouth and had, after stomping on it, thrown it to the crowd. Much like a baseball hit into the stands, I had assumed it made a nice memento for a lucky fan.

"Mankind, a fan wants to see you," a guard told me at the arena. "She says she's got something for you." Waiting for me in the back was a family of four with a small gift box. I opened the box, and to my surprise, found my front teeth looking up at me. "We thought you might have missed these," the lady said as her children beamed at me as if I was Indiana Jones with the Lost Ark safely in my possession. I didn't want to burst the family's bubble and tell them I hadn't used them in ten years—ever since I met Colette and she convinced me I looked sexy without them. Seeing as how "sexy" wasn't an adjective usually applied to my appearance, I took the damn things out immediately and stashed them in the ashtray of my '84 Chrysler LeBaron, where they stayed for many years. Come to think of it, if Colette thought I'd looked sexy without an ear, I would have lost one of those too. Which, come to think of it, I did.

The teeth in the ashtray came in handy during an argument with Colette in 1991. Knowing that I was wrong, I reached for the ashtray, but Colette immediately guessed my intentions and reacted in anger. "Don't you do it!" she yelled. But I was too fast, and in an instant had that bad boy out of the tray and into my mouth. "Fine," Colette said, "if that's the way you're going to be, fine." Later that evening I not only put the teeth back in storage, where they would remain for many years, but actually apologized for having the audacity to commit such a reprehensible act.

Back in the dressing room, Val Venis was lecturing on the foolishness of the American income-tax system, and was explaining how he, as a Canadian, was a member of the British Commonwealth, and was eligible to live in the Bahamas, income-tax-free. The Val Venis character may have been a porno star, but dammit, he was a conservative one.

Al was trying to explain to some of the other boys how he had not been fooled by Shane's popcorn talk, but the boys knew he was full of Snow. I noted that it was ironic that Al had been "selling" bags of massive amounts of popcorn, when usually it was his matches that caused popcorn vendors to do the same thing. Al admitted that the statement was clever, at which time I declared that Al was "Winger" to my "Hulka," in reference to the punch thrown by Warren Oates's Sergeant Hulka that dou-

bles over Bill Murray's John Winger in the movie *Stripes*. I then went a step too far by saying that Al was "Fosse" to my "Rose," a statement that was met by the blank faces of my younger cronies like Edge and Scotty 2 Hotty. When I explained that this was an allusion to the 1969 Major League All-Star Game where Pete Rose destroyed catcher Ray Fosse's career by running him over at home plate, even my cronies had to admit that the reference was a little too obscure to be effective. Later that year I had the chance to explain the story to Pete Rose himself, and baseball's all-time hit leader thought it was tremendous.

When I was eleven, I tried a Pete Rose face-first dive, when I attempted to steal third base as a member of Will Grey's Red Sox Little League team. Never mind the fact that I had the speed of a garden slug—I wanted to do the dive. One of the tricks of Pete's dive was to put the hands down first, which apparently I forgot, and by the time I realized I was "out" at third, I was "out" on the bench, where, with the help of smelling salts, I woke up to a standing ovation from my teammates. That may have been when I first realized "it doesn't matter if you win or lose, it's how painful things look along the way."

I stated earlier in this book that I had only been knocked out once in my career, but the preceding Little League story made me realize I was at least on the threshold of unconsciousness one other time. In June 1992, I was giving a fired-up interview about WCW wrestler Sting for an upcoming Pay-Per-View. Sting had legitimately hurt his ribs in a match with Vader, and I was attempting to convey my intention to assault the injured ribs. To do this, I had put a wooden crate on the ground, which I was going to try to break with a flying headbutt. This, I thought, would illustrate his ribs being broken. I knew that if I failed to break the crate I would look foolish, so I spent an hour in the dark, by myself, visualizing my stunt.

By the time I went on the air, I was fired up, and I just knew that the crate didn't stand a chance—my visualization was too strong. And I was right—my head went through the crate quicker than audience interest in a Posse match. Unfortunately, I hadn't visualized what would happen to my head once it went through the crate. What it did end up doing was bouncing off the floor like a basketball. I lay motionless for a moment, and then tried to stand, but fell back onto my ass, at which point Jim Ross (who at the time did play-by-play for WCW) asked me about my big match. "Ugh" was all I could say. Ross then tried to cover for me, and sounding as convincing as he could when talking about a semi-conscious man with his tongue hanging out and a glazed look in his eyes, yelled, "Cactus Jack is a dangerous man!"

Okay, I'm back from my tangent now—I hope you enjoyed the trip. When I started changing from my sweatpants and sneakers into my sweatpants and sneakers (when my knee was injured, I started wearing sneakers in the ring), The Rock walked up, and we shared a laugh over the previous night's match. "I was thinking," The Rock said, "it would have been funny as hell if every time I denied it, the imaginary dick would get bigger and bigger." "Yeah," I added, "and every time we went back and forth, the imaginary sucking action would get more passionate." So there in the dressing room, we laughed out loud as we conjured up the image of larger and larger imaginary phalluses, all of which climaxed (no pun intended) with The Rock on his knees holding something the size of a fully mature anaconda in both hands while vehemently denying he would ever commit this heinous act.

Just then The Godfather stormed in. It was the first time I'd ever seen him mad, and boy, he was livid. "Those fuckin' bitches," he yelled out, which is odd because he usually treated those Ho's with the utmost respect backstage. We tried to figure out what was wrong, but he just kept repeating the same line about the, um, bitches. The two Ho's tried to make peace, but The Godfather stormed out in front of their startled eyes. It turned out that the Ho's, who are always encouraged to show off their goods in a PG-13 type of way, had taken it upon themselves to raise that rating dangerously close to an X by making out with each other and feeling each other's breasts at ringside. As jovial a guy as The Godfather is, I guess deep down, keepin' those Ho's in line is difficult work. Because, as you know, pimpin' ain't easy.

I was looking forward to the main event, which I had a feeling was going to look eerily similar to the Vegas adventure, sans The Godfather tributes. Much of what's done in the ring is ad-libbed, but we had come up with a winning formula for the "Fatal Four-Way," and besides, we were 2,000 miles from Las Vegas—who was going to know?

Kane was introduced first, followed by The Rock, who went into his "trailer-park trash, big, red, retarded ass" speech. I was up next, and immediately grabbed the mike and prepared to give my "The Rock likes to talk about men's asses" speech. There was only one problem. After I got about half my spiel out, I thought of The Rock on his knees in the dressing room, two-handing the giant imaginary penis. His facial expressions were so vivid in my mind and the whole thing was so ridiculous that I cracked. The more I tried to hold it in, the more diffi-cult it became, and I finally exploded with laughter in front of the shocked crowd. I tried to regain my com-posure, but when I went to speak, I got only a word out when I was hit again by the thought of The Rock in action. I laughed until it hurt, and then I laughed some more. I looked at referee Earl Hebner, and his face was bright red from laughter, even though he didn't have a clue what I was laughing about. I looked at The Rock, and he was covering his face with his hands, trying to retain some degree of cool-ness. Kane's mask was jumping up and down. Then I looked out at the crowd. Ten thousand people had paid good money to see talented performers put on a hell of a show and they got this travesty. Guess what? I had never seen a crowd so happy.

I believe that deep down, the crowd wants to know that we are friends. And I think that they feel good knowing that we enjoy what we do. I don't think there was any doubt in Milwaukee that evening that the World Wrestling Entertainment main event was having the time of their life in that ring, and I think quite a few of the fans in atten-dance would say the same about watching it.

As a performer, I've become well aware of the fact that much of show business is an act. That may sound a little obvious, but I'm talking more about the public personas than about the work itself. I remember being devastated when I heard that Ray and Dave Davies of the Kinks sometimes barely spoke to each other before and after shows. I sat at a few concerts where the band would have their game face on, complete with orgasmic facial expressions, during songs and witty repartees with the crowd, only to turn around and suddenly turn off the face. Sometimes it's refreshing to know that performers actually love performing.

9: *Author?*

WRESTLEMANIA SHOULD BE the high point of a
wrestler's year. For me, both creatively and emotionally, it was among the lowest. A few weeks before
Mania, I had seen the poster for April's *Backlash*
Pay-Per-View, on which I was featured. I felt a little
funny about bailing out on a show that I was a focus
of as well as missing matches well on into May that
had already been advertised. I have a desire, border-
ing on an obsession, to never miss an advertised
date, which was probably instilled in me during my
DeNucci training days. For a guy who actually has a
T-shirt devoted to his vast array of injuries, I take
great pride in not missing a show due to injury in my
first eight and a half years of wrestling, and during
my years in the World Wrestling Entertainment only
missed the four shows following my *King of the
Ring* match in 1998. With my pride at stake, I
talked the WWE into letting me postpone my surgery until the end of May, when all of my advertised
dates would be fulfilled.

The World Wrestling Entertainment appreciated
my guts, pride, and dedication. My children appreciated that I would have my whole summer free, which,
in truth, had been more of a consideration in moving

my surgery date than that whole pride thing. So with visions of amusement parks dancing in my head, I limped through the next three months, including a *WrestleMania* matchup with the seven-foot, 450-pound Big Show Paul Wight that ranked right up there with my worst-ever Pay-Per-View offerings.

Show was a hot commodity from WCW who the World Wrestling Entertainment was counting on to headline *WrestleMania* 2000. A *Mania* matchup with Austin, it was thought, would set buy-rate records. To do that, however, Show would need to be a good guy for most of the next year so as to avoid giving the fans the proposed dream match too soon. So, almost from the start, when he appeared as Vince's hired corporate goon part, Big Show's babyface seeds had been planted. So in other words, no one really cared about my match at *Wrestle-Mania*, which carried a winner-referees-the-main-event stipulation.

I won by disqualification, after getting destroyed for most of the match, and Big Show turned face immediately afterward by punching Vince McMahon. I did get to make the three-count in the main event, after rushing back from the "hospital" where I had been treated for my "injuries." I've got to admit it was a thrill being out there for that match, as the crowd was in a frenzy, and I got to witness close up an excellent last few minutes of the Austin-Rock matchup.

So *WrestleMania* 1999 had not exactly been a high point of my career, but it stands out in my mind for one important reason: it was the day I found out I was going to be an author.

"Hey, did you hear the news?" I was asked by

John Nahani, one of our producers in the World Wrestling Entertainment, and the man responsible for the World Wrestling Entertainment's highly acclaimed Super Bowl commercials. "The World Wrestling Entertainment is going to do an autobiography on you, and my dad is going to write it." I was stunned, but in a happy way. I had often visualized my life story in book form, but had doubted it would ever become reality, especially because no large publishing house had ever shown an interest in previous wrestling books. The World Wrestling Entertainment, in an agreement with ReganBooks of the HarperCollins family, had changed that. "They're going to do three books," Nahani informed me, "Austin, Rock, and you, and yours is going to come out first."

I met John's dad Larry the next day. He came up to my room at the Airport Holiday Inn and began explaining the book publishing process to me. "It's very easy, Michael," he said, using the name that my mother had reserved only for when I was in big trouble as a child. "You tell your story into the microphone, and I turn it into a book." This all sounded a little too easy to me. I mean, shouldn't I have to actually do some writing to get my name on a book? But after all, Larry was a veteran of seventeen books, which included some of sports' biggest names of the 1970s, so who was I to argue?

Still, I was a little surprised by this news, because I had been an avid reader of sports autobiographies when I was a kid, and had always assumed that the star on the book's cover was the actual writer. Larry laughed when I said this. "Michael, none of these guys do any of the writing. They tell the story, and

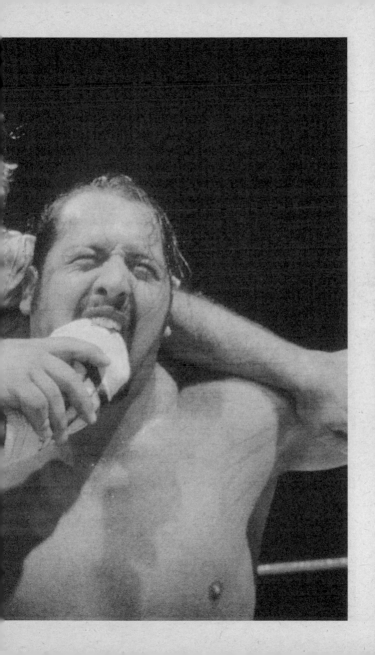

then I fill in the blanks, put in some quotes, and write the book. It's called creative license." I don't think I was this let down when I found out the tooth fairy wasn't real. "Larry, that somehow doesn't seem right," I said, although I had the feeling that my sense of right and wrong was not a concern of the publishing industry. Larry laughed. At sixty-nine years old, he had been around sports and its stars for his entire adult life. He knew better. "Michael, I wrote one baseball superstar's book after talking with him for half an hour. He was never going to write his own book—none of these guys are. That's just the way it is."

Grudgingly, I accepted this somewhat strange and more than somewhat dishonest news. I looked at the bright side, instead. Hey, I was going to be an author, wasn't I, and besides, it was at least going to be all in my own words, right? So, after rationalizing this whole autobiographical process in my head, I began telling my life story, and entrusting its outcome to a sixty-nine-year-old man who barely knew my name.

The next day I picked Larry up and we began our drive to the next town. He had a yellow legal pad with several paragraphs written on it. "This," he said with great pride, "is the beginning of your book." Like a kid on Christmas morning anxious for his big gift, I begged Larry to let me have an earful. My life was about to be immortalized on the printed page, and even better, I was going to be an author without actually writing a single word. With a little urging, Larry laid it on me:

"I was born Michael Francis Foley, a typical Irish name if ever there was one, but our family was not the typical Irish vision of free-flowing beer on Saturday and church on Sunday. Hell, I didn't even make my first communion until I was eighteen, an age when the other guys on the block already had their first girlfriends. After all, what kind of a girl would want to go out with a guy who hadn't had his first communion?"

I was a little shocked. I should have known right then that this partnership wasn't going to work out. "What do you think, Michael?" Larry asked. "I'll tell you, I'm a writing fool." When I spoke it was with great trepidation. I had genuinely liked Larry during my time with him the previous day and wanted to spare his feelings. But I couldn't let a book on my life begin this way. "Larry, I have a few problems with it. First off, most of the guys on the block have their first girlfriends at twelve, not eighteen. Also, I don't think having communion is a prerequisite for dating. I mean, I don't think girls would ever say, 'Hey, he's nice and cute and all . . . but he hasn't made communion yet.' "

Larry was not to be deterred. "That's okay, Michael, we'll change it."

I had a bigger problem, however. "Larry, I didn't actually say any of those things to you."

So let me get this straight. A "ghostwriter" takes a tape recording, fills in blanks, makes up quotes, and changes facts? Then a person who has never written a word of the resulting book gets credit for being an author? I certainly was surprised to find out that in many ways, the prestigious business of publishing books was, in truth, faker than pro wrestling.

10: *MMM,* *Beefy*

THE WORLD OF COMMERCIALS wanted me. Chef Boyardee felt that I, and I alone, embodied the qualities that made a man a "Boyardeeavore," a primitive beast whose only urge is to inhale as much of the quality canned pasta product as possible. I was ready.

I attacked the role with an enthusiasm that would have impressed Stanislavsky, and left in my wake an image of a Boyardeeavore that all future Chef pitchmen would strive to live up to. We shot the commercial at the Wild Animal Safari in Pine Mountain, Georgia. Along the way, I was not only exposed to exotic creatures from around the globe, but also attacked by a llama. I had no idea how to defend myself from a llama, so I did the only thing that a battle-scarred hardcore legend could do: I screamed and hid behind a tree. After all, none of my in-depth training at DeNucci's had included llama attacks. Thinking rationally, a guy really should be wary of any creature that would hang out with Michael Jackson—including that Webster guy. But of all the exotic beasts I met during the Chef shoot, none was more unique than Evan Metropolis.

I was introduced to Evan in my dressing trailer by

one of the World Wrestling Entertainment marketing representatives. "Mick, this is Evan," the rep said. "He is the head of all International Home Foods' marketing." International Home Foods was a multi-billion-dollar company, and standing in front of me was its head of marketing—a seventeen-year-old kid. "Hello," the kid said, "it's nice to meet you. It was my idea to use you in this campaign." I looked at him—fresh-faced, rosy-cheeked, and slightly chubby, and thought someone was playing a rib on me.

It reminded me of when I met Joe C., the three-foot-eight-inch Kid Rock sidekick, who claimed to not only have a "high-ass voice like Aaron Neville," but also a ten-foot member. I met Joe six years ago, when I was at an independent show in Detroit, and he was backstage using language that would have made even Dallas Page say, "Wait a minute, bro." When I reprimanded the little guy, I was told he was eighteen. I asked for proof, and he whipped out an official Michigan license with what looked to be a five-year-old's picture on it. Years later I saw his picture in *People* magazine and found out he had become a big rock star. Before his untimely death last year, Joe even traveled to shows with World Wrestling Entertainment wrestlers X-Pac and Road Dogg, and had become something of an unofficial World Wrestling Entertainment mascot.

Gradually, I learned that Evan was worth millions, that he actually produced movies, and was a regular on Howard Stern's radio show. I asked him where he hung out on weekends, figuring he'd say "at the arcade" or "with my buddies outside the 7-Eleven," and instead heard "either South Beach or the Greek isles." He even offered to fly me to Greece on his private jet. I had to decline, however, when he told me he liked to rumble on the weekends and that he'd never lost one of these fights. This kid didn't look like he could lick a stamp, and I told him so. "Come on, Evan"—I laughed—"how much do you pay these guys to do the job for you?"

Later I was told by the World Wrestling Entertainment rep that Evan had liked me because I was one of the only people who had ever disagreed with him about anything. I even got a chance to hit him with an empty ravioli can during the filming of a special International Home Foods video presentation. I hit him hard too. And then he hugged me. If anyone else had hit Evan with a can, they would be in the spoon position with Jimmy Hoffa about now.

The commercial was a big hit, and my tag line of "Mmmm, beefy" became an oft-repeated catchphrase for many months. I was even brought back later in the year to reprise my role as the Boyardeeavore, this time on a rampage in New York City. Evan and I hung out quite a bit on this shoot, and I even felt close enough to him to offer some genuine friendly advice. When I was told of Evan's fondness for sexual encounters with beautiful women, I was actually quite sad for him. When he told me of his quest to sleep with 1,000 women by his twenty-first birthday, I could feel his pain. When he told me he was already in the 350 range, I wanted to give him a friendly hug. When he told me that he'd actually nailed one of them while wearing the autographed Cactus Jack shirt I'd given him, I wanted to cry. With a shake of my head and gentle pat on the shoulder, and trying my best to invoke my inner role model, I spoke to him with the voice of wisdom. "Evan, one day you will learn that it is better to make love to the same woman a thousand times than to make love to a thousand women." I never heard anyone laugh so hard. Then Evan spoke with a wisdom that belied his tender age. "You never got laid when you were my age, did you?"

I have had a couple of other commercial-making experiences, but neither was as positive as the ones with Chef. Straight off my Boyardeeavore success, I was asked by the World Wrestling Entertainment to star in a spot for the Jakks' toys "Titantron," which many stores were counting on to make their Christmas. I felt up to the challenge.

The Titantron was a kind of stage that would play each World Wrestling Entertainment Superstar's music and announce their names when they were placed on it. The idea behind the commercial was that Mankind was only happy when he was having his name announced—he felt sad when he was out of the spotlight. So to combat his loneliness, he hires a guy named Ted to forever announce him in his everyday life. I loved the concept—Ted, with a megaphone, announcing me as I walked down the street, made a phone call, went to the bathroom, and so on. Unfortunately, I didn't love the director, who treated this children's toy commercial as if he were adapting Stephen Hawking's *A Brief History of Time* for a *Hallmark Hall of Fame* production.

The script sure seemed simple. "When I walk through the Titantron, I feel happy." Okay, here I go. "When I walk through the Titantron, I feel happy." Great. One take. What's next? *What?* I'm not capturing the mood? Okay, what kind of mood do you want? Now, the director, an overly arty New York prima donna with a Cosmo Kramer hairdo, offered his take on the line. "Okay, right now imagine that you lost your puppy. Now you found your puppy. You lost your puppy—you found your puppy. Give it a try."

I gave it a try. "No, no, no," the director yelled. "I didn't get any sense that your puppy was lost— nor did I feel any joy when your puppy was found. Come on now—I need that emotion." Twenty-four times I lost that damn puppy, and twenty-four times I found it. None of it was good enough for this guy, who probably would've been smacked around like Talia Shire in *The Godfather* if he'd tried to tell De Niro to find his puppy. The director made it clear that he was lowering his standards to work with me.

Next line: "I miss that feeling." Simple enough, especially since all I had to do was stir a cup of coffee. Ready and action. "Okay, stir that coffee. You love that coffee. Your life is that coffee." Take one. I stir the coffee. "Cut—I'm not sensing that you even care about that coffee. You've got to show me you love it. Can you show me?" I told him I would try. Eighteen takes later I still wasn't sure if I had accurately portrayed one man's love for a cup of coffee, but we moved on nonetheless.

The next line was the key. This is where I informed the world that everything would be all right now that I had Ted. "So I got Ted" was the line. Simple, right? But not apparently as simple as one might expect. "You're a mischievous little boy," the director explained. "You're eating cake before dinner, and you're getting away with it." I tried to be mischievous, and I tried to taste that cake as I delivered my line, but it wasn't good enough. The director was losing his patience with me. " 'So I got Ted'—come on, let me feel it." Actually, my own patience was now thinner than a *Love Boat* plot, and besides, I thought this director was overanalyzing this whole thing just a little bit.

"Listen," I said, "wouldn't this be the perfect time to slip into my Mankind persona?" The director looked dumbfounded. "What is the Mankind persona?" he asked. This guy had wasted a whole morning with meaningless takes concerning lost puppies and incredibly important cups of coffee. I wanted to yell, but kept my cool. Still, I couldn't let this pretentious prick off the hook without at least a few thoughts of my own. "You're making a wrestling toy commercial starring a wrestler, which will be seen by wrestling fans on a wrestling show. Shouldn't you at least be familiar with your talent?" The guy looked like he'd just lost his puppy. I then delivered one warbling Mankind "So I got Ted" and the crew applauded as if I was Carlton Fisk homering in the twelfth inning of Game 6 in 1975. Even the PP (pretentious prick) was impressed. I kept waiting for the commercial to air, and it never did. Instead, a spot featuring the action figures being held by kids' hands aired while "Now entering the Titantron" blared over and over. I felt so guilty. If only I had stirred that coffee a little better.

The other commercial-making experience was in reality nothing more than an audition in New York City, but was memorable nonetheless. I was working for Extreme Championship Wrestling during the spring of 1995, when Paul Heyman, the mad professor of sports-entertainment, told me about an audition for an American Express commercial starring Jerry Seinfeld. Only a few wrestlers were going to be there, Paul assured me, before adding that he felt I was the odds-on favorite for the gig.

It was a cattle call. Not only was every guy who'd laced up a pair of boots in the last ten years there, but every tattooed biker and musclehead in the tri-state area as well. I knew in all probability that it was much more important to look good than to actually be good, and with the knowledge that I carried about as much muscle on my body as an inactive twelve-year-old, I felt that my chances weren't all that good. Nonetheless, I waited my turn and changed into my working gear when called upon.

"You've got quite a few scars on your arms," the casting director noted quite accurately. I took this to mean that my chances of being picked were slimmer than Calista Flockhart surviving a hunger strike. "Where did you get all those from?" I tried to explain my propensity for Japanese barbed-wire matches as a means to paying my mortgage in as quick a way as possible, but the director's look of disgust lasted long after my story had ended.

"If we pick you for this story," the lady inquired, "what can you do to Jerry without hurting him?" In this situation, I did what every wrestler worth his salt would do when questioned about his talent. I lied my ass off. I rattled off the names of moves that I hadn't tried in years, some that I'd never even attempted, and some that hadn't even been invented yet. Hell, I think I even told her I could dropkick. Oddly, despite my stated mastery of every move ever performed, and my ability to perform them all without harming a hair on Jerry's head, I didn't get the part. In fact, nobody did, as the proposed commercial was scrapped.

A few days after the cattle call, I was talking with a few ECW wrestlers and comparing notes on the commercial audition. Like me, the other wrestlers' lists of moves they could perform without hurting Jerry ranged from slight exaggeration to outright

whoppers. All except Tazz, who at five-foot-seven and 270 pounds of muscle was known as "the human suplex machine." Tazz opted instead for the honest approach. "Hey, I told 'em I couldn't guarantee nothin'," he told us in his Red Hook, Brooklyn, accent. "I told 'em that if Jerry gets in there with me, he's kind of taking his chances."

11: *Bad Body, Britney, and the Boiler Room*

IN THE JUNE 1998 *King of the Ring* Pay-Per-View, the "Hell in a Cell" match had nearly ended my career. The Undertaker throwing me off the sixteen-foot cell onto the Spanish announcers' table has become the wrestling equivalent of the Zapruder film in that it has been seen, visually dissected, and talked about so often. The flight off the top certainly was a tremendous sight to behold, but ironically, it was a second fall that night (that garnered nowhere near the attention of the first) that nearly ended my career.

Following my Spanish announcer landing, I had somehow managed to climb off the stretcher I was being carted out on and return to action, at which point I immediately began scaling the immense structure again. The crowd's response was phenomenal, and I had chills running down my spine as I climbed the last few feet. The Undertaker was waiting on top, and put his hand around my throat to signal a chokeslam on top of the cage—a move we hoped would slightly tear a section of the steel mesh. Instead, the cage gave way instantly and sent me crashing violently to the canvas, where my unconscious body came to rest in an awkward, twisted pose.

The World Wrestling Entertainment's ring had been infamous for its lack of give. Dating back to 1985, when the World Wrestling Entertainment was on NBC on a monthly basis on *Saturday Night's Main Event,* the old rings had been replaced by rings that, in accordance with NBC's wishes, would not move when they were landed on. This, it was thought, would look better on television.

Perhaps these rings did look better on television screens, but there were other screens that did not benefit from NBC's solid-construction idea—namely X-ray and MRI screens. As a result, World Wrestling Entertainment wrestlers either cut down on their risks, or lived with the consequences. Backs were often injured, serious neck injuries became more frequent, and careers were cut short. New, safer rings had been rumored to be in the works for years, but no one believed it would ever come to pass.

I believe my "Hell in a Cell" match may have sped up the process, because in less than a month, we were throwing each other around these new rings at a level of general health that had previously been unthinkable. Ironically, these safer rings may have actually hastened the end of my career.

The new rings had a certain degree of bounce, which was good in terms of landing. In terms of running, however, I felt very awkward. It felt like running on an unstable surface, and was made worse during tag-team matches, when several wrestlers could end up in the ring at the same time. As a result, my knees took a pounding every night, which caused simple walking to become quite painful and made a flight of stairs my worst enemy. I couldn't wait for surgery, which I hoped would be a miracle cure. First, however, I had to get past the Big Show in a "Boiler Room Brawl."

I felt like I needed a match with the Show in order to complete the story we had begun before *Wrestle-Mania*, even though now as I write this, the only story I can remember is him being a lot bigger than me and beating the crap out of me. Russo and Vince were concerned, because such a match, they thought, would put Show in a position to be booed—a sound they definitely didn't want to hear. "What if we have it in the boiler room?" I said, in reference to the place that I used to call home during the early days of the Mankind character. The early Mankind was portrayed as dark and demented, and inhabited boiler rooms in arenas throughout the country. He rocked incessantly, pulled his real hair out in clumps, and called for his mommy. The evolved Mankind was more fun than dark and more dorky than demented, but somehow my ties to the boiler room had not been completely severed.

This locale, I felt, would be the perfect place for the Mankind–Paul Wight showdown, because fans would never be able to boo the Show since he'd never set foot in the ring. Vince and Russo saw the logic in this, and the second-ever "Boiler Room Brawl" was booked for the April *Backlash* Pay-Per-View in Providence, Rhode Island.

Now I had another problem. What the hell was I going to do in a boiler room with a 450-pound man? The first "Boiler Room Brawl" with the Undertaker in Cleveland in the summer of 1996 had been a memorable battle. Not everyone found it enjoyable, as it was twenty-seven minutes long with only a single camera and no audio from the announcers, but they found it memorable nonetheless. The brawl was memorable for a reason. We beat the hell out of each other in there. I had pushed my body to the limit, and had paid the price in painful mornings for the next several days. In April 1999, my mornings were already painful, even without a 450-pound man pummeling me. Big Show was going to need to be led through this thing, and at 450 pounds, I had a hunch that the match would not involve a whole lot of flying around on his part. No, for the second "Boiler Room Brawl" to succeed, I was going to need to absorb incredible punishment. Fortunately, I had an ace up my sleeve.

Richie Posner is a genius. The guy can do more things with his two hands than anyone I have ever met, and that's not including his love life. He has been responsible for the magic involved in the "Buried Alive" matches right down to making Mankind's referee shirt for *WrestleMania*, and even making balloon animals for my kids. He will hate being acknowledged in this book because he thinks "it will ruin the magic," but I feel he has to be singled out for his contributions. Richie had been a big help to me and we talked at almost every show, but Richie Posner knew better than to try to help out with my matches.

Three years earlier, when I was still fairly new with the World Wrestling Entertainment, Richie had approached me about using special-effects props for my "Boiler Room Brawl." I was almost offended. "Richie, don't take this personally," I told the eternally Hawaiian-shirt-wearing Posner, "but I don't believe in using special effects or props in my matches." Indeed, I was a believer in using what was available to me at the time—it seemed more real to me, and unfortunately for my body, it felt that way too. In 1999, however, my testicles no longer seemed quite so full of fortitude as they had in the past. Meekly, I approached Richie with a simple request. "Do you think you could come up with as much stuff as possible that looks painful, but doesn't hurt?"

So it came to pass that in April 1999, Mick Foley, the hardcore legend, used fake glass, fake steam, and even, dare I say it, *fake blood* in a match that turned out better than I could ever have expected. Don't get me wrong—I still got the hell beaten out of me, but it was a good kind of hell beaten out of me, and I sat back and enjoyed the rest of the show in Providence with the knowledge that I had done something special. Unfortunately, the long and successful marriage of Mick Foley and show-stealing matches came to a screeching halt following my "Boiler Room" victory. This painful divorce would last for nine months. At least I had Britney.

Nothing could make me forget about the pain like the opening chords of "Hit Me Baby, One More Time." Hey, say what you want about Britney's voice, boobs, or lip-synching—but don't try to deny that "Hit Me Baby" was infectious feel-good music that hadn't been heard since the summer of "MMM Bop" a few years earlier. The two songs shared something else besides a groovy beat and a hot blond singer: people over a certain age had to pretend they didn't like it. Especially when they were known as blood-and-guts, take-no-prisoners, ask-for-no-quarter-and-receive-none, hardcore legends.

So for a while I tried to lie, not only to others, but to myself as well. I wasn't really a Britney Spears fan, was I? Of course not. Then, in my mind, I would hear that driving backbeat and would hear Britney's sweet but not that innocent voice sing "In my mind, I still believe," before assuming the role of the chorus and loudly belting out "still believe." I felt so guilty leading this double life, until I finally came clean inside a rented Lumina on a road trip with Al Snow and the Blue Meanie. "You like that song." Al laughed disbelievingly, before quickly adding, "Me too." The Meanie was even more supportive. "I love that song—it's my favorite." Then, as if by magic, the driving piano of the opening chords came charging forth from the Lumina's standard factory stereo system, and we fired that mother up. Dancing in the car seats and singing out loud, we barreled down Interstate 95 on the way to another sold-out show.

I arrived several hours early for a show at Philadelphia's First Union Center that May. These days, all the arenas have corporate names. The Summit in Houston is now the Compaq Center, the Meadowlands Arena in New Jersey is now the Continental Airlines Arena, and the Scranton Catholic Youth Center is now, well, I guess that one hasn't changed. Actually, the World Wrestling Entertainment doesn't go to the CYC anymore, and I'm pretty much the guy to either blame or thank for that, depending on how you look at things.

The CYC is a tiny, dingy building that the World Wrestling Entertainment had been coming to for decades. It was a great place for atmosphere, and a great place to have fun, but somehow the fun didn't seem quite so fun when we got our Scranton payoff. The Catholic community was getting concerned about the World Wrestling Entertainment's bad-boy image in 1998, and as a result, when we came to Scranton that year, we were urged by road agent Jack Lanza to watch our language during the show. At least Lanza urged most of us. Even DX, a renegade band of hoodlums who were phenomenally popular, toned down their act, so instead of yelling their trademark "suck it" in a tag match against me and Kane, DX members Road Dogg and Billy Gunn let the crowd yell the offensive and somewhat graphic tag line. Unfortunately, Lanza hadn't spoken to me, because as he later said, "You were the last guy I would ever think would be offensive." Apparently he misjudged me, because as soon as the crowd yelled the two naughty words, I went into a panic. This is back when Mankind was still a little dark, and I had Paul Bearer, or "Uncle Paul," as my manager. "Uncle Paul," I squealed into the mike, "I don't want to suck it, don't make me suck it, I'm not going to suck it!" When I returned from my match, I was told that the World Wrestling Entertainment would never be welcome in the building again.

Anyway, while I was hanging out in Philadelphia, I began talking to a security guard, who informed me that Britney Spears was playing that night at the Tower Theatre in Philadelphia. I was caught completely unaware, and with my defenses down, let an "oh my God" slip out. Not a Joey Styles, ECW "OH

MY GOD" either, but more like a Moon Unit Zappa 1982 valley girl "Ohmigawd!" The guard was stunned to find out that the hardcore legend was in fact a fan of the current queen of bubblegum pop. His next question was a shocker: "Do you want to meet her?" I was shocked, but quickly regained my cool so that even while my mind was saying "Ohmigawd, can I? Really? For real," my mouth was saying, "Sure."

With visions of Britney's perfect choreography dancing in my head, I headed out to the parking lot with the guard (who knew a guard at the Tower) for what can only be described as a "pilgrimage." As I hopped into my car, I saw World Wrestling Entertainment star Edge getting out of his. Edge and I were pretty tight, and in fact our "white guy jumping high five" had put the frosting on many an "Al Snow joke" cake! Still, despite the bond that two men feel when they share a blind hatred for Al Snow, I debated asking Edge along on this journey. What if he laughed at me? I decided to go for broke. "Edgester," I yelled out jovially before proceeding somewhat less jovially, "want to meet Britney Spears?" In a flash, the Edgester was in the car, and after a similar encounter with Stevie Richards/Dancin' Stevie Richards/Big Stevie Cool, we were off to meet the Brizzard. Yeah, I know, that's a little weak.

As soon as we pulled into the Tower Theatre, we were met by throngs of yelling preteen and teenage girls, proving that being a Britney Spears fan and a World Wrestling Entertainment fan are not mutually exclusive. A few minutes later we were given our private audience with the singer, who . . . didn't know who the hell we were. She was polite and kind, but I couldn't help but feel a little disappointed. Up close, Britney looked suspiciously like any other eighteen-year-old. Granted, if she had suddenly broken into "Oh baybeh, baybeh, how was I supposed to know," I would have swooned like a hysterical chick at a 1964 Beatles concert, but we all felt a little let down as we headed for the door with our own Britney eight-by-ten autographed photos and three complimentary tickets to her show for our efforts.

This, however, was not the story that the puppy-love-struck Blue Meanie heard when we got back to the First Union Center. "Britney loved us," Stevie told the wide-eyed Meanie. "But especially Mick." Edge's next statement was brilliant. "Yeah, she nestled her head into his shoulder and gave him a big hug like he was a favorite uncle." A lesser man would have gone with a stupid "she nailed him right in front of us" line that would have ruined all credibility. Instead, by exercising wisdom and moderation, Edge had the Meanie believing every word.

That night, I wrestled "Bad Ass" Billy Gunn, who by now was a heel in the scheme of things. With my thimbleful of natural athletic ability further reduced by my problem knees, I had to resort to other means to entertain the fans. Like brown-nosing. Nothing is as gratuitous as wearing a Flyers hockey jersey for a match in Philadelphia, but then again, nothing is as cheaply effective. As had become my custom, I grabbed for the mike to try to cover up the lackluster performance that I was about to put on. "Billy Gunn, you call yourself a badass? Well why don't you take a look as I show all of Philadelphia what a real *bad*ass looks like." With that, I pulled my sweats down to my knees, and gave the City of Brotherly Love a look at my Fruit Of The Loom–covered buttocks. Even with white cotton covering my butt, the display elicited groans, followed by cheers. The fans in Philadelphia admired my guts, if not my ass.

Philadelphia has a long history for having the most heartless fans on the planet. The city's nickname was something of a misnomer, because in truth, there was not a whole lot of love there. With that in mind, I knew that I had to choose my next words very delicately. I could feel the knot tightening in my stomach, but dammit, I had to let my intentions be known. "I have a lot of history in this city. Whether I was Mankind, Dude Love, or Cactus Jack." The crowd cheered a little at the name of Cactus. "I have tried to put on the best matches that I possibly could, whether it was here in the World Wrestling Entertainment"—slight cheers—"WCW"— slight boos—"or in the ECW arena." A small but noticeable "ECW, ECW" chant began. "Over the years I have spilled a lot of blood, sweat, and even a few tears in this city." The crowd cheered appreciatively. I had indeed been in some wild contests in Philadelphia, and many of the fans remembered them fondly. I looked across the ring at Gunn, who seemed impressed by my heartfelt words. Actually my next words were the most heartfelt of all as I asked a favor of the crowd. "With that in mind, I hope you will all forgive me for tonight's match, because I have tickets to the Britney Spears concert, and I want to get the hell out of here as fast as I can!"

I looked back at Gunn, whose jaw had dropped in disbelief. Even with 18,000 fans booing, I could hear Referee Tim White's New England accent as he yelled, "Holy shit, I've never heard that one before." Yeah, the crowd was booing, but it wasn't a "boo Mitch 'Wild Thing' Williams so loud that he can't throw strikes anymore and has to retire" type of boo. This was a friendly boo. A "we admire your honesty" boo.

The bell rang, and while we didn't stink the place up, we didn't set it on fire either. After a few minutes of back-and-forth action, Billy had me from behind in a "rear chin lock," a position in which I could rest, but more important, a position from which Billy could flex his muscles for his own enjoyment. Then I saw him. Al. Walking down the aisle with something in his hand. When he got to ringside, I saw them. The Britney tickets. So close that I could almost touch them, but first I had Billy Gunn to dispose of. The crowd, sensing the urgency, and knowing that Britney, along with the Britney Spears Dancers, was already in full swing, started clapping in unison. Al started waving the tickets to the rhythm of the crowd. Strangler Lewis rolled over in his grave. With a superhuman effort, I fought back. It was almost as if I had channeled Britney's fresh-scrubbed, clean-living, teenage energy. I fired big lefts that had the "Bad Ass" reeling. He charged me with a clothesline, but I ducked it and caught him with a double-arm DDT. Now it was Socko time. I lifted my shirt and dramatically pointed to the front of my sweatpants. If I had pointed to the general vicinity of my genitalia even eight months earlier, the gesture would have been met with a combination of disinterest and nausea. Now, with "Sockomania" running wild, 18,000 people erupted. The eruption peaked when I pulled Mr. Socko out of my pants and slid him on my hand. Now, if I had pulled a flaccid, white object out of my pants eight months earlier . . . never mind. I clamped on the Socko Claw, and when the bell was rung, I threw Socko to the crowd, and hightailed it up the aisle with Al to take in a memorable last encore at the Tower Theatre.

Actually we never made it to the show, but what the hell—I've got creative license, right? The Britney Spears saga doesn't end there, however. Not with a dejected Blue Meanie to rib. With the help of Miss Kitty's (blond/black/red/blue-haired valet now named The Kat) little-girl, Southern-belle voice, I was able to continue this "favorite uncle" charade.

A few days after Philadelphia, I made sure I stood

near the Meanie when I was retrieving my messages on my cellular phone. I used to hate guys with cell phones, but as their popularity grew, I realized I would have to hate an awful lot of people. So using the old adage "If you can't beat them, join them," I became a stupid cellphone user.

After a few moments I let my eyes widen in mock surprise and said, "Meanie, listen to this." I played him the message, and he heard Kitty's tiny voice. "Hi, Mick, this is Britney Spears and I just wanted to say that I really enjoyed meeting you in Philadelphia. I really hope that I can see you again on my tour so I can give you a big hug. My cousin is a huge fan, and I was wondering if you could send him a picture. If you can, just mail it to the address I gave you. Okay, bye."

The Meanie was momentarily speechless. While he was regaining his composure, I took out Britney's address, which in reality had been written down by Miss Kitty as well. "Wow," the Meanie finally managed to get out, "that's really great!" He sounded a lot like the runner-up at the Miss America pageant, pretending to be happy for the winner.

I had an elaborate phone-message plan worked out that would include Britney gradually replacing her "favorite uncle" image of me for a somewhat less innocent relationship, culminating in a rendezvous in some romantic location. Unfortunately, at about that time my daughter Noelle became a big Britney fan, and I could no longer justify a sick, lust-filled affair with the teen pop sensation, even if it was make-believe.

A few nights later Test captured the Hardcore Title. A strange phenomenon occurred that night, the likes of which we may never experience again in our lifetimes. The moon was full on that spring night, but was almost completely blocked out by a huge cloud formation. When the formation passed, the moon disappeared. The wind began to howl, and the atmospheric conditions were such that even though the title bout had taken place in Connecticut, at the exact moment that Test's triumphant hand was raised . . . all the way from Amarillo, Texas . . . I could hear Terry Funk weeping.

12: *The Kiddie Pool at Munchkin Land*

I RECEIVED LARRY'S OPENING chapter on May 8, 1999. We had driven up and down the road during the previous week and had hit it off pretty well, and even though he still insisted on calling me Michael, I hoped for the best. I had convinced Larry that we needed to begin the book with something hard-hitting—something that would suck the readers in and leave them wanting more. A gripping account of losing two-thirds of my ear in Germany would be a perfect introduction to my life in the world of sports-entertainment. I couldn't wait to read how this seasoned literary veteran would capture every drop of blood, every ounce of emotion, and every thought in my mind in this opening chapter.

By the time I got to Larry's work, it was midnight following a grueling day of traveling and television taping. I began with the intention of just skimming a few chapters before nodding off. Instead, I woke up in a hurry, and stayed up for the next five hours, crossing out lines and making notes on every available space on the paper.

My life story was in big trouble. To say I was disappointed would be like saying the Battle of Gettysburg was a squabble. Everything about it was wrong. The first chapter was supposed to suck people in. In this respect, it was partly successful—it certainly did suck. I wanted people to know what it felt like to be me and feel the life being choked out of me—to actually feel like I was dying as the ring ropes held my neck in a viselike grip. I wanted the readers to know that the only way out was to use my remaining strength to squeeze out of ropes so tight that they literally pushed my ear off my head. I wanted the readers to hear every groan, to see the steady parade of blood droplets splattering the blue protective mats crimson. And I wanted Larry to explain how it felt to actually continue the match, only to find out later that I was without one auditory unit.

Instead, I got "the ropes were tight, and I could feel myself passing out. I pulled my head out, and saw that I was bleeding." I needed more.

My father came across in Larry's writing as a distant, coldhearted bastard. One line read, "My father was a man of few words. He liked to make his point and move on." My dad? A man of few words? My dad uses words like a needle uses thread. He loves to talk. He doesn't make points and move on. He makes points, explains them, elaborates on them, and then summarizes them. If I let this chapter stay as it was, I would be disowned.

Larry had explained the importance of telling readers what my favorite foods were. This came

across as "for a while, ham was my favorite food, and I could eat Boston cream pie every day. Mom made the best spaghetti on the block. Dad would never miss a meal at home simply because Mom was such a good cook." This stuff had about as much depth to it as the kiddie pool at Munchkin Land. Worst of all, Larry wrote about wrestling matches as if they were real, an error that readers would find inexcusable in the current wrestling atmosphere.

I had a sinking feeling as I tried to go to sleep. The next day I would be seeing Larry, and I knew we needed to have a long talk.

"Michael, what do you think? I told you I was a writing fool," Larry opened our discussion the following day. This was going to be hard. Larry was such a nice guy and he took his writing seriously. "Larry, I think we'd better sit down." Our discussion was interesting.

"Larry, I don't really think you made people feel like I was in a whole lot of danger when I lost my ear."

"Well, were you?"

"Yes, I was, and not only that, but when I was waiting for medical help, you made me sound like a whiner, when you write, 'Where the hell is the ambulance? How long am I going to wait here looking at a pool of my own blood? Why the hell won't anyone help me?'"

"Well, what would you say?"

"I would say, 'Could somebody please help me. I really need some help, please.'"

"Michael, you just lost an ear—you're going to be upset. You're not going to say please.'"

"Larry, that's what I did say. I always say please."

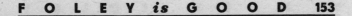

"Okay, I'll put it in, then."

"Now, Larry, my dad will be crushed if we print any of this. This isn't anything like my dad."

"Okay, we'll work on that."

"Now, about the girl I met during my first week of school—instead of saying, 'Her big breasts really turned me on,' how about, 'Her combination of sexy voice, swinging sweater puppets, and morally casual attitude, had me smitten?'"

"If you say so."

"Now, where you write, 'My idol when I was ten was Fonzie—I wanted to be like Fonzie'—maybe you should explain who Fonzie was."

"Who was he?"

"You never heard of the Fonz?"

"No."

"Okay, what if we said, 'My idol when I was ten was the Fonz of TV's seventies sitcom *Happy Days*. The Fonz was definitely the man. Fix a jukebox with a slap of his hand? No problem. And chicks—the Fonz had them lined up at the door.' And then at the end we'll add a 'Heyyy' with about three *y*s on the end."

"Michael, you can't do that."

"Why not?"

"Because 'hey' is not a sentence."

At this point I looked to Edge, tag-team daredevil brothers the Hardy Boyz, and Albert, a bald-headed hairy-backed 350-pound monster with thirty-three piercings on his body. "Hey, guys," I yelled, "what does the Fonz say?" Simultaneously they went, "Heyyy!" Grudgingly, Larry agreed to add it.

Next I brought up a story about my time in Nigeria, where I was shocked by the local custom of men holding hands. The quote itself was a good one, and Larry had printed it in its entirety. But after looking at the quote, I came up with a punch line to end it that I thought was pretty clever. Larry thought it was disgusting. I decided to read the passage, complete with new ending, to my esteemed panel of experts.

"I later came to see this gesture as the ultimate compliment, and was flattered to think that this middle-aged black man from Africa had embraced a young white man from another continent according to his local custom. It was a true gesture of friendship from a true gentleman." I then paused a second before delivering my last line. "Either that, or the guy wanted to hammer me." The wrestlers loved it, and their laughing seemed to hurt Larry's feelings. "All right, we'll keep it"—he shrugged—"but I don't think it's right."

We were making progress, but one thing was becoming readily apparent. Larry had told me that his talent was making his words sound like those of the person he was writing about. I had no doubt that he had made his words sound like Don Shula's in the mid-seventies. He was at that time a forty-five-year-old man trying to sound like a forty-five-year-old-man. I didn't read Larry's book on Shula and I'm not a betting man, but I would be willing to bet that Shula never said, "Man, every time Csonka bent over, I wanted to put some yardage in his backfield."

Larry had actually been a wrestling journalist decades earlier. Some people told me that he was the preeminent wrestling writer of his day. But in Larry's day, wrestling was covered as if the contests were real. This had to be changed, or else the readers would fart on *Have a Nice Day!* so loud it would sound like the bombing of Baghdad. This last subject really hurt Larry. He had gone from being wrestling's foremost journalist to being told that his style was all wrong.

When we parted ways, Larry agreed to make the changes I had proposed. He told me that in all his years of ghostwriting autobiographies, no one had ever taken such a hands-on approach. This statement struck me as being odd—after all, an autobiography should be a completely hands-on experience. In addition to the changes, Larry agreed to let me have a shot at writing the opening chapter, as well as the chapter on my dad. We agreed to speak a few days later.

I visited my aunt Ginny the next day in Daytona, Florida. She had been recently released from the hospital after a hundred-day stay, the result of a grading truck backing up over her as she waited behind it on her bicycle. The truck driver then panicked, and accidentally ran back over her in the forward direction. The accident should have killed her, but even at the age of seventy, she had battled back from critical condition and had begun walking several miles daily as a form of therapy.

She showed me the scars on her back, and I got weak in my stomach. All of a sudden my barbed-wire reminders didn't look all that impressive. Many people might consider me to be "the toughest SOB in the World Wrestling Entertainment," and given the video evidence that my career offers, there may be some truth in that statement. But after visiting my aunt Ginny and seeing the hell she'd been through and the positive attitude with which she had bounced back, I can't even lay claim to being the toughest SOB on my own family tree.

The next night in Orlando saw the return of Cactus Jack. Cactus had been my wrestling persona from my wrestling inception in 1985 until Vince McMahon put an end to the character upon my entry into the World Wrestling Entertainment in 1996. Cactus had been given a one-night revival in Madison Square Garden in September 1997, which had been incredibly successful, and a three-month stint, from January through March 1998, which had been somewhat less so. Still, with the World Wrestling Entertainment's ability to promote Cactus Jack as a somehow tougher, wilder version of Mick Foley, and with my ability to shift gears and cut some pretty believable heel promos, it was felt that Cactus Jack could draw big money in a feud with either Austin or the newly turned Rock. This show in Orlando was a way of refreshing the public's memory.

One opponent would just not do for Cactus Jack—he was just too damn tough—so I was put in a handicap situation. My opponents for the night were Mideon, the bizarre, tattooed tough guy who did an amazing Mankind imitation and knew all the words to "Forever in Blue Jeans" by Neil Diamond, and Viscera, a 450-pound black man with a blond Mohawk. In keeping with Cactus Jack's reputation, this was booked as a "hardcore" match.

Backstage before the show, I was introduced to tennis star Monica Seles. I told her of my former exploits on the tennis court, which included diving, yelling, and throwing my racket, and I think I detected the slightest sign of interest on her face. When the show began, the camera cut to a shot of an applauding Monica in the front row, and I came up with an idea. I grabbed Mideon, and together we formed a plan. I would get knocked down outside the ring, right in front of a concerned Monica. I would get up slowly and turn to Mideon, who would proceed to do a Mark McGwire impression with a steel chair as a bat, and my face as home-run-ball number sixty-two. The camera would then show Monica, who would no doubt be either disgusted or impressed, depending upon her personal tastes. Either way, I knew it would make for a tremendous reaction shot.

Yes, I know that Colette had put me on double-secret chairshot probation, but I felt that this occasion was important enough to override her decision. Besides, it was my theory that a steel chair to the side of the face did much less potential brain damage than a shot to the head, although this theory has never been proven by the medical community.

Cactus came out to a tremendous ovation, and in truth, I may have been too harsh when assessing my abilities earlier, because this match was actually pretty good. I went down from a double-team move right in front of the spot where Monica had been shown earlier in the evening. This plan was brilliant. Mideon had the chair. I turned slowly, and *crack*, he laid into me like he was a cop at the 1968 Democratic Convention. I went down to the collective "ooh" of the audience, including, I thought, an "ooh" with a slightly Yugoslavian accent to it. A moment later I pulled myself up to get a close-up look at Monica, only to find she was . . . gone! All that planning, all that sacrifice—for nothing. Oh yeah, I won the match.

That night I began to write about my dad. I had always been a decent creative writer, and at one point in my youth my mom had urged me to write a book, but I had lost interest when she said I couldn't use curses. I think I was ten at the time. A year later, when *Jaws* mania was sweeping the nation, I wrote about my exploits as a shark hunter, during which I referred to "that sonofabitch shark." My story came back with an F with the comment "this is not creative writing" written on top. That sonofabitch teacher! In my high school English class, each student was instructed to analyze a poem or song. I was so enthused about the project that I voluntarily wrote analyses for three other students. The results were interesting—3 A's and a C-plus. Guess who got the bad grade? As a college freshman, I actually had points taken away from my grade because a quote from a Dolly Parton song I used, "One is only poor only if they choose to be," contained improper grammar. In a quote! That teacher single-handedly ruined my love for writing—a love that I didn't rediscover until sixteen years later, with the writing of *Have a Nice Day!*

I'll be the first to admit that my grammar and punctuation is a little weak. As a seventh-grader in Norris Marshak's English class, I knew all my grammar and punctuation. Now, as a bestselling writer, I'll be the first to admit that I don't know a semi-colon from my colon. Thank goodness I have an editor who is paid to put all the doohickeys, thingamabobs, and whatchamacallits in the right places.

I know teaching is a demanding, often unappreciated job, but I believe that a teacher's job shouldn't end with the curriculum. Teachers need to instill a

love for learning in their kids. Granted, some kids simply don't want to learn, but others simply don't have the inspiration. I never dreamed that so many wrestling fans who purchased my book would be reading voluntarily for the first time in their lives. But inspiration comes from strange places. I became interested in the Civil War a few years ago, based solely on a Steve Earle song entitled "Ben McCulloch." I read seventeen books on the Civil War because of that song. Bret Hart and I shared many a historical conversation because of Earle's song. And in a roundabout way, that song helped me live out a dream.

A few months ago I sought refuge from the crowded Atlanta airport by slipping into the Delta Crowne Club room, which is reserved for Delta's most frequent fliers. Frequent fliers don't frequently look like me, which is part of the reason I like going in there. On this particular afternoon, the Crowne Room was quite crowded, so I sat in a chair that was next to a table at which two distinguished gentlemen were engaged in a detailed strategical discussion about the Battle of Gettysburg. No matter how much I read, I can never remember the strategies of the individual generals at distinct battles. These guys knew their stuff. For a moment I thought I was listening to a Kerwin Silfies PBS production. Then I heard it. A question that neither had an answer for. "Lee's second-in-command never was in favor of pursuing the offensive," one man said, before wondering, "What was his name?" The other man drew a blank. Believe it or not, I had visualized this scenario more times than I had ever envisioned becoming World Wrestling Entertainment champion. Not only did I know who it was, I had read the general in question's 640-page memoir, *From Manassas to Appomattox*. I could stay silent no longer. "Excuse me," I chimed in, "I believe the man whose name you're looking for is General James Longstreet." "That's it," one man exclaimed, and then asked me to join them, which I did for an hour of engaging Civil War talk. While we were chatting, a very wealthy-looking Wall Street type stopped by our table. "I just want you to know," he said, "that you coming up with that answer was the strangest thing I have ever seen."

Alrighty, then—I'm back from another tangent. Let's get back to my dad. I went to work on my writing. I wanted to convey how hard a worker my dad was, while showing how he always made time for his kids, while still showing his idiosyncrasies—such as collecting twenty-five years' worth of newspapers in our garage.

I churned out about 2,500 loving but somewhat humorous words on my dad in that one evening. For a guy who hadn't written anything larger than an autograph in fifteen years, this was no small feat. I was not computer literate, and my old Sears typewriter had bitten the dust years earlier. So I did it the old-fashioned, Thomas Jefferson "Declaration of Independence" way. I wrote it longhand. Which is actually how this book is being written as well.

I called up my brother John the next day to get his feedback on the idea of me writing my own autobiography. He laughed like hell, but brought up the possibility that my dad might not get quite as big a kick out of it as he would. I hadn't thought of that. Remember, I had asked for this assignment so as not to be disowned. My own writing would accomplish nothing if I was disowned anyway. In reality, my dad would never disown me, but if my writing hurt him in any way, I would regret it.

I hoped he would like it, or at least wouldn't mind, but nonetheless, this experience had proved one thing to me—I could write this book myself. Now I had to convince the World Wrestling Entertainment. I called Stamford, Connecticut, on May 12, 1999, and asked to speak to Jim Bell, the head of World Wrestling Entertainment marketing and the liaison between the Entertainment and ReganBooks. "Jim, I have a feeling that Larry's not going to work out," I explained. "Fine," Jim said, "we'll just get you another writer." This was going to be tricky. "Uh, Jim, I was thinking that I could write this book myself."

What followed was the type of silence usually reserved for a Pete Gas match. Finally, after what seemed like minutes, Jim spoke. "Maybe we could get Russo and Ferrara [another World Wrestling Entertainment writer] to help you." Was the thought of a guy who had suffered numerous concussions writing his own book really so strange? Of course it was. It was ludicrous. I finally spoke up with what seemed like a rational idea. "What if I write a few chapters and send them to you? Then you can tell me what you think." "Sure," Jim replied, while probably thanking his lucky stars for having bought himself a few days' time before having to crush my literary ambitions.

So there, in the stands of the Tallahassee Civic Center, which, for you trivia buffs, is the only town I ever ate lunch with Ole Anderson in, I began the

graphic depiction of my ear loss, complete with
what is, in my opinion, the greatest opening line this
side of Melville's "Call me Ishmael." The next day I
FedExed copies of the ear-and-dad chapters and
waited anxiously for a reply.

Two days later the phone rang. "Mick, this is Jim
Bell—we like it—we're going to go with it." With
that one call, and with Jim's sensitive heartfelt
words, I was going to be an author. Or at least half
of one. The book was supposed to be 60,000 words.
Larry had already written half of that, and covered
my life up to 1991. I intended to simply insert my
two chapters into the beginning and pick up where
Larry had left off.

I knew I had my work cut out for me. I had
30,000 words to write and a July 1 deadline—which
gave me exactly fifty days to finish. But first I had to
speak with my father.

When I told him of my plan, he wanted a little more information. "What are you going to write about?" he asked. "Oh, just general stuff," I said, "like how you used to take us to Yankee games, and how many hours you worked—and maybe a few stories too." My dad grew defensive immediately. "Stories—what stories?" Now he was becoming the Jack Foley who had intimidated Ward Melville High School students for decades. The Jack Foley who, as the school's athletic director, could silence a crowd of unruly basketball fans with one Jack Foley stare.

I tried my best to shrug off these stories like they were nothing. "Oh, you know, Dad, just little things like how you save all your newspapers, and how you used to curse a lot when you were working on your doctorate." These didn't seem like little things to my dad, who immediately reacted with, "Oh, Mick, I don't know—I don't want to be in the book—just leave me out of it, okay?" "Dad," I pleaded, "I don't think they make you look bad, they're just kind of funny." My dad cut me off in mid-sentence. "Let me think about it, Mick, I'll get back to you."

My dad did get back to me, about six hours later. He no longer sounded like the intimidating Dr. Foley of local legend; he now sounded like a mischievous kid. "Mick, I was thinking," he whispered as if he was trying to hide his bad-boy exploits from my mother, "I've got a bunch of great stories for your book. Like the time that Dick Dawe put new siding up on his house and I called up pretending to be the Three Village Historical Society . . ." The lure of immortalization in literature had been too much for my dad to turn down. He wanted in.

13: *Owen*

I BEGAN WRITING LIKE A MADMAN (no, not the wrestler). I wrote on planes, in dressing rooms, in hotels, at my kitchen table—anywhere I could find. I didn't read a paper or watch television for the next fifty days. My much-vaunted lovemaking skills, which usually combined a marathon aerobic workout with the secrets of the *Kama Sutra*, became merely perfunctory. During one trip back from England, including layovers and connecting flights, I wrote for eighteen hours. Thankfully, I had surgery scheduled for the end of the month, at which time I could concentrate on writing full-time while still having time to play Superdad at home.

I had come to two realizations as I worked on the book. One was that I was going to write the whole thing. As much as I liked Larry, I really wanted this book to be all mine. Our styles of writing were so different that to do the combined Foley/Nahani project would make *Have a Nice Day!* seem like two separate books. So in a somewhat backward way of doing things, I would finish the book first, and then write the first half.

My second realization was that this book was going to be way, way longer than 60,000 words. In truth, I had already written almost 50,000 and had only covered the period from 1991 to 1995. I had covered everything up until my first trip to Japan for the IWA, which would be a key chapter, due to the strange working conditions and inhuman suffering I had endured over there.

The May 29 *Over the Edge* Pay-Per-View from Kansas City, Missouri, would be my first PPV in ages that I would not play a major role in. I was mired somewhere in the middle of an eight-man tag team, a match that my performance was not going to make or break either way. Usually, I am full of ideas, and even take on a leadership role in these matches. But, hell, I was on a deadline, and I had barbed-wire matches with Terry Funk to write about. I decided to dedicate my day in Kansas City to writing and let the other seven guys worry about the match.

I was very happy with the way the day's writing was going as the Pay-Per-View went on the air. I was writing in an empty production office that had its own television monitor, which, due to my work, I glanced at only occasionally. In one of these glances, I happened to see an interview with Owen Hart in his Blue Blazer guise. Owen played the Blue Blazer as a bumbling superhero type, who claimed in this interview that The Godfather "makes my blue blood boil." Many people felt that this portrayal was forced upon Owen as a swipe at stereotypical 1980s babyfaces, and at his brother Bret as well, but I saw it simply as a harmless entertaining gimmick. The Blazer was a heel at the moment, but I felt sure that within months he would have a huge babyface run. I watched the interview (there was no audio) and smiled, as I usually did when watching Owen, before going back to work.

When I looked at the screen again, the camera was focused on a shot of the crowd for an extended time. I guessed that they were having technical problems, and resumed writing. Minutes later I looked at the screen again, and the crowd was still on-camera. As I wondered what was wrong, wrestling great Pat Patterson walked in. He was almost nonchalant as he asked, "Did you see what happened?" I replied that I had no idea. "Owen fell off the catwalk into the ring," he said, but still seemed somewhat calm. I had no idea what to think, but hoped that Pat, who liked to joke with the boys, was making a bad joke here. "Pat, are you ribbing?" Suddenly Pat burst into tears. "He's been lying in the ring for ten minutes. They don't know if he's alive or dead."

My whole body felt cold as I ran out of the room while Pat sobbed uncontrollably. I raced down the hall and crossed myself as I prayed for Owen. The backstage area was a collection of wrestlers either standing in stunned silence or crying openly. As I reached the entranceway, the gurney carrying Owen was wheeled to the waiting ambulance. An EMT stood atop the moving gurney and performed CPR as we all hoped against hope that Owen was still alive.

François Petit came through the curtain, and I rushed to meet him. "He's gone," François sadly said, "he's all gone."

I had no idea what to do. Nothing in my life had prepared me to deal with a situation like this. I realized that Colette and the kids had ordered the Pay-Per-View, and thought of how they were dealing with the tragedy. Dewey loved Owen, and I knew that he would be very upset. At this point I had no idea that most of the home audience had not seen the fall. Owen was supposed to descend from the catwalk via a harness, which had somehow become disengaged, and caused Owen to plummet nearly sixty feet into the ring. Even while falling to his death, Owen had warned the referee and a ring technician to move out of the way, and quite possibly saved their lives by doing so.

Jim Ross later told me that immediately upon impact, Owen had moved, as if trying to perform a sit-up, and then went limp, never to move again. Even though Ross and Lawler had continually told the audience watching at home that "this is not part of the show—this is not a wrestling angle," many viewers thought it was exactly that.

My family had no idea what had happened. They thought like I did, that there had been a technical problem, and had taken to playing during the delay. My phone call, then, came as a complete surprise. "Hello," Colette said, at which point I found myself unable to speak. My mouth was open, but no words would come. "Hello . . . hello," Colette repeated, and I feared that the silence on the other end would cause her to hang up. Finally, I spoke, and the most difficult words I have ever had to say came forth very softly: "I think Owen's dead." "OWEN'S DEAD?" Colette shouted, making me aware for the first time that my family had not known. Instantly, I heard Dewey break down in tears, and the next few minutes on the phone are just a blur to me.

I remember Noelle's gentle voice—too young to truly understand what had happened. "Where's

Owen?" she asked. "He's in heaven, honey, Owen's in heaven." Noelle still did not understand. "But where is him?" By this point I was crying, and my voice was shaking as I tried to explain. "Owen's with the angels, little one; he's with the angels in heaven." Noelle was crying now, more, I think, because she'd never heard her dad so upset than she was because of Owen. I really don't think she was able to fully understand the concept of death. "But where is him?" she sobbed, and then Colette was on the phone, holding Noelle and telling her everything was going to be all right.

In the arena, nothing seemed all right. Another match was in the ring. I wished the whole show could have been called off. Many people later said that the show continued because Owen would have wanted it that way. I have no idea what Owen would have wanted, or if anyone can really guess. After all this time I still don't know what the right answer is and I don't know if there is a right answer. Personally, had it been me, I would have wanted not only the show to stop, but the whole world as well. There is no real right or wrong, and in my opinion, no bad guy to blame. As much as I wish a sense of closure for the Hart family, I don't know if there is a true answer to what happened that night in Kansas City.

Owen Hart was pronounced dead shortly before my match went into the ring. The fans at home were told of the terrible news, while the live fans had no idea. Again, I don't know if that was the proper decision, or if a proper decision even exists. I do know that I dreaded walking out to the ring and taking part in a match on what was the worst night in our sport's history.

My senses all felt numb as I walked through the curtain. The referee warned us of a hole in the ring right near our corner. I stood in that corner for over ten minutes and never realized that the hole was where Owen had landed. I looked at the bloodstain no farther than three feet from my shoes, and had no idea that it was Owen's blood. I had a feeling of nausea, and a little feeling of hatred when fans actually cheered during our match. I remember Chyna in tears after her match, wondering what type of a person would yell vile insults at her in the wake of such a tragedy. Neither of us knew at that time that the live crowd was unaware of Owen's death.

I would like to think that wrestling fans as a whole are not coldhearted. I would like to give the fans in attendance that night the benefit of the doubt. Hopefully, they had no idea of what had happened to Owen. Possibly, they have seen wrestlers perform so many death-defying stunts and walk away that in their minds, they didn't feel such a tragedy was possible.

I believe that the wrestlers themselves block such possibilities out of their minds. I look back now at situations I put myself in that could indeed have been life-threatening, and realize that at the time I didn't allow such fears to enter my mind. Not only did they not enter my mind, but I had the ability to downplay my risks to others as well—putting their minds at ease in the process.

When faced with genuine examples of our own mortality, we don't seem all that accepting. We don't want to admit that tragedies happen. When Darren Drozdov went down with a neck injury at the Nassau Coliseum on October 7, 1999, every one of us thought he'd get back up. Then thought turned to hope and hope turned to prayer and prayer turned to reality. Darren Drozdov was taken away in an ambulance and hasn't walked since. We held a vigil for Droz in the hospital that night. At least twenty wrestlers, as well as the McMahon family, waited for word on Droz's condition. D'Lo Brown, who had been in the ring with Droz at the time of his injury, was beside himself with grief. After a few hours Darren was wheeled out on a gurney. He asked to speak to D'Lo. From my seat twenty feet away, I could hear Droz tell D'Lo not to blame himself—that it wasn't his fault. It may have been the gutsiest thing I've ever heard.

Later that night we got the news that Droz's X ray was negative—there had been no break. The doctor said he might regain feeling in his legs the next day. Every one of us, I think, took that to mean he *would* regain feeling the next day. The waiting room took on an atmosphere of jubilation. We wrestlers *were* indestructible after all. The feeling didn't return to Droz's legs that next day. Or the day after that.

I visited Darren twice in the hospital, and sent him two letters after that. Then . . . nothing. I think of Droz several times a day, but I never call. I can write for fifteen hours in a single sitting, but I never write to him. I was not an especially close friend of Darren's, but I was definitely a friend. I enjoyed his company, and will always remember his words to me in the dressing room following the *Royal Rumble*. I know he looked up to me and would enjoy hearing from me. I don't think I'm a coldhearted person, and I do think I care. I believe I haven't kept in touch with Droz for the same reason I haven't written to Owen's wife, Martha, and for the same reason I haven't talked to Owen's brother Bret. Because like most of the guys in this business, I'm scared. Scared I won't know what to say. Scared that I won't know what to do. But most of all scared because it could have happened to me.

The World Wrestling Entertainment dedicated their entire show to Owen the next night. Anyone who didn't feel like wrestling didn't have to. I did and found it healing. There were no angles or story lines on the show. Every wrestler who wished to was able to give comments about Owen that were then aired on the show. I wish that clips of Owen could have been shown, but I understand the reason for not doing so. Most of Owen's greatest World Wrestling Entertainment moments had come as a sneaky, despicable heel. It may have been in poor taste to air clips that had the announcers verbally slamming Owen on them.

I felt that the show was honorable in its intentions, but that too many of the people interviewed didn't know the real Owen. Some of them talked about how Owen lived to perform for his fans. Others said that the World Wrestling Entertainment wrestlers were like his second family. I feel like I knew Owen very well. Not as well as some, but well enough to know where his true passion lay. Owen liked to perform and at times even loved it, but he certainly didn't live for it. Owen liked certain wrestlers, maybe even loved them on a certain level, but they were by no means his family. He had a family—a wife, a son, and daughter who he loved, and it was for them that Owen Hart truly lived.

I attended Owen's funeral in Calgary a few days later, as did many of the wrestlers who had known him over the years. It meant a great deal to me to know that the Hart family appreciated my comments on the Owen tribute show. It meant even more when Martha Hart told me I had been one of Owen's favorites, and that he considered me one of the "good guys."

Owen Hart may be gone, but his memory remains. Stories of his legendary practical jokes are warmly recalled, and some of my memories of him still make me laugh out loud. Some still make me cry. My picture of Owen, Terry Funk, and me in an "old-time" photo dressed as Civil War generals still occupies a place of honor on my mantel, and every photo of the two of us together shows a shared smile or laugh. My children still ask if they can watch his matches, and both Dewey and Noelle have a picture of Owen on their wall.

I took Dewey on the road with me several months after Owen's death. Being the wrestling fanatic he is, Dewey brought his wrestling cards with him in his special notebook. When he opened up the book, I saw a picture of Dewey and Owen taped to the inside cover. Their smiling faces brought tears to my eyes. Somehow, Dewey's love for Owen makes me feel like a success as a father.

On the flight home from Owen's funeral I wrote

down my remembrances of a great man. While I was writing, words from a late seventies Charlie Daniels song entitled "Reflections" kept running through my mind. I paraphrased the words slightly and included them in my first book. I would like to do the same here.

And Owen my buddy above all the rest
I miss you the most, and I loved you the best.
And now that you're gone, I thank God I was blessed . . .
just to know you.

14: *Superdad*

I OFFICIALLY WENT ON THE SHELF on May 31 at the hands of a Triple H sledgehammer to the knee during a hardcore match. This would give me a ready-made program for my return and would also place valuable heat on Hunter (Triple H), who had been handed the top heel assignment following The Rock's defection to the babyface ranks.

The timing was perfect. Not for wrestling, but for my summer vacation. Florida schools had just gotten out, and following a little simple double knee surgery, I would be good as new. All I had on tap was a personal appearance for the day after my surgery, and then a lengthy vacation that would include both Hershey, Pennsylvania, and New Hampshire's White Mountains. Candy and coasters—my favorite combination.

I have become a master of the amusement park vacation. A famous baseball player (who apparently wasn't famous enough, or else I would remember his name) had a simple strategy: "Hit 'em where they ain't." Never mind that my college teacher would have deducted points for improper grammar in the quote. This theory was perfect for vacationing at theme parks. I call it "go when they ain't there." It's actually a simple philosophy that uses our country's educational system and geographical differences to my coaster-riding advantage. The schools in the North run from early September to mid-June. The schools in the South run from mid-August to mid-May. But almost every theme park in the country remains open full-time from Memorial Day in late May until Labor Day in early September. So I merely hit the Northern parks after Memorial Day, but before the end of school, and hit the Southern parks after mid-August, but before Labor Day. This was going to be easy.

Unfortunately, I had that nagging knee-surgery thing to contend with. One thing was certain: I would need to be writing every chance I got. I had been shocked—or actually, relieved would be more accurate—to see how vivid my recall was. I had been worried that the chairshots I had absorbed over the years would affect my memory, but instead, I, uh, um . . . what was I talking about? Instead, I was writing about events I hadn't even thought of in years, and as a result, the size of my book was swelling faster than Bill Clinton at an intern festival. My 60,000-word book was already up to 100,000, and I had only covered 1991 to 1998. With this in mind, I decided to skip right over any semblance of "Mom made the best spaghetti on the block" and start this saga at the age of eighteen, with my trip to see Jimmy Snuka inside a steel cage.

I was writing in my notebook until the moment I went under anesthesia in Birmingham, Alabama, on June 2. My instructions to the nurse before losing consciousness were simple. "Please don't give me any pain medicine." She warned me that I was going to be in great pain upon awakening. "That's okay," I said. "I've got to start writing right away."

Sure enough, I woke up and was in great pain. But I was true to my word. Despite the pain, I somehow summoned the guts, pride, and determination to fire off a decent Al Snow joke, and suddenly I felt better. I wrote for several hours in my little bed, while feeling quite sexy in my backless medical gown.

I had a sudden revelation when I tried to walk to the bathroom: there was no way I was going to feel up to riding roller coasters in three days. Sadly, I made the call home, and told the kids that we would have to postpone the trip for a couple of weeks because Big Daddy-O hadn't counted on not being able to walk.

Unfortunately knee surgery was not a miracle cure for me. Dr. Andrews (a noted sports surgeon) had repaired my radial meniscus and had cleaned up both knees, but unfortunately, there was no simple procedure to reverse fifteen years of pounding and abuse. As I lay in bed, it occurred to me that fifteen-foot flights off ring aprons onto concrete floors probably hadn't done a whole lot for the happiness of my knees. Yeah, I know, I hadn't come close to the fifteen-foot mark in years, but even my six-foot flights at a weight of 300 pounds hadn't been healthy. Simply weighing 300 pounds wasn't helping my cause either. Nor was my decision to stop wearing kneepads three years earlier.

I truly was "Superdad" two weeks later at Hershey Park. Up for breakfast at 9 A.M. Away to the park by ten. Coasters and candy until a midday break at two. Back to the park at four. Return to the hotel by eight. Bedtime story at ten. Then the people at the Hotel Hershey would allow me to use an office, where I would write until 5 A.M., at which point I would sleep until nine. I did this for three straight days.

Then it was off to Santa's Village in the White Mountains for some Christmas relaxation in June. It was here that I realized the error of my vacation plan. The trip should have been in reverse order. Let me explain. Vacations, much like wrestling matches, are a lot like Al Snow jokes. They are all a matter of timing and experience.

Too often, a wrestler will immediately go to the hottest moves in his repertoire in an attempt to get over with the fans. Often they will do these big moves at the expense of the in-ring story. They may get pops for the moves themselves, but the audience will find itself unable to become emotionally involved in this matchup, making it exciting, perhaps, but not emotionally fulfilling.

Instead, a wrestler should build a match from the ground up, in an attempt to whip the fans into a frenzy at the finale. That is the time to pull the death-defying, incredibly athletic moves out of the bag. That is where the moonsaults, the Swanton Bombs, the top-rope Hurricanranas, the Mr. Sockos, The Worms, The Stink Faces, the Ho Trains, and The People's Elbows come in. Hey, I know that the last five moves listed all suck, but people love them, and all of them are a credit to their inventors. Anyone can get a great move over; it takes real talent to make the bad ones work.

Al Snow jokes are the same way. I know why most of you bought this book—to see me score literary knockouts on "the crown prince of hardcore." But I can't knock him out too early—then it becomes like a Tyson comeback fight; you might get what you paid to see, but after it's over, you wish you had your money back. So I need to jab Al occasionally, throw a straight right once in a while that puts him on queer street (where I imagine he spends a lot of his time anyway), and knock him senseless in spectacular fashion when the time is right.

In that way, I am using Test and the Mean Street Posse as my tune-up fights. Let's put it in wrestling terms. I may give Joey Abs a literary hip toss, and I think the readers appreciate it. I may give Test a big literary boot to the face and he'll go down momentarily, and I believe the fans will enjoy that as well. I may even catch Rodney with a literary shot to the testicles that may seem hurtful and unnecessary, but I think deep down the readers will appreciate it. But Al? That's another story. What I have in mind for Al is the literary equivalent of Mr. Socko, The Worm, The Stink Face, The Ho Train, and The People's Elbow all being delivered simultaneously, and the effect will be devastating. So prepare yourself, Ray Fosse, because Pete Rose is rounding third and heading for home.

Hershey Park has a big, sprawling layout with world-class thrill rides and attractions—including eight coasters. Santa's Village is a small quaint park with only ten rides in the entire place. By the time Dewey and Noelle got to the Village, they had already been on the Superdooperlooper, the Wildcat, and many other rides beyond the scope of the imagination. Somehow Rudy's Rapid Transit Coaster no longer seemed like such a big deal. We still had a great time, and my mom enjoyed her first visit to the Village in thirty years, but the trip reminded me that my kids were growing up, which in some ways is a little sad.

In addition to the Village and writing whenever I could, I got to experience quite a bit more in the mountains of New Hampshire on this trip. Two of the experiences will stay with me for a while.

I love water parks. Unfortunately, water parks usually require me to be shirtless in public, and that is no longer such a good thing. Sure, I believe everyone should feel at peace with their body, but most people don't have to worry about their picture showing up on the Internet or on the pages of a tabloid. So these days, I tend to keep my pecs and lats and rolls and flaps confined to our backyard pool. Occasionally, however, I will lose my trepidation and my shirt simultaneously, as I did at the "Whale's Tail" water park.

School was not yet out in New Hampshire, so the crowd was at a minimum. I had my hair up under a hat and was sporting sunglasses for about the third time in fifteen years, and as a result, was somewhat incognito. My kids both love the "lazy river" at water parks, as do I, so the three of us grabbed our tubes and let the gentle rhythm of the water float us around the park.

I tried to sit on my tube, but it was too small. Instead, I put the tube over my head and let it rest underneath my arms. It certainly was relaxing . . . until it was time to get out. Then panic set in. I couldn't get the damn tube off my body. I was helpless and summoned a lifeguard for assistance; the lifeguard responded by getting on the public-address system and noting that a bather was in trouble. I wasn't in real trouble—I just felt kind of stupid. Then I heard a voice. "Isn't that Mankind?" With that, the secret was out, and I did my best to look cool for my fans while my mother and a couple of lifeguards began letting the air out of the tube. Now I knew how poor Pooh felt when he was stuck in that anal-retentive neat freak Rabbit's hole. (Entrance to his living quarters, that is.)

As I stood there, the irony of the situation dawned on me. Mick Foley, the "King of the Death Match," the hero of the "Hell in a Cell," the somewhat proud owner of a gruesome collection of scars, and the survivor of X-Pac's working punches, was getting his ass kicked, or at the very least his tits crushed, by an inflatable rubber tube.

This next story isn't about my second memorable White Mountain experience, but is a similar scenario, the memory of which was just triggered by my "battle of the tube" account. Prior to this, the painful memory had been somewhere in my unconscious, hidden deeper than the logic in a Jimmy Snuka interview. (Snuka was my childhood hero, but man, his promos were out there.)

It all went down at Six Flags Magic Mountain, in Valencia, California, in spring of 2000. Many of you may remember Magic Mountain as the cinematic locale of "Wallyworld"—the destination for the Griswold family in *National Lampoon's Vacation*. Others may recall *Vacation* for the wonderful shot of Beverly D'Angelo's beautiful boobs in the shower scene. The park is known for its coasters, so it was with fierce determination that I set out on a solitary trek to take them on. These days, when I go places

by myself, it makes me an "individual"; when I was seventeen and used to go to the movies by myself, it made me a "loser." In reality, I'm probably a combination of both.

I was there early, on a weekday during the school year. My planning was paying off, as I was able to ride several coasters without waiting. There were even some wrestling fans, one of whom couldn't stop proudly telling me of his sister's accomplishments in the world of adult films, who rode with me. As the day wore on, however, the crowds surged in, and I realized that long lines might make riding the park's premier rides, "Batman" and "Goliath," an impossibility.

As much as I like most wrestling fans, all it takes is one meathead with a couple of beers in him, forcing his theories on fake chairs and blood capsules on me, to ruin a day at the park. An hour in line with one or two or sometimes more of these guys is enough to make me want to seek refuge at a screening of the director's cut of *Heaven's Gate*.

As I headed for the exit, content with a good four hours of thrills, a park attendant suggested I go up the exit line on the big rides, and even offered to call ahead to make the ride operators aware of my imminent arrival. All right! With a smile on my face and a swagger in my step, I headed for Batman. As I headed up the exit, I thought of the resentment I might get from the people who had to brave the hour wait to be on the receiving end of the six inversions that this leg-dangling miracle of steel and science had to offer.

With a small case of line cutter's apprehension offsetting my adrenaline rush in a battle for emo-

tional superiority, I poked my head into view. In reality, most line cutters don't face this moral dilemma. By their very willingness to cut in front of people who have paid their line-waiting dues, they show themselves to be self-centered pricks, and as a general rule, self-centered pricks don't care a whole lot about the ramifications of their pricklike behavior. I did.

I sort of expected a "hey, the ugly guy's trying to cut," along the lines of "hey, the meat guy's sticking his head in the picture" during Rocky Balboa's meathouse training session in *Rocky*. Instead, I got, "Hey, it's Mick Foley," and "Foley is God," followed by a chant of "Foley, Foley, Foley." This was great. I was shown to the first row of seats—the best seats of all—as the crowd continued to chant my name. I suddenly had a new definition of success: "success is having the ability to cut an hour-long line for a roller coaster, and having the very people that you cut cheer you while you do it." I sat down right in the middle. Uh-oh!

Due to the dangling, inverted nature of the ride, Batman had a preshaped seat to hold the rider's buttocks and legs snugly. I suddenly guessed that the manufacturer hadn't had my buttocks and legs in mind when they made this ride. Who had modeled for his mold? I got up and looked down at a plastic ass impression that sixties supermodel Twiggy would have found challenging to fit in. I backed up and actually tried jumping in, hoping that my momentum would be enough to offset a lifetime of late-night pizza. I reached up and attempted to pull the safety harness into a locked position. The male and female parts looked to be a good five and three-quarter inches apart. I had been telling my wife for years that five and three-quarter inches was pretty darn big, but this time I actually believed it.

The ride operators tried to help out—all five of them. They looked like a pack of wild dogs going after a kill as they jumped on, pushed down, and hung off of the safety harness in an attempt to get the hardcore legend in motion. The crowd was no longer chanting my name; they just kind of stared in the type of silence usually reserved for funerals or Test matches. Slowly, I got out of the seat, a dejected, defeated man. There would be no Batman for me on this day. I felt humiliated, and just wanted to go someplace where no one would see me—like a WCW "Thunder" taping. It was then that I started a serious diet. Not to lower cholesterol, feel healthy, or any of those other reasons people deprive themselves of some of life's greatest pleasures. My intentions were far more noble—I wanted revenge on Batman's ass.

I did ride Goliath, which at 255 feet was the world's tallest coaster, until "Millennium Force" in Ohio's Cedar Point opened a month later at a towering 301. Goliath had made its inaugural run with AT&T pitchman and former WCW champion David Arquette in the front car. Now I know the image of David Arquette doesn't invoke a whole lot of fear, and his title reign may have been preposterous, but any guy who spends his honeymoon on a roller-coaster tour is all right with me. Besides, I want him to ask his sister Patricia if she wants to play Colette in the big-screen adaptation of *Have a Nice Day!* So I figure I'd better be nice.

Back to the White Mountains, and memorable

experience number two—this time at the venerable locale of "Clark's Trading Post." Clark's has been around for fifty years, and held some nostalgia for me, as I had been there as a four-year-old. The place was famous for its trained bear show, but also featured a genuine turn-of-the-century steam train that took hourly trips along the banks of the Pemigewasset River. As was tradition at Clark's, an odd, dirty, loincloth-clad, matted-haired creature known as the Wolfman would sporadically chase the train on an old three-wheeled motorcycle while firing gunshots in the air.

The Wolfman's story line is that he was protecting his gold from strangers. His real story is somewhat more impressive, as he apparently lives his gimmick, and even in the dead of New Hampshire's thirty-below-zero winters can be seen in local bars in his Wolfman regalia. The guy was pretty convincing. So convincing, in fact, that Dewey and Noelle were terrified of him as he sped after the train. Finally, the kids summoned the courage to yell, "Go away, you poo-poo head," and the train chugged safely back into the station.

A few minutes later, while strolling Clark's old-fashioned Main Street, I was approached by one of the Clark family. His words sent chills down Noelle's spine. "The Wolfman wants to meet you." The Wolfman, he explained, rarely set foot on Main Street, but had recognized me on the train and wanted to say hello.

My kids were in awe as their dad shook hands and posed with this local icon. Dewey even managed to step in for a snapshot. Noelle, however, clung to Mommy's leg. As we drove back to the hotel, it was

clear that the image of the gun-toting wildman was still very much alive in her five-year-old head. With great hesitation, she asked the important questions.

"Daddy—is the Wolfman coming to the hotel with us?" "No, honey," I assured her, "the Wolfman is not coming to the hotel with us." She thought for a second before asking, "Daddy, is the Wolfman going to eat dinner with us?" Again, I was there for her. "Of course not, little one—the Wolfman will not be eating dinner with us." Now came the big question, the one that had obviously been haunting her. She spoke in a voice filled with fear. "Daddy, is the Wolfman flying home with us?" This time I had to laugh. "I promise you, Noelle, the Wolfman will not be flying home with us." My answer seemed to put her mind at ease. She thought for a second, and it was almost as if a lightbulb turned on in her head and she realized the impossibility of her thought. There was absolutely no way the Wolfman could fly home with us, and Noelle knew why. "Yeah, him couldn't get on the plane with him nipples showing!"

Her statement got such a reaction from me and

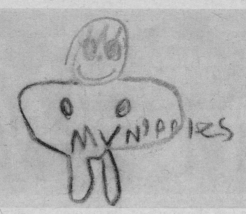

Colette that my daughter was suddenly like a wrestler with a new catchphrase. She even said the N word in *Beyond the Mat*. "Nipples" has been an obsession with Noelle for the last thirteen months. Come to think of it, they've been an obsession of mine for a whole lot longer.

Colette doesn't completely share my fondness for the parks, but she does tolerate it. Up until a few years ago I would never dream of going to a park without my kids; it would be like cheating on them. I find, however, that life on the road is just a little more tolerable if I look at it as a paid national amusement park vacation. Besides, my kids do all right. On a recent plane trip with Noelle, we made a comprehensive list of all the parks she'd been to, and how many days out of her life had been spent at these places. I thought the results were impressive. Twenty-six different parks for a total of ninety-three days all in a little over six years' time. An average of one park every twenty-five days.

I am a roller-coaster addict. I admit it. Sometimes I physically feel like I need a ride, like a junkie needs a fix. Here, then, is a somewhat unofficial list of my favorite parks and rides. So far.

MICK'S TOP TEN AMUSEMENT PARKS

1. *Santa's Village—Jefferson, New Hampshire.* What it lacks in rides, it makes up for in personal nostalgia, a beautiful location, and the magic of Christmas in the summer.

2. *Magic Kingdom—Orlando, Florida.* I know I bust on Disney a little, but an uncrowded day with a master touring plan makes me feel like a kid again.

3. *Hershey Park—Hershey, Pennsylvania.* Coasters and candy—a formidable tag team. Also the only park with a wrestling arena fifty feet from the exit.

4. *Disneyland—Anaheim, California.* Smaller and older than its Florida cousin, but this is the one that revolutionized the industry.

5. *Knoebel's Grove—Elysburg, Pennsylvania.* Great rides, low prices, relaxed pace.

6. *Universal Studios/Islands of Adventure—Orlando, Florida.* Where else can my kids take on King Kong and sing along with Barney five minutes later?

7. *American Adventures—Marietta, Georgia.* A sad day indeed, when I realized that my kids had outgrown it.

8. *Sea World—Orlando, Florida.* An educational experience and two great rides. Plus Noelle's classic question, "Are dolphins stronger than Chyna?"

9. *Dutch Wonderland—Lancaster, Pennsylvania.* A peaceful atmosphere in the middle of Amish country. A great time until the manager accused me of not paying for my lunch.

10. *King's Dominion—Doswell, Virginia.* Great coasters and landscaping. On the downside, too many screaming teenagers.

MICK'S TOP FIVE WATER PARKS
(Take into consideration that I have limited water park experience.)

1. *Blizzard Beach—Orlando, Florida.* I wouldn't dare go in the summer, but the "melted glacier" theme is beautiful and the variety of attractions is tremendous.

2. *Waterville, U.S.A.—Gulf Shores, Alabama.* Dewey claims this is my favorite, but he's wrong. Go to your room!

3. *White Water—Marietta, Georgia.* A beautiful place, and man, did we get our money's worth on the season pass in 1995.

4. *The Whale's Tail—Lincoln, New Hampshire.* Sure, I was humiliated, but until then, it was fun.

5. *Six Gun City—Jefferson, New Hampshire.* Actually, it's not a water park, but my kids used the two slides for hours. Besides, I love how

they give these plastic-and-steel slides names like "The Tomahawk Run" to somehow fit in with the western motif.

MICK'S TOP TEN ROLLER COASTERS

1. *Rock 'n' Roller Coaster—Disney/MGM Studios, Orlando, Florida.* I don't see how Aerosmith helps the Disney image, but its "limo trying to get to the show on time" makes the several inversions through a darkened "city" all the more memorable.

2. *Lightning Racer—Hershey Park.* A dueling racing coaster that is wild but smooth—especially for a woody.

3. *The Phoenix—Knoebel's Grove.* A classic out-and-back coaster, with the most airtime I've ever experienced.

4. *Volcano—King's Dominion.* The zero-to-sixty m.p.h. in two seconds sends the rider blasting through a volcano and then into multiple inversions.

5. *Twister—Knoebel's Grove.* An amazing thrill ride built by the park, using lumber from their own lumberyard.

6. *Kraken—Sea World.* An incredibly smooth steel monster that was marred only by Noelle's "I want to go! I want to go!" temper tantrum.

7. *Superman, Ride of Steel—Six Flags, New England.* The first 220-foot drop is almost straight down, and the rest of the ride feels like flying.

8. *Big Thunder Mountain—Magic Kingdom.* Incredible atmosphere puts this otherwise tame coaster on my list.

9. *Goliath—Six Flags, Magic Mountain.* Similar feeling to Superman, but despite Goliath's steeper drop, Superman's riverside location gives it the edge.

10. *Rudy's Rapid Transit Coaster—Santa's Village.* Sure, it's a kid coaster, but Dewey once rode it twelve times in a row and it's where Noelle kissed me because "you're a good man!"

MICK'S TOP TEN NONCOASTER RIDES

1. *Spider-Man—Islands of Adventure.* More amazing elements than any ride on the planet.

2. *Tower of Terror—Disney/MGM Studios.* Noelle couldn't stop talking about the "Towa-terra."

3. *Indiana Jones Adventure—Disneyland.* I had so much fun riding this with Al Snow that I temporarily forgot I hated him.

4. *Journey to Atlantis—Sea World.* Incredibly imaginative, but I learned to take the "You Will Get Soaked" sign seriously.

5. *Splash Mountain—Magic Kingdom/Disneyland.* Disney at its best, and great opportunities for Noelle to yell "I see him hiney" at Brer Bear.

6. *Yule Log Flume—Santa's Village.* It's not the drop, but the gentle music and beautiful mountain scenery along the way that add it to my list.

7. *Jaws—Universal Studios, Florida.* Mideon's Mankind imitation on this ride makes my memory of it even better.

8. *Steam Train—Clark's Trading Post.* For making "him nipples" a part of my life.

9. *Sports Cars—Miracle Strip Amusement Park, Panama City, Florida.* A long ride on a cool track that cuts through the woods, and a memory of Noelle dancing to "Rockin' Robin" while she drives.

10. *It's a Small World (Holiday Edition)—Disneyland.* Sure, the regular version is a little annoying after a while, but it is a thing of wonder at Christmastime.

This top-ten-list stuff is fun, so why limit it to fun parks? These lists are limited to my personal experience. I'm not trying to say that they're the best—just my favorites.

MICK'S TOP TEN FAVORITE MOVIES

1. *Rocky*—Still gives me goose bumps after all these years.

2. *Boogie Nights*—Forget the porno part; this movie's character development was what made it great. Plus, Reid Rothchild rules—yeah, he does!

3. *The Great Santini*—Robert Duvall's portrayal of a flawed marine colonel had me fighting back tears on my couch at age thirteen.

4. *The Iron Giant*—In a just world, this heart-warming kids' flick would have been a block-buster, and had a kids' ride named in honor of it.

5. *The Green Mile*—I saw it by myself, and had to fight hard to try not to ruin my "hardcore legend" status by crying like a baby.

6. *Schindler's List*—This should be required viewing for everyone.

7. *The Wizard of Oz*—I wish there was no video of this one so every kid would anticipate its yearly showing.

8. *Godfather II*—I like it a little more every time I see it.

9. *Taxi Driver*—I used to feel like I had a lot in common with Robert De Niro's Travis Bickle character—which is not really a good thing.

10. *Beyond the Mat*—Probably the only chance I'll ever have to sit in a theater with my family and see ourselves on the screen.

MICK'S TOP TEN TV SHOWS

1. *The Sopranos*—HBO's breakthrough show is the first one in years that I have watched regularly. I feel a strange kinship with Tony Soprano, with the exception of the cursing-every-other-word and killing people part.

2. *Happy Days*—The Fonz is still the man. Heyyy! Except when he grew a beard, taught auto shop, and got married. Whoa!

3. *The X-Files*—Now that I'm done wrestling, my goal is to catch every single episode. Also, my attraction to agent Dana Scully grows every day in a way that is almost stalkeresque.

4. *The Bob Newhart Show*—I love Bob, and you've got to respect a supporting actor named "Bonerz."

5. *The Incredible Hulk*—My favorite comic book was brought to life via Lou Ferrigno, who, when I met him twenty-two years later, was only interested in verbally blasting Vince.

6. *Seinfeld*—George Costanza rules! Yeah, he does.

7. *All in the Family*—Carroll O'Connor's lovable bigot is an American treasure. The first show I know of to use a flushing toilet for a cheap pop.

8. *Raw Is War/SmackDown!*—Sure, I'm on these two, but it's the giants before me—"The Pug," "The Goon," "T. L. Hopper," and "Freddy Joe Floyd"—who paved the way to Nielsen success.

9. *Hawaii Five-O*—While other teens were carrying condoms in their wallets, I carried a picture of Jack Lord's Steve McGarrett in mine—both effective forms of birth control. Lord, oh Lord, where has Jack gone?

10. *Thirtysomething*—Okay, okay. I know watching every rerun on the Lifetime channel makes me a nerd, but admitting to it makes me a brave nerd.

MICK'S TOP TEN WRESTLING MATCHES

1. *Terry Funk vs. Ric Flair, "I Quit"*—*November 1989, Troy, New York.* The Funker at his best in twenty-eight minutes of mayhem.

2. *Jimmy Snuka vs. Don Muraco, "Steel Cage"*—*October 17, 1983, Madison Square Garden.* This is not number two for its quality but for what it meant to me as a fan.

3. *Dynamite Kid vs. Tiger Mask—1981–1982, Japan*. Take your pick from about twenty great ones these guys had.

4. *Ric Flair vs. Ricky Steamboat, "Music City Showdown"—May 1989, Nashville, Tennessee*. The best match of their classic rivalry.

5. *Bret Hart vs. Stone Cold Steve Austin, Wrestle-Mania—1997, Chicago, Illinois*. The match that made Austin a superstar.

6. *Hardy Boyz vs. Edge Christian, "Ladder" Match at No Mercy—October 1999, Cleveland, Ohio*. One great match where four stars were born.

7. *Sgt. Slaughter vs. Iron Sheik, "Boot Camp" Match—June 1984, Madison Square Garden*. Both these guys were "busted wide open." A classic brawl.

8. *Bruiser Brody vs. Antonio Inoki—April 1985, Japan*. These guys brought out the best in each other. I'm just lumping the whole feud together on my list.

9. *Terry Funk vs. Jerry Lawler—1982, Memphis, Tennessee*. Funk was the personification of evil in this match. It is the standard that I tried to live up to as a heel but was never able to do.

10. *Al Snow vs. Big Boss Man, "Kennel from Hell" at Unforgiven—September 1999*. Just knowing this match existed and is on video makes me happy. So bad that I opted not to make fun of Al because of it—but knowing that I could makes me smile.

MICK'S TEN FAVORITE MATCHES THAT I'VE BEEN IN

1. *Mankind vs. Shawn Michaels, "Mind Games"—September 1992, Philadelphia, Pennsylvania.* This was the best shape I have ever been in. Great timing, psychology, and new moves that are still being stolen today.

2. *Cactus Jack vs. Terry Funk, "Barbed Wire" Match—January 10, 1995, Guma, Japan.* People go to jail for lesser things than we did to each other in this bloodbath in front of 180 fans in the forty-degree gym.

3. *Cactus Jack vs. Triple H, "Street Fight" at Royal Rumble—January 23, 2000, Madison Square Garden.* A great way to finish my career.

4. *Mankind vs. Undertaker, "Hell in a Cell" at King of the Ring—June 29, 1998. Pittsburgh, Pennsylvania.*

5. *Dude Love vs. Stone Cold Steve Austin, "Over the Edge"—May 1998, Milwaukee, Wisconsin.* The only time Dude Love will EVER show up on a best of anything list, but this was a blast to watch.

6. *Cactus Jack vs. Sting, "Falls Count Anywhere" at Beach Blast—June 1992, Mobile, Alabama.* For a few years, this was the match I tried to live up to. My big comeback after whooping cough.

7. *Mick Foley vs. Terry Funk, Raw Is War—May 1998, Richmond, Virginia.* I received twenty-

seven stitches in this wild fight for Mick Foley's soul. One of only two matches I ever wrestled under my real name.

8. *Cactus Jack vs. Eddie Gilbert, "Two out of Three Falls"—August 1991, Philadelphia, Pennsylvania.* This was ECW before there was ECW with the late, great Eddie Gilbert at his absolute best.

9. *Mankind vs. The Rock, Raw Is War—December 28, 1998, Worcester, Massachusetts.* Not our best match, but certainly my favorite.

10. *Dude Love vs. Owen Hart—sometime in 1997, San Jose, California.* Hey, the Dude made it twice. I've stunk up a lot of buildings in my career, but never had this much fun doing it.

TOP TEN CHRISTMAS SONGS

1. *"Little Drummer Boy,"* Emmylou Harris

2. *"O Holy Night,"* Nat King Cole

3. *"The First Noel,"* Colin Raye. I'm a big fan of Colin's music but an even bigger fan of the man. Knowing that people as nice as Colin exist in the world of entertainment is comforting.

4. *"You're a Mean One, Mr. Grinch,"* from *The Grinch Who Stole Christmas*

5. *"Little Drummer Boy,"* Bob Seger

6. *"Holly Jolly Christmas,"* Burl Ives

7. *"Have Yourself a Merry Little Christmas,"* Judy Garland

8. *"God Rest Ye Merry Gentlemen,"* Mario Lanza

9. *"What Child Is This?,"* The Judds

10. *"Little Folks,"* Charlie Daniels Band

15: *Rehab?*
What
Rehab?

I FINISHED WRITING *Have a Nice Day!* on July 1, 1999, in a trailer on the set of the USA show *G vs. E.* I had seen a few episodes of this rather odd, quirky science-fiction program, and was impressed. I really had only two problems: I was writing so much that I never learned my lines, and I was only a month out of double knee surgery, which made filming wrestling scenes a no-no.

The first problem was rather easy to solve. When in doubt, I did what wrestlers do best—I faked it. I pretended I knew what I was doing. Actually, through constant rehearsal, I managed to learn my lines, and even had the respected veteran actors on the show praising my work. "That was great," said Richard Brooks, whose work on *Law and Order* had been highly acclaimed. "How much acting experience have you had?" I thought his question over for a moment before saying, "I guess you could say I've been acting for fifteen years."

Up until a few years ago I would never admit to being an actor. Nothing bothered me more than a well-meaning fan saying, "Hey, you're a great actor."

Dammit, I didn't act out there; I *became* my character. In other words, I was a Method actor. Or else I would convince myself that I was the character, and I was just enhancing a certain aspect of my real personality for the camera. In other words, I was acting. In my present role of World Wrestling Entertainment Commissioner, I am often just being myself, which is in itself a form of acting. Hell, John Wayne made a pretty good living being himself in about a hundred movies. The Duke didn't have to change a thing, even as a Roman centurion uttering the memorable line "Surely thou wert the Son of God" in the biblical epic *The Greatest Story Ever Told*.

My second problem was a little more serious. My

knee was nowhere near ready, and I had a pretty intense wrestling scene to shoot. The World Wrestling Entertainment, for their part, had made sure that I had a stunt double, but I still felt just a little bit uneasy. Sure, I could barely walk, but my pride was on the line here. A stunt double for Mick Foley? That would be like having a Polish or Australian or Italian accent dubbed in for Meryl Streep, or a home-run-swing stand-in for Mark McGwire, or a stunt penis for Dirk Diggler. I don't generally consider myself a macho guy, but I do believe there are times that "a guy's gotta do what a guy's gotta do."

My opponent for the match was Testicules, who in the story line was an independent wrestler whose Faustian deal with the devil had given him amazing power. My job was not only to lick Testicules—wait, maybe I better rephrase that. My job was to not only defeat my demonic opponent, but get him to renounce the devil as well.

"What can you do out there?" I asked Testicules, who will now be known simply as "T." Think back to the Jerry Seinfeld story, and how I told the casting director I could do anything. That's what all wrestlers do when asked of their abilities. "T," who actually wasn't a wrestler but a wrestling manager, tried the honest approach: "I can throw a forearm across your back." Quickly, I sought out the Pate brothers, the twin creators/directors of the show, who looked like surfer dudes, and responded to good takes with "awesome, dude!" "Guys," I said, "I think we're going to need a stunt double for Testicules." "Do you think Andrew can do it?" they asked, in reference to the inimitable Andrew Bryniarski, of *Any Given Sunday* fame. Andrew had taken the role of an Australian bully that I beat up in a bar, simply so we could spend some quality hanging out time together. That scared me. Andrew, you see, is a little intense. When he used to come to the matches in Los Angeles, I at least had places to hide and thirty other wrestlers to deal him off to. I must admit, though, in a two-day period, I went from being afraid of him, to getting a kick out of him, to actually liking him. I was glad to work with Andrew on the wrestling scene. There was only one problem. Even though both Andrew and "T" were around six-feet-four, and both were around 280 pounds, they looked a little different. Andrew was pumped up and ripped to the bone, and "T," well, he wasn't. I could compare him to Ralphus of WCW fame, but I wouldn't want to offend Ralphus.

Fortunately, Andrew had connections with a good wrestling school in Los Angeles, and within an hour we had a great stand-in for "T." Our wrestling scene came across very well, even if doing take after take after take of move after move after move wasn't exactly what the doctor had ordered.

Actually, I had no idea what the doctor had ordered; I never saw one. I will admit to slacking off on rehab, which was odd, because I had always prided myself on how quickly I could charge back from injury. I'm always amazed how great guys usually look when they come back from injury. Not me. When I'm hurt, I look like I'm hurt. And on the rare few occasions when I've taken time off due to injury, I have the decency to come back looking like hell. I've never understood how guys can come back from arm injuries with arms that are bigger and better than ever. Actually, I understand it: they wait until they've had time to properly train and look good before returning. I just don't happen to agree with this approach.

In 1993, I had returned from a torn ligament in my knee in only three and a half months. The average time is six months, but I've known guys who milked it—I mean rehabbed it for up to a year. My progress had been swift because I trained like a man possessed. I know Mick Foley and training usually go together like *Ready to Rumble* and Oscar nominations, but three and a half months later I was back in action. Four months later I was tearing down the house with the huge wrestler Vader in a Pay-Per-View main event.

This time, however, I rehabbed a little differently: I sat on my ass all day. Now, granted, I usually had a pen in my hand and a notebook in front of me, as I wrote my memoirs, but I was on my ass nonetheless. Proper rehab includes ice and elevation. I strapped on the ice, but had no time for elevation. I was on a deadline. Unfortunately, as the size of my book grew, so did the size of my ass.

I will forever consider writing that book to be my finest professional accomplishment. As an author, I can accurately state that writing is a rewarding, therapeutic experience. It is not, however, a real effective form of aerobic exercise or a proven calorie burner. As a result, though I may have felt like Ernest Hemingway intellectually, physically I looked more like Ernest Borgnine.

Writing had another negative effect on me. My career, I felt, was over. Actually, this feeling wasn't negative at all—it was wonderful. I realized that writing my story had brought a perfect sense of closure to my career. I didn't need to prove anything to anyone; my career had been more successful than I'd ever dared dream. I looked at a list of goals that I had set for myself two years earlier and found that I had achieved them all. Sell out Madison Square Garden—check. Main event in a Pay-Per-View that does a 1.0 buy rate—check. Nail Barbara Eden—check. Okay, okay, so I haven't quite achieved that last one yet.

I only had one problem. Money. The World Wrestling Entertainment had become so popular that my bank account was expanding almost as quickly as my waist measurement. Financial independence had been one of my ultimate goals, and unfortunately, I was a long way from being there. I had made a million dollars in wrestling, but that figure was a total of my first twelve years combined. Even after being something of a star for seven of my thirteen years, I was averaging eighty grand a year. I have a friend who makes that much punching tickets on the Long Island Railroad—and he has both his ears.

Back when I joined in late 1995, the World Wrestling Entertainment was not quite the phenomenon it is now. Sports-entertainers didn't appear on the cover of *TV Guide* or host *Saturday Night Live* in 1995. A top guy, I was promised, could make between 300 and 500 grand a year. My first year had come nowhere close. A six-figure income was a lot of money to make, but not when Uncle Sam has his hand out, not to mention the Super 8s, Red Roof Inns, Cracker Barrels, and Ponderosa Steak Houses that wanted a cut for close to 300 days a year. My pay increased in 1997. It increased in 1998. Business was way up, and there seemed to be no end in sight. The year 1999 was shaping up to be even better.

I had been saving money since day one in the wrestling business. My thriftiness was legendary, with exaggerations of that thriftiness making it even more so. My payoffs had grown tremendously, but my road budget hadn't. Even when riding and rooming by myself, I still kept my expenses to under a hundred a night. I cut corners on the road like my high-school buddies buying a present for a birthday party. (One Springsteen album with six names on the card.) "That man at the bar would like to buy you a drink," was a statement I often heard at restaurants. "I'm not drinking, but he can buy my soup instead," was the answer many a waiter would return to the bar with. I had learned from some of the masters—Skandar Akbar, Bronco Lubich, Rip Rogers—that "it's not how much you make, it's how much you save." Over the years I had saved quite a bit, but . . . not enough. I felt like I owed it to my family to put in one more year.

Actually, I also owe it to my family to be a little more generous at home than I am on the road. So don't worry about my family—they're doing all right. If I'm guilty of anything with my kids, it's spoiling them. A recent road trip with Dewey (our yearly father-son bonding trip) saw the little guy do things other eight-year-olds could only wish for. In the span of a week he toured World Wrestling Entertainment headquarters, watched *The King of the Ring* at the World Wrestling Entertainment New York, was a batboy at a minor-league baseball game, made $43 signing his name on stick figures he drew, went to Six Flags New England, wrestled in the WWE ring, watched two WWE live shows, and nailed Barbara Eden (just kidding!).

Dewey may well be the world's biggest wrestling fan. In addition to his Entertainment action figures, his Entertainment video games, his Entertainment CDs, his king-size bed for wrestling, his trampoline for aerial moves, and his vast video collection, he has almost an encyclopedic memory for wrestling's recent past. When I decided to include the Al Snow/Boss Man match on my top-ten list, I drew a blank as to when it happened. This was not totally surprising, as most people who viewed the match have blocked it out of their memories—at least on a conscious level. Lack of memory shouldn't be enough of a reason to stop an Al Snow attack, so I decided to consult the master. "Dewey, what Pay-Per-View was Al Snow's 'Kennel' match with the Boss Man?" In about the time it takes for 30 percent of the viewing audience to turn the channel during a Tiger Ali Singh promo, Dewey had the answer. "*Unforgiven*, September 1999." I had to laugh. "How did you know that?" The little guy seemed almost embarrassed over his power of recall. "I don't know." He shrugged before revealing his source. "I read it in a magazine last month."

He can play with his figures for hours . . . only he's not just playing. I saw his D'Lo figure covering Hardcore Holly, and Dewey made a three-count on the rug with his hand . . . "one, two, three." As soon as he finished the count, he took out a pen and wrote in his notepad. I was intrigued. "Dewey, did you just write down who won?" It turns out that he does a lot more than just that. He writes down the winners and losers and keeps won/loss records and title histories for all World Wrestling Entertainment belts. "Do you want to hear my champions?" he asked. I assured him I did. "D'Lo is the Hardcore champ, Test is the European champ, Chyna is the Intercontinental champ, Road Dogg and X-Pac have the tag-team belts, and Austin has the World Wrestling Entertainment title—but don't worry, you're going to win it from him in a 'Three-Way Dance.' "

I try hard not to make my house a "look at me" house. There are only three mementos of my wrestling career in the main part of the house: a bookshelf with a variety of Mankind/Cactus/Dude toys, a plaque commemorating *Have a Nice Day!* as a number one bestseller, and a beautiful painting that a fan (who later became a friend) gave me outside an arena in Tacoma, Washington.

Dewey's room makes up for it, though. Dad is everywhere. Even when he's at school, for some strange reason, I find myself spending a lot of time in there. Staring . . . and thinking, *Look at me, look at me, look at me!*

So my book was done—or so I thought. In some ways, writing it was the easy part, but I'll get to that later. I had decided to wrestle one more year, but with knees that Joe Namath would have felt sorry for, and a body that made Colette feel sorry for herself, I wasn't all that eager to get back in the ring.

I weighed myself in mid-July and was shocked. At 311 pounds, I had actually lost a few pounds while sitting on my ass and stapling late-night pizzas directly onto my hips. "How could this be?" I wondered aloud. "I've done nothing but write and eat. I haven't worked out. But I weigh less than I did before. How can this be?" Colette tried to comfort me. She knew that I sometimes felt bad about my appearance, and wanted to ease my pain. Her choice of words failed in that respect. "Mick, you've lost a lot of muscle."

A visit to "Foley's Gym" confirmed this. Sure, I was benching somewhere around 430 (or quarter to five in the evening), but the results weren't all that impressive.

As July came to a close I began appearing at a few shows as an added bonus for the hardworking fans. My first night back was at the Meadowlands in New Jersey. It was one of the few nights in my career when I became flustered in front of a crowd. I was welcomed back with a nice ovation and decided to make my first public words an Al Snow joke. I picked the wrong one. This was actually a dressing-room classic, but its humor didn't seem to translate outside those confines. "Hello, New Jersey," I began—always a cheap, easy way to get a pop. "You know, right before I come out here, a kid asked me if I had seen Al Snow's last match. I looked at the kid and said . . . 'I certainly hope so!'" I waited to be bathed with wave after wave of laughter, but . . . nothing. A few groans, and a few courtesy laughs, but in general . . . nothing. I had told jokes that had failed before, but they had always been designed to fail—kind of like Carson or Letterman on late-night TV. This, however, was unnerving. So unnerving in fact that I had to resort to name-dropping.

Name-dropping is something I rarely do—a fact that my personal friend, *The Green Mile* Academy Award nominee Michael Clarke Duncan, would attest to—but at this point, I didn't know where else to turn. "I was talking to The Rock backstage," I yelled, to a tumultuous pop from the crowd, "and he said he's going to come out here and lay the smackdown on somebody's candy ass!"

16: *A Special Night*

ON JULY 30, 1999, I had the honor of participating in one of wrestling's greatest nights—the "Curtis Comes Home" card in Rostraver, Pennsylvania. The "Curtis" in question was Brian Hildebrand, who had managed and wrestled under the name Marc Curtis for over a dozen years before catching on as a referee with WCW in 1996.

Brian was perhaps my closest friend in wrestling. I had met him on the night of my first match, June 24, 1986, and we had hit it off instantly. That night in Clarksburg, West Virginia, also marked his last match under the "Professor Heimi Schwartz" moniker. The next morning he showed up at DeNucci's school, and despite the fact that he was a polished worker (performer) as well as a consummate manager (performer who helps make matches interesting, not an official money manager), he was a mainstay at the gym from that moment on.

If pro wrestling had offered a lightweight division in the mid-eighties, Brian would have been a big star. He could work in any style, be it classic American comedy, Mexican lucha libre, Japanese mat work, and later, submission. Unfortunately, Brian's metabolism was practically superhuman, and although he could keep pace at a buffet with the best of them, nature never let him get above 140 pounds.

Independent wrestling can be a tough row to hoe. Small crowds, bad payoffs, long rides, and worst of all, from a performance standpoint, no one in the audience knows who the hell you are. Guys who had received previous television exposure had a major advantage, but for no-name performers like we were in the eighties, getting over with the crowd was an incredibly difficult task. It was also a task that I never saw Brian fail at. The guy had the ability to generate heat and interest almost instantly and he stole many a show that I was on.

Unfortunately, the knock on Brian was that he couldn't cut promos. It was a knock that I disagreed with, but nonetheless, it kept him from getting full-time work for many years. In my career, I have seen managers land work who couldn't lace Brian's boots, and I've seen women with nothing to offer but a boob job become national celebrities. I wish someone would have realized that Brian Hildebrand was more than a manager and more than a wrestler—he was a teacher. He knew as much about the wrestling business as anyone I've ever met, and loved it with a passion that I've never seen rivaled. Many a young wrestler would have benefited from his guidance—as I did, and some promotion would have learned the value of his mind.

I got my first full-time wrestling job in the summer of 1988, in Memphis, the territory that was dearest to Brian's heart. We continued to stay in touch, and got together many times over the next several years. In 1992, he was brought to Tennessee by Jim Cornette, as a referee for Smoky Mountain

Wrestling, where, while holding the territory together with his many in-ring and out-of-ring talents, he found the time to fall in love with and marry a wonderful Virginia girl named Pam.

I worked quite a bit for Smoky Mountain in the fall and winter of 1994, and I was always a welcome guest in the Hildebrand home. Being a guest there was not always easy, however. Brian loved watching videos of Smoky Mountain house shows that his dad had shot with a single camcorder. He would watch these damn tapes for hours at a time. Unfortunately, I didn't share this particular passion, but never said a word for fear of hurting the poor guy's feelings. He would literally sit on the edge of his seat, as if the closer proximity would somehow improve the tiny, poorly lit images flickering on the screen. The word eventually got out on Brian (who had somehow assumed the nickname "Gerbil" in Tennessee), and "That Gerbil's a hell of a guy, but don't let him get you trapped on that couch with his videos playing," was a warning that was warmly given.

As I write this, I realize how similar that sentiment was in regard to former wrestler and current governor of Minnesota, Jesse "The Body" Ventura, who had been an announcer on WCW in 1992 and 1993. "Jesse's a great guy, but don't let him trap you in a corner with his stories about Verne [Gagne] and the Crusher," was a frequent locker-room warning. Now that he is one of the most famous people on the planet, I would like nothing better than to talk over old times at the governor's mansion. "Mr. Governor, didn't you work a program with the Crusher back in 'eighty-one?"

We all allowed Brian this one peculiarity, because he was a genuinely great human being. So it was with great sadness that I learned that Brian had been diagnosed with stomach and bowel cancer in 1997. He wasn't supposed to survive the year, but by mid-1998, it seemed as if he had the disease beat. In September 1998, I received terrible news. Brian's cancer was back and had spread to the point that he was given between one week and three months to live. I broke down in the dressing room when I told the news to D'Lo, Kane, and Al, who had been among his closest friends, and together, the four of us held something of a vigil for our friend. I flew to see Brian in the hospital the next day thinking it was my last good-bye, but the tough SOB proved me wrong, and I was privileged to see him many more times. During my short visit, Brian's phone was ringing constantly with best wishes from concerned friends.

WCW had a special surprise for him on November 28, 1998, when they turned a house show in Knoxville into a tribute to him. Even in his weakened state, Brian found the strength to referee the main event, and was presented with a replica of the WCW heavyweight championship by an unannounced Ric Flair, who was one of Brian's heroes. I made many comments in *Have a Nice Day!* about Flair that I felt were tough but fair, but the fact that he took a day out of his life to give Brian a wonderful memory is something that I appreciate a great deal.

By the spring of 1999, Brian was still hanging in. He was not only seemingly beating the odds again, but doing so with a grace and positive spirit that made him an inspiration within the wrestling world.

Even within the World Wrestling Entertainment, where he had never worked, his spirit was admired. Top stars asked about him frequently, and Earl Hebner, our top referee, who had overcome his own brush with death in early '98, checked with me on his progress almost daily.

His friends stayed in constant touch. I was always scared when I dialed that number, fearing that I wouldn't know the right things to say, but I always seemed to have a sense of wonder about me by the time I hung up the phone. He was never down. Never. Everyone who had contact with him was amazed by his attitude. Brian Hildebrand was a dying man; it was just a matter of time. His cancer had been too devastating to even attempt surgery. The doctors merely sewed him up and passed a death sentence on him—but Brian refused to accept it.

In June, I received a call from Brian while I was eating lunch at a *Raw* taping. As always, I was glad to hear from him. "How are you?" I asked, and his answer gave me goose bumps. "I'm up to a hundred and twenty-one pounds!" I didn't know what to do, so I just yelled out "Brian Hildebrand is up to a hundred and twenty-one pounds!" Only a few people in that room had ever met Brian, but everyone had heard of him, and a loud cheer went up. I distinctly remember thinking, *He's beat it, he's really beat it.*

Marc Keenan was a big reason why. Marc was a fellow DeNucci student, who had worked full-time in Memphis and Dallas in 1990 before a serious neck injury ended his career. Marc had remained a good friend of Brian's and had come up with the idea of promoting the Rostraver show as both a benefit for, and a tribute to, Brian. Brian had been involved in every aspect of the show, and on July 30, 1999, he was beaming with pride. He looked vibrant and healthy, although in truth, he had very little time left to live.

Other than the match I refereed, I don't remember a whole lot about the wrestling. I do remember that it was unbearably hot, with no air-conditioning in the building. The humidity seemed so thick it could be cut with a knife, but the love in the air was even thicker. I don't throw around the *L* word all that often—ask my wife, who had to practically pry it out of me back in 1990—but I sure felt a lot of it on July 30. The event served as a DeNucci graduate reunion with Dominic, Shane Douglas, Marc Keenan, Preston Steele, Dick Flanagan, and me all swapping exaggerated stories of our ring abilities. WCW had allowed future World Wrestling Entertainment stars Eddie Guerrero, Dean Malenko, Perry Saturn, and Chris Benoit to come; and the World Wrestling Entertainment had sent Al Snow, D'Lo, Terry Taylor, Chris Jericho, and me to Rostraver, at their own expense. Longtime friends Lord Zolton, Jim Cornette, Sandy Scott, and Les Thatcher were there, as well as Bruno Sammartino, who was even smiling!

I could see Shane smiling a mischievous smile as Dominic, looking fit and trim at sixty-three, prepared to enter the ring to do battle with Zolton in a "legends" match. Now, I like Zolton, but if you consult your *Webster's* for a definition of "legend," there is a good likelihood that Zolton's photo won't be included. "What the hell are you laughing at?" I asked Shane, who was one of my closest friends in the business. "Just wait," he managed to sneak out in between laughs. I then heard Hank Hudson (who had given me my "Truth or Consequences, New Mexico" hometown before my first match) announce Dominic and his music began.

When Dominic was a star in the sixties and seventies, entrance music was unheard of, but, my goodness, he had it on July 30. Within two beats of the music, I realized why Shane was laughing. Dominic DeNucci, the guy who had attended the school that burned down before the "old school" was built, was walking to the ring to the strains of "Tequila"—the song that Pee-wee Herman had danced on the bar to in *Pee-wee's Big Adventure*. I could just picture Dominic saying, "Shane, you sominabitch!" as he walked for what must have seemed like miles to the ring.

I had the pleasure of refereeing a great match between D'Lo and Al, but not before getting the mandatory verbal knockout on Mr. Snow. D'Lo held both the Intercontinental title and the coveted European title at the time of the show. Al had been the Hardcore champion (and a good one) until dropping the belt only five days earlier to the Big Boss Man. I decided to make him suffer, but not before paying tribute to Brian, who watched the whole show from a table set up next to the ring. Al and D'Lo followed suit with tributes of their own. Now it was time for fun.

"Ladies and Gentlemen, as you know, this is a very special night. Because of that, I have decided that not only are D'Lo's European and Intercontinental titles on the line here in Rostraver, but I'm putting Al Snow's Hardcore belt up for grabs as well."

I could see Al's jaw drop. He had felt he was safe on Brian's big night, but he was wrong. I looked at Brian, and he was grinning while shaking his head in disbelief. Al was coming around now and was yelling "you two set me up" repeatedly. Actually, he was wrong; D'Lo hadn't been in on it, and in truth I wasn't planning on burying Al, but was merely following my instincts. A shark swims, eats, and makes baby sharks. It's instinct. I make fun of Al—instinct.

D'Lo played along, though, and pretended to "inform" me of my mistake, while I did my best Bob Newhart imitation, using the house mike instead of a telephone. "What, what's that? You say Al doesn't have the belt anymore. You say that ho-ha, Al lost to the ho-ho, oh-ho-ho Big Boss Man?" Then I broke into a full-blown fake laugh, and the crowd laughed along. Al, for his part (and despite what he says, he does enjoy playing his part), did the slow burn while mouthing a silent "I hate you."

The two of them put on quite a show for Rostraver, but more so for Brian. The match culminated with Al and D'Lo bullying me, at which point I somehow managed to subdue them both with a "double Socko Claw," at which point I slowly lowered them to their backs. Brian seized the opportunity and made his way into the ring to make a three-count on both fallen men. D'Lo and Al were remarkably good sports about the devastating loss, and in a moment I'll never forget, the three of us paraded Brian around on our shoulders while the 2,000 in attendance chanted his name.

When the matches were over, all of the participants returned to the ring. Speeches were made, gifts were presented, and tears were shed. Brian was as happy as I've ever seen a human being. Pam's tears fell freely as she hugged us and thanked us for our support. I looked at Pam in her beautiful white dress, overwhelmed at the emotion surrounding her. I looked at Brian and saw the smile that will always be the first thing I think of when I remember him. I thought of my career, and some of the prestigious venues I had performed in. Madison Square Garden, the Tokyo Dome, the Georgia Dome. Inside that small stifling gymnasium, in a suburb of Pittsburgh, with perspiration pouring from me, I had a revelation of sorts. I turned to Marc Keenan, who had worked so hard on a show that Pam feels extended her husband's life, and told him how I felt. "Marc, I have never felt quite this proud to be a wrestler in my life."

Brian Hildebrand passed away on September 8,

1999. He was thirty-seven years old. I was able to see him a few days before he died, and am grateful that I was able to say good-bye and tell him how much he meant to me.

I asked Pam recently if Brian had ever let his illness get him down, and told her of my amazement at his tremendous strength in the face of such suffering. She told me that he never felt sorry for himself, but sometimes felt sorry for her, because of the pain that his illness was causing. In the end, Brian left this world doing what he had been best at—teaching.

In dying, Brian taught us all a little bit about living. He taught us about courage in the face of death. He taught us hope in the face of insurmountable odds. And he taught us that in a business filled with giants, a 140-pound man could walk tallest of all.

17: *Chapter Seventeen*

THE VERBAL FAILURE AT the Meadowlands was followed by an even greater setback—my first match since surgery. Even though I was part of a six-man tag in Baltimore and was therefore able to get away with doing very little, the little I did do made it painfully obvious that I was a long way from healthy. At that point the fact that I had written my life story on 760 pages of legal paper seemed somewhat insignificant, while the fact that my knees throbbed and my belly shook seemed significant as hell.

I had my first singles match back on August 5, 1999, at an amphitheater at Kings Dominion Amusement Park in Doswell, Virginia. It was there where, after riding many hours of coasters, I turned in a performance so rotten that I could practically imagine my kids in the audience denying any knowledge of their lineage. "Hello, Virginia," I began with a standard suck-up line that's only slightly behind "USA, USA" on the cheap-pop ladder. "Now, I know that a lot of you out here tonight saw me in the park earlier, didn't you?" Another cheap pop. "But while I was out there, I also saw my opponent tonight, the Big Boss Man." Cheap boo. "Yeah, I saw him all right—throwing up after riding the Scooby-Doo [kiddie] coaster." The place went nuts, and the Boss Man played it up big time before getting on the mike. When he did, he was classic. Most heels would have tried to deny it, but the Boss Man seized the opportunity. "Hey, I wasn't feeling good even before I went on that ride! Haven't any of you ever had a stomachache before?" To the tune of 8,000 people chanting "Scooby-Doo, Scooby-Doo" while the Boss Man covered his ears in anger, I tiptoed my way through a horrible affair that offered about as much physical contact as a Bobby Fischer training session. Luckily, I had Mr. Socko, and when I pulled him out, a large portion of the crowd forgave my performance. In fact, for a large percentage, forgiveness wasn't necessary; they thought they'd seen a hell of a match.

I sometimes find it ironic that some of my greatest matches have taken place in tiny gymnasiums, musty armories, dusty racetracks, parking lots, and even an odd fruit stand or birthday party. At these less than prestigious venues, with no pyro, lighting, or thousands of cheering fans, a performer's weaknesses can really stick out. I've seen many a muscle-bound stiff who looks like a million bucks in the gym suddenly look like the emperor with no clothes when he locks up in a ring.

On the flip side, fame can hide weaknesses. Don't get me wrong, with four hours of new programming every week, top guys have to work hard and earn their spots, but once there, a certain amount of coasting is acceptable. I myself was counting on doing a whole lot of coasting while my knee got stronger, but was shocked out of my comfort zone by a knee injury to Stone Cold that threatened to shine a big neon light all over my weaknesses.

On the August 9 *Raw* in Chicago, Stone Cold suffered a torn posterior cruciate ligament in his left knee, an injury that threatened to ruin the much-anticipated *SummerSlam* showdown between Austin and Triple H. *SummerSlam* had always been considered the World Wrestling Entertainment's second-biggest show of the year and this year's event, slated for August 22 in Minneapolis, with Minnesota Governor Jesse "the Body" Ventura as the special referee for the main event, was expected to be huge. Austin's injury put the whole thing in jeopardy. The World Wrestling Entertainment needed a miracle. Instead, they called me.

In my heart, I knew I wasn't ready for a match of this magnitude. In my wallet, I knew that this one match could make up for two months of missed work. The wallet won out over the heart, with my head helping out by convincing me that I could find a way through it.

Austin, it was felt, would not be physically able to complete the classic singles matchup that the situation called for. By making the match a "three-way dance," surely we could add enough intangibles, including some surefire Ventura physicality, to make it exciting.

A few days later I was called into the World Wrestling Entertainment offices for an emergency meeting. Bad news. Jesse, they'd been informed, didn't want to get physically involved. He had been getting heat from every news source ever invented for even being present at the damn match, let alone actually getting involved in it. This was a major wrench in the works of sports-entertainment's second-biggest day of the year. With a top star who could barely walk, an addition whose two butt cheeks had different zip codes, and a troubleshooting referee who didn't want to shoot down any trouble, this match was going to be difficult to pull off. Actually "difficult to pull off" is a little optimistic. "Suck" was a more realistic expectation.

A special referee had to get involved. That's what he was there for. Muhammad Ali had been a wrestling referee. He got involved. Mike Tyson was a referee. He got involved. Once, I had a seventy-two-year-old referee in Italy who had been a wrestler years earlier. Even he got involved. He didn't just get involved either. He threw a dropkick and a flying headscissor and followed it up with a cartwheel into a standing ovation.

My favorite experience with a special referee was Dave "The Hammer" Schultz, the infamous goon of the Philadelphia Flyers glory years of the seventies. As the epitome of the "Broad Street Bullies," he was brought in by WCW in May of 1994 to referee a "Broad Street Bullies" match with me and Kevin Sullivan against the Nasty Boys. Schultz came up to us several hours before the match. Now in his mid-forties, he still seemed fit, but no longer looked like the bane of the NHL, as he had twenty years earlier. He also looked out of his element and quite nervous.

"Hey, guys," he politely said, "I know I'm going to get involved tonight, and I thought one of you might teach me how to throw a fake punch." We all laughed, because we knew that the match was going to be extremely intense and that faking punches wouldn't be high on the list of that evening's priorities. We all assured Dave that faking his punches wouldn't be necessary. Dave looked flustered. I tried to put him at ease. "Dave, this is a big match for us. We're going to be hitting each other pretty hard. The last thing we want to do is have you ruin your reputation by throwing punches that don't look good." Schultz looked over at Nasty Boy Jerry Sags, who was to be the recipient of the blows. Sags gave him a goofy grin and assured him that it would be okay.

From that moment on Schultz looked like a different guy. Looser, cooler. He even drank a couple of beers. He actually appeared to be looking forward to it. And when he got the chance to go, he looked like "The Hammer" of old. He pulled Sags' shirt over his head, hockey-style, and with a sneer on his face, threw about a half-dozen uppercuts that damn-near knocked Sags out. More importantly, the crowd went wild, and long after Sags' headache had gone away, it still looks great on video.

So, Jesse didn't want to get involved? What could I do? Nothing, besides try to get in shape in twelve days and try to hide my weaknesses, which, at that point, was like trying to hide Roseanne Barr/Arnold/just plain Roseanne in a thong. Besides, we had two whole days to explain this entire scenario, which included getting me, who hadn't been seen in two months, back not only on TV but into the title picture.

In the wake of Austin's injury, a quick, somewhat preposterous, but creative scenario had been set up concerning the number one contender spot for *SummerSlam*. A three-way contenders' match with Undertaker, Hunter and Chyna had ended with Chyna winning the match on a fluke and being awarded the number one contender status. Now, in my first show back, Hunter desperately wanted that status back from his real-life and on-screen squeeze. She refused. He got mad and so did she, and they agreed to their own number one contender match.

This is where I entered the picture. In the midst of a very good match, Mankind returned, hit Triple H with the stairs, and helped Chyna attain the victory.

I had always had a special relationship with Chyna. Upon her entry into the World Wrestling Entertainment in early 1997, she had run into many World Wrestling Entertainment Superstars who were unwilling to sell for her during matches. Despite the fact that she had a phenomenal build and could outlift many of the guys (including me) in the weight room, she still carried the stigma of being a woman in a man's business.

To this day, Chyna (real name: Joanie) gives me credit for helping change that. Hunter and I had engaged in a memorable feud in the summer of '97, and it was enhanced greatly by the creative and hard-hitting maneuvers that Chyna was a part of. I had been secure enough in my manhood to sell for a woman, and soon everyone else followed suit.

I decided to publicly call her on that favor by inviting her down to the ring later in the show. "Chyna, we both know that there has always been a vague sexual tension between us. You with your revealing outfits—and me with mine." Hey, I can't remember what I said next, but I somehow asked for a match and climbed to the second turnbuckle to milk some audience support.

Look, I can't take it anymore. I've been living a lie, and I can't continue any longer. Talking about

Chyna and thinking of her in those studded-leather sexy outfits has been too much for my system, and though I may regret writing this, it has to be better than the pain of pretending it never existed. This book is about the truth, and sometimes the truth hurts. But you see, at one time Chyna and I were more than just friends. We had a . . . relationship. A relationship that included a great deal of contact with her hand and my genitals. Sure, her hand was usually balled up in a fist and was traveling at high speeds when the contact was made, but what the hell, it's my book and I'm going to count it!

While I stood on the ropes, the memories of our relationship must have been too much to resist, and she made contact again and I slumped to the canvas in an awkward fetal position. "Does that mean no?" I managed to gasp out, and even from a distance, I could see Chyna laugh as she stepped back through the curtain.

We did have a match, and it was strange because, as well as I knew her, and as helpful as I'd been to her career by letting her get physically involved, I really felt strange about having a match with her. She and Hunter had torn into each other only minutes earlier, but I really didn't know what to do. So I did what came naturally: I stunk up the place and then put Mr. Socko on her.

Since that time Chyna has gone on to have matches with many of the guys, and I feel like a wimp for not giving her a little better matchup. She has been the Intercontinental Champion, and I think she has done a tremendous job. Even more important, she is Noelle's idol and she treats my daughter with a kindness that is truly touching. I may be Big

Daddy-o, but when Noelle comes to the matches, she wants nothing to do with me. Instead, it's Chyna holding her hand on the way to the girls' dressing room for some quality bonding.

In 1997, Chyna wasn't allowed to be hit at all—even by accident. Now, after being suplexed, punched, and kicked by the top guys in the game, she definitely wrestles like one of the guys, but more important, is accepted as one of the guys.

Following my victory over Chyna, Shane McMahon insisted that I wrestle Triple H to find out who the number one contender truly was. Shane, who at this point in time was the head of "The Corporation," whose crown jewel was Triple H, insisted he be the referee. Commissioner Shawn Michaels, however, insisted that he himself referee. This led to a compromise that allowed for two referees, each of whom, at the end of the match, saw a double pin differently and awarded the number one contendership to two different people. So we headed into *SummerSlam* with two number one contenders, a champion with a torn ligament, and a governor referee who didn't want to get involved.

I was given the honor of throwing out the first pitch at the Twins–Yankees game on the night before the big show. I was even allowed to take a little batting practice at the Metrodome. I hadn't swung a baseball bat since I was fifteen, back when I used to dominate my brother in driveway stickball. I hadn't swung at a real baseball since I was twelve. This was not a problem, as I was simply going to tap a few grounders and bloop a couple of fly balls before retiring to a luxury box to watch my first professional baseball game in twelve years.

Right? Screw that, I was going to hit one out of the park!

The first pitch came in and I sent a screaming liner down the third-base line. A few of the Twins clapped and I saw a couple of Yankees nod in appreciation. Another pitch came in, and I took it deep to left. Man, that baby was gone, and I knew it! Unfortunately, the ball didn't know it, and dropped about ten feet short of the wall. Still, it was a hell of a drive for someone who hadn't swung a bat since the Carter Administration. A few more swings and that ball would be jumping over the fence; after all, I'd visualized just such a thing. Too bad I didn't visualize how damn far those fences were, because no matter how hard I hit the ball, it always came up short.

I should have walked back to the dugout, accepted a few handshakes for my hitting—which really had been pretty good—and watched the game in comfort. Instead, with one of the biggest matches of my career on the horizon, I became obsessed . . . with hitting a home run. By the time I left the field I was exhausted, soaked with sweat, and vaguely aware that I had just screwed up big time.

People who watch wrestling often wonder how we are able to accept so much punishment. The answer is simple—training. In the same way that a marathon runner trains to run long distances, wrestlers train to accept punishment. Baseball players train too. An inexperienced kid who jumps into a wrestling ring and attempts to have a match is an idiot. A thirty-four-year-old man who takes 200 home-run swings with no warm-up is probably an even bigger one.

When I woke up on the morning of *SummerSlam*, I was in tremendous pain. My right hand throbbed, and would be incapable of a handshake for two weeks. My lower back was spasming. And my oblique muscle was the worst of all. My oblique! I didn't even know I had one of those.

The backstage area was covered with security for the governor. For hours we didn't see him. In the days leading up to the event, criticism surrounding Jesse's participation had been extremely harsh, and we sensed that he was going to be miserable to work with. The participants gathered in one dressing room to try to salvage the match, but expectations were low. "Here comes Jesse," Shane announced, and moments later a bevy of official-looking men ushered in Governor Ventura. "Hello, Cactus," he said in

that incredible voice. Yes—the governor remembered me! His next words were even more uplifting. "I wasn't going to get involved," he boomed, "but I've been getting blasted so bad by the press that I figure SCREW IT—I'll do anything you want!" This was like music to our ears. Suddenly we had a second chance. The governor had issued us a pardon. We had been handed down a "crappy match" sentence and Jesse Ventura had overturned it.

He even came up with some ideas of his own, and truth be told, they were among the highlights of the match. At one point Jesse grabbed an intruding Shane and threw him over the top rope, to the thunderous roar of the crowd, and ad-libbed a line that I'm sure stuffy Washington insiders must have loved: "That's for your old man, you little bastard." The match itself was pretty good, and yeah, I even managed to hide those dreaded weaknesses. Best of all, I won the damn match. In a move that was a surprise to just about everybody, I defeated Stone Cold with a double-arm DDT—becoming the first guy in almost two years to score a clean win over "The Texas Rattlesnake."

In a move that was something less of a surprise, I dropped the title to Triple H the following night in Iowa. I was the World Wrestling Entertainment Champion for a third time, although it lasted less than twenty-four hours. I think over time I will gradually forget about that last little fact, and when my grandchildren ask about my career, I will simply point to a huge poster with the governor of Minnesota raising Grandpa's arm in the air.

18: *Size Does Matter*

MY BOOK WAS IN BIG TROUBLE. Quality wasn't the problem. My editor had read the manuscript and been very impressed. Content wasn't the problem, either. The problem was sheer mass. ReganBooks had wanted 60,000 words for a reason: it was easier to sell that way. Easier to sell to bookstores, who already doubted that wrestling fans could or would read—and easier to sell to fans as well.

My editor broke the bad news to me on the phone one afternoon, and just about broke my heart as well. He explained that a book my size would price itself out of the marketplace in many of the larger book outlets. Sadly, he explained that a great deal of content would have to be removed.

Colette could tell that I was crushed. When I told her the news, she was just about in tears—along with me. "What are you going to do?" she asked. Immediately I thought of an old magazine article I'd read in 1976, where Sylvester Stallone said he would rather have buried the *Rocky* script in his backyard and let the worms play Rocky than sell the script and let studio favorite James Caan have the role. Maybe I wasn't willing to bury it, but I told Colette that I would rather keep it in the attic than allow it to be sold in a bastardized state.

Several hours passed before I received a call from Judith Regan, the namesake of the Regan division of HarperCollins. Her brief conversation with me made my world a happy place to live in once again. "We're going to keep it in its entirety," Judith informed me, "and we're going to keep the price the same. But I've got to tell you; we're counting on your enthusiasm to help us sell a lot of books." Enthusiasm, I assured her, was not going to be a problem.

What exactly is "a lot of books"? Larry Nahani had told me that 100,000 copies sold was a huge amount. Judith Regan had been the editor in charge of Howard Stern's *Private Parts*, which in 1993 had shocked the literary world by selling more than a million copies. Since then, Judith had played a part in many successes, but her biggest-selling celebrity autobiography had been Marilyn Manson's *The Long Hard Road Out of Hell*, which had sold somewhere around 150,000 books. Autobiographies by people I considered to be major stars, such as Fran Drescher and Meat Loaf, routinely sold in the neighborhood of 50,000 copies. Outwardly, my editor hoped to sell numbers comparable to Manson's. Privately, he probably felt that Fran Drescher would give me a literary spanking.

When I look back on it now, I can understand Regan's concern. I can even stretch myself to understand, if not agree with, the fears of the book world. Books tend to frighten people. Big books terrify them. Most wrestling fans don't read books, but neither do a great majority of the public. I once read a report that claimed 70 percent of all adults never read a single book after completing school. I believe it. So most people, when they do decide to read a book, don't want to be overwhelmed. I guess it's kind of like an old guy tiptoeing into the shallow end of a pool instead of attempting the Triple Lindy of *Back to School* fame.

Personally, I enjoy reading. Back when I was making monthly forays to Japan, I was a reading machine. I stayed in small rooms with no English television, rode for hours on buses, and flew with all the perks that seat 26D includes. But even for me, a book like *Moby-Dick* looked ominous. My mom had recommended a book called *The Physician*, but at 1,100 pages, I had self-prescribed several hours of *Nick at Night* instead. A big book is like a serious relationship; it requires a commitment. Not only that, but there's no guarantee that you will enjoy it, or that it will have a happy ending. Kind of like going out with a girl, having to spend time every day with her—with absolutely no guarantee of nailing her in the end. No thanks.

A few days ago I saw a man in the Okaloosa Regional Airport reading *Tuesdays with Morrie* by Mitch Albom, which at this point has been on the bestseller lists for more than 120 weeks. Two complete years. Maybe this sounds cruel, but I'm usually a pretty good judge of character, and this airport guy looked like he'd be more comfortable flipping burgers at the Waffle House than flipping through a story of "an old man, a young man, and life's greatest lesson."

I made a quick assessment of this Albom reader and guessed that this was his first journey into literature since high school, or at least since the twentieth-anniversary *Best of Jugs* hit the newsstand. So why *Morrie*? Well, probably for the same reason I read *Morrie*—a little spiritual uplift and a two-hour time killer, all in one easy flight. Yeah, it's a good book—but is it really that good?

Tuesdays with Morrie is 30,000 words, 30,000 F'n words. Now usually I'm the first guy to jump up and say "size doesn't matter," or "it's not the size of the dog in the fight, but the size of the fight in the dog," or "it's not the size of the wave, but the motion of the ocean," but this was different. This was about *books*. And being the author of a big book, I felt that size did matter. But a 200,000-word *Morrie* would have killed its success. Tuesdays with the guy was just fine. Wednesday, Thursday, Friday, Saturday, Sunday, and Monday would have been too much, and the book would have spent about as much time on the bestseller list as Mideon on the crunch machine.

Thirty thousand words? Hell, I could have written a book like that. As a matter of fact, if I had taken *Have a Nice Day!* and removed the graphic depictions of violence, Al Snow jokes, obscene language, sexual references, sophomoric humor, and other various offenses, about 30,000 touching words is exactly what I'd have been left with.

Who Moved My Cheese? Fifteen thousand words, and the thing is selling like Emo Phillips merchandise at a losers' convention. About 100 pages long with writing so large that Mr. Magoo could knock it off in an hour. Hell, I've got 15,000 words of advice hidden somewhere in my book also.

I find the fact that these books are eligible for the bestseller lists a little distressing. I think they need to fall into different categories. The *New York Times* already had different lists for Fiction, Advice, How-to and Miscellaneous Nonfiction, Self-Help, Diet, and as of July 2000, Children's. I think the book world was a little concerned that J. K. Rowling's Harry Potter series had a monopoly on all the top fiction spots and was thereby not giving the "real" authors a shot at number one.

So now we've got Rowling's 300,000-word *Harry Potter and the Goblet of Fire* at the top of the children's list and the 15,000-word *Who Moved My Cheese?* at number one in nonfiction. What the hell is wrong with that picture?

So if the *New York Times* is willing to create a new children's list in their newspaper, why not add a few more lists? *Tuesdays with Morrie* could move to the "Inspirational Pamphlet" list and *Who Moved My Cheese?* could move to the "Informative Brochure" list.

I guess like a lot of things in life, the size of a book can be compared to sex toys. I was going to use the *D* word, but I realize that some of our younger readers may not know what that is, and I don't want to be responsible for little Jimmy asking about a dildo at the dinner table.

Back in 1987, while on a disastrous wrestling tour of Wyoming, Idaho, Montana, and the Dakotas, a bunch of us DeNucci students hit a twenty-four-hour "adult" store just to look around. A former World Wrestling Entertainment wrestler used to hit these places and do more than look around; he'd drop a couple hundred a week in them. But I swear, I was just looking around.

At one end of the store, on shelves that seemed to

go on forever, stood the largest collection of fake penises known to mankind—the species, not the wrestler. Some of these things were grotesque. One looked like a king cobra with a vein running through it. Another looked like a baby's arm holding an apple. A few of us, including "Moon Dog" Tony Nardo and Dave "Crusher" Klebonski, approached the salesgirl as if we were looking at late-model Chryslers. "Excuse me, ma'am, which of these fine phallic forms would be your most popular model?" The lady smiled and pointed at a rather innocent-looking number. I think my mom used to take my temperature with thermometers that were bigger. It didn't even look like the real thing.

The lady could see our surprise, and as an expert in the field, decided to give us a little insight. "Most women who come in here have never used a sex toy before. They find this model . . . less threatening." With her simple words, this woman had not only given me a way to describe my own "less threatening" member, but a philosophy of life as well. Certainly it can be applied to my experience in the book world.

For a book to be phenomenally successful, it has got to appeal to people who don't normally read. Therefore, many people stepping into a bookstore are doing so for the first time in a while, and are looking for something "less threatening"—like *Tuesdays with Morrie*. *Morrie* was less threatening. My book was a baby's arm holding a damn apple.

19: *Legal Issues*

I HAD OVERCOME THE SIZE PROBLEM, but there were other problems rearing their ugly heads as well. Not the least of these was my writing, which was atrocious. Not the content or style, but the actual penmanship, which was, at times, barely legible. As a result, the 760 pages of legal paper that I sent in was returned to me as being in something less than a state of completion.

Upon the manuscript's arrival in New York, a team of people had been assigned the arduous task of deciphering my words. I think digging up and assembling the "Fighting Dinosaurs of Mongolia," which were on display at the Museum of Natural History, had taken fewer hours than typing my project. My handwriting itself was borderline horrible, but it was the cross-outs, arrows to the top of the page, insertions of "page 724A," and notes in the margin that made things extra difficult.

During especially long writing sessions, my penmanship would get even worse. I estimated that I had averaged seven hours a day of writing over the fifty-day course of the project. Seldom was it actually a seven-hour writing day, however. Due to scheduling conflicts and the pressures of being a wrestler, a husband, and a father, sometimes I was not able to write at all. Sometimes I wrote for two hours and sometimes for twelve. On a trip from England, for example, I wrote for eighteen—a number I hoped to beat on my aforementioned Asia trip. After writing for fifteen straight hours, though, we arrived in Vancouver, and my energy fizzled out quicker than an Al Snow entrance pop. I slept from Vancouver to New York.

Even now, as I write these words, it's 1:43 A.M., since I have to wait for my family to go to sleep before I go to work. I hope someday to have a house with my very own office so that I can go about accomplishing my ultimate goal of becoming America's foremost author of children's Christmas books.

The chapter in *Have a Nice Day!* on meeting my wife was especially troublesome since Colette insisted that I be drunk when I wrote it. So I loaded up in the Delta Crowne Room and boarded a plane, where a combination of loving thoughts, inebriation, and airplane turbulence caused my pen to jump around, like the results of a Pinocchio polygraph test.

When the manuscript came back from the typist, a good 5 percent of the words were either left blank or written incorrectly. A section on Terry Funk stands out in particular. Since he is my idol and mentor, I wrote quite a bit about Terry, who I affectionately referred to as "The Funker." The manuscript came back with every Funk reference written as "The F—ker." The woman must have felt that she was typing up a book for Diamond Dallas Page, what with all the *F* words in there.

Page, or D.D.P. for those who don't know, is a

walking, talking cartoon character, whose overbearing ways and eyeball-rolling-inducing clichés are matched only by the size of his heart, his love for wrestling, and his loyalty to his friends—a group that I am proud to include myself in. D.D.P. is also the key player in *Have a Nice Day!*'s perennial favorite "cookie story," which I plan to make a major part of my projected film version of the book.

D.D.P. wrote a book himself, but unlike mine, which was written off the top of my head, Page's was meticulously researched. Unlike mine, which took fifty days to write, D.D.P. worked on his for years, conducting hundreds of hours of interviews with friends and wrestlers from all periods of his life. And unlike mine, which printed all curses in unedited form, D.D.P.'s book used the star method of editing all his f**k words. So, as a result, Mick Foley, who uses the *F* word only in traffic jams and on special occasions in the Foley bedroom, comes off like Tony F**kin' Soprano, and D.D.P., who uses at least two *F* words to describe a newborn puppy, escapes F-free on an editorial technicality.

So I read the manuscript, corrected the mistakes, crossed out parts I didn't like, and sent it back. I received a corrected manuscript in a few weeks' time, went through a second correction and crossing-out process, and sent it back again. At this point official editing began.

Certain structural suggestions were made, most of which I accepted and some of which I fought. More important, the editor suggested we cut out things that made me look like a jerk. It has been said that "the pen is mightier than the sword," and I could easily see why. In fifty days, I had been able to settle all the scores, right all the wrongs, and get back at all the people who had screwed me along the way. Much of it, I know, was a little severe. Many people thought that I was rough on Ric Flair, a certifiable wrestling legend and possibly the most respected performer of the modern era. For those people, and for Ric himself, who I heard was hurt by it, I can only say that it's a good thing you didn't see all my words. I remember writing for six straight hours about Flair and then throwing it all out in the morning because it was a little *too* brutal. As brutal as it was, though, it was very therapeutic to get my feelings down on paper. I can honestly say that I have never had any ill will toward Flair since then, so it's too bad that he hates my guts now.

It's too bad that gangs and world leaders can't get their hatred down on paper. The world would be a better place.

Even though I had done quite a bit of self-editing, quite a bit remained to be done. By the end of the process, happy Mick was well represented. Cranky Mick was eliminated. For those interested in the writings of cranky Mick, check out the bonus chapter in the paperback of *Have a Nice Day!* He's all over it.

The book was scheduled for an early October 1999 release. Printing and editing were a big concern, but they seemed to get resolved. Only one hurdle remained—but it was a big one. Legalities. I thought I was safe on lawsuits; after all, this was an autobiography and these were my opinions. For example, I just read in *The Weekly World News* that I was predicted to be the recipient of a sex-change operation. That was the opinion of well-respected

Nick, it was great seeing ya!
collette, Dewey
and Noelle,
much love
and SEASON'S GREETINGS.
happiness to you! we miss you!
Kim and Page... and Gerry

sports psychic Sonny Meers, and I wouldn't be so foolish as to think I could sue him for it. Besides, if it weren't for the fact that I'd make a real ugly chick, I'd start shopping for estimates.

The attorneys involved thought that Vince McMahon would have problems with criticisms that I had written about him and the World Wrestling Entertainment. Instead, they were stunned when Vince responded with "don't gut the book, if that's the way he feels, then print it." Other issues were not resolved quite so easily.

In the book, I was quite critical of a particular wrestler's talents or lack thereof. I had also made small jokes about the wrestler (let's call him *what's-his-name*) and his wife, who was something of a celebrity. I really didn't know what to do about this. I needed a punch line for my jokes, but already knew I was dangerously close to overutilizing Al Snow. Remember Al jokes were my big finishers, so I couldn't go there too often.

As I stood for hours at the phone, in a sweaty arena in Texas, speaking with lawyers in their air-conditioned offices in New York, I saw the answer to my problems: the Mean Street Posse—Joey Abs, Pete Gas, and Rodney—heading toward me. In an instant I whipped up a batch of false sincerity. "Hey, guys, how would you like to be in my book?" The Posse looked quickly at each other and all agreed that being in the book would be cool. Now I had to tell them in what context they would be appearing. "I'm going to make fun of you in it." Again they looked at each other. "Okay, that's cool," was the unanimous decision. With that one quick conversation, *what's-his-name* was out and the Posse was in.

I like the Posse. There, I said it, and I'm not afraid to admit it. I like their gimmick of being tough guys from the mean streets of Greenwich, Connecticut—and I like the guys as well. Two of them, Rodney and Pete, are high-school buddies of Shane McMahon. Joey Abs is actually a veteran of the Carolina Independent scene who was brought in to be the "worker" of the group.

I'm not sure if Pete and Rodney were actually supposed to be wrestlers. Originally, they were used to hype Shane's match with X-Pac at the 1999 *WrestleMania* XV Pay-Per-View. In the midst of telling outrageous stories about Shane's exploits in Greenwich, they started getting over, and even though they'd never wrestled, actually had more heat than most of the heels on our crew.

They had heat in the dressing room as well—especially Rodney. Pete seemed like a nice guy, but Rodney? Not only was he sporting a hairstyle that was repulsive even by sports-entertainment standards, but he was unbearable to be around. Then he started growing on me. Sure, they were horrible and hadn't paid any dues, but they were working hard and I genuinely got a kick out of the gimmick, which saw them going to the ring to do battle in loafers, chinos, and blue sweater vests. I liked it so much that when I saw the guys growing wild facial hair I tried, so to speak, to nip it in the bud. "Look, guys," I explained, "you guys don't want to look like tough guys. We have enough of those. The preppier the better." They actually listened. Pete shaved off his beard, and Rodney covered up his tattoos so that the Posse gimmick remained pure.

The guys had been practicing in the "World

Wrestling Entertainment Dojo," which was actually at the television studio in Stamford, and while their improvement was not noticeable, they were still a long way from even being poor when I found out I was to wrestle all three members on a late August episode of *Raw*.

Rodney and Pete politely asked to talk to me before the match. They had been informed that I was going to lay out all three of them with chair-shots to the head, and they were understandably nervous. Oddly, they weren't nervous about being hurt. They were nervous about *not* being hurt. "Listen, Mick," Pete Gas said softly, "we know that we're only here because we're Shane's friends, and we know some of the boys resent us for it." I nodded in agreement. Personally, I didn't resent them, but I could understand those who did. Rodney then spoke up. "We've never gotten hit with a chair before, and we don't want everyone thinking that we're afraid to. So . . ." Rodney's voice trailed off, and as he searched for the proper way to phrase his next words, Pete stepped up and made the strange request. "Do you think you could hit us really hard with the chair?" Rodney nodded and they both looked at me as if I was "the great and powerful Oz" contemplating their brain and heart requests.

I thought it over. They had been very polite about it—and besides, I had been planning on blasting them anyway. "Sure, guys, I'll do it," I said, and was rewarded with sincere handshakes and heartfelt gratitude.

Sure enough, I lived up to my word, and sure enough, the Posse was deeply appreciative.

Hey—I give the guys a lot of credit. They took

whatever bookings they could get and even moved to Memphis to improve without the spotlight of the World Wrestling Entertainment on them. Maybe someday, when Rodney is the new "most electrifying man in sports-entertainment," I can point to the TV and say, "I gave that man his first chairshot."

Unfortunately, the Posse wasn't there to clear up *all* the legal questions about my book. Difficult questions. Soul-searching questions. Questions like:

What's the basis for your belief that Flash wanted to hammer Foley? Was Esterly found sitting Indian-style naked, eating brownies? Who are The Godfather's Ho's and what do they do?

All in all 325 legal questions were raised, including whether my saying that I had seen seventies adult film star Kay Parker perform oral sex on a videotape was slanderous to her reputation. The toughest question of all, however, was the following: What is the basis for stating that Scorpio is a "genitalactic" freak of nature?

"Can you repeat that, please?" I asked, not quite sure of what I'd heard. "What is the basis for stating that Scorpio is a genitalactic freak of nature?" they repeated. I asked the attorneys on the phone if they were serious and they assured me that they were. Actually, these were the World Wrestling Entertainment attorneys and were merely reading a list of questions that had been written by an outside law office.

This was the type of question that was so simple it was hard. It was like a "who's buried in Grant's tomb" question. I decided to answer in the easiest way I knew. "Um, because he has a large penis?" I actually answered in the form of a question. They gave me a follow-up: "Is this true?" I assured them it was. "Would you be able to find witnesses to corroborate your statement?"

This was too much. I half expected to have Allen Funt walk up and point to a hidden camera. Of course I could find witnesses to corroborate my statement. Entire dressing rooms had seen the damn thing. Besides, I asked the lawyers, "Is this really the type of thing I'm going to get sued over?"

Really! Is this guy going to file a suit claiming that

he's been wrongfully charged with having an enormous pecker? Is he going to claim damages based on mental duress and pain and suffering? I wish somebody would slander *me* that way. Besides, if I know Scorpio, he's probably got that page framed on his living-room wall.

I stuck to my guns on the penis problem, but ended up giving in on a few others. Unfortunately, a few of the things I had to give in on were not legal matters, but were important personal points.

Have a Nice Day! should be called *Blood and Sweatsocks*. In truth, I never said "have a nice day" all that much, and certainly never in the first eleven years of my career. I had to fight just to get the name "Mick Foley" on the book. My editor didn't seem to grasp just how important this was to me. "You're better known as Mankind, aren't you?" was his somewhat baffled reply to my request. "Maybe," I said, "but I didn't write the book with my leather mask on rocking back and forth and calling for my mommy." I also pointed out that Mankind doesn't show up until page 373 of a 503-page book. Granted, the White Whale didn't get his big scene until the last few pages of Melville's *Moby-Dick*, but he was talked about the entire book. Besides, I'm tired of all the scholarly comparisons that already exist between my book and Melville's.

In the end, we compromised. It was too late to change the title, but we did add *A Tale of Blood and Sweatsocks* as the subtitle. Mick Foley did get credit as the author as well, even if the name does appear awfully little next to the nearly Scorpio-size MANKIND that dominates the spine of the book.

I had a chance to see our legal system at work in

May of 2000 when I was a defendant in a lawsuit filed by a fan based on an October 1995 incident at the ECW arena in Philadelphia. The fan received first- and second-degree burns on his hands and face as a result of the incident, and was treated at the hospital and released less than forty minutes later. When I saw the fan in the dressing room, he appeared not only calm but almost ecstatic at having been the center of attention. Indeed, he was freely taking the credit for "putting out" Terry Funk, who had accidentally caught on fire during the match.

That was the last I saw of the fan until we stepped into that courtroom. Ten months after the fire incident, the fan, William Sandborn, had been involved in a terrible motorcycle accident that resulted in the amputation of one leg and over a dozen operations. In all, he was in the hospital for over a month, one week of which was spent in a coma. Despite the severity of his injuries, it was his attorney's contention that the ECW incident had caused greater mental duress and more pain and suffering. I found that to be ridiculous.

I wish that Sandborn had come to ECW with the facts, or at least the facts as I believed them to be. "Look, I was at your building and I got burned. Sure I'd had a few beers and sure I reached over the guardrail, but I was trying to help out and I got burned." I have no doubt that had he done so, he would have gotten a small settlement, and more importantly, received what seemed to be of utmost importance to him at the time—free tickets for life.

Instead, Sandborn let his lawyers present him as an innocent victim, someone who was minding his own business when a burning chair flew onto him in the crowd. Sandborn, they claimed, was then pushed onto the burning chair and was an emotional wreck afterward. So emotional that he hung out in the back and asked for free T-shirts after the incident. So emotional that he was able to drive his truck, with a stick shift, home that night.

I took the stand on the third day of the trial. I saw his counsel pull out my book, which he proceeded to quote from as if it were gospel. I will reprint a few pages of that incident from *Have a Nice Day!* so that you can gain a better knowledge of the incident in question and also familiarize yourself with what I was hearing on the witness stand.

I should point out that there is one lie printed in this story of the fire. Keep this in mind as you read, and try to picture the attorney reading in a decidedly unpleasant voice, especially concerning profanities, which he made extra grating. After every profanity, he would apologize to both the judge and the jury— just to make it clear that it was my offensive language and not his. Here we go:

> *Funk got on the mike and attempted to lure me into a fight using the same psychology he'd used on Bullet Bob Armstrong. "Cactus Jack," Terry bellowed, "you're a goddamn coward, you son of a bitch." I remained in the back. "Your wife is a whore." Still in the back. "Your mother is a whore." Nothing. "Your children are both whores." That should have done it. But . . . nothing. I could not be broken. The Funker had one more ace up his sleeve. "Bischoff is a homo." That did it! I was out from behind the curtain in a flash to defend my*

main man's honor. I meant business as I hit the ring, but as I got to the blasphemous Funk, Dreamer stepped in front and started peppering me with big rights. BAM, BAM, BAM, BAM—the crowd was exploding, and I was doing my best to make each one look its most devastating. . . . Our quest for righteousness was not to be denied, however, as referee Bill Alfonso (who had been taken to the back after suffering his one-punch knockout) reemerged with a weapon of his own. It was my old Japanese standby—the fire chair! I was handed the unlit chair and knocked Terry down with a nice shot to the head. Dreamer turned as well and was dropped with a crushing blow to the skull that was lessened only slightly by the kerosene-soaked towel. Raven touched Funk's iron to the towel, and the fire chair lived again in the ECW arena. . . . Before my shocked eyes, I saw our plan fall to pieces. What appeared to be a giant fireball flew off the chair and instantly ignited Terry, who was bent over by the ring apron. My first thought was to save him. I completely abandoned my character and my story line and dove through the ropes to try to put out Terry. I knew that flames had about three seconds of contact time before they really did their damage. Terry was up to at least two. I took off after Terry, but he was running like a madman. To this day, I try to relive these events in my mind and try to figure out why I couldn't catch him. Was he moving too fast to catch, or was I simply a coward under pressure? The question still haunts me. I do remem-

ber thinking, "I've got to catch him." And then wondering, "What do I do once I'm there?" I had no answers. I wish I could point to a burn on my body and say, "This is where I saved my hero, Terry Funk," but all I have to show for it is a heavy conscience.

The guy had read a few pages from my book, but had managed to completely crap on the spirit in which it was written. I had seen the guy operate the past few days and had to admit that he was very good. Short and stocky, with a suit that looked a good two sizes too small, he used the bully approach with witnesses. He would seek out the slightest discrepancy between witness testimony and depositions taken a year earlier and attempt to exploit it as well as a witness's own nerves and insecurities. I knew that he would attempt this with me as well.

Several minutes into his inquisition, he asked me about the accuracy of quotes that I had attributed to several people. I informed him that I had written about the incident several years after it took place and was using my memory and "creative license" to attribute quotes. "Aha"—he thought he had his opening!

"'Creative license', huh, Mr. Foley," he bellowed while making those stupid quotation marks in the air with his fingers—a move that should be reserved only for Dr. Evil. From then on every question was followed up with "Is that true, Mr. Foley, or are you using 'creative license'?" with the annoying finger quotes. Finally, I cracked and admitted that there was one small lie in my *Have a Nice Day!* story. He jumped all over me like Clinton DNA on a Gap dress.

"So, you're telling me that you lied in your book?"

"Yes, sir."

"You're telling me that you have deceived this jury by passing off your book as the truth, when in actuality you knowingly lied?"

"Yes, sir."

"Mr. Foley, you swore in this courtroom to tell the truth, the whole truth, and nothing but the truth—*so help you God!* Do you remember that?"

"Yes, sir."

I looked at the judge. Her eyes were locked on me. I looked at the jury. For the past two and a half days they had looked attentive but completely humorless. I had not seen a single one smile during the proceedings. For the first several minutes I had seemed so sure of myself, but now this legal genius, this master of the spoken word, had me on the ropes. Then he made a mistake. In the legal drama *A Civil Action*, John Travolta's lawyer character admits to making the mistake of asking a question that he doesn't know the answer to. Apparently, this attorney hadn't seen the movie, because he made the same mistake.

"Mr. Foley, would you care to tell the members of the jury what part of your story isn't true?"

"Are you sure?"

"Yes, Mr. Foley. Give us the truth. Don't use 'creative license.'"

The last finger quotations did it. He deserved to be made a fool of. The lawyer had served up a big fat softball and I intended to hit it out of the park.

"Well, sir, Terry really never did call Bischoff a homo."

The jurors broke out in laughter, and even the judge chuckled. The tough-guy attorney, for his part, looked like he wanted to crawl into either a hole or a WCW "Worldwide" television main event—someplace where he could be hidden from the public.

Five days later the verdict arrived. I had been wearing the same suit for every session and had tried to fool the jury by switching ties. The poor Funker looked exhausted. He had feared the worst—and the worst, he felt, could be pretty bad indeed. Terry felt that the jury might well look at us and assume we were loaded and then look at that poor bastard without a leg and pretty much give him everything we'd ever worked for. I thought he was being a little paranoid, but I certainly felt like I was going to have to open up the purse strings and wave bye-bye to several years' worth of money saved on the road.

Before excusing the jury to make their decision, the judge had informed them that their job was to determine who was most at fault. If the plaintiff (Sandborn) had been more than 50 percent to blame for his injuries, she explained, they would not have to award damages.

The jury returned and my heart started pounding. I had been calm for the duration of the trial, but now the reality of the situation was sinking in.

"Ladies and gentlemen of the jury, do you find Extreme Championship Wrestling liable for Mr. Sandborn's injuries?"

"No, we don't."

"Ladies and gentlemen of the jury, do you find Paul Heyman [ECW owner] liable for Mr. Sandborn's injuries?"

"No, we don't."

"Ladies and gentlemen of the jury, do you find Terry Funk liable for Mr. Sandborn's injuries?"

"No, we don't."

This left only me. In the ten seconds it took to ask the question and get the answer, I foresaw the worst. All the blame was going to be placed on me!

"Ladies and gentlemen of the jury, do you find Michael Foley liable for Mr. Sandborn's injuries?"

Drumroll, please. "No, we don't."

Yes, yes. After four and a half years I could finally put this thing to rest. I was finally free. Free to light more chairs on fire. Free to burn more fans. What the hell! I was free to relax with a big thick steak and a victorious plane ride home.

I couldn't help but feel bad for Sandborn and his wife as they sadly walked away. I also couldn't help but feel a little sad for our justice system, and how it can be abused.

During my time in the courtroom, I had witnessed testimony that differed from my recollection of the events, bullying of weaker witnesses, taking quotes out of context, misrepresenting facts, and not substantiating claims. Yes, indeed, the United States legal system can be—you got it—faker than professional wrestling.

20: *Rock 'n' Sock*

I HAD BEEN SPENDING a great deal of time thinking about the future—mine as well as my family's. I knew I had about a year left as an active wrestler, but how I spent that last year depended, in large part, on me. I had been presented with a great opportunity to turn heel a while back, but had felt not only physically unable but mentally unprepared. As the proud possessor of half a thimbleful of natural athletic ability, I had depended on a great deal of physical risk and mental energy to excel in a business where gifted athletes were the norm.

At age thirty-four, I had more than fourteen years of paying the price for my physical risks. I simply no longer felt I could perform at a top level on a regular basis. My past successes as a heel had been the result of a combination of high risks, quality matches, and an ability to dig deep to come up with and showcase the ugly side of my personality.

Some call it acting, and sometimes it was. Sometimes, though, it wasn't. Much of my anger was very real, and while therapeutic to vent, it often left me emotionally exhausted. In my 1995 ECW interviews, it had been easy to be angry. I had left a six-figure job with a major company, I was getting physically decimated by participating in barbaric "death" matches in Japan, my family was living in a sweatbox with no air-conditioning, and I was performing regularly in a converted bingo hall while wrestlers in other companies who couldn't hold my jock (or at least wouldn't have enjoyed doing so) dwarfed my salary with a fraction of the effort.

In 1999, getting angry would be a little more difficult. I had been the World Wrestling Entertainment champion three times, every store in the country carried my action figures, and I was being paid more money than I ever dreamed of. Hell, I was one of the guys that the 1995 Cactus Jack would have been pissed off at.

For me to be a heel in mid-1999 would have meant digging even deeper for some real hatred to grab hold of. With my body no longer able to cash the checks that my mouth would be writing, I turned down the heel opportunity and focused instead on making Mankind as lovable as possible.

The lovable Mankind, however, was stuck in a career hole. With Austin and The Rock miles ahead of me on the babyface food chain, I had resigned myself to never getting any bigger than I already was. From an ego standpoint, that was fine. I had no problem being number three. But from a financial standpoint, being number three was not fine. Being number three meant never truly making the big Pay-Per-View money.

I looked at our top heels, and the list was small. The Undertaker had finished a long run with Austin, and both his character (which he had stretched to its limits by introducing satanic elements) and his body needed a rest. Triple H was making great strides as a heel and was looking to embark upon a series of matches with Austin. He had already engaged in many Pay-Per-View contests with The Rock, and that rivalry needed a rest.

As I saw it, there were two ways to make truly big money in the World Wrestling Entertainment, and neither one involved being a lovable but broken-down babyface. The Rock and Austin were the way to go. I had great history and chemistry with each. Austin and I hadn't had a match of magnitude in over a year. My rivalry with The Rock was still etched in people's minds, but a reversal of roles would make the whole thing seem fresh again.

I knew that turning heel would require two things that I hadn't shown in a while: physical conditioning and some real anger. With my family's financial security on the line, I knew that I could summon the fortitude to get my ass in the gym. The anger was going to be a problem to tap into and channel, but I was willing to go to those dark places in my mind because in the long run, with a fat pile of cash in front of me that I could wallow naked in, I'd be happier.

Now, what reason did I have to hate these guys? Veteran wrestler Michael Hayes had taught me long ago that every heel needs to believe he is justified in his actions, no matter how wrong the logic behind those actions may be. My best promos always came forth when I knew I was right, and at least some of the anger was legitimate.

I thought back to the point in the "Hell in a Cell" match when I managed to get back to my feet after a second devastating fall. Jim Ross was at his absolute best there, as he called the action with legitimate passion and emotion. "My God, he's got to be the toughest son of a bitch in this type of environment that I've ever seen!" Something about this call had always bothered me, but for months I couldn't put my finger on it. When I did, I knew that I could draw big money with Austin.

"He's got to be the toughest son of a bitch . . . in this environment." *In this environment?* What exactly did this mean? From a character standpoint, I knew what it meant. It meant that Ross, in complete honesty, was in the middle of calling me the toughest son of a bitch he had ever seen, period, when something had stopped him. Something made him add on that ridiculous "in this type of environment." Jim Ross had to add those words because, from a marketing and story-line standpoint, Steve Austin was the toughest son of a bitch in the World Wrestling Entertainment. As Mick Foley, a guy who knew his role, I understood why Ross needed to qualify his statement. But as the heel Cactus Jack, I would find Ross's glorification of Stone Cold's character at the expense of my real-life "Hell in a Cell" performance to be inexcusable—and I would take it out on Steve.

I needed The Rock to get to Austin, but in truth, I felt like The Rock needed me. In the three months since he had turned babyface, The Rock had been on an incredible roll. His interactive audience-participation promos were highlights of our television shows, which now included a two-hour Thursday show on the fledgling UPN network. The Rock was like wrestling's version of singer Ray Charles in that he could come up with a catchphrase on Monday and have an entire crowd repeating it on Thursday. He was undoubtedly the heir apparent to Steve Austin, who was showing signs of fatigue after his phenomenal run on top of the World Wrestling Entertainment.

I could only see one thing getting in the way of The Rock's rise: his character was mean. As a heel, part of The Rock's appeal was watching him humiliate people. It was a guilty pleasure—kind of like watching Louis Gossett, Jr. chew out young officer candidates in *An Officer and a Gentleman*. As a babyface, The Rock continued this practice and the crowd roared its approval, but I could definitely see the day when fans would stop perceiving it as cool. Sooner or later I felt The Rock was going to have to show signs of inner decency to go along with his slick persona—and I thought lovable Mankind would be the guy to bring it out of him. Then, when The Rock actually accepted this homely Mankind guy, *BAM*, I would turn on him and show the World Wrestling Entertainment audience a side of Mick Foley they never knew existed.

Why would I turn? This one was easy. The *Royal Rumble*, January 1999, and The Rock's dressing-room no-show would provide all the anger I needed.

I sat down with The Rock in the dressing room in Iowa State University on the evening of August 24, 1999—one day after my title loss. I explained to him my feelings, my ideas, and my belief that in a year's time there would be no Austin, Undertaker, or Mankind in the World Wrestling Entertainment and that the company would be his to carry into the future. He was very open to my thoughts, and together we brought the idea to the Vinces—Russo and McMahon.

During the discussion, I laid out a tentative timetable for an October teaming, a December heel turn, and a series of matches that would take us through February. Austin, I hoped, would be the Holy Grail—the 2000 *WrestleMania*.

Six days later The Rock tapped me on the shoulder, and I turned to see him smile. "We're teaming up tonight." "Tonight," I said, a little surprised. "Wow, that was kind of quick."

So, on August 30 in Boston, Massachusetts, The "Rock 'n' Sock Connection," as it came to be known, began one of the most unique and humorous journeys in sports-entertainment history. We even won the Tag Team Championship from Undertaker and the Big Show on that very night.

The act was a natural! We rarely talked about what we were going to do, relying instead on our chemistry together to guide us. Much of it involved my theft, or at least my borrowing and adjusting, of The Rock's catchphrases. On our first night in Boston, The Rock was looking for revenge on 'Taker and Show, who had left him lying earlier in the broadcast. He stepped out on the stage and began spouting Rockisms as he walked down to the ring and insisted that he wanted to take on both culprits.

While he stood in the ring, my music hit and I stepped onto the stage. I proceeded to run off The Rock's spiel, but put my own personal touch to it.

I implored The Rock to let me be his partner with the words "The people want Mankind to be The Rock's partner, the people need Mankind to be The Rock's partner, and tonight in Boston, Massachusetts, Mankind is asking to be The Rock's partner." The Rock accepted on a one-time-only basis under one condition: "Never—and The Rock means *never*—steal The Rock's catchphrases again!"

The match was to be won with the People's Elbow, a point that I had a problem with. There was no way, as a fourteen-and-a-half-year veteran, I was going to let a match against the legendary Undertaker and the world's largest athlete end with a move as stupid, as infantile, and as horrible looking as the People's Elbow—unless, of course, I got to do it, too. So together we dropped our elbows, with The Rock's grazing Show's triceps and mine landing squarely on his nuts. The first title reign of wrestling's odd couple had begun.

Perhaps most amusing of all was a twenty-minute impromptu celebration in the ring that took place after the show went off the air.

The feedback the following day was phenomenal. The wrestlers loved it, the Internet was buzzing over it, and most important, Vince loved it. This was going to be an incredible pairing that would translate into incredible heat and box office when the dastardly turn took place.

Yes indeed, Rock 'n' Sock mania was running wild, and as it turned out, at the next night's *SmackDown!* taping in Worcester (*SmackDown!* is taped on Tuesday and aired on Thursday), it was running everywhere. "Seven times?" I moaned to The Rock. "They have us on the show seven times." Together we went to Russo with our concern about too much of a good thing and came to an agreement that we had to limit our appearances. That night, however, we gave Worcester enough Rock 'n' Sock to last them for quite a while.

A memorable promo occurred when The Rock went to the ring to address the issue of Shane McMahon's forcing the connection to fight each

other on that night's program. I guess Shane felt that the People's Elbow and Mr. Socko would be simply too much for the rest of the WWE to withstand. While he was out there I strolled to the ring and told him that I thought it would be cool if he threw the match and allowed me to win in Worcester, the same city where I had beat him for the title. The Rock saw it differently.

"Yeah, that would be cool," he said with a smile. "But you know what would be even cooler? If The Rock took your tag team belt"—oh no, I could smell what he was cookin'—"shined it up real nice"—the crowd smelled it now too—"turned that sumbitch sideways"—this was going to hurt—"and stuck it straight up your candy ass!" The crowd loved it. The Rock had gotten me with one of his classic lines, and the audience roared its appreciation. The Rock, you see, threatened to turn everything sideways—Triple H's nose, the Stanley Cup, his foot, and a plethora of other things never meant to be used in the sphincteric vicinity—and shove them up people's asses. Apparently, he still had that ass fixation that I had diagnosed several months earlier.

Everyone sold this threat in the same way—with anger. I decided to sell it a little differently—with fear. As if I was afraid that he would actually make good on his threats of anal anguish. I looked at my belt in disbelief and slowly picked up the mike. Slowly I spoke. "Rock . . . um . . . I don't think . . . that this thing will fit up there."

With that, the audience broke out in laughter, but The Rock never cracked a smile. Instead, he uttered a Rockism and cocked his head back to prepare for his "if you smell what The Rock is cookin'" line.

When he did this, his glasses fell off and plopped unceremoniously to the canvas. He was at a loss for words or actions. He couldn't very well pretend to be cool and deliver the line without his glasses. That would be like the Fonz saying "Hey" after falling off his bike. He couldn't bend down and put them back on. That would be like Michael Steadman and Elliot trying to fool Hope and Nancy into thinking that . . . never mind, a *thirtysomething* reference isn't really appropriate here.

Finally, after what seemed like minutes but what was probably only a few seconds, I bent down, picked up the glasses, and put them on The Rock's head myself. This time The Rock smiled, a huge smile, and said "The Rock thanks you for that," before asking me if I detected the aroma of his culinary efforts.

When we stepped through the curtain, we were both besieged by the boys in the back, who thought it was one of the classic moments in sports-entertainment. Two nights later I watched the show, eagerly anticipating this special moment. Here it comes—belt up the ass, it won't fit, if you smell what The Rock is cookin'. . . . Wait, what happened to our great moment? I never found out who made the final call, but the word I got is that it had been edited out because it wouldn't have been good for The Rock's character. Not good? It would have been great. What better way to show some warmth in his character than with an unplanned moment that we couldn't duplicate if we tried. Somebody had dropped the ball.

I know that The Rock's style works for him, but in issuing threats, I believe in adhering to a certain sense of reality. For example, if former Ultimate Fighting champion Ken Shamrock said, "I'm going to tear your shoulder out of its socket and then snap your Achilles tendon," I'd be likely to believe him. If World Wrestling Entertainment wrestler/human mannequin Steve Blackman said, "I'm going to dismember and decapitate you and dispose of your body in an abandoned mine shaft in eastern Pennsylvania," I would tend to believe him as well. But a championship belt turned sideways and shoved someplace never meant for that kind of storage capacity? No way.

So, kids, when using threats, always make sure you can back them up. Otherwise you'll sound as preposterous as people who actually use the following two threats. In theory, they may sound tough, but in practice, I just don't see the odds of bringing them to fruition being all that good. To illustrate the absurdity of these threats, I am going to insert fictional detectives Bill Tuesday and Fox Scully into a fictional hunt for two missing bodies. Imagine, if you will, a dark alley in a bad part of town. The smell of urine permeates the humid summer night as the detectives' flashlights cut through the darkness like swords.

"Hey, Fox, I think I've got something here. There's a human head and a trail of human feces that leads to the body . . . oh no, it seems as if someone has ripped off his head and shit down his neck!"

"Tuesday, this could be even worse. I've got a body here with both eye sockets exposed. There seems to be a proliferation of some type of white liquid . . . oh my goodness, this man has had his eyes pulled out and has been skull-fucked to death!"

21: *"This Is Your Life"*

THE SEPTEMBER 27, 1999, edition of *Raw* was a monumental show, both as a success and a failure. "This Is Your Life" with Mankind and The Rock would represent not only the high point of The Rock 'n' Sock Connection and Vince Russo's last great World Wrestling Entertainment idea, but an example of a great opportunity lost as well.

I had participated in the "Six-Pack Challenge" main event of the *Unforgiven* Pay-Per-View a night earlier, along with Kane, Triple H, Big Show, British Bulldog, and The Rock. During the buildup of the show, I had agonized over what to do should I find myself face-to-face with The Rock and had even claimed to "know how Meryl Streep felt at the end of *Sophie's Choice*." Granted, a great deal of our audience had never seen the movie, but I still thought it was a clever line—until seeing *Sophie's Choice* again a few nights ago. Somehow, after watching Streep's heart-wrenching performance, it no longer seemed like an appropriate punch line at a wrestling show. Toward the end of the match, I had surprised The Rock with a double-arm DDT for a near win (Triple H got the win) and felt horrible about it the following evening.

So horrible in fact that I prepared a special surprise.

The segment was supposed to last fifteen minutes, and was set to start off the ten o'clock hour, but was teased with little vignettes throughout the opening hour. After every match, the camera would cut to me holding balloons and a giant book, with a mystery figure cloaked under the secrecy of a blue bedsheet. "Wait until The Rock sees you," I told the mysterious sheet wearer, "he's going to go BANANA!"

"Banana," with no *S* on the end was my tribute to wrestling legend/stooge Pat Patterson. Patterson was of French-Canadian descent, and despite having lived in the United States (or United *State* as he would say) for over thirty years, he had never completely mastered the difference between singulars and plurals. As a result, he had once told a small group of wrestlers that "at this point the Undertaker will go completely banana," to which I responded, "Will the crowd then go absolutely NUT?"

Pat's plural problem had once led to me having my hopes dashed, when, in the mid-eighties, my parents informed me that Mr. Patterson had called my house and wanted me to work for the World Wrestling Entertainment. At the time Pat was Vince McMahon's right-hand man, and a call from Pat was like a trip to Shangri-la for a young wrestler. Still, I sensed it might be a rib. I knew how to weed out a Patterson impostor. "Dad, did the guy mess up his singulars and plurals?" I asked. My dad's answer made my day. "Oh, the guy's English was horrible." Yes, it really was Pat. Hooray!

I called Patterson's office every day for two weeks and left messages. When I visited my parents at the end of that time, my mom played me the message, and I knew right away that I'd been had. "Hellos, this is Pat Pattersons calling to tell you that we thinks you is one of the greatest wrestler we have seens." It was Shane Douglas, speaking English that was even worse than Pat's, playing the always-funny trick of fooling someone into thinking that their dream has come true.

Only about six people in the world even knew what the joke was, but a one-out-of-every-million ratio seemed reasonable to me. Finally, after an hour of making the world wait, I made my way to the ring, along with my trusty mystery sidekick. Rumor had been rampant about which Superstar could be beneath the sheet. Abdullah the Butcher? Terry Funk? Spaceman Frank Hickey? Only I knew for sure.

Recently, The Rock too began paying homage to Patterson's unique verbal stylings by calling his "spinebuster" move the "pinebuster."

I picked up the mike and asked for The Rock. The "Great One" made his way to the ring and demanded to know the meaning of this intrusion. I explained that I was sorry about the DDT at the "Six-Pack Challenge" and this was important, this was historic . . . "This Is Your Life."

With that, balloons fell from the ceiling, confetti filled the air, and the strains of "Happy Days Are Here Again" burst from the speakers. I then proceeded to pull out names from The Rock's past, and upon their arrival into the ring, The Rock would systematically tear them apart with his verbal skills. One by one, they were sent on their way. Betty Griffith, his home-economics teacher. Gone, because she wouldn't allow The Rock to make pancakes. Everett

Hart, his high-school football coach. Gone, because he took The Rock out of the game before he could own the state single-game sack record. Joanna Imbriani, his high-school sweetheart. Gone, for cutting The Rock off as he tried to cop a feel on the couch.

In reality, these people were all actors and their names were all taken from my own life experiences. Everett Hart was the name of Ward Melville High School's football coach. Betty Griffith was my kindergarten teacher. Joanne Imbriani was my tribute to my buddy John Imbriani, who I had also paid tribute to in *Have a Nice Day!* by spelling his name eleven different ways.

These actors were a little bit shocked to see that The Rock and I didn't rehearse for a fifteen-minute segment. I introduced them to The Rock a half hour before the segment, and he asked me how I wanted to go about doing it. "Rock, I'll say something to bring out the home-ec teacher, and then you say something to get rid of her, then I'll introduce the coach, and you'll get rid of him. And then the girl-friend will come out, and you'll get rid of her. Okay?" And that was pretty much it. Unfortunately, it wasn't "pretty much it" for the segment, which had already run its allotted fifteen minutes, and still had plenty left to go.

First, I unveiled the mystery guest, who turned out to be ... drumroll please ... YURPLE! That's right, the lovely clown who had accompanied me to the hospital for the birth of Mr. Socko. Together we presented The Rock with his presents—matching Rock 'n' Sock Connection jackets, and a "Mr. Rocko" sock with a tremendous image of The Rock on it—before regaling him with a 20,000-strong sing-along of *Happy Birthday to You*.

"That's great," The Rock said with disgust, "but there's only one problem. It's not The Rock's birthday, you idiot." I wasn't so crazy about the "idiot" reference, but it was The Rock's next reaction that was going to make this whole segment and get us where we needed to go, angle-wise. I put my head down and slowly spoke like a child who's just been yelled at. "I know, Rock, but it's just that every day I get to spend with you feels like somebody's birthday."

Okay, here it comes. The reaction I'd been waiting for. The big smile, the amused laugh. Okay, Rock, I'm ready. But they never came. So we lost the opportunity to further our angle—to plant a seed. I needed those seeds, or else I couldn't turn heel. I also needed to have a little respect shown to me which, by refusing to be gracious, The Rock didn't do. The Rock 'n' Sock was a huge success, but hell, The Rock by himself was already a huge success. We didn't really need to be teaming unless it was going to lead us somewhere.

As I write this, I am currently the "Commissioner" of the World Wrestling Entertainment. It is truly the easiest job in the business, as I get to have all of the fun with none of the pain. On my first night back with the company, The Rock approached me and we reminisced about the days of The Rock 'n' Sock Connection. He even gave me what almost sounded like an apology. "Mick, when we were teamed up, I was new to being a babyface, and I almost felt like I was walking on eggshells. But I just watched some of that stuff we did, and man, that

really was some funny shit. If we were to do things together now, I'd be up for anything."

Eight days after that talk, we were back in the ring. The Rock had a catchphrase that consisted of asking a person a question and then cutting him off with "it doesn't matter what you think/want/say/wear" and so on. Personally, I hated the phrase, because there was always some yahoo at a personal appearance who would use it, and it was really annoying. On this night, however, The Rock suggested that I use his own phrase on him.

"Rock, congratulations on being a three-time World Wrestling Entertainment Champion. In my opinion, this has to put you up there with the greatest World Wrestling Entertainment Champions of all time. I was wondering if you could tell me what you think about that." At the moment The Rock got his first syllable out, I was there for the cutoff. "IT DOESN'T MATTER WHAT YOU THINK!"

With that, I jumped up in the air and pumped my fist like an out-of-shape white guy with a Slick Watts seventies-style headband sinking a three-pointer at rec league. "Yes, yes." I then took off for a celebratory lap around the ring while the crowd chanted my name. "Foley, Foley, Foley." As I was running, I looked up at the ring and at The Rock. He was sporting a huge smile and was shaking his head in disbelief.

That's it, I thought, *that's the look*. If The Rock had given me that same look in September 1999, my whole career would have taken a different path.

"This Is Your Life" was not a total disaster. While sitting in the lunchroom the following day, I heard The Rock's voice behind me. "Did you hear?" He paused for a moment before revealing a very important number. "Eight-point-four." Eight-point-four? That was unheard of. "EIGHT-POINT-FOUR?" I yelled out in a "this is too good to be true" type of voice. "Eight-point-four," The Rock repeated.

The 8.4 in question was the rating for our "This Is Your Life" segment on *Raw*. It was, to the best of my knowledge, the highest-rated head-to-head wrestling segment in history. I say "head-to-head" in reference to WCW airing its *Nitro* show at the same time as *Raw*. Over the course of several months *Raw* had been averaging close to a six, which made it the most-watched show on cable television. *Nitro* had been averaging a three or so, but "This is Your Life" had taken a great deal of their viewers. Not enough, however, to fully explain the huge rating. Together, Rock and I tried to figure it out. I could only come to one conclusion. "Rock, that number is so big that people had to literally be calling their friends and telling them to turn on their televisions." Our happiness was such that there was only one appropriate and mature thing to do—rub it in Vince's face.

When we tracked Vince down, he reacted as if he were Superman looking at two towers of kryptonite. He was literally cowering. "Too long, Vince, huh?" The Rock said with a sneer. Vince had known this was coming and he was trying to laugh it off, but man, he hated being this wrong about something. Rock stayed on him. "So it dragged, huh, Vince?" Suddenly I broke out in an uncontrollable coughing fit. "Huh, huh, huh, eight-point—huh-huh—four, huh, huh." Finally, Vince cracked. "All right, all right, I was wrong. From now on you guys can go as long as you want."

Unfortunately, although The Rock's chemistry with me remained amusing, I not only saw our chances of spinning off into a Cactus Jack/Rock feud dwindling, but also felt my own reputation suffering. I felt that there was a fine line between allowing myself to be a comedic figure and looking like a complete idiot. Writing my book had let me relive all of the sacrifices I had made, and all of the battles I had fought on my way up the wrestling mountain. With The Rock 'n' Sock Connection not leading us to where I hoped it would, I began to seriously consider getting out of it and letting the two of us go our separate ways.

Upon my arrival at the Meadowlands Arena (it was called the Meadowlands, not the Continental Airlines Arena, when I hitchhiked to see the Kinks there in '81, so it will always be the Meadowlands to me) on October 5, I was told that Vince Russo had left the company. Not just left it, but left it for WCW. The day felt completely dismal, as we had lost not only our head writer, or writers, as Ed Ferrara had left also, but a good friend as well. I had loved Russo's ideas—well, at least most of them. Aside from his tendency to come up with sexual ideas that drew no money and put heat on the company, I thought he was tremendous.

The departure of Russo would be a tremendous loss, but Russo felt his leaving was necessary. Not only because he felt overworked and underappreciated in World Wrestling Entertainment, but because he felt he could cement his reputation by pulling WCW out of the ratings gutter.

Sadly for Russo, the reputation he ended up cementing was Vince McMahon's. McMahon responded by taking an even greater interest in the writing for TV, and after a few shaky weeks, the World Wrestling Entertainment programs were as seamless as ever. The whole company pulled together, with Shane playing a greater part in production and the wrestlers themselves contributing a great deal.

Russo, on the other hand, never seemed to get off the ground. He was not prepared for the backstabbing atmosphere backstage at WCW, or for the system of contracts and the politics that were designed not for success but for maintaining the status quo. Even worse, he put himself on television and pushed himself as the company's top heel. He took the lead role in angles that should have been left to actual wrestlers, and had such great ideas as teaching actors how to wrestle because "anyone can." You can tell the guy's job wasn't going well by the number of times Vince McMahon was asked, "Is Russo still secretly on our payroll?"

Before Russo left, he wrote one last week of television. It was the worst stuff he had ever written, including a segment where I was to ask The Rock to marry me. Alas, the nuptials were not to be, and on October 18, in Columbus, Ohio, The Rock 'n' Sock "marriage" was annulled in powerful fashion.

During the show, I presented The Rock with a copy of my book, which was due to go on sale two days later. "Great, that's great," The Rock sarcastically stated, "just sign it to 'the Great One' and leave it over there."

Several minutes after this Al Snow found the book in the garbage and handed it back to me. I headed for The Rock's room and proceeded to give older fans a reminder of who I used to be, and newer ones a glimpse of a Mick Foley they never knew existed.

"How could you?" I softly asked The Rock. He didn't respond or even look up. "How could you?" I yelled, which prompted a "The Rock doesn't know what you're talking about." I gave him a hint. "I give you a gift, something that means a lot to me, and you throw it away?" The Rock still didn't seem concerned, as he said, "What is this about your book?" *Voom!* I threw off my mask and followed it with my Rock 'n' Sock jacket. I was about to enter a zone of intensity the likes of which the World Wrestling Entertainment fans had never seen from me. "Goddammit! I'm not talking about my book, I'm talking about my life—my blood, my sweat, my tears—and you take all that and you piss on it. I say piss on you—you self-righteous, self-centered, egotistical SON OF A BITCH!" My adrenaline was rushing now and I had entered that special place where one's own disbelief is lost. The Rock's eyes were wide, since this verbal diatribe had come as a complete surprise to him, and he tried to fire back. "You barge into The Rock's room and you interrupt The Rock. Well, The Rock says this. . . ." I never did find out what The Rock had to say since I cut him off in a manner that no one had dared to use before. "No, I say this. I SAY THIS! I don't want to know you, I don't want to work with you, I don't want to fight you, Dwayne. I don't want to even know you exist. You live with that—and GROW UP!"

Even the cameraman, sound guy, and producer were a little blown away. They had known me for over three years and had never seen a "real" Cactus

Jack promo—which was essentially what the scene had been. The angry 1995 Cactus Jack revisited.

The promo had been ultra-effective in letting our audience know that the book was not only real, but meant a lot to me as well. It also effectively ended the first era of The Rock 'n' Sock Connection. The Connection never did what it was designed to do—sell tickets and boost buy rates. It did, however, help sell a snowload of books.

22: *Bestseller*

IN *HAVE A NICE DAY!*, I detailed my dad's curious collection of some twenty-five years' worth of newspapers that occupied over half the Foley garage. When my dad found interesting articles, he often underlined them and sent them to me. With my book's publication on the horizon, my dad had been kind enough to send me an article written by an author who described the perils of a book-signing tour that nobody showed up for.

This was my greatest fear. I had suffered through a few embarrassing autograph catastrophes in the past and still felt the pain somewhere deep down in my ego. Fortunately, none of those incidents had occurred since my babyface turn of '98, which seemed to most fans like a distant memory. This was different, however. This was a book tour. Maybe the experts were right. Maybe wrestling fans wouldn't read a book. I mean, who was I to argue with the infinite wisdom of the publishing world?

I brought my family to New York with me for my three days of publicity there. With publicity tours of New York and California occupying my off days, I was looking at nineteen straight days on the road. That's a long, miserable time to pretend to be happy.

Besides, Colette had always enjoyed New York, having grown up and modeled there until the Foley charm swept her off her feet in 1990. I had been somewhat apprehensive when I heard words like "Saks" and "Bloomingdale's," which generally hit me like Quint's nails on a chalkboard in *Jaws*, but I eventually gave in. With one stipulation—no Louis Vuitton!

I brought Dewey with me for my first book signing while the girls spent a night at the ballet. I did the Conan O'Brien show en route to the signing, and had a good time. Conan's sidekick, Andy Richter, was a big fan and apparently had briefed Conan on some fast Foley facts. Everyone agreed that it went well, and then it was into the long, black limousine for a ride to the Virgin Megastore in Times Square for my big signing debut.

There is no money paid for book signings, but the perks are great. First-class hotel, good restaurants, shiny limos. After about a week I graciously asked Jennifer Suitor, my HarperCollins publicist and newest friend, if we could downgrade to a Lincoln sedan or Cadillac. To me, there's a fine line between classy and pretentious, and a thirty-seven-foot car for two or three people falls firmly in the latter category. I can understand the whole image thing, but in my case, that image is pretty much shot the moment I step out of the vehicle anyway. For some reason, flannel shirts, saggy sweats, and $150,000 cars don't go together all that well. Besides, they are a pain in the Test to get into and out of, the TV never works, and the climate control only has two settings— Saharan Journey or Arctic Discovery.

On the way to the store, Jen told me that the store

had hosted successful signings where more than 250 books were sold. I would have been delighted to sign that many. I could feel my heart pounding as we inched closer in the sluggish city traffic. Not only was I fearing bomb-scare-like attendance numbers, but this was going to be my first time inside a Virgin . . . store, that is.

All my fears were soon washed away. The line was huge. They were chanting my name as I got out of the car. A few even chanted for Dewey, who seemed overwhelmed at the mass of Foley fanatics. The little guy sat down and drew pictures of his favorite wrestlers while Dad signed away. Mankind, Kane, D'Lo, Al Snow. *Al Snow?* The crowd stood in hushed silence while I pulled down my son's pants and gave him his first spanking since '95. Just kidding—Dewey loves Al, and I've learned to live with it.

After two hours I was told that we had shattered the signing record. Total tally: 760 books. I was contracted to do six of these signings, in New York, Long Island, Los Angeles, Chicago, St. Louis, and New Jersey. By the time I was done promoting, I had done an extra fourteen, all with no pay. I had written the book, was proud of it, believed in it, and wanted to see it do well.

Which didn't mean I didn't stoop to ridiculous levels to promote it. The St. Louis signing was unique in that I would be going to my book signing immediately following my match. So when I stepped out into the ring to face Chris Jericho, I took advantage of a tremendous marketing opportunity. "Jericho," I bellowed into the mike, "if you want some more of me after this match, then I dare you to show up at the Wal-Mart on Fourteenth Street, where I will be signing copies of my book, *Have a Nice Day!*, from seven to nine P.M." I lost the match that afternoon, when Jericho used my 503-page book as a foreign object for the pin, but I definitely was a big winner at the book signing. Over 1,100 copies signed in two hours—a new HarperCollins record!

In the St. Louis case, I had a financial motive behind my microphone goofiness, but in a lot of towns, I did it just for the boys in the back, and to get a rise out of World Wrestling Entertainment road agent Jack Lanza. Lanza had spent most of his career in the Midwest, and may actually rival Governor Ventura for most stories told about Verne. He had also been a longtime partner of Blackjack Mulligan, and as Blackjack Lanza had enjoyed a long and successful wrestling career. Lanza actually made a rare on-camera appearance in 1997 to introduce Justin Bradshaw and Barry Windham as the "New Blackjacks." As a general rule, the word "new" in front of anything in wrestling spells doom, as in New Rockers, New Midnight Express, and the New Originals. Unfortunately, the New Blackjacks didn't do a whole lot to change that general rule. Christmas that year was nearly ruined when Dewey opened up one of Santa's gifts to find a "New Blackjacks" tag-team doll set. The little guy was only five then, and he looked almost saddened at what he perceived to be a catastrophic error in judgment by the all-knowing Santa. "Dad," he sadly said, with little tears welling up in his eyes, "doesn't Santa know that I hate the New Blackjacks?"

Miami represented an all-time highwater mark for these Lanza-goading promos for the boys.

Miami is The Rock's hometown, and at the time, October 10, 1999, The Rock 'n' Sock was still together. So, with The Rock's wife and mother looking on from the front row, and with Lanza and the boys looking on from the curtain, I gleefully began the worst promo of my life.

"I would like to dedicate this next match to a young man who couldn't be here tonight. Earlier today, I got together with The Rock"—cheap gratuitous pop—"and soaked up some sun, and rode the waves at South Beach. On our way out, I saw a man running toward us with a pen and a picture of The Rock 'n' Sock Connection"—another cheap pop. "By the way he was running, and by the urgency in his eyes, I knew that he was our biggest fan. Unfortunately, just as he got to us, he slipped in a puddle of suntan lotion that had dripped off my oiled-up body, and hit his head. He temporarily lost consciousness, but I stayed with him as we waited for medical help. As he was being loaded into the ambulance, this huge fan opened up one eye and spoke to me. 'Please,' he said, 'tonight in Miami, just one time, go out and win one for the slipper!' "

Sixteen thousand fans groaned, and Lanza, I was told, was beside himself. "Jesus Christ," he yelled, "that's the worst shit I've ever heard!" I, however, was thrilled. So what if 16,000 fans hated it? Six of the boys in the back had loved it. Six out of sixteen thousand? I'll take those numbers. Besides, the fans in Miami appreciated the honesty that followed. "I'm sorry," I said, "but the wrestlers in the back bet me I wouldn't do it." This time they cheered. So what if the story was horrendous; it was the courage to purposely fail that they admired.

Howard Stern was my next stop on the New York publicity tour. There was actually some history here, as back in 1991, I had been the first wrestler to ever appear on Howard's nationally syndicated radio show. It had been a risky venture then, because Howard hated wrestling, and in truth, I was only there because I was Fred the Elephant Boy's favorite wrestler. Who the hell is Fred the Elephant Boy? Fred is something of a normal guy who happens to have a speech impediment that makes everything he says sound funny. That peculiar talent, and a willingness to divulge every facet of his personal life, has been enough to keep Fred as a quasi-

celebrity and a semi-regular on Howard's show for ten years.

At one time Fred was the most famous person I knew. He and his brother even attended my wedding. Yes, it's true, and I have a photo of myself as Elvis in a white jumpsuit that was never meant for a 300-pounder, and Fred and his brother in prison outfits and inflatable guitars singing *Jailhouse Rock*, as a painful reminder.

Yeah, for a while I used Fred to get over in casual

This time I mean it. Looking out at the crowd after my last match at WrestleMania 2000.

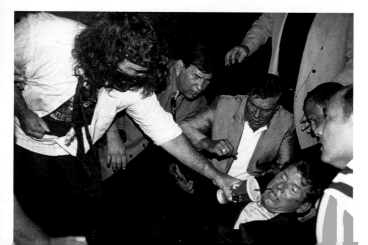

conversations, but our friendship became somewhat strained when he lent me a video of Howard's *Butt Bongo Fiesta* Pay-Per-View. Colette had come down and caught me in the middle of the night watching Howard use girls' buttocks as bongo drums, and had accused me of watching porn—which was a definite no-no in our house. I tried telling her it was a comedy tape, but she wasn't buying that poor excuse, and as a result, *Butt Bongo Fiesta* had mysteriously vanished. Unfortunately, I couldn't put the episode behind us, since Fred began calling regularly and driving me crazy with those three words spoken in his own inimitable way: "Butt Bongo Fiesta."

I still remember sitting in the green room back in 1991 and hearing Howard blast wrestling while I waited to be brought out. When I did set foot in the studio, he sized me up and made the following observation. "Cactus Jack, it looks like you're missing a few teeth there." I adjusted the headphones and responded with, "Well, Howard, they're gone, but I don't miss them." And he laughed. Howard Stern laughed at my opening joke. From that point on, it was easy, as I think I dispelled Howard's preconceived notions of big, ugly, stupid wrestlers. Sure, two out of three of those preconceptions were right on the money, but the whole thing went very well. I even made another appearance with Fred, later that year, which also went well, but then people started paying Fred to be on the show, and Howard got a little fed up.

Now, eight years later, I was poised for my return, and Howard had arranged for Fred to be brought in as a special surprise guest. There was only one problem: Fred insisted on seeing me before the show, and in a dramatic charge that was captured on video for Howard's television show, the Elephant Boy broke free and into my waiting arms. Hey, it was just a quick manly hug.

Actually, Fred wanted to inform me of some strange scandal that he'd been involved in that had to do with lewd acts and a video camera—which apparently had upset him a great deal.

As it turned out, we had a lot of fun with the whole scandal, and the show in general was fun as well, and I think Howard was genuinely touched to see that I still liked Fred after all these years. I even invited Fred to come visit Colette, although I made it clear on the air that I wouldn't let him near my children. All in all, it was a very successful appearance, and we were able to plug that evening's book signing in Long Island, which did even bigger numbers than the one in New York City.

Several weeks later I heard that Howard had been asked about some of his favorite guests, and was flattered to discover that my name was mentioned in very complimentary fashion.

I find the whole talk-show experience to be a little odd. Meeting people you barely know, or have never met, acting like good friends while the cameras roll, and then sitting awkwardly during commercial breaks. Then the commercial ends, and *bam*, you're best friends again. I have heard and read of many stars who have a great on-screen rapport with a host, and have actually never had an off-screen conversation with them. I know I probably shouldn't write this, because I definitely will want to appear on these types of shows again—hopefully to promote the new book—but in a lot of ways, the whole talk-show appearance is faker than pro wrestling.

When it comes to interesting talk-show appearances, *Roseanne* took the cake, and probably ate it as well. I did *Roseanne*—the show not the woman—the day after *Martin Short*. The Short show had been a great experience; it was very professional and Marty and I seemed to hit it off. I think I may even have pieced together a few clumsy sentences during the commercial break.

Roseanne was filmed in the same building, so I hoped for more of the same. I began to get a sense that something was amiss when her producer pulled me aside. "Okay," she nervously began, "we wrote up a bunch of questions for Roseanne, but she's not very good at asking questions. So if you can, try to get her into a conversation. She's pretty good at that." I was a little stunned, but tried to play it off with an "All right, I'll try to do that." The producer wasn't done yet. "We have some great clips of you, but Roseanne isn't very good at calling for clips, so if you want it to be seen, you should probably call for it." This was going to be some adventure.

I sat in the green room and watched a little bit of this special Halloween edition that had Roseanne dressed like a witch. She sang a rendition of *I Put a Spell on You*, which actually wasn't half-bad until she started screeching in a way that made me long for Quint's fingernails on a chalkboard.

Now it was my turn. The show's director had wanted me to come down the stairs and walk through the audience, jump up on a platform, and strike a biceps pose before sitting down with the host. I explained to him that my knees were too shot to do the big jump, and that I didn't really have biceps worth showing off. So instead I merely walked up to Roseanne, shook hands, sat down, and tried to engage her in conversation. I think I would rather have had a conversation about human body disposal with Steve Blackman.

Whereas Martin Short and Conan had gone out of their way to make me look good, Roseanne, it seemed, wanted me to look bad. Her questions were rude and dull, she cut me off before I was through with answers, and at one point repeatedly spoke when I tried to answer. She began talking about how her husband was an Ultimate Fighter and how Ultimate Fighting was much bigger than the World Wrestling Entertainment. Five times I tried to answer her, and five times she butted in. I have a lot of respect for Ultimate Fighters, despite the fact that no one I know has ever heard of Roseanne's husband being one. But Ultimate Fighting's popularity was on the wane, and high-school kids weren't really knocking down doors to get to Dan "the Beast" Severn merchandise. I tried five times to politely answer with something like, "The World Wrestling Entertainment actually learned a lot from Ultimate Fighting, and we've tried to incorporate some of their style into ours." I couldn't even get two words out. Finally, I looked at her and politely but firmly said, "Roseanne, you're not letting me talk," to which she shrieked, "I can do that, because it's my show, and it's HALLOWEEN!" While her audience meekly applauded, and Roseanne sat back with a contented smile on her "neck and neck with Michael Jackson for most cosmetic surgery done in a lifetime" face, I silently wondered what qualifications were necessary to host a talk show.

When my segment ended, I was greeted with a strange reaction from Roseanne's staff. They were actually applauding me, but it wasn't a "Foley is God" type of applause. It was different. It was as if they were applauding the survivor of some type of disaster, which is exactly what I was.

I had a similar "survivor" feeling about Larry King after doing *Larry King Live* a few months later. I had been asked to be on the show several weeks earlier to discuss *Beyond the Mat* but had opted not to do so after Vince McMahon turned out to be about the only person in America who hated the movie. Maybe he didn't hate it, but he interpreted the movie to be a downer (which I disagreed with) and also felt used by Lions Gate (which was distributing the film), which expected the World Wrestling Entertainment to promote the film with no financial reward for doing so. I understood Vince's point but also understood the concern of the studio, which felt they would be compromising the film's integrity by making a financial deal with the World Wrestling Entertainment.

As a result, the King show was set to feature director Barry Blaustein and WCW wrestlers Hulk Hogan, Roddy Piper, and Ric Flair, none of whom was in the film. I called Vince and shared my belief that the show would turn into a one-hour indictment of the World Wrestling Entertainment. After much persuasion, and with Vince's blessing, I called the King people and was booked immediately for the program.

After the program, I called Jim Ross (J.R.) at World Wrestling Entertainment headquarters. He asked me how the show had gone, and I think I accurately summed up the experience when I said, "It would have been a hell of a lot worse if I hadn't been there." Indeed it would have as our panel of guests (with the exception of Hogan, who was appearing via satellite from Florida) seemed eerily reminiscent of King's Republican Presidential Candidate show with Blaustein as the stoic John McCain, Piper as the overtly loquacious Alan Keyes, and Larry King as Larry King trying to maintain some semblance of order—and me. For lack of a better comparison, I guess I would be George W. Bush, looking mighty confused and just trying to sneak in a point whenever Piper stopped talking.

I came off reasonably well, but Hogan was definitely made out to be the big star, despite having recently drawn a Pay-Per-View buy rate that rivaled David Hasselhoff's recent special for biggest all-time PPV disaster. Amazingly, when I watched the show a few nights later, Larry King came off as if he really knew a lot about the business, and I guess therein lies his unique talent. He *appears* to know everything.

I have often been asked my opinion about Hulk Hogan, but the truth is, I barely know him. I used to watch him in Madison Square Garden as a teenager, and while never being a full-fledged Hulkamaniac, I certainly enjoyed his act. He was entering WCW at the same time as I was leaving, and over the years I have rarely had occasion to speak to him. When I have, he has always been friendly, and I have heard through the grapevine of many compliments that he has directed toward me.

Even well past his prime, he is still among the two or three highest-paid performers in our business. Is he worth it? Probably at one point he was. His presence on WCW lent instant credibility to their product, and helped both television ratings and buy rates tremendously. His heel turn in 1996 was instrumental in leading WCW *Nitro* to a long run on top of the Monday-night wrestling wars. But at this point? Probably not.

Without a doubt, Hulk Hogan has carved out a place for himself in the annals of pro wrestling history. He was the biggest drawing card in the business in the eighties, and was able to reinvent himself and become a vital part of the nineties. With each passing appearance, in the past two years, however, his value has steadily decreased. Sure, he makes a lot of money. But at some point he needs to step back and realize that he is the captain of a ship that is sinking, and the only way to fix the damn thing is for him to jump off, swim away, and let some newer, hungrier guys take control.

I pulled into Springfield, Massachusetts, on October 26 with tremendous news. *Have a Nice Day!* had made its debut on the *New York Times* bestseller list at number three! Two weeks later it would go to number one! This was unbelievable, for no one had predicted it or seen it coming—least of all the book world. Unfortunately, this brought on a several-week period of frustration, as the booksellers needed to play catch-up in a big hurry. I actually went a period of five weeks without ever seeing the book in a store because they were all gone.

As Dickens said, "It was the best of times; it was the worst of times." The best because *Have a Nice Day!* was known within the book industry as the greatest sales surprise since Stern's *Private Parts* ten years earlier. It was the worst of times because no books obviously meant no sales, which obviously was not good. A few days after my book's peak at number one, the Oprah Winfrey–produced movie *Tuesdays with Morrie* was broadcast to twenty million on network television, and the book version of *Morrie* replaced Mankind on top of the list. So, yeah, I guess you can say when it comes to *Morrie*, I'm still a little bitter. Especially when I essentially went down without a fight because of lack of available books. I lay awake for a few nights with the same thought running through my "former #1 bestseller" mind: *If only it wasn't for that damn Oprah!* Then I looked at the cloud's silver lining. *Hey*, I thought, *how many guys in the world can stay up at night thinking, "If only it wasn't for that damn Oprah," and really mean it?* Besides Phil Donahue, I can't think of any.

Oprah. Oprah. Oprah. Oprah. Of course, that was it. I would be a guest on the Oprah Winfrey show. How ingenious. Sure, that indeed was the ticket. It was a natural. After all, Oprah loved to make young writers' careers, and she and I would hit it off fabulously. Certainly, an avid reader like Ms. Winfrey would be able to look past the blood, vulgarity, sophomoric humor, and multiple penis references and see the tender heart within my book. Certainly she and I would share an ironic laugh over her movie causing my tumble from the top of the charts. I suggested it to Jennifer, my publicist. She nearly spit out her sandwich.

"What do you mean, Oprah wouldn't want me?" soon turned into "Why wouldn't Rosie O'Donnell like me?" to "Why doesn't Letterman like wrestlers?"

to "What do you mean Leno won't book World Wrestling Entertainment guys?"

At least I had an ace up my sleeve: with my book a former number one, the book critics would have to review it, and would obviously be pleasantly surprised by it, which in turn would lead to rave reviews and translate into increased sales. As the author, I knew the book was actually more about sacrifice, hard work, and chasing after dreams than about professional wrestling, and now the book critics of the world were going to spread the word. "After all," I said to Jen, "that's the way it works, right?" I thought she was going to choke.

Sadly, she told me the rules of the game. I felt like a kid being told about the birds and bees, but instead of asking, "They put *what, where*?" it was "You mean they only *review* what they *want to*?" Professor Bob Thompson, a former teacher of mine at Cortland College in central New York, who has gone on to much bigger and better things at Syracuse University, volunteered to review it for the *New York Times*. As one of the country's foremost experts on the medium of television in modern culture, he has been quoted dozens of times in *USA Today* and *TV Guide* as well as many top newspapers across the country. In addition, he has been featured on television shows ranging from *48 Hours* to *MacNeil-Lehrer* to the *CBS Evening News with Dan Rather*. Professor Thompson had also reviewed several books for the prestigious *New York Times*. So when the esteemed professor offered to review the book for them, you would figure they would jump at the chance, right? Come on, as the Quaker State oil commercial says, "you know better."

"Sorry," they told Professor Thompson, "we're not going to look at that one."

So what exactly do book critics do? I haven't quite figured that out yet. I know that movie critics review movies—including popular ones. I know that television critics review television shows, including popular ones. I know that wrestling critics review wrestling matches, including popular matches. So what do book critics do? Well, after further thought, I guess they make a living not just by judging books but by prejudging them as well.

At least some of them do. Quite a few gave the book a try, and their words were almost unanimously kind: for them I'm thankful. Even some backhanded compliments were appreciated. The *Village Voice*, an artsy publication if ever there was one, said, "If one can get past the sophomoric humor and penis references, there emerges the touching (if somewhat drawn out) tale of a creative young man chasing his dreams." Hey, I'll take it, because on the flip-side of that assessment, I can proudly state, "Once you get around all that sappy stuff about a young man chasing his dreams, there's some pretty good sophomoric humor in there."

23: "Foliability"

MY BOOK HAD HIT number one, but sadly, I was wrestling like number two. You know, as in one for pee pee and two for . . . well, you know.

I was lucky in the sense that I was in an angle that I enjoyed—the completely fictional story line of being Al Snow's best friend. Al, you see, had been there to console me when The Rock 'n' Sock had split up, and I was likewise there to console Al when he became the focus of a national news story that resulted in the Al Snow action figure being pulled from various stores across the nation.

The whole thing was preposterous beyond belief. A couple of teachers from Kennesaw State College in Marietta, Georgia, had made a stink about how Al's doll was a "textbook for spousal abuse," due to the severed head that Al carried to the ring. So, of course, Al's action figure came with a little tiny severed head. Immediately Al's figures were banned in many major department stores across the nation, causing them for the first time to actually be worth something.

I only saw one problem with the whole situation: Al didn't carry a severed head. He carried a mannequin's head that he looked to for guidance and companionship. Yeah, I know it sounds stupid, but at the very worst, it elicited a "we want HEAD" chant. Sure, it was a cheap pop, but it beat the pop that Al had been getting, which was close to unchartable. The truth is that Al's "head" had never been portrayed as, nor was ever even hinted as being, a severed human head.

It was a sad day indeed when I proudly showed off a little tiny article about me in *Time* to Al and he was able to humble me by opening up to a two-page spread on his predicament in the very same issue. Didn't anyone even do any research before banning the figures, or did they figure that with Halloween on the horizon, a tribute to the Salem Witch Trials would be appropriate? What about the two teachers raising the ridiculous stink? I swear, I lived one mile from Kennesaw State for five years, and I never even considered it as being a real college.

Speaking of Halloween, Dewey dressed up as Al Snow. He looked great, but looked just a little too handsome to really do Al justice.

Fortunately, Al and I were able to have a lot of fun with this rather bizarre hand that paranoia and hysteria had dealt him. We were able to do some great promos about the subject, including one where Al acted so forlorn that he threatened to buy a shotgun and live ammunition at one of the stores that wouldn't sell his figure and do himself in. In one show, I was able to serenade Al with a 15,000-strong sing-along of "He's a Jolly Good Fellow" after yet another Snow loss. The teaming helped Al to the point that if the wind was still, and the alignment of the stars was just right, you could almost hear him get a crowd reaction.

A short while later a movie called *Sleepy Hollow* was released. I had always been a big fan of Washington Irving's "The Legend of Sleepy Hollow," upon which the movie was based, and so attended the cinema with high expectations. I wasn't let down, as Tim Burton's dark imagery, tremendous special effects, and a fine cast made for a memorable viewing experience. Plus, that Christina Ricci has grown some rack on her since her days as Wednesday Addams. Particularly memorable were the gruesome beheadings that seemed so lifelike as blood dripped and tendons hung while the demonic horseman clutched these gruesome heads in his hands.

The film was expected to be a huge success, and so it was no surprise that a line of merchandise, including action figures, had been manufactured prior to its release. I was surprised, however, to see an action figure gripping severed heads, complete with dripping blood and hanging tendons, in the same stores that had banned the evil Snow dolls.

With Al by my side, I shamelessly carried my book wherever I went. I took Al on a "vacation" in Las Vegas to cheer him up, and the book went, too. UPN enjoyed our chemistry so much that they requested us to host a *World Wrestling Entertainment's Greatest Hits* show that had even my normally cranky brother John raving over our ridiculous performances. I even brought the damn thing to the premiere of Arnold Schwarzenegger's *End of Days*, which saw Rob Reiner dis (as in disrespect) me when I tried to talk *Spinal Tap* with him. In all fairness to Reiner, he probably gets asked about *Tap* more than I get asked about the "Hell in a Cell," but that doesn't stop Chris Jericho from frequently asking about the time Marty DiBergi (Reiner's name in the film) dissed me.

For the most part, Al and I stood around the party and felt like jerks. A group of women who worked for Universal Studios, which produced *End of Days*, approached me with reverent looks in their eyes. They were not wrestling fans but had been touched by *Beyond the Mat* (which Universal had financed) and actually treated me as something even a little better than a World Wrestling Entertainment Superstar, as a good dad who happens to make some big mistakes.

When the women left, Al and I went back to not fitting in, and after witnessing the expert schmoozing and ass-kissing for a while, Al made a stunning observation, "And they call our business fake?"

I even got to tour the White House for the World Wrestling Entertainment cameras, along with Jerry "The King" Lawler and Miss Kitty, and of course brought the book with me. I even managed to slip it into the Presidential Library, after getting the okay from the Secret Service. Upon leaving, I even signed it for President Clinton and was assured that it would get into his hands. Whether he read it or not is anybody's guess, although my good buddy Evan Metropolis offered to give Chelsea a call to find out. Out of respect for the First Family, I didn't check to see if Chelsea was on Evan's list.

Now for the bad news. After almost fifteen years of blood, sweat, and tears, I came to the sad realization that I now sucked as a wrestler. Sure, I had Mr. Socko, and I had dozens and dozens of fans. At my core, however, I had always considered myself a good in-ring performer, and I no longer felt that was true. Even on days when my work was not up to par, I had always worked hard, but my body could no longer tolerate the grind. While playing soccer with my kids, I had realized that if the ball wasn't kicked directly to me, I really couldn't get to it.

While I stood there on the grass, I assessed my physical skills. I couldn't run. I couldn't jump. I couldn't move side to side. I couldn't squat down. I had trouble bending over. Sometimes I could barely walk. To make matters worse, I felt like my mind was starting to slip.

I seemed to lose my train of thought more regularly. My sense of direction seemed even worse than usual. For three months running, I had made huge mathematical mistakes in my checkbook ledger. Colette had to take over my duties as Foley record keeper. For a long time I feared that I was going to pay a serious price for the risks I had taken, but the writing of my book seemed to reaffirm the adequacy of my brain. But now I wasn't so sure.

I had been working a series of matches with Val Venis since The Rock 'n' Sock breakup that actually stemmed from the "This Is Your Life" segment. Later in that same *Raw* episode, a hidden camera had caught Val pulling Mr. Rocko out of a garbage can. As a former adult film star (at least in story line), Val knew just what to do with Mr. Rocko. He rolled him up and stuffed him in his trunks.

So I set about trying to get Mr. Rocko back, which led to a memorable moment in Trenton, New Jersey. As the bell rang, I immediately jumped on Val and attempted to pull Rocko out from his hiding place. I have always been very verbal in the ring and am often imitated by the other boys for the nonsen-

sical grunts and yells I give out during the course of a match. On this night in Trenton, the grunts and yells went something like this; "Hasa, heh, hah, ass-aba, ah, hasa, oops, sorry, Val." Yes, in the process of digging for Mr. Rocko, I had mistakenly unearthed Val's Mr. Cocko.

I couldn't help but feel upset after the match, and it wasn't just because I'd touched another man's penis. No, deep down, I was sad because I knew I had become the thing I dreaded most—a liability. For most of my career, I had the reputation of being a guy who could make other wrestlers look good. I always felt that I was a guy that others liked to work with—especially the younger guys—and now I could sense that feeling slipping away. The World Wrestling Entertainment roster was filled with young guys willing to work hard and I could almost imagine them talking about me:

"Hey, who are you working with tonight?"

"Mankind."

"Oh no, not Mankind."

"Yeah, I know. My mom and dad are here. I really wanted to have a good match."

"Sorry, man, what are you going to do?"

"What can I do? I'll let him talk for a while and then I'll wait for him to pull that stupid sock out."

"Heard one of the guys say he used to be a legend. Is that true?"

"Mankind? Legend? Oh, that's a good one. Oh, ho, ho, ho."

All right, so maybe I'm being a little harsh, but "used to be" doesn't count a whole lot in the fast-paced world of sports-entertainment. The Road Warriors are a perfect example. I'm not trying to be mean, because I respect them for all the money they drew, and I like both the guys, but jeez, they went from main-event stars to locker-room punch lines in a year's time.

When I look back on my career I will always consider the Val Venis program to be my biggest failure. I met Val (or Sean in real life) in Arkansas in 1994 when he was working for twenty bucks a night. I saw him again when he came to the World Wrestling Entertainment in 1997, and for months was convinced that he didn't know my name. Every time I saw him I got a "hey, buddy" or a "what's up, pal?" and even an occasional "how ya doing, chief?" In other words, all the things I say when I don't know someone's name.

Val was a strong worker with a great look and a good gimmick, but for some reason he had remained mired firmly in the middle of the card. The Mankind angle was his highest-profile series of matches, and I hoped to boost him up a notch because of it. I had always prided myself on my track record of moving guys up the card, or at least solidifying their top spots. When my program with Val was over, I unfortunately could make no such claim. For Val Venis and for the World Wrestling Entertainment, Mick Foley was not a stepping-stone to better things. He was instead a liability.

24: *November 2, 1999*

MY CAREER FELL TO an all-time low on November 2, 1999, in Philadelphia. Actually, a lot of the day was quite fun as we taped several humorous vignettes documenting my "search" for Val through a gentlemen's club and a seedy adult complex. I had actually been somewhat concerned about my image inside the questionable establishment, which was like a one-stop shopping trip for all "adult" needs, including a store with a variety of sex toys that rivaled my Montana experience for sheer number of fake penises, a dance club, a private shower viewing area, an impressive array of peepshows, and a baby-sitting service. All right, I'm just kidding about the baby-sitting service.

Al and I had included a stop at the Cheetah of *Showgirls* fame as part of our Vegas vacation, and I didn't want to get typecast as a strip-club fanatic. On that Vegas visit, Al had hit the jackpot on a slot machine, and we had shown up at the club, ready to tip with his mountain of quarters. This had resulted in a classic moment where, after rewarding a buxom babe with a quarter for her efforts and reminding her that "there's plenty more where that came from," the offending coin came flying back and caught me square in the eye. "Oh, my eye," I screamed in a manner reminiscent of Marcia Brady's "oh, my nose" moment in that memorable episode of *The Brady Bunch*.

An even better moment had occurred when the exotic dancer in question caught me by surprise with four quick slaps to each side of my face with her massive, man-made mammaries. Not only did the blows from her rock-hard hooters jar me like a series of Austin comeback punches, but I was almost busted open by her multiple nipple piercings. "That was really great," I said to the proud performer, "but you need to wait for the camera to be set up, and you have to put your top on to be on the show." The disappointment on her face was eerily similar to my children's when I make them clean up their room.

After throwing the quarter and being thanked for her time, the girl informed us that she now had to make a living and headed for the Lapdance Lounge. Having never seen an actual lapdance in a live setting, I couldn't help but give an extended glance at the prestigious lounge on my way out. It was like a traffic accident; I didn't want to look, but I had to. My goodness, there had to be twenty of these unusual gyrating, grinding lap extravaganzas going on simultaneously. In the right far corner I spotted our "quarter" girl riding some customer like Ron Turcotte at the Belmont Stakes.

Because this had been taped for the World Wrestling Entertainment, I had been able to slide by Colette's "no strip bar" stipulation on a technicality. Quite a few of the wrestlers frequent these types of places, because, as Dallas Page put it in his book,

Positively Page, "It's a place where guys like the boys and I can go and not be the center of attention." I've got to admit that theory does sound solid. It was that exact rationale that I'd explained to Colette back in '91. She didn't buy it then. She still doesn't.

Now, in all fairness to my wife, I have to say that she's practically a saint. It takes a special type of woman to tolerate a well-known husband on the road, and Colette's trust and understanding make my life a whole lot easier, and her powers of forgiveness far outshine those of mere mortals. Especially with the knowledge that her husband has within the past few years become known as "cuddly, cute," and to a small twisted minority, even "sexy." Hey, I know that sounds crazy, but for a few years my favorite sign from a fan was a simple MANKIND IS SEXY. Later, at a book signing in Montreal, a fan showed off a sign that was a little less innocent: I WANT MORE THAN MANKIND'S SOCK IN MY MOUTH. I really didn't know what to say, so I gave her an embarrassed "what would your boyfriend say?", at which point the guy behind her said, "It would be cool because it's you; you're our idol." I pretended to be merely amused and was thankful for the table at which I sat, which hid the evidence to the contrary.

Colette asked me a few years ago if I had "been to one of those places" recently. I had been to one, and only one, in Montreal several months earlier and decided to admit this indiscretion. "Just one," I said. Colette seemed hurt and wanted to know why I would do such a thing. I hoped that honesty really was the best policy, because I was about to hit

Colette with a dose of truth that most husbands would never dream of administering. "Well, I heard they were going to have live lesbian sex acts onstage, and I wanted to see what it looked like." My wife's eyes opened wide and her jaw dropped low. She was speechless for close to a minute. When she did speak, her voice was soft and forgiving. "Okay," she said, "just tell me next time."

I became an instant hero in the dressing room with that story of spousal love and understanding and was often asked to repeat it. "Just tell me next time?" That sounded like a free pass to me. A short while later a wrestler, who knew of my *Boogie Nights* admiration, told me that adult film legend Nina Hartley was appearing in a club that night about a hundred yards from my hotel. Hartley, besides her ability to ad-lib nonstop dirty talk that would make even D.D.P. blush, is known, believe it or not, for her warmth, humor, and intelligence. She played the insatiable nympho whose cheating ways caused her husband to blow both her and himself away at the pivotal party scene in *Boogie Nights*. I thought about it for a long while. Nina Hartley, film legend and star of *Boogie Nights*. I decided to use my free pass.

The next day I told my loving wife about my Hartley adventure without even a twinge of guilt. Colette was not pleased. "Mickey, last night was our anniversary!" I am now officially out of free passes, and unlike the Montreal lesbian story that made me a locker-room legend, I chose to keep this one to myself.

Business was business, however, and in Philadelphia, on November 2, 1999, business required me to

visit these locales on my quest for Val Venis. *Okay, I'll do it*, I thought, but inside I knew I had to keep my kid-friendly image from being crushed. Bruce Prichard, the producer of the vignettes, wholeheartedly agreed and assured me that I wouldn't be made to do anything to compromise my image. He later laughed and admitted he knew he wouldn't have to make me do anything because he knew I couldn't help myself.

"Wouldn't it be a great idea if I looked for Val in a peep booth and pulled out the wrong guy?" Some-

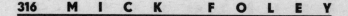

how, I managed to talk our production assistant, Warren, into posing as the pervert who actually had his pants down to his ankles during his surreptitious viewing. "Oh, sorry, you're not Val," I explained, after yanking him out of his booth with words like "sicko" and "sinner" to describe his moral character. Then, with Warren out of the way, I saw the video and quickly changed gears. "Hey, is that Kay Parker?" I blurted out with an innocent squeal. "Is she still around?" With that, I shut the door and the camera tilted up and faded out on the word "OCCUPIED" above the booth.

"Hey, Bruce, can you get me about a hundred quarters?" I asked as we prepared to shoot our final vignette, in which I was to run after a truck that was towing my car. "Sure," Bruce said, "but what for?" "That way," I explained, "when I run after the truck, all the quarters will fall out of my pockets and it will seem like I've been in that booth forever." Bruce smiled and got the quarters. Sure, lovable Mankind came across like a stumbling, bumbling sicko with a weakness for pornography, but what the hell—it was fun television. Besides, that same image didn't hurt Jimmy Swaggart all that much, and he's a man of God.

Even before my "near-slanderous" remarks about Kay Parker were published, word had spread into the adult film community about my past fondness for the fair-skinned British beauty with the naturally big boobs and the one crooked tooth. I ran into porno mainstay Tom Byron at a home-video convention in Los Angeles a year ago and was asked about the subject. "I heard you like Kay Parker," Byron said with just a hint of amusement in his voice. At that moment I remembered Byron's scene with Kay in a video that I had watched at John Imbriani's house back in 1982. That feature had helped make Byron's career. Suddenly I had access to a person who had intimate details of my porn idol's life. "What was she like?" I asked. "Come on, tell me everything. Was she nice? Was she funny? Come on, tell me!" "I don't know!" said Byron, with a shrug. "That was one of my first films. I don't think I've seen her twice since then." Wow, that was kind of disappointing. It would be kind of like running into Larry Hagman or Bill Daily, or Hayden Rorke, and finding out they didn't remember a thing about Barbara Eden. Suddenly Byron's powers of recall seemed to kick in. "Oh yeah," he said, "I remember she smelled like my grandmother."

Let me get this straight; there's no Easter Bunny, wrestling's not real, and Kay Parker smells like Tom Byron's grandmother? Life isn't fair.

Unfortunately, when I got back from the bowels of Philadelphia's entertainment district, I had to wrestle. With Al no less. I barely had time to warm up when we were out for the first match of *Smack-Down!* against the team of Hardcore and Crash Holly for the World Wrestling Entertainment Tag-Team Championship. The vignettes we had just shot would be inserted into the show as if they had transpired after the match.

The match had its high points. Al insisted that we debut our "pattycake, pattycake, baker's man" double elbow, but I had questioned the move, thinking it a little too dumb. "You don't think a sock puppet is dumb," Al asked, "or a man talking to a mannequin head?" Both valid points. We did the move, and the crowd loved it. We even won the match—and the titles. Al Snow and Mankind, the "Best Friends," as Kevin Kelly phrased it in the greatest exaggeration in sports-entertainment since WCW's claim of having "close to 90,000 fans" in a nearly empty Louisiana Superdome. We even did the jumping-white-guy high five, and the fans cheered that as well.

The match had its low points as well—me. If I had been a liability with Val Venis, I was a downright embarrassment here. I did a move where I shot Crash into the ropes and went for a kick to the gut. Crash grabbed my foot and spun me around. I was looking to come out of the spin with a big clothesline, which had always elicited an enormous response from the crowd.

I could legitimately lay claim to inventing the move in 1990, and Diamond Dallas Page could legitimately lay claim to stealing it in 1994, about eleven seconds after my departure from WCW. He's used it so much since then that a lot of people actually think it's his. "Bro," he tried to explain when I called him after viewing a WCW television match that looked like *Cactus Jack's Greatest Hits*, "you're not on TV anymore"—which, at the time he made the remark, was true. "No," I agreed to the man who claimed to have never had a bad day in his life (his disastrous match with the Big Cat in Fort Myers in '93 notwithstanding), "but I plan to be on TV again someday."

I have since gotten Page back many times without his knowledge. Every time I wrestle Dewey on the bed, I hit him with Dallas's "Diamond Cutter," and I tell him not to sell it.

This clothesline didn't elicit quite the same reaction from the crowd. I fell down while attempting it. It wasn't a first for that move, either, as I had suffered a similar fate in recent house-show matches. I fell over one other time in the title win over the Hollys as well when my knees simply could not support my weight. As a result, when the match aired two nights later, much of my part in it was edited out. It wasn't the first time that I had been edited. During the course of my career, my matches had been edited several times for being too long, too violent, or too bloody. In fifteen years of wrestling, however, it was the first time that I had been edited because I sucked.

We had a locker-room celebration following the victory that included Edge, Christian, and The Blue Meanie. Al had a quart of milk and explained that he was going to dump it over his head as a humorous variation on the victorious champagne tradition. I turned to Edge, who Al liked to refer to as my crony, and spoke disbelievingly. "Is Al Snow really going to dump a white liquid all over his face and not expect me to say anything?" Sure enough, when the cameras rolled, Al poured the milk and I drilled him with an incredibly easy joke, but despite the laughs at Al's expense and Al's "okay, okay, you got me," my heart wasn't really in it.

My part of the show was over and I was free to go home, but I felt that I needed to talk to Vince. Vince is incredibly busy at these tapings, so I stopped by his office before the taping and asked if I could speak to him about something important afterward. The two hours that followed seemed to last an eternity. When I came back to his office, it was to make the most important decision of my career.

"Vince, I think it's time that I stopped being an active wrestler." I had been thinking about this moment for a while, and Colette and I had been preparing for it since the physical fallout from "Hell in a Cell," but I had no idea that the words would be so hard to say. Halfway through them my voice cracked with emotion, and upon completing them, my eyes filled up with tears.

For his part, Vince didn't try to talk me out of it, but merely asked, "Why?" At that moment I felt inside almost as if he'd been expecting this day to come and was surprised that it hadn't come sooner. Critics who have never met Vince have written some terrible things about him, at one point even likening him to *Silence of the Lambs'* murderous cannibal, Hannibal Lechter. Unlike these critics, I *do* know Vince, and in four and a half years of working closely beside him have never seen even a hint of these characteristics. Indeed, the Vince McMahon who sat before me on November 2, 1999, thought not of the World Wrestling Entertainment at this time but only of my personal interests.

I told Vince of the realization I'd had while playing soccer with my kids and how I felt that my physical quality of life was extremely poor. When I told him of my mental problems, he cut me off in midsentence. "Mick, you've just had your last match." I was a little stunned. I had actually been thinking of a *Royal Rumble* send-off at Madison Square Garden in January, and told him so. "Why risk it?" Vince asked. "If you finish tonight you could go out as a champion—and you deserve that."

Together, we talked things over for a long while, and after careful consideration of my desire to have one last match, we settled on *Survivor Series* in Detroit on November 19 as my final date. I had twelve more days to go.

25: *A Change in Plans*

I WALKED INTO THE Bryce Jordan Center on the Penn State campus, fully expecting to begin my last week as an active wrestler, but was instead met by Jim Ross and some shocking news. Steve Austin's career, it seemed, was over. Austin had suffered a serious neck injury in 1997 that had kept him out of action for several months but he had come back and led the World Wrestling Entertainment to levels of prosperity that few could have dreamed of. Beneath his "Stone Cold" persona of flipping birds and downing beers, Austin was, at heart, a work-horse of a performer, and therein lay much of the problem. By working so hard night in and out, Austin's neck never got a chance to fully heal. After undergoing a series of tests as a result of recurring pain, Austin's initial prognosis was that he should retire immediately.

This made my *Survivor Series* retirement a problem on two levels. From a loyalty standpoint, I would have a tough time bailing out on a company that was losing its biggest star. From an ego standpoint, not a whole lot of people were going to care about Mick Foley's retirement if it coincided with Steve Austin's. Make no mistake about it, I wanted people to care. A year earlier Terry Funk had bestowed one of his great Funker teachings upon me: "The fans do love us, but they sure don't miss us when we're gone." I wanted to go out proving the Funker wrong. The fans definitely did love me in a rugged, platonic type of way. But I wanted to be missed when I was gone. With those two factors in mind, retirement was pushed back until the December Pay-Per-View in Fort Lauderdale, Florida.

Al and I dropped the tag belts to the New Age Outlaws that same night at Penn State and came up short in a rematch at *Survivor Series*, during which I dislocated my shoulder. The "Best Friends" would never relive their glory day of November 2, when I stunk up the ring and Al Snow was foolish enough to pour white liquid over his head on-camera.

Word started to leak out concerning my departure from the company, and wrestlers and office personnel alike began stopping by over the next few weeks to wish me well. I've always been flattered by the respect and friendship given to me by the younger wrestlers who, I believe, may have viewed me as some type of really homely bridge between wrestling's "old school" and the new generation of stars.

I had put Matt and Jeff Hardy in my *Three Faces of Foley* video back when winning matches wasn't part of their résumé. They had been very appreciative of the screen time, and now that they're big stars my decision to include them looks pretty wise indeed.

Edge had been my partner in "Al Snow crime" for quite a while before the fans really took to him, so I feel like something of a proud father when I watch him and Christian tear down the house. I told the four of them (Matt, Jeff, Edge and Christian) that I felt like I was watching four stars being born when they stole the show at the *No Mercy* Pay-Per-View with an unforgettable ladder match.

Well, maybe I ought to stop patting myself on the back since, after all, I'm the guy who thought The Rock just didn't "have it" back in '97. Speaking of The Rock, it was he who was chosen to be my opponent for my "new" retirement match. Vince wanted a "babyface" match for the Foley finale, a move that would be tough to pull off on several levels. A babyface match was a tough sell in this day and age. The modern wrestling fan is drawn to the fast pace and excitement of sports-entertainment in an "action-adventure" television format. Classic babyface matches of the past usually took a while to unfold, employing a storytelling formula that many modern fans simply don't have the patience for.

During my World Wrestling Entertainment career, I had been in many matches that lasted more than twenty minutes and crowds had reacted well, but they were always the result of good guy/bad guy angles that were driven by animosity between the opponents. I considered myself adept at those long matches, but quite honestly didn't feel I had the talent or physical skills left to pull one off and leave Fort Lauderdale and my career on a high note.

Despite my recent lackluster ring efforts, my popularity had never been greater. Not nearly as great as The Rock's, however, and that posed another problem. Fort Lauderdale was only twenty minutes from The Rock's home of Miami, and I was really not looking forward to being booed on my last night in the business.

Nonetheless, the wheels for the match went into motion, and I've got to admit the next few weeks of television were among my all-time favorites as The Rock 'n' Sock Connection returned, despite the objections of a bitter and jealous Al Snow. The Rock, it seemed, had not thrown my book out, and his ability to quote passages from it seemed to hint that he had purchased another copy, although his pride wouldn't allow him to admit as much. So if The Rock hadn't thrown out the book, who had? Who had motive to do so? Who in the World Wrestling Entertainment stood to gain the most from the breakup of The Rock 'n' Sock Connection? A curious nation wanted to know.

The Rock 'n' Sock Connection got back together, but Al was still my best friend . . . or was he? An interview for *SmackDown!* on November 23 was among the best of my career, and not because it was all that good or even memorable in itself. The premise was simple: Al and I could continue to be best friends, but I would no longer team up with him. This premise had Al understandably upset as the cameras rolled. "I can't believe you're doing this," Al said, "turning your back on your best tag-team partner." "Hey, that's not true," I assured my bitter buddy. "I've got a match with The Rock later in this show." Al was forlorn as he said, "I don't even know how you can stand him; he treats you like garbage." At this point I became Al's consoling pal as I gently explained the facts of life to him. "Al, you're still my best friend, but I just seem to get a much better reaction from the crowd when I team up with The Rock."

That's what I was supposed to say, except I

couldn't get the words out. Five times I tried to finish that final sentence, and five times I failed. I couldn't stop laughing. Each time I laughed, Al got a little angrier. "Why do you keep laughing?" he demanded. "It's not even that funny." "I know," I admitted, "it's just that in what other business can a guy get away with telling the truth, crush his friend's feelings, and claim it's just part of the show?"

I've got to give credit where it's due, and I will give Al credit for one of the classic ribs in wrestling history. While working a program that culminated in the infamous "Kennel from Hell" match, Al's dog Pepper was kidnapped by the sinister Big Boss Man. Before I get to the rib, let me get to the "Kennel from Hell," which turned out to be a rib in itself. During the course of the angle, the Boss Man invited Al to his room, where he would "give Pepper to him," but not before the thoughtful Boss Man insisted on serving Al some Chinese food. After a few bites, the Boss Man revealed that Al had actually eaten "Pepper" steak, which set the stage for the "Kennel from Hell" at the *Unforgiven* Pay-Per-View in September 1999.

This match employed the "Hell in a Cell" cage which contained within it the standard steel cage that, as most fans know, is built directly onto the ring. This left a four-foot space between the two structures that would be patrolled by vicious, wild attack dogs. The object was to escape from both cages, which meant that Al and the Boss Man would be risking life and limb with these wild animals running amok. That, at least, was the theory. The truth was that the cameras could barely show the animals, which spent the match peeing and pooping and at one high-point actually humping. Yes, indeed, actual canine carnal knowledge in front of 20,000 fans.

Still, even with the general consensus that it set new lows, deeper even than any Test has ever sunk to, the "Kennel" match did nothing to tarnish the reputation of Al's rib. The rib took place during the "kidnapped" part of the angle when poor Al appeared on television with a poster of the missing Pepper that featured a reward and a number to call with information on the dog's whereabouts.

A bunch of the guys watched the interview from the dressing room with moderate amusement. Almost immediately, Val Venis's cell phone rang. "Hello," Val said, in his deep Val voice, followed by, "Sorry, you've got the wrong number!" A moment later the phone rang again. "Hello . . . sorry, wrong number." Val seemed to be confused as he walked from the room.

The next day he showed up looking for Al. "Okay, you got me," he said, "but payback is going to be hell." The number that Al had given was actually that of Val's cell phone, and apparently over the course of twenty-four hours, Val had gotten almost a hundred calls, all offering information on Pepper's whereabouts. As of this writing, no revenge has been exacted.

The Al Snow jokes in *Have a Nice Day!* were actually my own way of reaching out to Al and attempting to mend our friendship. By 1999, our private game of insult one-upmanship from back in 1997–98 had turned ugly when we took it to the World Wrestling Entertainment Internet show and

then made the giant leap onto World Wrestling Entertainment television. There, I had the clear advantage because I had the privilege of more microphone time, and it was with that advantage that the camel's back was broken in East Lansing, Michigan. Let me tell you about the straw that did it.

First, the background behind the straw. "Selling," as I mentioned earlier, is the art of making a move look more devastating by . . . um . . . uh . . . pretending it hurts more than it does. For example, it might be used in, "Wow, did you see Hunter sell that punch?"—or as my son Dewey has said, "Dad, why does Big Show only sell for Billy Gunn?" Of all the things a wrestler "sells," a chair might well be the easiest. Why? Because it really does hurt. Believe me, you don't need to be Sidney Poitier to sell a chair. On one memorable occasion, however, Al sold four chairshots as if he were Superman taking a Lex Luthor punch to the solar plexus. *Bam*, the Road Dogg nailed Al with a chair, and down he went. Amazingly, Al was up within seconds and was laughing. *Bam*—another shot, another fall, another laugh. Then another, then another.

The boys in the back were irate. When Al came back, I was the first one to ask him about his new superhuman powers. Amazingly, Al pleaded innocent. "I don't remember a thing after the first one," he said with a slight slur in his words. "I was knocked out."

Hey, maybe he was. But that didn't stop me from ribbing him about it. I told him that he should challenge the Undertaker to a "No Sell in the Cell" match, and that he and I should shelve Kevin Kelly's ridiculous "Best Friends" moniker for the more dynamic tag-team name of "The Sellers, Best and No." Unlike most of my jokes, Al didn't take these well and asked me nicely not to rib him about the ridiculous chairshots in front of the boys. At one point he even got down on his knees and begged me. Damn, I was going to make a comment about this not being the first time that Al was on his knees, but out of respect for younger readers I'm not going to do so.

I knew Al was sensitive about the incident, but I pushed too far, and will admit right here in print that I was out of line for burying Al in a national television interview.

The scene was East Lansing, Michigan, and the event was Mr. Socko's birthday party, although in reality it was more of a "birthplace" party, as Mr. Socko was still a few months shy of the big day. Yurple was there, and there were balloons and music as well, and amidst all the hoopla, Jim Ross stepped into the ring to congratulate me. "Thank you, J. R., but the man who really deserves our congratulations is Al Snow, for landing a lucrative endorsement deal with the La-Z-Boy company, which is strange, because Al usually doesn't sell chairs."

Yes, it was a pretty good line and a definite one-punch knockout, but I scored the KO at the price of breaking my word. Even worse, Al felt pressured to respond, and when he did so the following night, he was not only unfunny but was reprimanded by Vince for ruining an entire segment of the *Raw* show.

So yes, there was some tension there for a while, but the insults and jokes about Al in *Have a Nice Day!* seemed to build a bridge between us, and even though Al will never publicly or even privately admit to it, deep inside his soul he knows that the book helped his career. I'm glad that he and I are on good terms, or else I wouldn't dream of exposing the truth behind the legend of the Penis Suplex!

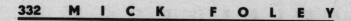

26: *The Legend of the Penis Suplex*

UNTIL NOW, THE EVENTS of November 21, 1999, have been shrouded in mystery. Until now, no one has had the courage to come clean about just what they saw inside that arena in Montreal on that chilly afternoon.

The seeds of the mystery had been sown several weeks earlier, when, inside a rented Chevrolet Lumina somewhere along a lonesome stretch of Interstate 71 that runs between Columbus and Louisville, a voice had been heard. Not just any voice, but a majestic one, a voice of love and understanding. The voice of Nat King Cole.

Nat was singing about a night, but it was not just any night that he sang of. It was a holy night. A night where the stars were brightly shining. A night divine. The words were truly beautiful, until two not-so-beautiful voices joined in on the chorus. "Fall on your knees; O, hear the angel voices."

A third voice then made itself heard, a voice of anger. Its corrosive energy cut through Nat's "O Holy

Night" like a sword of vulgar lethality. "Goddammit, it's too early for Christmas music!" The voice belonged to Bob "Hardcore" Holly, and its owner was not happy about what he perceived to be an error in holiday etiquette. The two voices in the front seat were momentarily silenced, and a quick turn to the left on the dial marked "volume" nearly silenced Nat's voice as well.

The voice on the passenger side of the Lumina spoke up, but in contrast to Holly's near-Neanderthal nitpicking, this voice was filled with kindness and reason. The voice was mine. "Bob, it's only ten weeks before Christmas, that's certainly not too soon for Christmas music. Besides, 'O Holy Night' is appropriate for year-round listening." I then tried to expound my philosophy of Yuletide music, which allowed that while such songs as "Rudolph the Red Nosed Reindeer," "Frosty the Snowman," or "I Saw Mommy Kissing Santa Claus" were more in tune with a December time frame, spiritual hymns like "What Child Is This," "Silent Night," and Nat's song in question were suitable for all-season entertainment. I then pointed out that they just don't make good songs about adulterous Christmas Eve voyeurism like "I Saw Mommy" anymore.

Holly was not swayed. "Turn that crap off." I looked into the rearview mirror at this modern-day Ebenezer Scrooge. Beneath his soiled NASCAR cap lay a receding line of close-cropped, bleached-blond hair. But what lay beneath that? What caused him to eat almost thirty egg whites a day? Why did he refuse to go on even the most innocent of midway thrill rides?

Some speculated that he had grown curmudgeonly after being saddled with a World Wrestling Entertainment gimmick that resulted in him being called "Sparky." Others felt that he had never completely forgiven office management for forcing him to lose to Mankind back in 1996 without getting any offense in. Whatever the cause, I made a solemn vow to myself in that rented Lumina at that very moment. I would find a merry prankster living deep beneath his regimen of two-hour daily workouts and a three-to-one protein-to-carbohydrate ratio.

We traveled in silence for several minutes, at which time I decided to make a stand. I wanted Christmas music, I wanted it now, and I didn't care about Bob "won't go to the carnival" Holly. "Al, pass me the *Elvis Christmas*!" Suddenly a voice boomed out from the backseat. A happy voice! A "you've got Elvis!" voice. Five minutes later I looked in the rearview mirror at Bob. He was bobbing his head and snapping his fingers. And the mouth that had been so angry only minutes earlier was now curled up in an Elvis-like sneer and was singing "Here comes Santa Claus, here comes Santa Claus, right down Santa Claus lane."

Over the next few weeks a change seemed to come over Bob. It was almost as if he were Scrooge and Elvis had been the Ghost of Christmas Yet to Come. "Hey, Cactus, tell the story," he'd say, and then would stand there as giddy as a schoolboy as I did my "Bob doing Elvis doing 'Here Comes Santa Claus' " routine. The smile on his face let me know that he was indeed capable of helping me in my quest for Al Snowtopia.

Let us go back now to the day of November 21, 1999, and the events that until now have remained

hidden deeper than the reasoning behind the booking of Brisco and Patterson in an evening-gown match.

When wrestling in Montreal, all the boys share one room, but it is a large one. Unlike our fictional television scenarios, and unlike WCW's real-life hierarchical star system, there are no "star" dressing rooms in the World Wrestling Entertainment. Everyone more or less piles into one or two dressing rooms and coexists rather peacefully. Even if such star dressing rooms did exist, it is unlikely that Al Snow would be allowed in one.

So it was in this close dressing proximity that I noticed something rather odd as Al pulled up his one-piece wrestling singlet. He wasn't wearing any underwear beneath it. Strangely, I felt compelled to ask him about this rather unusual choice in costuming. "Underwear shows lines, and it doesn't look good on television," Al explained, which didn't explain too much since this was not a televised show. "Well, aren't you afraid of . . ." I started to say before breaking out into a big grin. "What?" Al asked, but I just shook my head as if to say "never mind."

I had an idea, but I needed an accomplice. Someone who could get in the ring with Al. Who were we wrestling that night? I looked at the lineup for the show. A four-team elimination match with Snow and Mankind vs. the Dudlez vs. the Acolytes vs. Crash and Hardcore Holly. Bob! He was the man.

"Bob," I began, laughing in a really transparent phony way as I sat beside him. "Hey, do you remember that time when I asked Al for the Elvis tape?" Bob burst out at the mere mention of the wonderful story. "Hey, tell it to Bubba," he exclaimed, and in accordance with Bob's wishes, I did my best to entertain Bob and Bubba, that blatant Cactus Jack rip-off. Although as blatant Cactus Jack rip-offs go, he is pretty damn good. The cool thing is that Bubba will take this as a compliment.

As soon as Bob finished saying, "Isn't that a great story?" I made my move. "Jeez, I love that story, Bob. Hey, you want to help me out tonight?" Al actually caught us in mid-conspiracy but gave up easily when we assured him that our laughter was not about him. He hadn't been so wrong since he believed that Avatar would get over back in '95.

I was still laughing when my music played. "I know you're up to something," Al kept saying, but I denied it as if I was a big-tobacco executive being interviewed on *60 Minutes*.

The bell rang, and I watched Acolyte Bradshaw sell Crash's punches as if he were Al Snow taking a Road Dogg chairshot. Bubba came in and brought Crash into a corner. Once there, he seized the five-foot-six Elroy Jetson look-alike up for a chop and *smack* brought his big hand down on Crash's pectoralis major with full force. The smacking of hand on flesh that echoed throughout the arena gave me an idea. "Keep him there," I said to Bubba, and moved to the timekeeper's table as fast as I could. In other words, it took me forever. I climbed up on the apron and headed for the corner. Bubba seemed somewhat apprehensive as he wondered what the hardcore legend might do. "Chop him again," I yelled, and as Bubba reared back, I placed the house microphone right next to the approximate area where contact would be made. *WHACKKK!* The sound was awesome and the crowd went BANANA!

Bubba then tagged me in, and the current and future hardcore legends shot young Elroy into the ropes and combined with a devastating multigenerational, um, something or other. I then proceeded to go to work on Crash in a style eerily reminiscent of the early-eighties Lou Albano, which is not exactly a good thing to be compared to. I wasn't concerned about my effort, however. I was only concerned about the next two tags. I took Crash into my own corner and gave him a good old-fashioned "Beale toss" toward his. Crash got up and tagged in Bob. I walked over and tagged in Al.

Innocently, the poor bastard walked in, unaware that his life was about to be turned upside down, literally. He was smiling his stupid "look at me, I'm nuts" smile and had his stupid HELP ME painted backward on his head, so it read EM PLEH. It should have read RETHGUALS OT DEL GNIEB BMAL, because that's essentially what he was.

Bob greeted Al with a stiff boot to the stomach. Everything Bob does hurts like hell, so why should this boot have been any different? I saw Bob hook Al's arm around his head in preparation for a vertical suplex. He then grabbed the short legging of Al's singlet, as most people do to execute the move correctly. Al suspected nothing. In an instant Holly made his move. With one quick yank, he moved the left legging over to the right side of Al's crotch, exposing his privates in the process. It should have been a milestone in my life, Al being publicly humiliated, but it wasn't. Instead, I felt strangely sad.

A singlet, you see, is tremendous for protecting the testicles. A singlet is not tremendous, however, when it comes to displaying the dimensions of the male reproductive organ in a complimentary way, which is why the first thing a singlet wearer does when he removes that particular article of ring attire, is give the organ in question a quick but firm tug to free it from its "childlike state." Unfortunately for Al, he was locked in suplex position by the powerful Holly, and was not able to get a secret tug into the night's agenda. Therefore, as Holly lifted Snow into the vertical position, it became obvious that, as George Costanza once put it on *Seinfeld*, "there had been significant shrinkage."

To make matters worse for Al, he didn't subscribe to the rather new male trend of grooming his bush, and as a result, in front of 20,000 fans, I saw what appeared to be a sparrow's egg peeking out of a vulture's nest. A small family of koala bears could have lived in there.

Part of me wanted to put an end to it. Bob wasn't just administering a simple suplex. He was holding him up there. For seconds . . . maybe ten of them. Al was trying to pull his singlet back over, but Bob was just too strong. It was almost as if every workout suffered through and every fourteen-egg-white omelette ever ingested had led him to this one moment. At that instant Bob was sporting perhaps the biggest smile of his entire miserable life.

Al's body finally crashed to the canvas. I looked to see his expression, which I was sure would be one of fury. Instead he was laughing. If he had seen things from my vantage point, I'm not sure he would have been.

After the match, we gathered in the locker room. Together, all of us vowed never to reveal the tragic

events of that afternoon. We looked almost like the kids, vowing never to tell of the body they found in *Stand By Me*, another film directed by Rob Reiner, the guy who had snubbed me at the *End of Days* premiere. True to my word, I have kept that vow until now.

The story you have just read is true. Not even the names have been changed to protect the innocent. Pass it on to your children, and to your children's children. Teach them the legend. The legend of the Penis Suplex.

27: A Second Chance

I ANNOUNCED MY RETIREMENT on Canadian television on the day that followed the legendary suplex. I knew the show would be broadcast two days later and that the news would be somewhat old by then, as I planned to announce the same decision on *Raw* later that very night. *USA Today* even wrote, "Mankind makes shocking announcement" in their television schedule. My announcement was not made that night, as a last-minute decision pushed the speech back another week. I look at that decision now as a blessing, because as I went home for the Thanksgiving holidays I was bothered by a persistent feeling that something about the retirement wasn't quite right.

For some reason I kept thinking about a boxing match from more than twenty-five years ago. The "Thrilla in Manila." It was a fight that many consider to be the greatest of all time, and the images of it haunted me as I tried to sleep that week in late November. An exhausted but jubilant Muhammad Ali, with his arms in the air, in a gesture of victory. A battered and beaten "Smokin' " Joe Frazier, sitting on his stool in the corner, his head hung low in defeat.

I was eight years old when the historic fight took place in the Philippines. Back in those days, world title fights took place in cities other than Las Vegas and Atlantic City. I remember glancing at the pictures of the ring warriors in one of my dad's *Sports Illustrated*s. With swollen eyes and blood and sweat, they had earned their way into my memory long before I had ever seen the actual fight. Now, late in 1999, those same memories kept me awake.

I saw the fight several years later, and my respect for the two men grew even deeper. The battle seemed to drain the very life out of both fighters, and quite possibly could have been the last great fight in each man's career. The Thrilla in Manila might very well have made a great movie, except for the ending. A movie would have seen both men throwing punches as the final bell tolled. It would have seen the brave fighters fall into each other's arms in a gesture of true respect. Except this wasn't Hollywood, it was Manila, and the reality of the fight is that Joe Frazier had been too badly beaten to continue.

Or was he? Frazier was and still is a man of enormous pride, and I wondered how he felt deep down about the famous fight. I wondered how he felt about finishing his greatest fight sitting on a stool. And I wondered how many times over the last twenty-five years he wished he could have gone that one final round.

Just one round. Three more minutes. A small price to pay for the lifetime of peace of mind that would have followed.

I realized why "Smokin'" Joe had been on my mind. I felt a strong connection between his career and mine, and it bothered the hell out of me. In a way, I felt as if I was Joe Frazier, and I was going out of my career sitting on a stool.

Now, I know true sports fanatics will probably think my analogy to be near blasphemous, but they haven't lived my life. They haven't hitchhiked to the Garden as teenagers to watch the "Superfly" soar off the steel cage. They haven't slept in their cars en route to barely attended armories or sat in an emergency room while their own ear was thrown in a garbage can as they stared with open eyes. Most of all, they haven't decided to end their careers by taking the easy way out, by sitting on a stool.

I saw the "Thrilla in Manila" as if it were my career, with each round representing a year. Fourteen years of reaching for the stars followed by one last year of reaching for a sock.

Steve Austin's injury had left a big void in the World Wrestling Entertainment that had yet to be filled. The Big Show had just won the World Wrestling Entertainment title and had been slated to face Triple H at the *Royal Rumble*. Logic seemed to dictate that Triple H and The Rock would lock horns at *WrestleMania*, a little over two months after that. *WrestleMania* is touted as the biggest show of the year, but in truth, without the proper buildup, it is just another Pay-Per-View. Nineteen ninety-seven's *'Mania* had proved that, as injuries had destroyed the buildup and buy rates plummeted.

The World Wrestling Entertainment, as I saw it, was in trouble. The Big Show was trying hard, but the fans were just not behind him as a champion. Triple H was fast becoming the best heel in the business, but without the proper promotion he would arrive at 'Mania flat for the biggest match of his career.

I spoke with Colette at length about my life and career, and about how, when it was all over, I didn't want to be saddled with a lifetime of "what-if's." I felt in my heart that I could come up with one more big match. I needed the World Wrestling Entertainment, but in truth, the World Wrestling Entertainment needed me as well. *Give me Triple H at the Royal Rumble*, I thought, and in return I would give the World Wrestling Entertainment plenty of heat and the Triple H they wanted, ready for The Rock at *WrestleMania*.

I called Hunter aside on November 29 in Los Angeles and told him of my plans. His eyes lit up. Together, we planned and plotted, and pulled Vince aside to tell him about our big idea. He shot it down. I honestly don't remember why, or even what was said, but I do remember feeling the agony of defeat as I left his office.

Meanwhile, The Rock 'n' Sock was entertaining as hell, and unlike our first incarnation, The Rock seemed to be showing small signs of actual warmth for Mankind. Maybe I could still get in my one last big-money match with the People's Champ.

I did a lot of thinking on my way home from California. I came up with a Plan B. Whether I liked it or not, I was going to get booed when I fought against The Rock in Fort Lauderdale. Hey, if I was going to be treated like a heel, I might as well be a heel. Besides, I might be able to get that one truly big payoff that had somehow eluded me for my entire career. I had heard of monstrous checks given out for the main events at blockbuster shows but had never been the recipient of one. A matchup with The Rock, fueled by what had happened during the "I Quit" match of January 1999, which in truth still bothered me, could possibly be my way.

Plan B was foolproof. Instead of a match against each other at the December 12 PPV (which had yet to be announced), The Rock and I would team together against the Outlaws. At that show, I would turn on The Rock's candy ass, and then, using some deep-down feelings of real pent-up anger, would promote the hell out of the return of Cactus Jack for the January 23 *Rumble*. A furious contest at the *Rumble* would lead to a return match in February, where odds were I would leave without my arm in the air. I would then announce *'Mania* as my last match, and the fans would be able to say good-bye to the hardcore legend in a classy way.

I visualized the entire scenario, until I could literally feel it, and then sprung it on Vince at the December 4 house show in Madison Square Garden.

He shot it down. I was frustrated as hell. I knew deep down that I had at least one good match left in me and hated Vince for not allowing me to have it. "Why, Vince, why?" His answer hurt me perhaps worse than any chairshot I've ever received, but at the same time it opened up my eyes to the logic of his answer, which made hatred a great deal more difficult to feel. "Mick, you're huge." I tried to defend myself, but with a body that seemed to support his accusation, I was left speechless. He continued his assault but did so as gently as possible. "Maybe you two could have a good match at the *Rumble* if we promoted it correctly, but a rematch in February would require you to put in a lot of time"—he was referring to the length of the match—"and I really don't think you can do it."

My weight had been steadily increasing for the last few years, and on December 4, at around 320, I certainly was terribly out of shape. I had always been able to get by on a blend of guts, knowledge, and luck, but now, as I looked at Vince, I felt like my luck had just run out. For most of my time in the World Wrestling Entertainment, heavier wrestlers had been encouraged to lose weight, but somehow I had always seemed to slip by. "Hey, it's your gimmick," other wrestlers used to say, and at 280 pounds that may have been true. Cactus Jack and Mankind had not gotten over because they looked good. Cactus Jack and Mankind had gotten over because they were wild, they were funny, they were smart, they had guts, and they gave the fans a hell of a show. Nowhere in that list of accolades, however, does "fat" appear.

Wrestlers spend a great deal of time at the gym. Historically speaking, so have I. My body is not genetically predisposed to carrying large muscles, and I have never taken any pharmaceutical steps to change that. As a result, my gains in the gym have been minimal. Poor genetics combined with a slow metabolism and a ring style that over fifteen years has made working out secondary to trying to heal my injuries have seen to that.

When I did show up at the gym, I would get ribbed by the boys. "Hey, you're going to kill your gimmick," they would joke in a friendly way, and would respond similarly if I was caught with a protein bar, or any other such health food. Over time, I began to rationalize my dwindling appearances at the gym and more frequent trips to the buffet line as a way of actually helping my career. Also, by an odd coincidence, my pay seemed to expand with my waistline.

When my body began showing greater signs of wear and tear from years of abuse, my greater weight made recuperation more difficult. I had always prided myself on being in shape for the big matches, but injuries made putting forth the effort necessary for cardiovascular training almost impossible.

While I was completing my career by writing *Have a Nice Day!*, I was actually ruining the last year of it by neglecting my body. Once I was back on the road, things got even worse. Partially due to my overindulgences at the dinner table, my pain became even greater. While I refused to take pain medicine, I certainly agreed to a slice of pecan pie at 2 A.M. at the Waffle House. Maybe I could "just say no" to drugs, but I simply said yes to jelly dough-nuts. And Hershey bars and cookies, and above all else, I said yes to virtually anything that had the word "pumpkin" in it.

I think pumpkin is to me what shrimp was to For-rest Gump. Maybe he could rattle off seventy-eight things to do with shrimp, but I could come up with about forty recipes that employed pumpkin—and I loved them all.

My experience with drugs is very limited. I never used marijuana or cocaine, even though one of my best friends was a dealer in college. I have sat around while people I like snorted it, licked it, smoked it, and rubbed it inside their gums and butt holes. I have never smoked crack, and the sight of people doing so makes me sick to my stomach. I have never used hard drugs, nor have I had even the slightest urge to try.

I didn't even have a cup of coffee until I was twenty and barely drank alcohol a dozen times until I turned twenty-one. Despite a ring style that was revolutionary in its perceived recklessness, I didn't take a pain pill until my sixth year in the business. Since then, my use of them has been minimal. I have thrown out entire bottles of pills that have passed their expiration date, and was able to get through my entire double knee surgery and rehabilitation period with only one pill.

This past year, though, has been tough, and I have had to use pain medicine with slightly greater frequency to get through it. On rare occasions, I have borrowed a pain pill from a friend, which I guess technically makes me a criminal, so that I won't have to wait for several hours at a doctor's office to be given the same damn thing. I even tried GHB a few times, back when it was sold in health-food stores and was supposed to build muscle and burn fat. Then Colette found it in my bag and made me throw it out, because she knew intuitively what all GHB users know deep down: if it makes you feel good, it's a drug.

I see an actor like Robert Downey Jr., who has been jailed and is ruining the peak years of his career because of drugs, and I am at a loss to understand it. This guy has lost millions and has been sent to jail simply because he can't control himself, because he can't say no to drugs. I look at a guy like that and have no empathy, until I realize . . . if I had to give up pumpkin pie for an entire fall and winter, with the threat of jail time if I lapsed . . . I think you'd have to lock me up.

I now have a great deal of understanding for drug addicts, because just as they crave a joint or a snort or a needle or a spoon, I crave those damn pumpkins. Got to have my pumpkins.

When I look back, I will always consider my September 1996 "Mind Games" match with Shawn Michaels to be the greatest of my career. Not coincidentally, it was also the *only* time in the last ten years that I *knew* I was in shape. Sure, I still looked like hell, but at 280, after a brutal cardiovascular training regimen, I was able to go full tilt for twenty-seven minutes with a smaller, quicker, better athlete than me. I wonder how many good matches could have been great, and how many great matches could have been all-time classics if I had only won my battle of the bulge. My career certainly has given me a great many things to be proud of, but the ability to "just say no" has not been one of them. After a fifteen-year battle, it seemed that food had not only kicked my ass, but had made it wider and decorated it with dimples.

Fortunately, I had an angel on my shoulder. A seven-foot-tall, 450-pound one named the Big Show. This is going to break the poor guy's big heart, but the sad truth (at least for him) is that the lack of reaction for Show from the Garden fans had caused Vince to reconsider the *Rumble* main event.

"Mick, can I talk to you?" Vince's voice sounded stern, as if I had screwed up, but in truth, his succeeding words became something of a professional salvation to me. "I'm not going to go with Triple H

and Show at the *Rumble*," he said. "The reaction's just not there. I'm going to go with you and Hunter, but not as a retirement match, we can do that later." I thanked Vince up and down for his decision, but he wasn't quite through yet. "Mick, I want you to get in shape," he then told me. I had six weeks to get there.

28: *Drugs and Choices*

THERE IS A DRUG PROBLEM in wrestling. With that being said, this will probably be the most difficult chapter I will ever write. Difficult because it may be perceived as casting a negative shadow on a business I love and people I care about, and difficult because in order to write it I've had to ask myself questions for which there are no easy answers.

Yes, there is a drug problem in wrestling. There are also drug problems in football, baseball, hockey, and basketball, all of which have been well documented. There are drug problems in Hollywood, drug problems in music, drug problems in cities, drug problems in schools, and drug problems with everyday citizens as well. I read about them every day, and I see them every night on the evening news. Drugs are by and large a societal problem, and wrestlers are a part of society. But that doesn't let us off the hook.

I have no desire to write a tell-all book about drugs, nor am I the man to write such a book. I think it's low class and a breach of trust to go that route, and it's not what my life or career has been about. I don't go out to bars, and I don't know who's taking what. The only time I hear about someone's drug use is if it's bad or if their behavior seems suspicious, including telltale physical signs.

For years, heavy drinking was considered a sign of a wrestler's manliness. I don't think wrestlers have gotten any less manly, but at the same time I don't hear nearly as many stories of drinking prowess. Sure, I hear a few, but I'm much more likely to hear wrestlers comparing the merits of their protein shakes these days than their favorite beers. Maybe the guys still jam the bars and just don't tell me about it. But as a guy who keeps his ears open all the time, I just don't hear a whole lot about heavy drinking.

I don't know a single wrestler who uses hard drugs. I think a heroin user would be an extreme rarity in the business. Personally, I don't know of any. Cocaine was huge on all levels of society in the eighties, and therefore was huge in wrestling. Guys who made $300 a week would snort $300 a week, and guys who made more snorted more. Guys snorted in the dressing rooms and guys snorted in their cars. It has literally been years since I've seen or heard of anyone in our business snorting cocaine.

Crack was on the rise when I was in WCW. I used to hear a few of the boys talk about it, and even was in a car on a road trip when the driver made a detour through M.L.K. (Martin Luther King) Boulevard in a strange city to "get some rocks." I started picking my driving buddies a little more carefully after that. I did ask the driver how he knew where to buy crack in a strange city, and his answer was simple: "You just go to M.L.K. in any city, that's where all the rocks are."

For some reason, when Dr. King said, "I have a

dream," I don't think having streets named after him where "all the rocks are" was quite it. The people I knew who used crack spoke about the experience as if it was heaven, literally. That's the word they used, "heaven." I wonder if they feel the same now, as most of these crack users have lost their homes, families, and jobs as a result of their fondness for the heavenly stuff. I can honestly say that I don't know of a single crack user currently in the World Wrestling Entertainment.

Marijuana . . . well, that's a different story. I know some of the guys in wrestling smoke a little pot, and as soon as I see evidence that its effects go beyond making people happy and mellow, I'll let you know. Professional wrestling is a high-stress job that causes its participants to be on the road a great percentage of the year. Without a release mechanism, some would find it unbearable. Maybe my thinking is a little too liberal here, but in my book (and this is my book) there are bigger problems in today's world than a grown man smoking a joint in a hotel room after being thrown around a ring and driving a couple hundred miles.

I would be a fool to think that there's not some steroid use in the World Wrestling Entertainment. In my opinion, if someone looks too good to be true, he *probably* is, but again, I am probably the worst person to pass judgment because steroids have never been part of my life.

A lot of the guys in the business today—not just the World Wrestling Entertainment, but WCW and ECW as well—make their bodies their top priority. The dedication they put into their training and diet is incredible, as is their attention to dietary supplementation. To hear some of them talk is like trying to use a computer for me; it's a foreign language. The World Wrestling Entertainment at one time included a bodybuilder who had placed fifth at the Mr. Olympia contest, the bodybuilding industry's most prestigious showcase. He may have been a terrible wrestler, but would have made a fine scientist, as his knowledge of anatomy, kinesiology, chemistry, and physics was phenomenal.

This knowledge is what makes testing for steroids so difficult. A steroid test, even a surprise one, is not going to catch all steroid users, only the chemically uneducated ones. Only a complete idiot would fail an announced test. The users are too smart now, and their methods for passing drug tests border on ingenious. In his 1996 book, *The Dark Side of the Game*, former NFL football player Tim Green described the extreme measures that players sometimes resorted to in order to pass drug tests, including catheterizing clean urine into their bladders. If someone wants to beat a test bad enough and has the knowledge to do so, they will.

Look, when I see a wrestler who looks a lot better in a big hurry, I *guess* that he's on steroids. But that's all I do—guess. The same way I guess that a Hollywood actor who muscles up dramatically for a role is on the gas (steroids) as well. The same way that I guess the reason the average NFL lineman's weight has gone from 250 to 300 over the past twenty-five years, while his time in the forty has decreased, is chemical in nature. But they're all guesses.

When I broke into wrestling, steroid use and talk about it was in the open. Guys jabbed each other in the ass with needles and compared dosages and

effects as if they were exchanging cake recipes. If there is steroid use in the World Wrestling Entertainment, I don't in all honesty actually *know* about it. I have not seen an injection, discovered a discarded needle, or even heard someone admit to taking steroids in the nearly six years that I have been there.

Someday someone will come along and write the definitive history on drug use in professional wrestling. He will name names, remember dates, and document dosages. To do so, that person will have to have firsthand knowledge of such drug use and a willingness to destroy people's lives. I have neither.

If putting a finger on the steroid use in wrestling is difficult, pointing a finger of blame on the real drug problem in wrestling—prescription drugs—is even more so. Why? Because such drugs are legal. They can also be deadly. Four wrestlers of prominence have died in the last five years as a result, at least in part, of the effects of prescription drugs.

A recent article on ABCNews.com listed sixteen wrestlers' deaths in the last seven years, with the insinuation that wrestling was a deadly business. I found the article to be extremely biased, especially since most of the wrestlers listed were either retired or had died of causes ranging from cancer to suicide to domestic violence. Surely the wrestling business cannot shoulder the blame for all of these.

In 1998, I was thrown off of a sixteen-foot-high cage. I have never once felt the need to exaggerate its height, because I feel that the truth is impressive enough. In the same way, I don't feel the need to sensationalize the number of deaths in wrestling, because the truth is bad enough. And the truth is that the deaths of four wrestlers in the last five years—Brian Pillman, Louis Spicolli, Rick Rude, and Bobby Duncum Jr.—are suspected, at least in small part, to have been caused by prescription drugs. Undoubtedly, many more in our business have problems with these same drugs.

I knew all four of these men. Pillman and Rude I knew well. Spicolli I knew a little, but had not seen in five years, and had only met Duncum Jr. a few times in passing. Of these four, Brian Pillman was the only wrestler to die while he was involved in the World Wrestling Entertainment, and Duncum Jr.'s death was due to drugs that were given to him by someone else.

There are a lot of reasons for prescription drug use in the world of wrestling. The demands of the road and of the ring often lead to pain, sleeplessness, depression, and anxiety. On a larger scale, much of the world experiences pain, sleeplessness, depression, and anxiety, but for a wrestler, the job demands greatly intensify the symptoms.

- **Pain.** Whether it be sport or show, wrestling is physically demanding work. Even when done correctly, a certain amount of soreness and injury are inevitable. I have never approved of the word "fake" as it pertains to professional wrestling, because the pain and injuries are very real, and at times, do require medication.

- **Sleeplessness.** The schedule of a wrestler is sometimes mind-boggling. In one five-day stretch in April 2000, I flew from Los Angeles to Atlanta,

Atlanta to Pensacola, Pensacola to New York, New York to Cleveland, Cleveland to Las Vegas, Las Vegas to Salt Lake City, Salt Lake City to Atlanta, and Atlanta to Pensacola. In those five days, I had actually landed in seven different time zones. Needless to say, my internal body clock was screwed up worse than a Test vs. Rodney match and I had difficulty sleeping on three consecutive nights of red-eye flights. It has been a long time since I have used a sleeping pill, but oftentimes when I am unable to sleep knowing that I have a 4:30 A.M. wake-up after a midnight hotel arrival, I question my judgment. Four hours of pill-induced sleep would certainly beat the horribly tired day I spend traveling home to see my kids and pretending to be superdad on minimal sleep once I do get there.

■ **Depression.** The rigors of the road, an ultracompetitive job, and the family problems that a combination of the two cause may lead a wrestler to battle depression. But hell, a large part of the world is depressed, and a large part of the world takes medication to deal with it.

■ **Anxiety.** Believe me, living in a fishbowl with a job that never ends and no real place to get away from it all can make even the best of us anxious. Fans at the hotel when we wake up, fans in the restaurant when we eat, fans wanting autographs while we're pooping, fans waving from their cars as we drive, fans at the airport when we fly, fans calling us at the hotel, fans driving past our houses, and fans with computers and apparently

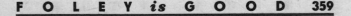

no real lives trying to access our personal information are somewhat anxiety inducing. I refuse to ask for anxiety medicine because of the negative stigma I feel is associated with it, a "he can't deal with life" stigma. Sometimes I take a pain pill before I go to an amusement park. Feel free to judge me if you want, but it's the difference between yelling, "Hey, I'm with my family" rather than, "Sure, buddy, what's your name?" when a fan wants an autograph.

Without question, I can see why wrestlers use drugs. Unfortunately, the step between use and abuse is a small one, and it's an awfully easy one to take. I've heard it said that nobody sets out to be a drug addict. I have personally never run into a single wrestler who said, "I never really wanted to be a wrestler, but I knew if I wrestled, I would get hurt, and then I'd get pain medicine." Wrestlers take medication because they legitimately need it. They continue taking the medication because they like it.

In 1994, I suffered a serious shoulder injury at the WCW *Spring Stampede* Pay-Per-View. I was in so much pain that I couldn't sleep at night, and in the daytime I was in so much pain that I was a miserable SOB to be around. At that point I had been in the wrestling business for nine years. It was the first time that I was given a prescription for pain medicine. Prior to that, I had taken one pain pill for broken ribs in 1991 and two more pain pills for more broken ribs in 1992. This was actually the first bottle of my own, and when I took a pill something strange happened. Not only did my pain subside, but the world became a wonderful place to live in. I smiled a beautiful, mouth-hanging-half-open, tongue-sticking-out smile and waited with happy impatience for four hours to pass so I could take another one. Within two days I felt I was becoming addicted, if not physically, at least mentally, to these pills. The next day I stopped taking them and didn't look at them again until I used them for my "Hooked on Being Hardcore" ECW promo a year later.

I was smart enough and lucky enough to realize that the medicine was getting a hold on me. Most people don't realize this until it's too late.

If I had used my entire prescription at the recommended rate of "one or two every four hours," I would have been out of pills in a week. Meanwhile, if I, at 300 pounds, was zonked on one pill, what kind of guy takes two? I'll tell you who—a person with a built-up tolerance for drugs. If I had called my doctor after a week and asked for a refill, I hope that he would have objected. Apparently many doctors don't.

Have you ever seen the list of drugs found in Elvis Presley's system at the time of his death? My goodness, Betty Crocker doesn't have that many ingredients in her cupboard. What about Sonny Bono's autopsy? What the hell did Sonny ever need pain medicine for? Sure, he was married to Cher, but I never saw him married to Chair. You know, as in Chair Schott.

Obviously, these guys either had an awfully generous doctor, a number of different doctors, or a combination of both.

Wrestlers are no different from anyone else, and quite honestly, this is the part about prescription drugs that I find most confusing and bothersome.

Aren't there restrictions on how much medicine one doctor can prescribe? And shouldn't there be some sort of national data system that ensures that the same drugs are not prescribed to the same person by multiple doctors? I've been trying to find out for weeks now, and it seems like the answers to both questions are no. Why not? Well, I don't have an intimate knowledge of the pharmaceutical business in this country, but it would seem that the answer would point to money. The more drugs they sell, the more money they get. So we can send a man to the moon, we can have five-year-old kids access hardcore pornography on their computer, but we can't stop a drug addict from getting the same legally prescribed drug in multiple states?

Brian Pillman was, in my opinion, an accident waiting to happen. Always a tremendous athlete and an exceptional wrestler, Brian's popularity had peaked when he began his "Loose Cannon" persona in 1996, in which he managed to not only convince the fans but most of the boys in WCW as well that he was legitimately out of control. I saw him during this time, and despite our having been good friends prior to the birth of this character, I had little to say to him. He either had a screw loose for real or was doing a convincing job of pretending to. This character had made Brian a hot commodity right at the time that his contract was ending, but a near-fatal auto accident put his future as a wrestler in jeopardy.

Brian did return to wrestling, but he was never the same. His ankle, especially, was badly injured, and he took a great deal of medicine to mask the pain. He signed with the World Wrestling Entertainment, but a variation of his "Loose Cannon" personality never really took off. His behavior was erratic and his ring work was at times embarrassing.

Brian was my second opponent when I entered Wards WCW in late 1989, and a tremendous match with him, and his words of praise for me to the office helped my standing in the company immensely. Our ring chemistry continued over the years but by no means were his matches with me a highlight of his career. Indeed Brian Pillman was a constant show stealer, with his series of singles matches with Japanese star Jushin Liger, and his tag team exploits as one half of the Hollywood Babes, along with a pre-"Stone Cold" Steve Austin standing especially strong in my mind.

I was scheduled to wrestle him the following day in St. Louis on the *Badd Blood* Pay-Per-View. To be quite honest, I had great apprehension about the match because his condition had been so poor and his ring work had sunk so far from its previous levels.

Brian never made it to that show. He was found dead in the same Super 8 Motel that I had slept in that night. An enlarged heart was detected, and was ruled as the official cause. Some have claimed that the World Wrestling Entertainment should have checked for such a defect. Actually they did. As did the National Football League, as did the Canadian Football League, as did World Championship Wrestling. The defect never showed up.

Progress has been made. The rings have more give now, and the days of twenty-five-day road trips are gone. In the World Wrestling Entertainment, we are on the road four days a week. It's not easy, but it's

not impossible either. I have had a lot of pain to deal with in my career, and I know that I will have some degree of it for the rest of my life. When the pain gets too bad, I take a pill, but never more than once a day. I don't blame wrestling for the way I feel. I don't blame the World Wrestling Entertainment and I don't blame Vince McMahon. Vince didn't force me to get into wrestling. He didn't push me off Danny Zucker's roof in 1985. I am a grown man, and I take full responsibility for every decision that I've made.

The decision to take drugs or not to take drugs

ultimately is my own to make as well. To claim otherwise is to live in a world of denial. Wrestling is in many ways a world of fantasy, but inside that world, some very real decisions need to be made, including the decision whether or not to take drugs. Vince McMahon doesn't make those decisions. We do.

29: *The Boy Who Saved Christmas*

"WHAT PAIN THIS LITTLE BOY had known, what suffering for a child, but the thing that touched dear Santa most was the magic in his smile."

I wanted everything to be perfect for my big reunion on December 7 in Boston. I was having a little party for a special person, and I had asked some of the wrestlers to join me. Edge and Christian were there, as were Ivory, Albert, and both Hardy brothers. We gathered in a backstage room and waited for our little visitor. The door flung open and his eyes met mine. With all the speed that his four-year-old legs could gather, he ran to meet me with open arms. I met the little guy with a giant hug and picked him up in the air. His smile was magical. I looked at my fellow wrestlers and could see beaming smiles on each face. Without saying a word, this little boy had touched them all.

I had first met Antonio Freitas on December 4 at a shopping center in Somerville, Massachusetts. It was not a book signing but a free autograph session, and as a result the store was packed and a line ran out deep into the brisk New England night. In a situation like this, conversations need to be kept to a minimum and signing is done as quickly as possible. With almost 2,000 people to get through in my two hours, a rate of one autograph every four seconds is a necessity. Sure, I wink, nod, and throw out a lot of "pals," "buddies," and "chiefs," almost like a Val Venis conversation, but an event like an autograph session is the last situation at which I thought I'd meet a special friend.

He was a tiny little guy, but he certainly wasn't hard to spot. Part of his face and a great deal of his head were covered with thick scar tissue. I could tell instantly that he had been burned and had suffered through many difficult operations.

There was something else that touched me, even deeper than his obvious wounds. The child had the face of an angel and a smile that could melt the coldest of hearts. I asked if the little boy could be brought up to the front, and despite the length of the line, and the length of time that some people had been on it, not a single person voiced an objection. I signed a picture for the child and asked him his name. Antonio's stepfather said that I was his favorite wrestler and that I had played a special role in his life.

Antonio had been two when he had pulled a boiling pot full of frying oil on top of his own head. He was feared dead, but was revived on the way to the Shriners Hospital for Children, where he remained for three months. As part of his treatment, Antonio was required to wear a mask, which he had objected to vigorously. His family had pointed out that Mankind wore a mask, and as a result, the child began wearing his too.

I had enjoyed talking to the boy, and his stepfather's story had flattered me greatly, but unfortunately I still had 1,500 fans to please. I gave the boy a thank-you and he wrapped his little arms around me tight and walked away. I waved as he grew smaller in the distance, but somehow felt like I had failed my own self. It was almost as if Jiminy Cricket was slapping me upside the face and was screaming, "What's wrong with you?" I got the picture. "Antonio!" I yelled, just as he was about out of earshot. I was relieved to see him making his way back, his stepfather holding his hand. As he got closer, I asked him a question that would cause a small but profound change in my life. "Would you like to sit on my lap?" With that, the little guy jumped up on my leg as if it was a big comfy couch, and we talked about wrestling and children and Christmas as I signed my name once every four seconds. When he left a while later, the crowd cheered for a solid minute with smiles so warm it was as if a bit of Christmas magic had touched us all. I continued my rapid signing pace, but I took pleasure in a special feeling that bathed me in tranquillity the likes of which I'd rarely known. After a while I identified the feeling. Antonio Freitas, a four-year-old boy, had made me feel like Santa Claus.

Our reunion in Boston three days later was a wonderful time, and his family members were deeply grateful. His mother, Rhonda, handed me a card with touching words of heartfelt thanks. Her eyes held tears that nearly fell as she said, "I'll never forget you for what you've done for my son." "I don't think you understand," I explained, with eyes that welled to match her own, "that he's done just as much for me."

I have been a wrestler for fifteen years, and with a few glaring exceptions, I think I have done my job well. My brother is a supervisor for UPS. He puts in long hours and does his job well. My dad was an athletic director for thirty-five years in the Three Village School District in Long Island and is considered something of a legend among his peers. In our respective fields, I probably am about on a par with my brother and can't compare with my father, who worked every day as if the Pay-Per-View cameras were rolling. Of the three of us, however, I'm the one who signs autographs, and on rare occasions can make a difference in a child's life.

As wrestlers, we have critics who call what we do immoral. If the choice was theirs, professional wrestling would not exist. I wish one of these people could be on hand to see the smile on a dying boy's face when Steve Austin says hello, or see an ill child's family cry when The Rock raises an eyebrow to pose for a picture. I don't believe that we are necessarily role models, but we have been given an unbelievable gift by our fans—the chance to make a small difference in some special people's lives.

I have recognized this fact for the last ten years, and at age thirty-five believe that I have wasted far too much time without truly giving back. A number of people across this world would disagree with my self-critique, and those particular people would be correct, for over the years I have been involved in what I would call random acts of great kindness. Unfortunately, I can't help feeling that when my face stops being televised and my name stops meaning quite as much, I'm going to realize that one of the biggest opportunities of my life has passed me by. I sometimes think of Liam Neeson at the end of *Schindler's List* thinking that he could somehow have done more. I can do more, and in all fairness to myself, I have tried. But I haven't tried hard enough. I believe I needed something special to inspire the best of me to make itself known, and I honestly believe that my initial meeting with Antonio Freitas was that "something special."

Writing my book had opened up doors that I never knew existed. I approached ReganBooks with the idea of doing a children's Christmas book, and they had actually seemed interested. I had stated my goal of being known as "America's foremost author of children's Christmas books" and relished the thought of growing old, watching my kids grow, and warming the hearts of future generations with my beloved tales of the true meaning of Christmas. I only had one problem. I had writer's block.

For weeks and then months I had hoped that the words would come to me. I was certain that the book should be done in rhyme and didn't want to resort to sitting down and saying, "Let's see, what rhymes with 'stocking.'" True art, I felt, couldn't be rushed, it had to flow naturally. Unfortunately, a natural flow and an approaching deadline sometimes don't go together all that well. On a few occasions I even began to write but just came up flat. I needed an idea. I needed inspiration.

On a flight from New York to Houston, inspiration hit me. It came in the form of a four-year-old boy, and it hit me hard. For the next two hours I fired off rhymes about naked elves and arrogant reindeer and managed to make rhymes out of "flatten 'em" and "triple platinum." In my poem, various North Pole hassles had poor Santa feeling down, to the point where he actually threw in the towel and called off Christmas.

I had set out to make a book for children that would make grown-ups cry. I wanted to write a story that was fun but had a genuine heart in the middle of it. While I sat in my hotel room the next night, I had Antonio on my mind, and as wild as it may sound, I believe I got the help from someone up above as I wrote about the special little child who changes Santa's mind. I believe the last few pages of what turned out to be *Mick Foley's Christmas Chaos* to be the best writing I have ever done. I have read the story to several wrestlers, and though I've yet to see one cry, I have seen something equally touching. I see them making a genuine effort not to.

A portion of the proceeds from *Christmas Chaos* (which benefits greatly from Jerry "the King" Lawler's illustrations) now goes to the Shriners Hospital for Children, but more importantly, I am hoping that it is raising awareness for the cause. Until recently, when I thought of the Shriners, I thought of the guys in the funny red hats. They are a whole lot more. They care, they save lives, and all treatment is free to children under eighteen years of age.

My wife loved *Chaos*, and upon hearing it came to an immediate conclusion that had completely escaped me. "You know you were writing about yourself, Mick, don't you?" she said. I didn't have a clue of my own, so Colette explained. "Santa Claus is you, Mick, the North Pole is your world, and you feel like you need to save it." I thought about her hypothesis and then about the cold night in Somerville. I then read the book again and realized the wisdom in her words. Let me try to explain with my own crude attempt at self-analysis. Happy Mick is the predominant author of the book you are reading. Sad, unloved, underappreciated Mick is Santa Claus in *Christmas Chaos*.

30: *Here Comes Santa Claus*

OH MY GOODNESS! Al Snow turned out to be the culprit. Like a jilted suitor, envious Al had stolen the book from The Rock, thrown it out, and then "found" it, in an attempt to throw a monkey wrench into The Rock 'n' Sock machine. Al's confession to the crime was eerie in its delivery, and was without a doubt the best interview he had done in some time.

I don't want to sound like a broken record, but . . . wait a second, does anyone even know what a broken record sounds like anymore? Let me try again. At the risk of sounding repetitive, I am a big believer in some semblance of legitimacy in an interview. No, I'm not talking about WCW's repeated use of "shoot" interviews that 98 percent of the audience don't understand, but a foundation of genuine emotion upon which to build up story lines. Therein lay the strength of Al's interview. He had no problem sounding bitter, jealous, and resentful of me, because he, um, well, he *is* bitter, jealous, and resentful of me.

Actually, I was happy for Al, as the interview not only helped him but me as well, as our "Falls Count Anywhere" match on December 14 in Tallahassee was my best outing in a while and gave me a shot of well-needed confidence. Colette and the kids were with me, and I was able to run straight from the ring into our car and didn't slow down until Disney's Magic Kingdom was in sight.

As I mentioned earlier, I do my homework before these trips, and as a result am able to get a little more bang for my Disney dollar. I even take advantage of "early entry," which is available to all Disney resort guests, and as a result was able to get on the new Winnie-the-Pooh ride without a wait. The ride included a depiction of a happy Pooh smiling joyfully, with his face covered with his beloved honey. I snapped a picture of the touching scene, which I then used as a visual aid for an Al Snow joke.

My kids are at a wonderful age for Disney theme parks. They love the big rides but are still young enough to enjoy the simple pleasures that Walt's vision offers. Colette and I spoke at length about our growing children on this trip, and about Christmas, Santa Claus, and the inevitable conclusion that each child eventually comes to about Father Christmas. I dreaded that thought. No Santa would be a disaster. No Santa would mean no Santa's Village, and who knows what that could lead to?

Every year I find it harder and harder to be a good liar. The kids are getting smarter, and the holes in the entire Santa Claus theory make the psychology of a Posse match seem airtight by comparison. The blame for this lies squarely on the deceased literary shoulders of Clement C. Moore, the author of

"A Visit from St. Nicholas," which is more widely known as "The Night Before Christmas." No, this is not going to be a rant against the poem just because I've written one of my own, but just a wish that Moore's vision of Santa Claus hadn't been so preposterous.

Moore's poem, you see, is the basis for the modern-day Santa Claus. Before that, Santa Claus, originally known as Saint Nicholas, which turned to Saint Nicklause and then to Santa Claus, had been a kindly old gift-giver clothed in long robes. Moore's story gave rise to the vision of Santa as a "ripe and jolly old elf," a vision that was made even more popular by Coca-Cola's ad campaigns featuring Santa. Unfortunately, "A Visit from St. Nicholas," which in all fairness to Moore was originally written just for his children, has also taken the art of parental lies to new heights because of the vast implausibility of the story. Moore, you see, invented the theory of flying reindeer and Santa coming down the chimney, not to mention the eyes that twinkled and the dimples so merry. Look, I don't blame Moore completely, because other whoppers concerning Rudolph and the North Pole made things even worse, but he's the guy who started the whole thing.

With that in mind, here is my top-ten list of reasons that the legend of Santa Claus is completely at odds with any logical thought process:

1. What does Santa have against Jewish kids?

2. If Santa "doesn't care if you're rich or poor, 'cause he loves you just the same," how come the rich kids get more presents?

3. Doesn't Mrs. Claus get angry when Santa comes home with an empty sack?

4. What kind of a reindeer coach can Santa be when a new reindeer hasn't cracked the starting lineup in over a hundred years? Even WCW gives young guys more breaks than that.

5. How come no child I know has gotten a wooden train, when that is all the elves seem to know how to make?

6. What if you don't have a chimney?

7. How does Santa get his fat butt down the chimney?

8. Do Santa's reindeer jump, as "Rudolph the Red-Nosed Reindeer" claims, or fly via magic feed corn, as "Santa Claus Is Coming to Town" would lead us to believe?

9. If each kid gets an average of twenty-five toys a year, and each home has an average of 2.2 kids, how does Santa fit 110 billion toys into his one sack?

10. How does Santa find the time to visit two billion kids in one night?

Two Christmases ago Dewey recognized that Santa's handwriting was the same as Mommy's. "Santa is awfully busy delivering toys," Mommy explained, "so he counts on us to help him write the name tags." Last year he woke up at midnight and said, "If Santa hasn't come yet, how did my stocking get filled?" We covered that with "Grandpa Jack is Santa's stocking helper." I covered his "How does Santa travel to every house in the world in one night?" question with some bull story about how traveling through the time zones actually gives Santa more than twenty-four hours to do his thing.

In addition to the growing number of their questions, Noelle seemed intent on "catching" Santa in the act. Dewey insisted that he had seen Santa three years ago and had actually hugged him, and Noelle was desperate to do the same. Colette told me of Noelle's strategy of drinking Sleepy Time tea in the afternoon so she could take a nap and thereby stay awake all night in order to nab Saint Nick.

The dwindling threads of reason that held the Yuletide fib in place had me nervous as hell on Christmas Eve 2000. To make things even worse (for a reason I'll get to later), I was exhausted, but still kept pushing the delivery hour back so as to better my odds of successful present presentation. I kid you not when I say my heart was pounding harder during Christmas Eve toy distribution than it was before I was thrown off the cell in '98.

When I finally went to bed, somewhere around 4 A.M., or to put it another way, twenty minutes before I woke up, Dewey's pile of toys had a stuffed Tigger on top of it, and Noelle's had a stuffed Pooh on top of hers. Magically, the stuffed animals had switched places when I came out to the living room, and I listened to my son serve up more whoppers than a pimply-faced Burger King employee as he insisted that "Santa had left them this way."

The Santa Claus dilemma had me worried during that Disney trip. "Colette, if the kids want to know the truth about Santa, do what you've got to do, but don't tell me that they know." Colette tolerates my year-round Christmas fascination and even thinks it's kind of cute sometimes, but my very real obsession was starting to worry her. "Mick, someday the kids won't believe in Santa anymore. There's nothing you can do about it."

Maybe she was right. Maybe it was inevitable that Dewey would reach the dreaded conclusion first and then, sadly, my little one, my tiny creature, the child whose very name means "Christmas" would find out too. That would be it. No more children to share the magic of Christmas morning. No more children to tell Christmas Eve stories to as their eyes danced and gleamed with the wonder of holiday surprises. No more children . . . no more children . . . no more . . . That's it. The answer. It had been so simple and made such sense. Why hadn't I thought of it before?

"Honey, my love, Colette," I said with as much

charm as I could muster after a ten-hour day of rides, walking, and mice with heads the size of Maytag washers. "Would you like to have a baby?"

Colette absolutely loved the idea, and we made plans, big plans, for her time of ovulation, which, as luck would have it, fell on Christmas Eve and Christmas. There were two ways that this coincidence could be looked at. We could take it as an omen that our beautiful child was to be conceived at the holiest time of the year. Or we could try to figure out how we were going to nail each other six times in two days with my parents in the house.

It wasn't easy, and in truth, our "I need to talk to you" and "let's watch a movie" and "my back hurts, I need to lay down" probably fooled nobody. By the end of day one, I was running out of steam, and running into another problem that I had not foreseen. Just as a person who runs a lot can become a marathon runner, I was becoming a marathon man in the game of love. Which is great if you're on your honeymoon but not so great on Christmas Eve with the threat of kids walking in, the knowledge of parents hearing the effects of their little boy's athletic prowess, and the haunting specter of a Santa Claus exposé coming soon in the Foley living room.

By Christmas day I was begging for mercy, and Colette responded by wearing outfits that The Godfather's Hos might find offensive. Still, I found the testicular fortitude to get both a post–present opening and a pre-Christmas-dinner rendezvous into our Yuletide agenda.

By eleven, I was a beaten man. I had officially had more sex in two days than I had managed in my first twenty-four years. At least I was safe. Colette hadn't stayed up past eleven in two years, including New Year's Eve. I slipped into bed, as quiet as a 300-pound one-eared mouse, and tried to drift off to sleep. Colette began to stir. Oh no, please don't wake up. She started to move toward me. Say it isn't so. Suddenly she placed her hand on my minuscule member and breathed a sexy "one more time, big boy." The woman was insane. Not only was I officially out of ammunition, but my penis was showing less signs of life than a Garden crowd during a Test comeback.

Hey, I wasn't embarrassed. I had proven my manhood over the last two days, and my wife deserved the truth. "Colette, I'm sorry, but I've got nothing left. I am tired, I am sore, and I just want to get some sleep." My wife wasn't sad; it wasn't as if she had even a thimbleful of desire left for me at this point, but she had her reasons. "Please," she begged, "just one more to make sure." I told her as gently as I could that nothing she could do would make me change my mind. Her next five words proved me wrong.

"Want to watch a porno?"

A porno? Was she serious? "Yes," she assured me, she was serious. Don't get me wrong, I'm not a porno connoisseur, but these unexpected words had awakened my sleeping giant. Okay, so it's not a giant, but that's how the damn phrase goes, so I'm sticking with it. Colette hated porno. I would never get a chance like this again. My wife agreeing to porno was like Gandhi agreeing to a Big Mac. It was like the pope agreeing to join the Ho Train, it was like The Rock agreeing to put Pete Gas over for the title.

There was only one problem. "I can't watch a porno on Christmas," I whined, and despite her objections, I stood my moral ground. I had faced the same problem on the night of Christmas in 1978, when I had run into stacks of my father's old magazines. No, my dad didn't have smut in his house, he had *Sports Illustrated*. About ten years' worth. Now if the year 1978 and the words *Sports Illustrated* don't ring a bell, it's obvious that you don't remember that year's scandalous Swimsuit Issue that featured Cheryl Tiegs in a fishnet bikini that showcased nipples that were roughly the size of a good pair of buckwheat pancakes.

Sure, the current issue was the phenomenon, but my dad's innocent cache was to a horny teenager what finding a Mickey Mantle rookie card would be to good old J.R.—nirvana!

No one else had access to a young, pre-nipple-exposed Tiegs in exotic locales wearing skimpy bikinis. I looked at the clock on that Christmas night so long ago. Ten-thirty P.M., an hour and a half left until the official onset of December 26. An hour and a half until I could do what my thirteen-year-old hormones were truly telling me needed to be done. I had lasted in 1978, and by golly I could last in 1999.

The minutes seemed to pass like hours, until finally, midnight. Yes! Let the games begin. I don't remember even thinking about a baby as I watched Christy Canyon's bouncing boobs and used verbiage in that bedroom usually reserved for the Cross Bronx Expressway during rush hour.

31: *Anatomy of an Angle*

AN ANGLE IS THE CORNERSTONE of sports-entertainment. Wrestlers need good angles and angles need good wrestlers. It's a true relationship. In truth, the angles might be more important than the wrestlers because a bad wrestler can get by on good angles a lot better than a good wrestler can get by on bad ones. I should know since I've been a part of some bad ones ("Lost in Cleveland") that nearly led to a career in pool cleaning, and I've been involved in some good ones (Mankind vs. Undertaker, Dude Love vs. Steve Austin) that led to an increase of human asses in cushioned seats. In my fifteen years in the business, I do believe that the buildup to and the execution of the *Royal Rumble* 2000 was the best angle that I've ever been a part of.

First, a little background. Triple H took the World Wrestling Entertainment title from the Big Show and raised the stakes in his feud with Entertainment boss (and at this time babyface) Vince McMahon by, of all things, marrying Vince's daughter Stephanie the night before her nationally televised wedding to Test. It seems that Stephanie had been slipped a Mickey (no, not me, a sleeping pill) during her bachelorette party in Vegas, and the despicable Hunter had married the unconscious girl at the drive-thru lane at a local wedding chapel. (The wedding was part of the story, but the drive-thru lane really does exist.) Then, at the Test/Stephanie wedding service, Triple H unveiled a videotape in front of a distraught Stephanie, a furious Vince, and a really dumb-looking Test.

Usually, I'm a big fan of World Wrestling Entertainment stories, but this wedding thing (and unfortunately for Test, his part in particular) was a little ridiculous. First, as a wedding present to his future son-in-law Test, Vince was generous enough to "give" him a match with Hunter about an hour before his nuptials took place. As a result, poor Test showed up sweating to a degree that not even Richard Nixon approached in the famed Kennedy debate. Not only that, but he was actually announced coming down the aisle to his wedding ceremony as "Test"; not Andrew Martin, as Stephanie called him several times on TV, but Test. To raise the ludicrousness level even higher, he came down the aisle to his ring music. It was hideous. After seeing him destroy the nuptials of the sweating, wedding-day-ring-music-playing, gimmick-wrestling-name-using Test, I'm surprised Triple H wasn't an instant babyface. I know the boys in the back were cheering him.

I realize now that while I have previously explained my use of both the Mean Street Posse and Al Snow in oft-repeated punch lines, the origin of Test's role in this same respect has been untold. Probably because I don't know why I pick on him. I just like it. Actually I like him too, and I think his ring work is impressive. His "Love Her or Leave

Her" match with Shane McMahon at the 1999 *SummerSlam* in particular was excellent. But Test is an easy target, a man virtually void of any and all quick comebacks. He gets no mike time, so I don't have to worry about on-air retaliation, and his chances of writing a book are right up there with England's Queen Mother getting a nipple ring. Once in a while he tries to make a verbal comeback in the locker room, but him trying to get over on me is like shooting spitballs at a battleship.

Recently, as Commissioner of the World Wrestling Entertainment, I had a chance to pull a good one on Test. He and his partner, Albert (together known as T&A), were set to come into my office for a taped preshow interview. Before they arrived, I told the producer and cameraman that I was going to play a joke on Test and to go along with it. Test had some scripted lines, but because I am generally given the freedom to say whatever I want, none were written for me. Test came into the office, asking for a match with the huge Samoan wrestler Rikishi, and showing some of the worst acting skills this side of Richard Grieco. When he was done with his request, I picked up my official Commissioner's gavel and began to speak.

"You see what this is? It's a gavel, right? And do you know what this gavel means? It means I'm the Commissioner. Which means I make the rules. So I guess you could call me a ruler, right? And you know what they say about rulers, don't you? They've all got twelve inches. So why don't you bend over my desk so I can rule your ass. Now be off with you!"

I fully expected Test to break out in laughter and

say, "Okay, good rib, now let's do it for real," but he didn't. Instead, he simply yelled "thank you" and left the room. The second he heard "cut," I heard him ask, "Were those his lines?" to Albert. "All right," the producer said, "that was good. Let's take a look." A bunch of the boys who were in on the joke gathered around to watch the playback. I was holding in my laugh much as I'd done in the D.D.P. cookie incident, but Test didn't seem to notice. After we saw it, he *still* didn't realize it was a joke. To his credit he took it well, but even after the real interview was taped, he maintained he liked the first one better.

Enough about Test. Back to the *Rumble* angle. In a valiant attempt to defend his daughter's honor, overmatched fifty-four-year-old Vince took on the World Wrestling Entertainment Champion at the December 12 *Armageddon* show. After taking more punishment than any CEO of a major corporation has in a long time (at least since Bill Gates's last visit to the barber), Vince was defeated when his own daughter turned on him.

Since that point, the "McMahon–Helmsley Era," as it came to be known, had taken to stacking the odds against the company's top babyfaces. Such was the case on December 27 in Greensboro, North Carolina, the site of "This Is Your Life," when they forced the members of The Rock 'n' Sock Connection to battle for their very careers in the first-ever "Pink Slip on a Pole" match. In this epic struggle, the first man to climb a pole in one of the ring's corners and grab the pink slip attached to the top of it would be the winner. The loser would be out of a job. Yeah, I know, usually the person who gets the

pink slip is out of a job, but this is wrestling, where an "if Kane loses, Tori has to spend the holidays with X-Pac" stipulation was actually enforced. So please work with me on this.

The match was actually quite good. As part of my *Rumble* training, I was no longer required to work at nontelevised shows, and the extra healing time helped greatly. I had been working extremely hard at the gym in addition to my marathon cardio sessions on Christmas Eve and day, and the results were obvious. Not only was I getting slowly but surely a little lighter, but my ring work was looking better.

I had my chance to win, via an Al Snow run-in, but being the sportsmanlike SOB I am, I refused to win that way. Instead, I blasted the cheating bastard and it cost me. The Rock won the match, and Foley was gone . . . kind of.

My actual absence lasted two weeks, but in truth I was all over every show. The *SmackDown!* that aired three nights later was my very own tribute show, with several "Foley moments" aired through-out the program in addition to a solemn at-home interview that was actually taped in World Wrestling Entertainment road agent Dave Hebner's house. Usually I'm a stickler for reality, but after realizing that I would have to go from Richmond to Pen-sacola via Atlanta, and then back to Washington, D.C., the following day, I came to the conclusion that two minutes of reality would cost me twenty hours of traveling. "Besides," I explained to Jim Ross, who was actually going to fly with me for the interview, "no one knows what my kitchen looks like anyway." So yes, I will admit that I pretended to be in my house! I lied! I faked it!

The January 3 *Raw* from Miami saw me ring in the New Year by ringing all four DX members' bells when I ran in on a three-on-one "Handicap You're Fired" match to save The Rock. I was firing chair-shots so quickly that I didn't have time to line up for X-Pac correctly and I knew when he went down that I'd caught him with the edge of the chair, which is a definite no-no. I waited for him to come through the curtain, and sure enough when he did, the skin on his forehead looked like a tin of sardines that's been opened a third of the way. He took it amazingly well, and it sure did look good on tape.

Throughout the course of the show, a series of "Have a Bad Day" vignettes featuring Triple H and a fake Mankind were shown. Mankind was played by my old buddy Dennis Knight, who is better known as Mideon, in what was surely one of the crowning moments of his career. I had been trying for years to incorporate Dennis's uncanny Cactus/Mankind imitation into several different shows, and "Tex" really got to show his talents off here. Special-effects wizard and all-around magician Richie Posner actually made his mask out of masking tape and spray paint, and the parade of parodies was off and running.

Each skit saw Hunter, dressed in ridiculous disguises and using such aliases as Harry Sacks and Oriental Dr. HungLo, destroy the pathetic Mankind as he went progressively from a job interview where he admitted he had no skills, to a children's hospital where no kids wanted to see him, to a book signing that no one showed up for.

From here we headed to Orlando for *Smack-Down!* tapings, but, more important, for a trip to

Universal Studios Islands of Adventure. Knowing that I would be leaving the company sometime in the near future, I had set up a park visit with Edge, Scotty 2 Hotty, and the Hardy brothers as kind of my going-away present to the younger wrestlers. On the eve of our departure, Al Snow got wind of it and more or less invited himself along. No one had the heart to tell "old fifth wheel" that it was a special day, so we endured his presence and his stories about how he used to "sell that son of a bitch out." Wait a second, that's Ricky's line (don't worry, only about ten people in the world will understand that reference, but those ten will love me for it). "Brother, you've never seen so many people."

We had a guide named Shawn who I had met years earlier when my kids took the Nickelodeon tour at Universal Studios. He admitted that upon our first meeting, he had not known who I was but thought I "must be someone famous in order to have a hot-looking wife like that." Actually, when I met Colette I was making $400 a week as an independent wrestler, so I sleep easy in the knowledge that she didn't marry me for my money. Come to think of it, I'm not sure why she did marry me.

We had a tremendous time on our nostalgic park trip, and in truth Al was not a "fifth wheel" but had been included from the start. Many of the rides were incredible, with Spider-Man standing out as perhaps the greatest ride anywhere. Up until this ride, Shawn had seemed proud to be hanging with us, but our singing of "Spider-Man, Spider-Man, does whatever a spider can. Spins a web any size, catches thieves just like flies" caused whatever respect he might have felt for us to visibly melt away.

"Look, there's Spidey," yelled Edge, at the real-life-costumed Spider-Man who was leaving an autograph session as we exited the ride. Edge is an especially big Spidey fan, and his enthusiasm must have startled the web-slinger slightly, for, in one of the more bizarre incidents in my life, the startled Spidey walked into a lamppost and required medical attention. "Is he strong, listen bud, he's got radioactive blood . . . look out, there goes the Spider-Man!"

When I showed up at the arena, I received tremendous news. I was being dispatched to Universal Studios to supervise some Bogus Mankind vignettes being filmed in the park. As creative supervisor, I was asked what locations would be best for these vignettes. "Hell," I said, "we need to do one on the *Jaws* ride." And so it came to pass that while taking the boat ride five times for "scouting purposes," the Bogus Mankind (his actual credited name) was filmed on the famous ride detailing the magnitude of his courage in the midst of a boatload of park visitors who couldn't have cared less.

"Boy, let me tell you, before Triple H fired me, I was somebody. I wasn't afraid of anything. I jumped off the top of the Hell in a Cell. The Undertaker almost killed me, but I wasn't afraid. No, do you hear me, no, I was not afraid. Because I am Mankind, the craziest, most fearless wrestler in the history of the World Wrestling Entertainment. There isn't anything that scares me, not one thing in the entire world, do you hear me?"

At that point the mechanical shark jumped out of the water and the most fearless wrestler in the history of the World Wrestling Entertainment went into hysterics. "Oh God, oh God," he yelled as he alter-

nately clutched his heart, his head, and disgusted riders. Finally, after about twenty seconds, Mankind regained his composure. "Boy, I'm sure not afraid of that anymore," he claimed . . . as the clip faded to black.

The vignettes reached a humorous but physical climax when the Bogus Mankind exited the *Back to the Future* ride. The Bogus one's words upon entering had hit hard. "I know," he said, "I'll set the hands of time back to December 28, 1998, the day I won my first World Wrestling Entertainment title." (Yeah, I know, *Back to the Future* is a motion simulation ride that has nothing to do with setting back the hands of time, but continue working with me here.) His next comment was out of line, but not out of the story line. "Or better yet, March 15, 1982, the last time my wife found me attractive and let me

have sex with her. Boy, that sure was a great day."
Uh-oh, a remark about my family. Retaliation was
definitely called for.

When he came out of the ride, that call was definitely answered, as the real Mankind was on the
scene and was one angry man. He was even angrier
when the impostor explained that the ride had made
him sick to his big, giant belly. "Are you talking
about my wife?" I asked with anger, which caused
the fake guy to come out of character. "Hey, man, I
was just—" I cut him off with a scream: *Are you
talking about my family?*" Again, the fake Mankind
tried to explain. "Listen, Triple H hired me—" I cut
him off with a forearm and then proceeded to
destroy him in the first, and until someone does a
better one, best wrestling fight ever staged at the exit
of the *Back to the Future* ride.

The January 10 *Raw* was a major turning point
for me and the angle. It began with The Rock threatening a mutiny of every Superstar in the company
unless changes were made, which included bringing
me back. Moments later I was back on World
Wrestling Entertainment television, even though I'd
really never left, and was issuing a challenge to
Triple H for the *Royal Rumble* in Madison Square
Garden. We also booked a *Raw* main event pitting
the four members of DX (Hunter, Road Dogg, Billy
Gunn, and X-Pac) against the A.P.A. (Faarooq and
Bradshaw) and The Rock 'n' Sock Connection. It
would be my best showing by far since my knee surgery seven months earlier. But first, some good old
American sports-entertainment BS, and I mean that
in a good way.

The Bogus Mankind, you see, needed to be taught

a lesson. And what better way to teach a lesson than by tying him up and torturing him? First the Chinese water torture. Then hot coffee to the face. After that, I untied the poor guy, but did so with the warning that he not leave the room. This led to one of my favorite and most uncharacteristic skits of my life.

Tori, the young woman who had been forced to spend the holidays with X-Pac, was (in our story line) the somewhat unstable girlfriend of the massive Kane. She had once been a competitive bodybuilder and still had a phenomenal build, which was augmented by a magnificent set of boobs. Hey, I know that sounds crude, but those boobs were the focus of the skit. I was going to talk about them and I was even going to spank her, and best of all, it was part of a story line, so I couldn't get in trouble at home. Yes!

I caught up to Tori in the hallway and flagged her down. "Tori! Tori! Hey, Tori, it's me, Mick!" I yelled as she cowered in fear. "Hey, I've been looking for you all night. Listen, we don't get a chance to talk like we used to, so I'd just like to tell you that I really admire your sweaty, heaving, voluptuous breasts." She was terrified, but I continued with an interesting fact. "I know that you've heard I'm a good kisser, but in addition to that talent, I've composed a list of about seventeen other things that I'd really like to do to those bad boys." Now she was mortified. I don't think she wanted me anywhere near those bad boys. Still, I decided to let her mull it over. "Hey, if you want to go over that list, I'll be in my dressing room." With that, I gave her a playful but firm whack on her muscular buttocks that provoked a roar of surprise from the crowd and sent

Tori scampering for safety. Still, I wanted her to know that the offer still stood. "In case you didn't know, that's dressing room number three—number three, okay? Bring a friend, because there's plenty of Mankind to go around." As Tori stopped scampering and started running away, the camera panned back to me for a hokey thumbs-up that would later become my trademark, and an even hokier extended "yeahhh!"

When the show came back from break, the terrified Tori was pointing dressing room number three out to her stoic, masked boyfriend, and in an unfortunate miscarriage of justice the Bogus Mankind ended up paying for my inappropriate remarks. My match was next. The Tori skit yielded a humorous Foley family moment when a few days later Noelle asked me when her "bad boys" would grow.

I spent most of the contest standing on the ring apron, knowing full well that the entire angle's success or failure depended in great part on what I did with my tag. Fortunately, when the tag came with Triple H in the ring, "what I did" was better than I could have imagined. My first few punches were nothing special. Then I put Hunter in the corner, and as was my trademark, began throwing forearms to his head. Usually I throw five or six, sometimes a little more. Sometimes they come in slow and deliberate, sometimes a little faster. On this night in St. Louis, the forearms were somehow better. I started slow and picked up the pace. By the time I got to ten, the crowd was behind every one, and Hunter was sliding down, but was encouraging me with every one. "Come on, Mick, come on," he said as my wristbone connected with his skull at ever-shorter intervals. By the time I was done, I had thrown twenty-two forearms and had moved at a speed that belied my years of physical wear and tear. From that point on, I tried to relive that moment in the corner in all of my remaining matches, but could never quite recapture the magic.

I backed away and then sprinted in for a running knee in the corner. I knew I was running faster than I had in years, and my belief is backed up by a video of the match that I still find hard to believe. *Wham*, I nailed him, with what is more accurately a "running inner thigh" than a knee, but that somehow doesn't sound as brutal. Unfortunately, my increased speed led to a problem that I had not encountered in some 400 previous attempts at the move. My chest hit the top turnbuckle with tremendous force, and I knew immediately that I was hurt. The injury would later be diagnosed as a bruised sternum, and would not completely heal for several months.

The pain caused me to slow down, and the match temporarily lost its focus as I tried to take deep breaths to recapture the wind that had been knocked out of me. Hunter tried to make a tag, but in keeping with a subplot in the show, DX was falling apart and none of his buddies would tag in. Eventually, they walked off on Triple H and A.P.A., and The Rock battled them up the ramp. The stage (or ring) was all ours. I caught Triple H with a double-arm DDT, which was my standard setup move for the dreaded sock. The crowd went wild as I pulled out the cotton icon, and even wilder when I pulled an interfering Stephanie into the ring. Triple H cut me off.

He pursued me to the outside, where he sent me into the stairs and forward into the announcer's table. As I turned slowly toward him, he picked up the timekeeper's bell. *Clang!* He caught me with a mighty shot that sent me tumbling over the table. The crowd was eating it up and in the midst of the action, I called an audible "pedigree." With that one word, Triple H administered his finishing move on the announcer's table and the table shattered upon impact, and sent us down to rest with the ruined lumber and mangled monitors. Blood ran from a small cut on my head as he rolled me into the ring. One pedigree later and the match was over. "Dammit," Jim Ross yelled with great emphasis, "I can't believe this night has turned out like this." Actually, the night wasn't through turning.

Triple H continued pounding on me as the blood began to drip down my mask. He brought me to the corner and worked on me some more. He turned his back to me to yell at the referee, and when he faced me again I was waiting with the stiff forearm that sent him down hard. I pulled off my mask in a symbolic gesture and threw it on the ground. The blood was more visible now, and stuck in a coagulated mass to my forehead and nose. Throughout my career, I had been known as a heavy bleeder, but in truth, this was one of the few times in my four years in the World Wrestling Entertainment that I was, to quote the late, great Gordon Solie, "wearing the crimson mask." It was the most important blood that I had ever shed.

I threw Triple H to the outside and gave pursuit. I had nothing planned and let instinct and emotion take over. It's no secret that a great deal of what we do is planned ahead of time, but I am still a great believer in the spontaneity of the truly great moments of our sport. When I shouldered the ring stairs and met Triple H at full force with the steel, I felt as if I was living one of those great moments. More ad-libbed ass-kicking followed, and I then rolled the World Wrestling Entertainment Champion into the ring.

I cannot overstate the importance of selling or my frustration with those who either won't do it or don't know how to do it well. I am thankful that Triple H had both a willingness to do it and knowledge of how to do it well, because when I clotheslined him over the top rope, his sell made the angle complete. He sold it as if he'd seen a ghost. And in a way, he had.

An interview is often only as good as the guy who is reacting to it. Too often I've seen great promos

negated by an opponent who instantly belittles the great promo that has just been given or belittles the guy giving the promo, which is just as bad. For example, I've never believed in treating my opponent like a piece of garbage, because if I win, all I've done is beat a piece of garbage. If I lose, well, certainly I can't be that good, since I lost to a man who I have built up to be nothing.

Just as bad are the guys who don't react at all. I worked with a famous announcer in WCW (not Jesse Ventura) who made a hell of a lot more money than me but continually undermined the wrestlers by not selling what was said. As a heel, it didn't mat-

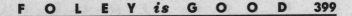

ter how convincing you were on the mike because a sneaky little comment from that guy would kill any heat. As a babyface, it was tough to leave a lasting memory when the guy was always waiting with some stupid comment designed to get himself over.

I try to remember that guy when performing my current duties as Commissioner of the World Wrestling Entertainment. I know that I'm supposed to be entertaining and that the job description calls for me to occasionally get the verbal best of our heel performers. But at the end of the day, I try to remember that my primary job is to get the angles and, to some extent, the wrestlers involved in them over.

Our next night's *SmackDown!* interview was vital because it contained the metamorphosis of Mankind into Cactus Jack. My main concern in doing this entire angle was whether or not the fans would buy into Cactus Jack as some kind of mythical superhero instead of the same broken-down guy wearing a different shirt. If Hunter had sold the transformation as the latter, the *Rumble* angle would have joined Kelsey's nuts on the "dead" list. Instead, the interview "made" the angle by "making" Cactus Jack, and as a result we both went on to "make" some pretty good money.

The interview angle began with Triple H calling Mankind out to the ring. Instead of the real deal they got the bogus guy, who immediately got down and groveled at Hunter's feet. This mockery brought out the genuine article, who definitely did not appear to be having a nice day. The words themselves were not all that memorable; but the actions, reactions, and crowd response certainly were.

"Triple H, that is enough," I began with intensity fueling my thoughts. "Is this what you get off on, making fun of me?" Triple H just smiled smugly. "You take my job," I continued, "then you bring this idiot out here"—pointing to the bogus guy—"and you take away my dignity." Hunter smiled, smugger still. "Then Monday night in what should have been the greatest night of my life when I was reinstated on *Raw*, you take me and you ruin my shirt"—which was splattered with blood—"and you ruin my face." Hunter smiled at the memory. "I'll be honest, when I stepped into that shower and I let the cold water run down my head, and when I looked down at the blood as it swirled around the drain, I started thinking a little bit about what Mankind was.

"Now, Mankind is an entertaining son of a gun. Mankind is a pretty damn good author. Mankind is one tough SOB, and Mankind is one hell of a fighter." I then continued in a slightly quieter tone. "So it saddens me to say that after the beating you gave me on Monday night, one thing that Mankind is *not*, is ready to face you in a street fight at the *Royal Rumble* in Madison Square Garden." Hunter broke into a larger smile, which grew larger still with my next sentiment. "Because you are without a doubt 'the Game,' you are the best in the business right now. And Mankind in some way is just a beaten-up pathetic fool. But I think the World Wrestling Entertainment fans deserve a substitute in that match." The fans cheered and I knew I had to be careful. Logic and experience told me to milk the anticipation and let their interest peak. Instinct told me that if I waited too long, the crowd would start chanting "Rocky" and would ruin my surprise. So I charged right in. "So what I'm going to do, Triple H, is I'm going to name him right now.

"I think you know the guy," I said with increasing tempo as I pulled off my mask. The crowd started to stir. I ripped open my Mankind collared shirt to reveal the infamous "Wanted Dead" shirt underneath. "His name is Cactus Jack"—a pop as big as any I've ever been a part of—"and his first official act as part of the World Wrestling Entertainment is to kick your teeth all over Chicago."

As I mentioned earlier, the effectiveness of this startling pull-off-a-shirt metamorphosis all hinged on Triple H. If he had laughed it off, our *Rumble* buy rate would have done Hasselhoff numbers. Instead, Hunter sold the transformation as if he were Pam Ewing and just saw her dead husband Bobby walk out of the shower in the *Dallas* season cliffhanger.

I stormed the ring and went after Hunter. The punches were nothing special, but the reaction was. After nineteen forearms, I raised my hand in the air and caught a hard chair to the back courtesy of the Bogus Mankind. A chair to the back is different from a shot to the head in that one has a little more creative freedom in how they choose to sell it. Which is my way of trying not to sound like a hypocrite for choosing not to sell it at all. At least I didn't laugh. The Bogus one went for another shot, but I caught the chair with my hands and threw it angrily to the corner. Too angrily, as it turned out, since when I went to pick it up moments later it was gone. I was convinced that it was a part of some conspiracy as I looked for the missing seating device

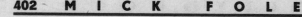

while cursing audibly in the ring. (In addition to traffic, the bedroom, and *The Sopranos*, the F word is also appropriate when trying to find a missing chair in the middle of a Cactus Jack angle.)

It turned out that no one had taken, stolen, or hidden the chair. I had merely thrown it too hard and it had skidded out of the ring. It was finally handed back to me, and after knocking the Bogus Mankind onto the announcer's table with a sliding kick, I picked up the chair and delivered a devastating elbow/chair off the apron to the chest of the impostor.

Triple H, who had taken a powder (bailed out of the ring) after the first chairshot, continued to sell the vision of Cactus Jack as if he was a monster. Unfortunately, I landed hard on my knee while performing the move and it swelled to grotesque proportions. Two moves and two injuries for Cactus in two days. Maybe Hunter was putting Cactus Jack over as some mythical madman, but in truth, I was getting my ass kicked by my own self.

In addition to the tremendous execution of the angles, part of the interest that began mounting came from the dramatic departure from the lovable Mankind character. Fans were able to suspend their disbelief and accept Cactus Jack as the darker, pissed-off side of Mick Foley—the ass-kicking side. Vintage clips from Japanese death matches on the following week's *Raw* further enhanced the public's perception of Cactus Jack, and in a strange way, so did my absence from televised matches.

"For one show, I can convince the fans that Cactus Jack is something special," I had told Vince when we planned out the idea, "but if I wrestle on

royal rumble

TV, they'll know I'm the same broken-down guy they've been watching for years." So with Cactus Jack temporarily relieved of his on-air wrestling duties, I threw all of my thought into this huge Pay-Per-View match.

I had a lot of thoughts to throw. For hours every day I thought of ideas to incorporate and then made mental notes of what I thought was best. Then, for the first time in my career, I made actual notes and wrote down my ideas. That's right, after years of hearing about wrestlers using scripts in their matches, I actually proved them right.

For the first time in years I felt like I was in shape when I stepped into the ring in Madison Square Garden for the *Royal Rumble*. I had been training hard and I knew I was prepared.

I walked back into the dressing area twenty-seven minutes later with a half-dozen thumbtacks stuck in the temple area of my head, barbed-wire holes in my back and stomach, sweat pouring out of my body, and a feeling of total professional redemption. I wish it had been my last match. It was that good. Triple H was at his absolute best here, and I was only a small step behind. The *Rumble* match was a brutal, beautiful, emotional affair, and in many ways was like a dream come true.

Unfortunately, I woke up.

32: *From the Penthouse to the Doghouse*

"HERE COMES CACTUS JACK," yelled a fired-up J.R., "and business is about to pick up. My goodness, he's got a two-by-four, he's got a two-by-four! This is going to be a slobberknocker. He raises that two-by-four over his head, and ooh, that looked kind of crappy. Another shot, and damn, that one sucked too. My goodness, King, he's forgotten how to work, Cactus Jack has forgotten how to work!"

Wrestlers should be entitled to their day of glory. A day to bask in the glow of appreciation and adulation that follows a triumphant Pay-Per-View match. St. Louis Rams quarterback Kurt Warner got to yell "I'm going to Disney World" after his Super Bowl win. A pro basketball player gets to have sex with one of several willing women who will probably bear him a son that he won't ever see. But wrestlers? Unfortunately, unless you're lucky enough to have surgery scheduled, the most likely answer to "you've just main-evented a Pay-Per-View in one of the greatest matches of your long career" is "I'm driving to Philadelphia for a pressure-filled live television broadcast of *Raw*!"

I spent the afternoon in Philadelphia in time-honored fashion: watching the previous night's match sitting side by side with my opponent and hoping for that rare postmatch ovation from the boys. Okay, here's the end of the match, will we . . . yes, they're cheering, we did it!

The *Royal Rumble* match was a success on the rarest of levels. The challenger (me) had come away being more over than when he went in, and the champion was a better champion. We were able to help "make" each other.

Unfortunately, later that night I did some more "making" with my disastrous two-by-four run-in. I "made" people feel sorry for me when I tried to run down the ramp. I "made" fans cringe with some of the worst-looking offense this side of a Posse match, and I "made" the glorious Garden effort look like a

distant memory. Man, I wished I had called it quits after the *Rumble*.

The *Rumble* show just about coincided with the release of *Beyond the Mat*, which was in serious contention for an Academy Award nomination. (It didn't get one but did garner a nomination from the Directors Guild.) Reviews were almost unanimously great, and the film should have helped make this twilight of my career even greater. It didn't. The World Wrestling Entertainment's decision to not promote the movie was theirs to make, and although I didn't agree with it, I understood it. What I didn't understand and could not tolerate was an executive (who is no longer with the company) telling ABC's *20/20* (my old friends were doing a feature on me) that the footage of my family had been a setup expressly for the movie.

It takes quite a bit to really make me mad, but this guy managed to do the trick very nicely. Following a phone call in which I used the word "bullshit" seven times in two minutes, *20/20* received a call during which the executive in question apologized deeply.

I promoted the movie on *Good Morning America* a few days later—a fact that had me losing favor rapidly with the World Wrestling Entertainment office. I was halfway in their doghouse. The *20/20* show pushed me in completely. (On the positive side, Diane Sawyer liked me and thought I was a good father despite letting my kids watch me get pummeled.)

I had been told by the producer of the piece, a grizzled news veteran named Lenny Borin, that *20/20* wanted to do a "positive" piece. Great. He also told me using a word that would come back to haunt me, that ABC needed some "heat" to go with it. In other words, a happy story wasn't good for ratings.

My interview with correspondent Chris Cuomo went well, as did a seven-hour day during which the crew followed me around at Disney/MGM Studios (filmed during our fateful December vacation). Following the Disney day, ABC filmed an interview with Colette and me during which Colette talked about the toll that too many headshots had taken while I attempted to provide a little levity to the proceedings. Unfortunately, the levity was cut, while the spousal concern made the air.

I watched the program from a hotel room in Philadelphia, and I knew I was screwed before my segment ever aired. The "heat" that Lenny had talked about manifested itself in morbid teasers that promised to look at "the dark side of wrestling" and promised to explain "the trouble with Mankind." It wouldn't have mattered if the piece itself was about my relationship with fuzzy bunnies, because the audience was preconditioned to thinking it was a "dark, trouble-filled" segment.

Lenny was upset when he heard I didn't like it. "Mick," he said over the phone, "I thought we showed you in a very sympathetic light." I agreed. I came off as extremely sympathetic, but I felt *20/20* erred in two important respects. First, they made the extreme punishment I had taken in extreme circumstances seem like it happened much more frequently than, in fact, it had, and second, the show made wrestling itself, and the World Wrestling Entertainment by inference, the focus of the blame.

I thought it was going to be a happy story,

because, in truth, that's what my story was. Sure, I visited a few emergency rooms in my day, and sure, maybe I'm a veteran of a few too many Norman Bates showers, but the rest of it is happy . . . the part about chasing my dreams, overcoming odds, and retiring on top of the business . . . not to mention writing a pretty good book about it.

If anything, the World Wrestling Entertainment had taken steps to prolong my career. I had been well compensated for basically being a washed-up sock wearer and had never been *forced* to do anything. I had *almost* been forced to work a program with the "Wildman" back in '97, but had somehow managed to dodge that career-threatening bullet.

My style has been described as "high risk," but I feel it would be more accurate to term it "high impact." Over the years I have certainly done some things that were a little bit risky, but for the most part I have tried to limit the real risks. Instead, I focused on a style in which risks of career-ending injury (neck, back, knees) were low, but probability of lifelong discomfort was high. I mean, it didn't take a genius to look at a twenty-three-year-old guy diving twelve feet off a ring apron onto concrete to say, "Hey, that guy's going to have a little trouble walking when he gets older." Likewise, a genius wasn't required to look at the '99 *Rumble* and say, "Eleven chairshots can't be all that good for his brain." So I guess you could say from day one that I knew the truth and accepted the consequences.

On the heels of my *Good Morning America* appearance, I knew the World Wrestling Entertainment was not going to be all that happy with the attention the media was giving Mick Foley.

Fortunately, Eddie Guerrero dislocated his elbow in a manner that placed him right up there with Joe Theismann for most hideous televised sports injury. I guess it wasn't all that fortunate for Eddie, but it created a tremendous opportunity for me. Eddie had come in along with Chris Benoit, Dean Malenko, and Perry Saturn as "The Radicalz," a band of talented but underutilized castaways from WCW. Talent is not actually given high consideration when looking at the WCW hierarchy, and so the Radicalz decided to jump ship and swim over to the World Wrestling Entertainment. I was supposedly the guy who brought them in.

As "owners" of the World Wrestling Entertainment, Triple H and Stephanie had played Wizard to their Dorothy by granting them their wish, on one condition—members of the Radicalz had to defeat members of DX in two out of three matches on the February 1 *SmackDown!* show in Detroit. It was thought that a controversial finish in the decisive third match would lead to an eight-man matchup at the February 27 *No Way Out* Pay-Per-View. Guerrero's injury, however, led to the Radicalz dropping three straight falls, but more important, to dropping right out of the *No Way Out* main-event picture.

Vince called me on my cellular phone on February 6. I had my kids in the car and wasn't in any mood for a verbal confrontation, so I never mentioned *20/20*, but its aura hung heavy in the car, like a White Castle fart, nonetheless. "What do you think we should do about the Pay-Per-View?" Vince said. Now, I consider my relationship with Vince to be a good one and at times to be a close one, but he doesn't make a habit of consulting with me about

Pay-Per-View ideas over the phone. I generally give the World Wrestling Entertainment some good ideas and they always give me a great deal of creative freedom concerning interviews and angles, but this particular call was a little out of the norm.

Fortunately, I had been giving my potential retirement match a great deal of thought and had an idea on tap. I had regretted not retiring after the Madison Square Garden show and feared hanging around much longer. I had successfully battled my "Joe Frazier on a stool" vision, but didn't want to defeat Frazier just to turn into Leon Spinks.

I had actually met both of these fighters at separate times. "Smokin'" Joe had showed up at the hotel where the ECW wrestlers stayed in Philadelphia and was in the bar watching the ECW show, and he was loving it. The legendary fighter was laughing out loud at the wild action, and cringing a few times too. My match came on and Joe went absolutely NUT! I decided to take advantage of this unique coincidence and introduced myself. He responded with a blank, uncaring stare followed by the weakest of courtesy smiles.

Spinks was another story. From the moment he defeated Muhammad Ali, Spinks was a legendary figure in the boxing industry. Sadly, he was not a legend in the financial industry, and he was not in the greatest shape, financial or otherwise, when I met him at the ECW arena in February 1996. Leon was no stranger to wrestling, since he had even main-evented a match at Sumo Hall in Tokyo against Japanese legend Antonio Inoki. The match was so bad that Japanese fans actually rioted afterward. I've been to Japan well over a dozen times, and I think I know the Japanese fans pretty well. They dress well, they're polite, they bow, they take a lot of pictures, they buy a lot of Cactus Jack T-shirts, and they respond to big moves by yelling "oooh." They do not riot. The Spinks/Inoki matchup had to have been extraordinarily bad for rioting to occur, and in truth it was. I rioted when I saw it too, and I was in my own house.

Despite the Sumo Hall fiasco, Spinks continued to dabble in wrestling. He refereed a few matches in Memphis for Jerry Lawler's CWA and even went on a few tours for Japan's FMW. So certainly the guy would know Cactus Jack, right? Well, yeah, if you count a glassy stare and a little stream of drool as signs of recognition.

Leon was in ECW to begin a program with Taz, who was still bamboozled as to why he didn't land the Seinfeld gig. Taz was touted as a legitimate tough guy, and part of that touting was based on winning matches with legitimate fighters. Spinks was supposed to be videotaped in the crowd watching Taz's match as step one of a planned feud. The feud never got to step two because the somewhat simple step one was never completed.

"Get a shot of Spinks," yelled ECW owner/mad scientist Paul E. Dangerously. "We can't show Spinks," Paul E. was informed. "Why not—I need the shot," the scientist yelled. "Because Spinks is puking" was the answer. Indeed he was, and Taz and Leon never got a chance to get it on. Which in retrospect is probably a good thing. If Japanese fans had rioted because of Spinks, there was a pretty good chance he wouldn't have made it out of the ECW Arena alive.

By the time the phone call was done, we had booked the *No Way Out* main event. Cactus Jack against Triple H in a "Hell in a Cell" match with the loser being forced to retire. I had intended to go out at the *WrestleMania* with a nice send-off, but I actually liked this idea better, wrestling my kind of match in a Pay-Per-View main event.

The waters were again calm in the Foley/McMahon ocean, but a mere five days later storm clouds arose that threatened to sink our relationship for good. But hey, I had six good days to enjoy, which included an innocent little incident that in all likelihood the world of sports-entertainment will never again see. Before the *Rumble*, I had not wrestled on television or in house shows. Now, with *No Way Out* on the horizon and with my body finally recovering after our brutal MSG battle, I began to wrestle a little more. *Royal Rumble* had been built on good promos and the Cactus Jack mystique, but another big show would require some in-ring wrestling angles to keep the momentum rolling. In addition, I agreed to wrestle a few shows within driving distance of my Pensacola home.

Mobile, Alabama, was the host of a Cactus Jack and Kane vs. New Age Outlaws main event. I was actually quite nervous before this showdown because of the mythical Cactus Jack buildup. I had been able to pull it off at the *Rumble*, and had even followed it up with a few good television matches, but this house-show thing had me worried. What was I going to do?

I came out to the ring to a great reaction. The people in Mobile sure loved the hardcore legend. Boy, were they going to be disappointed. I looked out into the crowd and I saw Pam Johnson, who was both Dewey's former and Noelle's present kindergarten teacher. I smiled and waved, and tried to look like what I thought a hardcore legend should. The New Age Outlaws music played and the Road Dogg and Billy Gunn entered the ring and did their "ladies and gentlemen, boys and girls, children of all ages, D-Generation X is proud to bring you its World Wrestling Entertainment Tag-Team Champions of the Wooooorldd!" routine that they did whether they held the belts or not.

I looked out at the audience again, and when I saw Pam Johnson a lightbulb flashed on in my mind. In addition to being both Dewey and Noelle's teacher, Mrs. Johnson had actually taught the Road Dogg when he was a child as well. I swear it's the truth, or as former Olympic champion Kurt Angle would say, "It's true. It's true." This was a coincidence that was too good to be true. It would be like a big boxing match between Lennox Lewis and Mike Tyson with an announcer saying, "I know that Tyson threatened to eat Lewis's children, but Lewis's children and a young Mikey Tyson actually all had the same kindergarten teacher . . . and my goodness, she's sitting in the front row."

I knew it was a tremendous coincidence, but the crowd had no idea, so I made it a point to inform them. I then pointed out that "Mrs. Johnson looks like she is awfully disappointed in the Road Dogg, because he looks like he wants to touch Billy Gunn in an inappropriate way." Road Dogg, who until my announcement had no idea that she was in attendance, and in truth hadn't seen her since he was in school, responded by first waving and then climbing out of the ring and playfully yelling at her. All of a sudden Mrs. Johnson was the center of attention in the front row and she took advantage of the spotlight by rearing back and slapping the Dogg. I then hopped out and began brawling at ringside, and the crowd ate it up. Back in the dressing room, the other boys refused to believe that the whole thing hadn't been set up.

A few days later I received a phone call from a friend, who told me that Vince had been on a radio show in San Francisco and had compared my wife to a beautiful and famous Hollywood actress. That was the good news. Maybe he meant the grace of Audrey Hepburn. Or maybe the coltish charm of Julia Roberts. Or maybe the timeless beauty of Barbara Eden. Unfortunately, it was none of the above. The bad news was that my boss, Vince McMahon, had publicly compared my wife to Robin Givens.

With the news my heart dropped to somewhere around my left ball while my dinner simultaneously rose to somewhere around my larynx. I knew exactly what Vince was referring to, and it made me livid. Vince was comparing my wife's comments on *20/20* to Robin Givens's infamous comments about then-husband Mike Tyson on a Barbara Walters special. In the Walters interview, Givens had said that her marriage was "like hell," that her husband was a "psychopath," that he had beat her, and that she was "scared for [her] life." All my wife had said was that she was worried about my health.

I didn't have Vince's home number, so I called J.R. to get it. I told him of the comments, and of my feelings about them. He gave me the number. I got Vince's machine and left him a little message. I didn't yell and I didn't curse, but even a man without Vince's mental acumen would have detected a little anger. Then I called my own phone and changed the message on my machine. If Vince was going to call, I didn't want him to be the recipient of a standard Foley goofy spiel. I wanted him to feel my pain.

He did indeed call. And he did indeed get my morose message. And he didn't try to claim he was misquoted either. He apologized. He also tried to explain that his comments were not a knock on Colette, but a comparison between me and Mike Tyson, who he felt had both looked like sympathetic figures during our respective interviews. With that assessment, I would have to agree. Mike had looked either doped up or like he'd watched a Steve Blackman interview. I looked the way a typical father looks after a seven-hour day at Disney with two kids, except with the added bonus of dealing with thousands of wrestling fans. In what won't go down on my top-ten list of career compliments, the ABC cameraman had marveled that I'd drawn more attention than former New Kid on the Block Joey McIntyre. So I guess Vince was right. Right? Except Vince hadn't publicly compared me to Mike Tyson. He had compared Colette to Robin Givens, and as the proud owner of two testicles, I couldn't just let that fact go.

Our face-to-face conversation took place on Valentine's Day, February 14, in San Jose, California. Unlike Vince, who had a huge wrestling company and a new football league to worry about, I had all weekend to think about the Givens comments. In addition, I had thought about all the little things that had been bothering me for a while. At its

most basic, the problem, I felt, was about respect. Although I put myself in the same league as Austin and Undertaker in terms of long-term value, I doubted that Vince would have made similar comments about their families, no matter what the circumstances. When his door opened up and we met face-to-face, I was armed with more notes than a *Tuesdays with Morrie* sequel.

When the door opened back up an hour later, the air had been cleared, and Vince was bleeding internally. Just kidding. Actually we handled it like gentlemen, and I was actually glad to have been able to get a lot of negative thoughts out of my mind. He apologized to me and he apologized to Colette, so what else could I ask for? Except a raise, which was a point I brought up as well. Vince would actually call the Foley house with several apologies but continually got the machine, until Colette, who, like a lot of people, is intimidated by Vince's larger-than-life persona, finally picked up the phone and accepted Vince's words.

All right, so Vince isn't perfect. With that being said, I have great fondness for him and consider our relationship to be one of the most important in my life. I have rarely met a man with his mind, and I have never met a man with his energy and his drive. A lesser man would have closed down the company in the face of the enormous losses of the early nineties. A lesser man would have settled for second place when WCW had the hot hand in 1997 and '98. But that's not Vince McMahon.

I sometimes wonder where I would be if Vince had not rescued me from my bloody Japan and ECW existence. When he brought me in I had been offered a big raise in Japan. Fifty-one thousand dollars for 150 days of work overseas . . . long bus rides . . . coach-class airline seats . . . blood . . . burns . . . bombs . . . scars. After taxes, I would have brought home less than a tenured custodian.

WCW would have probably brought me in eventually, but I likely would have been pushed with all the authority of a prepubescent boy's first bench press. A few miserable years of dealing with egos and office politics and then, as they say in Japan, *sayonara!*

I wasn't Vince's buddy when I came in. I wasn't Vince's buddy a year later when most of our conversations were limited to "hello," "good-bye," and Vince's favorite, "good to see you." Still, in that time of Steve Blackman–like vocal workouts, I was pushed harder and was made a bigger star than I had been at any point in my career. Gradually the conversations grew to the point where I now consider Vince my good friend, workout partner, and spiritual mentor. Okay, so maybe I'm laying it on a little thick, but I do consider him to be a good friend. I consider his children, Shane and Stephanie, to be good friends as well, despite the hatred they show for me on TV, and the fact that Vince's children actually like him and like being around him actually gives me hope as a parent.

I sometimes question Vince's judgment, especially about the bringing in of talent. I have often seen him bring in talent that looks to be of little use. No, he doesn't headline Pay-Per-Views with them like WCW does, but he does give them jobs. While traveling with Terry Funk back in 1997, I brought up the subject of a very questionable piece of talent and asked why Vince would even bother paying the guy. The Funker not only has known Vince for a long time, but is very intuitive as well, and his answer seemed to make perfect sense. "Cactus, sometimes Vince does things just to be nice."

I used to hear horror stories about the way Vince treated talent. I have yet to experience this firsthand. Actually, I have yet to see him even yell at a wrestler. The atmosphere in our dressing room is casual and friendly, and that has to be in great part because of the boss himself. One of the biggest compliments I can offer Vince is that he allowed *Have a Nice Day!* to be printed complete with criticisms of him, and I suspect that he will allow me that same privilege here. I certainly don't agree with every decision he makes and I had to be restrained from striking him when Test won the hardcore title, but in the end, it's his company and he can do with it what he wants. He's like the big kid with the football, and he lets me play with it. But damn, I got to play for a long time.

Before my nose gets too far embedded up Vince's ass, let me make one final point. Or more accurately, let me ask one final Vince question: What other owner of a major company, whose personal net worth is rumored to have more zeros in it than a Snow family reunion, would allow heavily muscled employees (not me, but work with me here) to blast him with steel chairs?

So in the end, Vince and I are cool, but yes, the sea was a little rough there for a while. And do you know who I blame for it all? Blaustein! Blaustein and his critically acclaimed movie, *Beyond the Mat*. Without him there would have been no tension. There would have been no cursing at World Wrestling Entertainment executives. There would have been no *Good Morning America*. There would have been no *20/20*. There would have been no Robin Givens comparisons. And there would have been no fears that for the rest of my life my beautiful wife would be known as "the lady who cries."

Maybe I'm being a little too rough on Barry. After all, he was responsible for writing the "giant hamster humping the professor" scene in *Nutty Professor II: The Klumps*. If "that which does not kill us makes us stronger," then Barry Blaustein is responsible for making the Foley/McMahon bond stronger than it's ever been. Yes, that was a wrestler quoting Nietzsche.

33: "Good-bye, Cactus"

HOW DOES A PERSON live up to something that is impossible to live up to? The June 1998 "Hell in a Cell" had almost become a part of folklore. It was frequently cited as "the greatest match of all time," which seems somewhat akin to calling the maiden voyage of the *Titanic* "the greatest cruise of all time." Like the *Titanic*, the '98 cell match was a disaster, and its appeal lies in the courage of its survivors. Unlike she did for *Titanic*, I will refuse to let Celine Dion sing its theme song in the big-screen version.

I promoted the 2000 version of "Hell in a Cell" with the promise of once again coming off the top of the cage. This time, however, I promised to come off with an elbow on top of Triple H. Was I really going to dive a legitimate sixteen feet, which in wrestling circles would be billed as thirty? No way. But I didn't feel like I was lying. My rationale may seem almost Clintonesque, but my feeling is that as long as, within the scope of the story line, there is the intention of fulfilling the promise, then no lie has been told.

I had used this philosophy in the cell scenario in a little-remembered match against Kane in September of '98, and no one had complained. I promised to come off the top in that one too, and saw my promise shot down by the Undertaker, who pulled me off as I reached the halfway point of the structure. The fall was supposed to be broken somewhat by the announcers' table below, but instead, my ass merely grazed the thing and most of the impact was taken on my shoulders and head—which was actually meeting the concrete from a distance of fourteen feet. I was actually a lot more devastated physically by this landing that no one remembers than by the infamous first flight in Pittsburgh.

I had no problem covering a lie made with honest intentions. Covering a lie that my predecessors had made with dishonest ones was a bit more of a problem. Retirement matches, once practically cause for national mourning, were now a joke. They were used to spike buy rates or to boost ratings and had an actual return-to-action rate of about six weeks. The few people who did retire were wrestlers who no one had any desire of seeing anyway.

So I was faced with the problem of trying to look like Abe Lincoln amid a sea of Pinocchios. I wish that I had simply stated that "win or lose, this is my last match," but it was too late for that. On February 24, I gave my last promo before the big match. In it, I tried to distance myself from the retirement rip-offs, and without blatantly saying, "I'm going to lose," tried to convey the feeling that I was indeed going to.

Some experts felt it was the best interview of my career. Some of the wrestlers cried backstage as they listened. Personally, I was disappointed. I felt so full of emotion backstage, but when the music hit and the crowd popped, I became a performer. I wanted to tell a story but gave in to the current pressure for catchphrases and instant gratification. I think I lost my nerve. I told the story, which included my Joe Frazier analogy, but I yelled too much, and while I was doing it I felt I was failing myself by turning a special situation into a "wrestling promo." Above all else, I used a word that would come back to haunt me . . . "prostitute."

"Prostitute." As in, "I'm not going to be like those other guys who prostitute their name in a retirement match only to come back after a six-week vacation." I wanted the word to be strong. I wanted "prostitute" to tell fans I was serious about the match stipulations. I wanted "prostitute" to increase buy rates. Most of all, I wanted the word "prostitute" to save me from becoming a real one. Wrestling may not have been my first love in life, but it was certainly the first one to love me back. I honestly didn't know if I could leave it. "Prostitute" was my insurance policy.

I felt pressure all around me during the final days before *No Way Out*. I wanted this match to live up to its famous father but knew I had to do this without the huge risks associated with the first one. *Beyond the Mat* and *20/20* had shone a public spotlight on my laundry list of injuries, and the last thing I or the World Wrestling Entertainment needed was a major mishap in my final match.

I also felt pressure as a result of my recent falling-out with Vince, the wounds from which had not yet completely healed. I was also working on a bonus chapter for the paperback edition of *Have a Nice Day!* I thought it would be intriguing to chronicle my final days as an active professional wrestler. In one respect, it turned out to be a fascinating portrait of my thoughts, hopes, and reflections during a tense and somewhat historic time. In another respect, it was a big mistake, as it tarnished the humor of the original. Sure, it's intriguing, but so was finding out that Judy Garland was an alcoholic and drug addict. We know the truth, but wouldn't it be better if everyone remembered her as Dorothy?

I was actually writing for a good part of February 27, as it seemed to take my mind off the pressure of the match. For hours I alternated writing with stretching and taking walks around the backstage area. I cursed my decision to book a personal appearance in Huntsville, Alabama, where I had spent the previous day. Sixteen hours of traveling was not the way to prepare for a match of this magnitude. The traveling had left my legs feeling tired, so that unlike January's *Rumble*, my physical condition was weighing heavy on my mind.

I put my pen and paper away only minutes before the match and did one last session of warm-ups before heading for the entrance. I watched the end of The Rock vs. Big Show matchup and thought about my career. I don't know if God cares about sports-entertainment, but I said a small prayer anyway. I have often prayed for safety, but on this night I also hoped to leave after an effort that I could be proud of for a lifetime.

I heard the screech of tires and the crash that followed and I knew my time was at hand. I heard the opening guitar chords and I stepped out into the Hartford Civic Center. I looked out at the sea of fans and I looked up at the ominous cell structure that was still hanging from the ceiling waiting to descend. I thought of my recent miserable performances and longed for the confidence that I had taken into Madison Square Garden. I felt like the smallest, most insignificant 300-pounder that the world had ever seen.

Triple H's music played, and he stepped through the curtain with the lovely Stephanie at his side. Please, I thought with an urgency that bordered on prayer, let Hunter be at his best here. I'm going to need all the help I can get. He stepped into the ring and the cage began to lower. If there is such a thing as a silent buzz, such a thing was running through the crowd as the cell steadily descended. As the structure came closer to the Hartford concrete, something seemed amiss with the door; it was locked in at least a half-dozen different ways. How was I going to escape from the cell to complete my promised elbow from the top?

While I was looking, Triple H attacked from behind, but I turned to thwart him. We exchanged decent punches, an exchange that I got the better of. Hunter went down to a hard right and I was atop him in speedy fashion and bounced the back of his head off the canvas several times.

Triple H briefly stopped my momentum, but a backdrop over the top rope put me back into control and in pursuit on the outside of the ring. I grabbed a steel chair from ringside, but as I prepared to use it, Hunter rolled into the ring to safety. I climbed the ring apron with the intention of bringing my chair with me, but a high Triple H knee to the chest sent me flying off the apron and into the somewhat forgiving cage.

Hunter seized the advantage and whipped me hard into the stairs. I took them hard with my mid-thighs, and the momentum whipped my body over the top of them with an impressive flip. Whips into the stairs are commonplace in the World Wrestling Entertainment, but everyone seems to drop down and take them with their shoulder, which is impressive but somewhat out of line with the body's natural motion. I don't want it to look like I'm trying to hit the stairs; I want the effect of the stairs altering the course of my progress.

Hunter continued his assault by running my head into the steel ring post, a blow I may have taken a little too hard, as I temporarily forgot what I was doing and lay on the ground for way too long, while my opponent waited for me with the ring steps on his heavily muscled shoulder. The collision was worth the wait. *Boom*—the impact echoed throughout the arena and was impressive enough to merit three different instant replays. The force of the stairs may have seemed overly brutal, but in fact it had to be. We needed that stair "spot" to stand out in people's minds for future reference.

While I lay on the ground, Hunter placed the weapon/stepping device over my head and proceeded to come down mightily on it with several chairshots. No, it doesn't hurt, but it looks impressive and plays havoc with the eardrums. Hunter rolled under the ropes with the chair still in his possession as I gamely struggled to my feet. I too then rolled into the ring. Triple H was waiting.

Wham—he caught me in the back. *Wham*—another one brought down with a force that elicited a gasp from the crowd. The second blast had only seemed to piss me off, and as I turned to face my rival, the crowd buzzed with anticipation.

CRACKKK—a giant baseball bat swung to the side of the face sent me down fast and the crowd's buzz along with it. A good match is like a roller coaster, and we had just brought them up a small lift followed by a steep drop.

Triple H went for the cover, but oddly, my kick-out elicited barely a reaction. A DDT put me down again. Another kick-out, another barely audible reaction. Why? He picked up the chair again, and as he turned to me I got to my knees. I waved him on with my hands and a nod of my head, as if to say, "Come on, let's see what you've got." The crowd was alive with a "Cactus Jack" chant, which made their lack of reaction to the pinfall attempts seem even stranger. The chant seemed to inspire Hunter, who charged with the chair held high overhead. *Boom*—I stopped him with a punch to the stomach, which caused him to drop the chair in between his legs. I reached for the weapon and brought it up into his crotch and followed the nut-cracking move with a double-arm DDT onto the chair. One, two, kick-out—no crowd reaction. The lack of response was really concerning me. A Russian leg sweep brought his head down backward on the chair for another two-count and another lackluster response. The response was no longer concerning me; it was down-right bothering the hell out of me. What the hell? This wasn't a Posse match. This was "Hell in a Cell" with my career on the line. I knew we were having a hell of a match. So what was wrong?

I took Triple H into the corner and threw the fast stiff forearm that had helped make this entire angle

work. It wasn't as fast or as stiff as it could have been, but by now I was distracted by the crowd. I charged at Hunter, but he sidestepped me and took me down with a drop toehold that brought my head down hard onto the very chair that had already seen action.

It was good for another two-count and another weak response. Triple H clotheslined me over the top rope to the floor, where, fortunately, business, and the reaction as well, was about to pick up.

I went to work on Hunter with what is pretty much standard fare in cage matches—head into the cage, punches—but the intensity was tremendous and the crowd ate it up. A Beale toss into the cage left Hunter down for a while, and as he lay there, I finally got my hands on a chair. The audience "oohed" in anticipation.

With my chair in hand, I climbed the apron. I tried to mount the second turnbuckle that faced Triple H but couldn't gain my footing. I momentarily panicked. Luckily, my second attempt was more successful. I paused to bathe in the warmth of the Hartford fans before going for the chair/elbow. *Wham*—300 pounds dropping from seven feet with a chair is a tremendous force, and the consequences were steep. Hunter told me later that the force nearly knocked him out. It did its damage on me as well, as my face smashed into the chair and I broke my own nose in the process. The agony of the moment was washed away with chants of "Foley, Foley, Foley." The tepid two-count reactions of only minutes ago seemed far, far away.

I stood up slowly and basked in the "Foley" glow, and a realization came upon me: this match could be a classic. With Triple H still down from the effects of the elbow/flying nosebreaker, I planned my next move . . . the stairs. Now, with Hunter hurting, was the time for payback. I hoped the crowd would remember the awesome force of the first stair collision, for I wanted the fans to *need* Hunter to feel that same force. Their reaction as I shouldered the steps let me know they remembered. Hunter stood up slowly and I began my charge, approaching fast and with bad intentions. When I got within a few feet of impact, I threw the stairs with a strength that defied my physique. At the last moment, however, the champion moved to his right and the steel instrument of destruction whizzed mere inches from his head and crashed harmlessly into the mesh of the cell. The crowd, however, reacted with a buzz that grew and grew until it became a legitimate sustained pop. Why? Because the stairs that had crashed into the fence had actually caused the cell to rip. A panel of the mesh was torn. I had access to the outside world.

I milked that reaction for all it was worth. My promise was about to be fulfilled. I would climb the cage after all. As the milking of the reaction went on, I suddenly realized why our two-counts had garnered such weak reactions. Not a soul in the place believed that the match would end inside that cage. Not until we got outside of it, anyway. Now with access suddenly granted, the crowd was on its feet.

Despite the huge pop, I was disappointed. I had hoped that the fence would give the stairs a better fight. Richie Posner had seen to it that the mesh would tear, but I was hoping for a better struggle. I wanted to throw those stairs four or five times. I

wanted the initial fight to get outside to be nearly as intense as my subsequent fight with the champion. I wanted to throw my body at the fence. I wanted that fence to fight me toe-to-toe. Instead, I knocked it out with one punch. I decided to give it one more blow anyway, and with a running start, I put my shoulder into it and dove into the world outside. When I stepped back in to bring my prey outside, I had blood running down my arm. With a handful of hair, I grabbed Hunter and flung him through our newly constructed exit. I climbed through as well. Chants of "Foley" were there to greet me. In a way, it seemed as if the in-ring action had taken place in dull and dreary Kansas. Once outside, everything came alive. We weren't in Kansas anymore, Toto.

I pulled Hunter up onto the table and pile-drove him with my own quick stump-pulling style. The table didn't break, but I didn't panic. Instead, I moved my head slowly toward the cage and slowly looked up. I gave that top of the cage a long and loving look. The partisan Hartford crowd was on its feet and was exploding with enthusiasm in anticipation of a promise to be fulfilled. Slowly I began to climb. I was following my own special yellow brick road and was off to meet the Wizard . . . when the Wicked Witch cut me off. Stephanie grabbed my leg, then pulled it, and eventually hung on to it until I finally let go of the cage.

I stalked the Witch to a great response, and caught Triple H with a punch when he tried to intervene. I then threw timekeeper Marc Yeaton to the floor and reached under his table for a surprise. The sight of a two-by-four wrapped in barbed wire brought the crowd to another level. Adrenaline surged throughout my body as I held it aloft in the air—basking in the cheers of the fans as the blood made its way in tiny rivers from my triceps to my wrist.

Triple H tried to flee into the crowd, but I caught him by the trunks and pulled him back. *Whaamm*— I caught him with the wood. The roar of approval was monstrous.

I had regretted using two separate two-by-fours at the *Royal Rumble*—one wrapped with barbed wire and one wrapped in a different wire with soldering metal taking the place of the barbs. The shots I took to the back and stomach had been done with the legitimate wood, and a shot that Hunter took to the head had involved the other one. Afterward he still had holes in his head and regretted not being hit by the real deal. This time he was.

The Cactus Jack mystique was alive and well in Hartford, Connecticut, on February 27, 2000. The fans weren't looking at a broken-down, sock-puppet-toting loser. They were looking at an indestructible madman. Hunter couldn't stay and fight—he'd be destroyed. He had to flee. Selling the effects of the beating and the image of Cactus, he began climbing the cage to get away.

Okay—this is where suspension of disbelief becomes a necessity. Why would Hunter not simply run around the cage and up the aisle? He'd have had possibly the slowest man in sports-entertainment giving chase. I don't have an answer. Fortunately, the crowd didn't demand one, as they were completely caught up in my pursuit (with two-by-four in hand) of Hunter up the ominous cell.

As I neared the top of the cell, I made something

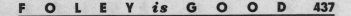

of a tactical error by placing the two-by-four in a spot that allowed Hunter easy access to it . . . and me. He took full advantage of this by raking the wire against my head, which is more or less a mandatory gross-out move for that particular type of weapon. I resisted the urge to look below me at the table where I knew I'd be landing. The memory of my shoulder and head landing in September '98 was running through my mind as Triple H began stomping on my hands. *This is it*, I was thinking, *time to let go. Crash*—the sound of a perfectly broken table was like music to my ears, and I lay on the floor exhausted and hurting, but thankfully not injured.

"Foley" chants filled the Hartford air again as I struggled to my feet. With fire in my eyes, I picked up a metal chair and flung it up on top of the cell. No, I didn't. I tried, but the chair came up short. Damn, I'd cleared it by several feet earlier in the afternoon, but apparently the twenty-plus minutes of intense action had drained the strength from me. Three more times I tried and three more times I failed, each one accompanied by collective groans of disappointment from the crowd. DAMN, I needed a chair up there; its presence was essential to my future cell plans. I began scaling the cage to the delight of the fans while I tried to formulate a Plan B.

As I reached the top, Triple H stood ready with the two-by-four. *Whack*—I took a shot to the back and the crowd reacted with a combination of excitement and sympathy. *Wham*—another one—this time to the stomach. I wished I had the chair, but as I fell to my back, I decided to resort to an old standby—a kick to the nuts.

I took the offensive to the tune of "Foley, Foley" and silently thanked Richie Posner for the reinforcement of the cell as I suplexed Triple H on it and followed this up with a double-arm DDT. The cell match of '98 had seen the mesh rip several times by accident, even before the chokeslam that knocked me unconscious.

With Triple H down, I eyed the two-by-four. The crowd was buzzing. As I picked up the board, the buzzing grew in volume. "Oh no," Jerry "the King" Lawler yelled on commentary, "what could be worse than a two-by-four wrapped in barbed wire?" I had the answer. With a flick of my lighter, the barbed-wire board was set ablaze and the response in the Civic Center was deafening.

It almost didn't happen. When I had picked up the hidden lighter, my hands began shaking. A few attempted flicks yielded no spark, since my hands were simply shaking too badly to control; in fact, I almost dropped the lighter. Luckily, I found the ability to calm my hands, and the blazing two-by-four was alive and well in Connecticut.

Hunter staggered to his feet and was met with a shot to the head that sent him back down. The actual blow was a little weak, but as far as shots to the head using a two-by-four wrapped in barbed wire and set on fire go, I felt it was pretty impressive. Not as impressive as our next move, however.

I placed the burning weapon on top of the cell and signaled for a piledriver. I grabbed Triple H and placed his head between my thighs. The crowd was in a frenzy. I hooked my arms around his waist in preparation for the liftoff. My heart was pounding as the potent cocktail of adrenaline and terror

coursed through my veins. There was going to be a landing, all right, but it wouldn't be Triple H on the two-by-four.

With a quick burst, Hunter lifted me into the air. *Oh no*, I thought, *I'm going over too quickly, I'll never land on my back*. I pushed off his lower back, and as his back body drop was completing, I prayed that the cell would give way as I'd been promised. As I hit the mesh, I felt an entire panel give way and I plummeted toward the canvas, which was a good twelve feet away. *Twoooam*—I hit the ring and a good portion of it collapsed, as, fortunately, a team of experts had been preparing diligently for my landing while Triple H and I had fought on top of the cell. The fall knocked the wind out of me but left me in enough control of my faculties to relish the impressive "holy shit, holy shit" chant that echoed throughout the arena.

For his part, Triple H reacted as if I was dead. He wore a look of shock on his face that continued as he climbed down the hanging mesh panel and into the ring. He kicked at me as if he was checking on the status of fresh roadkill. Suddenly I moved my arm. Hunter was livid. "I don't believe it," J.R. hollered, "the crazy SOB is moving." I was moving, but not so well, as Triple H began putting the boots to me. I got to my knees as the chanting of my name grew louder. Maybe, just maybe, I had a miracle left in me. Hunter hit the pedigree. I was fresh out of miracles. One, two, three.

As was his custom, J.R. provided the perfect words to complete the scene. "This man gave us everything. What more could any of us have asked for. We have just seen the last match of Mick Foley.

At thirty-four years of age, the career of Mick Foley is over."

I needed only to walk up the aisle. A simple twenty yards. It was a long twenty yards and it may have been the saddest walk of my life. The happiest as well. I looked like *Death of a Salesman*'s Willie Loman as I turned my back for the final few yards. Then I turned to look back at not just the crowd, but at fifteen years of memories. My eyes welled up and my face began trembling. The scene was perfect—looking out at my career with a face full of blood, sweat, and tears. Slowly I turned, and just like the heroes of old, I rode off into the sunset.

I felt an immediate sense of joy when I walked through the curtain. Vince wrapped me in a big hug despite my bloodied state and his expensive jacket. Hunter was through next and he hugged me as well. Even Stephanie was up for a hug, even with the knowledge that her dress would be history. Al Snow attempted to hug me, but I just said hi instead.

The first minutes after a big match are a special time. A time to relax and a time to reflect. In some ways, I guess it's like smoking a cigarette after great sex, even though I wouldn't know anything about that. About the smoking, I mean. Also, after sex, paramedics don't come into your room and stitch you up—at least not when it's been done properly.

While the cleansing and stitching process was being completed, I was informed that my father and brother were outside. I spoke for a while with them, remembering when my wrestling dream was in its infancy and the chances of success seemed so slim and far away.

My hotel was directly across the street, and at

$120 a night was a good $40 above my usual limit. What the hell—a guy only retires once, right? So I splurged for the room, had my car valet-parked, called home, where the kids had stayed awake just to say "I love you," and prepared for my fattening celebratory meal and Pay-Per-View movie. Instead, I had a protein drink and fell asleep with a smile on my face for a match and a career well done.

In a business where performers often allow their dignity to be stripped for the sake of a few bucks, I had been able to leave with my head held high. In an industry where competitors refuse to acknowledge their own limitations and hang around past their effectiveness to the point of pity, I had left the World Wrestling Entertainment on top. Not on top of my physical game, but in a blaze of glory that has known few equals. I had walked back through the curtain with blood on my face and tears in my eyes, but with fans on their feet and chants of "Foley" in my ears. (Or at least in one of them.) For the rest of my life, I could look back with pride on my final match.

34: *"Hello, Mick"*

SIXTEEN DAYS LATER I called Jim Ross just to say hello and to find out what plans the World Wrestling Entertainment had for me over *Wrestle-Mania* weekend, which was still several weeks away. I fully expected to remain a vital part of the company, and in fact had suggested myself for an on-air "Commissioner" role several months down the line. In the meantime, there was the World Wrestling Entertainment New York entertainment complex to help out in, paid appearances to make, and public relations to lend a hand in. I fully expected J.R. to tell me about helming the Chef Boyardee booth at World Wrestling Entertainment Axxess, or some other prestigious position.

Instead, he started telling me about the *Wrestle-Mania* main event. Everyone in the company was banking on The Rock vs. Triple H, but apparently Vince had a different idea. "What Vince was thinking of," J. R. began, "was a four-way match with Hunter, The Rock, the Big Show, and . . ." For the life of me I couldn't think of who. Maybe Rikishi. He'd been getting an incredible reaction from the crowd, and a slot in the 'Mania main event could make him a bona fide player for years to come. Or maybe Benoit, who had all the necessary tools except big-time interview skills (which he has since improved greatly). Or maybe Test. Or maybe I've taken too many shots to the head. As Dustin Hoffman might have said in *Rain Man*, had he watched the World Wrestling Entertainment instead of Judge Wapner, "Not Test, definitely not Test." Who then? Or as legendary one-hit Australian wonders Men at Work once sang, "Who Can It Be Now?" J.R.'s next two words answered that question, but opened up the door for many more: "Mick Foley."

Mick Foley? He couldn't wrestle. He was the guy who'd just retired. With dignity—on top—in a blaze of glory. Besides, he'd pretty much spent the last sixteen days helping rid the world of pork ribs, one barbecued rack at a time. I didn't know what to say, so I just reached for the obvious. "J.R., I just retired." "I know, Mick, but Vince has got an idea to bring you back for one last match. Give him a call."

Generally speaking, a wrestler considers finding out he's just been picked to be in the main event at *WrestleMania* to be good news. Good? Hell, it's the best news possible. It would be like answering your door to find Ed McMahon standing there with a six-foot check in his hands. It would be like stumbling upon a bottle on a beach and finding out Barbara Eden lived in there. For me, however, main-eventing at 'Mania sounded like a disaster, a disaster that would turn me into a . . . prostitute.

I called Vince and tried to convince him of the error of his ways. Vince can be a little stubborn. As far as *WrestleMania* was concerned, Vince usually knew his way and committed very few errors. By the time I hung up the phone, I was convinced of the greatness of Vince's idea. About five seconds later doubts began popping up like a teenage boy with a 1978 *Sports Illustrated* Swimsuit Issue.

I had two major issues working against me. First, Vince was convinced that this was the way to go. I had tried to remind him of the previous years' "it's got to be a one-on-one matchup at *WrestleMania*" mentality, but he was ready with a comeback. "Mick, just because that's the way it's always been doesn't mean it's the way it always has to be." Wow. Wasn't that another Nietzsche quote? I was ready with another one. "Vince, I was pretty strong in my interview about never coming back. Don't you think that there will be a backlash against me?" His answer both made sense and boosted my self-esteem. "Mick, the fans love you. They never wanted you to leave. They will love to have you back." He was right about that. They love me . . . they really love me.

The other major issue was my own words. In building up the *Rumble* and *No Way Out* matches, I had spoken fervently about my desire to main-event at *WrestleMania*. Sure, the honor would have been nice and the payoff even nicer, but in reality, I knew it was not going to happen. I will admit to being crushed at not headlining '*Mania* in '99, but that was because it had already been in my hands and was then snatched away. This year's '*Mania* was never mine to hold, so I never became attached to it. All of my talk about "living out my dream" had been done in order to put more heat on Hunter when he ended my career.

I don't want to downplay the importance of

WrestleMania as the premier showcase in sports-entertainment. But neither do I want to downplay how satisfied I was with the way things turned out for me at *No Way Out*. I had never let the magnitude of a show dictate its importance to me and I didn't want to start now. Which is why I was more pumped for an ECW Arena show in front of 1,000 lunatics in 1995 than I was at a Tokyo Dome show in front of 64,000 one week earlier.

In my conversation with Vince, I had raised several objections, but I had never once flat out said no. If I had told him flat out that I didn't really care about the show, I believe it would have hurt his feelings. *WrestleMania* was his baby, which he had fathered back in 1985, and to tell him the show wasn't important to me would have been like telling him his kid was ugly. I just couldn't bring myself to do it.

As the next few days went by, I began suffering from the tag-team attack of "conscience" and "prostitute." My conscience kept telling me that I was a fraud, and my memory was running "prostitute" through my mind as if it was Charlie Sheen's living room. In a hotel room in New York, with the thought of the match making an afternoon nap impossible, I decided on another approach. I'd talk to Hunter, and if necessary, I'd talk to The Rock. *WrestleMania* was almost like their birthright—surely, they would hate me being in it.

Triple H was oddly accepting of the situation. Vince and his damn logical philosophies had brainwashed him. Something about how 'Mania was like our Super Bowl, except the football players didn't have TV the next day and a Pay-Per-View a month later to think about. Vince could hold off Hunter and The Rock for another month (which in hindsight was a brilliant move, as that next Pay-Per-View event did huge numbers). "Sure, I'd like to have the match for myself," Hunter said, "but I'm fine with the four-way." I decided to call Vince for one last plea.

I called the McMahon home and Linda told me that Vince was talking to The Rock and would call me back at my hotel. Yes! The Rock had a good sense for business; surely he would straighten out Vince's monkey ass. The hotel phone rang minutes later. I sprang out of bed like a kid on Christmas morning and picked it up. "Hey, Vince, what did The Rock say?" His answer was not quite what I had expected. "He loved it!" I sat in silence for a moment, with the handset to my ear, hoping to hear that familiar Vince deep-voiced "huh-huh" laugh, followed by an assurance that The Rock had talked him back to his senses. It never came.

Vince then ran off a long list of respected people who loved it as well, and with each passing "Patterson" or "Brisco" I could see my chances slipping away like the sands in the Wicked Witch of the West's hourglass. You know the one that lets Dorothy know how much time she has left to live. Dewey was three the first time he saw *The Wizard of Oz*. It was the first full-length movie that he ever saw in its entirety, and the viewing was a major event in our family's history. He asked me what the hourglass was for, and when I told him, he came out with a pretty good question. "Daddy, why doesn't she just turn it upside down?" I didn't have an answer for him. And I was out of questions for Vince. I was in the match.

Since my "retirement" at *No Way Out*, the fans I had met had asked several questions of me. Actually, it was the same question over and over. "When are you coming back?" When I replied that I was retired, they would look at me like I was crazy. "I know that, but when are you coming back?"

No one had believed that I was actually retiring—except me. My colleagues before me had killed off the retirement match the same way Teddy Long and Paul Ellering had killed off the "hair vs. hair" match ten years earlier in WCW. "Hair vs. hair" is a match where one guy is bald and the other has a crew cut. This nonbelief factor had weighed heavily on my mind before finally giving in. Since there was no "real" retirement in wrestling, I would in fact have been breaching my contract by refusing to do a match.

As I write this now, it seems ridiculous to think that the World Wrestling Entertainment would have enforced that issue of my contract. It's a slap to Vince McMahon's face to insinuate that they would have kept the money that I had coming to me. But when I thought of the money I was owed, money I had already earned, I became worried to the point of paranoia. I had a hell of a lot to lose.

The *Royal Rumble* and the *No Way Out* Pay-Per-View payoffs stood to be the biggest ones by far of my career. At the time of this *'Mania* madness, I had yet to be paid for either. *Have a Nice Day!* had at that time been on the *New York Times* list for twenty-one weeks and was still hanging in there. I stood to make more in royalties than I'd made in my first twelve years in wrestling combined. But I had yet to see a single penny. The fruits of all my fifteen years of labor were just waiting to be harvested. As a husband and a father, I just could not take a chance—any chance—on letting my harvest freeze.

In a paranoid worst-case scenario, I actually envisioned my breach-of-contract case going to court. "Your Honor," I would say, "I gave my word to the fans that I would retire if I lost at *No Way Out*." The judge would think it over for about a half a second before making his ruling. "Retirement? That was just a wrestling angle. Get your ass back in the ring."

I returned to the World Wrestling Entertainment on March 20 in Chicago on *Raw* to the loudest reaction of my career. In an interview on the following evening's *SmackDown!* I got a sustained standing ovation simply for mentioning my new haircut. In truth, the fans didn't hold my words against me because they had never believed them in the first place. But in one way, I certainly had proved to be a man of my word. I swore I wouldn't be like those other guys who "prostitute" their name only to come back six weeks later. And I hadn't. I came back three weeks later.

I did suffer a major backlash from a minority of the audience who felt what I did bordered on blasphemy. The criticism hurt. Partially because I agreed with them and partially because they were the same type of fans who had believed in me when nobody knew who I was. It bothered the heck out of me until I thought about the proverbial shoe being on the proverbial other foot. I was catching a lot of flak for making a decision that had been very difficult, but I finally saw the truth. Vince McMahon was a very difficult man to say no to. The guys criticizing me the most wouldn't have been able to say no to Vince McMahon if he asked them to mow his lawn, let alone main-event the biggest show in the history of sports-entertainment.

Come on, guys (and you know who you are), admit it. If you received a call that began, "Hello, pal, this is Vince McMahon, and I'd like you to cut my lawn today," you'd be overjoyed. You wouldn't tell him to kiss your ass. You wouldn't tell him that your wedding was that day. You wouldn't tell him you had Yankee tickets. You would run to your car and would be pulling the cord on the mower in Greenwich, Connecticut, with a smile like Bob Holly giving Al Snow the Penis Suplex.

So I did the match. And to tell you the truth, it wasn't too bad. In fact, the match went pretty well. Sure, I was once again over 300 pounds and hadn't hit the gym since *No Way Out*, but I did okay. I even brought the family with me as a way to correct my mistakes of fourteen months earlier at the '99 *Royal Rumble*. This time we would do Disneyland the right way—after the show. In fact, it was the Disney visit that was on my mind when I came up a good three feet short on an attempted elbow from the second turnbuckle to the table, which nearly crushed my sternum. *Oh no*, I was thinking as I lay in a fetal position clutching my midsection. *I don't think I'm going to make it to Disneyland.*

Oh, don't worry, I made it. Even after a sleepless night spent with a bag of ice dripping down both sides of my body, "superdad" somehow managed to find the strength to ride Splash Mountain, the will to board Pirates of the Caribbean, and the testicular fortitude to conquer Indiana Jones. We had a won-

derful time. But in the end, it wasn't a ride that I recall most fondly. It was Mickey Mouse.

I really don't quite understand how Mickey Mouse got over so big with the public, with his ridiculously high voice and his ultranerdy persona. But I'll tell you, there is something special about meeting Mickey. I actually get nervous when it's my turn to pose with the Mouse, and a Foley family portrait with Mickey in the middle rests on a special place on our mantel.

A Disney employee once told me a heartwarming tale of a dying young boy whose last wish was to see Mickey Mouse. Sadly, the boy took a turn for the worse while at the Magic Kingdom and an ambulance was required to rush him away. Mickey climbed in and held the boy's hand en route to the hospital—a destination that the child never reached alive. He died with his hand in Mickey's and a beautiful smile on his peaceful face. His parents, I was told, had cried tears of joy knowing that their child's last moments on earth were also his happiest.

When I heard this story, I looked back at my wimp of a wife, who had tears streaming down her face. Her tough-guy, hardcore-legend husband, on the other hand, was able to turn his head to face the window before anyone spotted tears of his own.

Mickey Mouse is far from perfect, however, as I found out firsthand on a Disney Cruise in 1999 as part of the World Wrestling Entertainment's "Wrestlevessel." The cruise itself was great—my parents came with us, Disney's own Castaway Cay was gorgeous, and Colette and I were able to spend quality time together while Dewey and Noelle played at the Kids Club.

On our way back from lunch one day, we happened to pass by a room that was holding a "vegetable car" rally. What the heck—it sounded interesting, so we headed in to see families working vigorously on making small cars out of carrots, cucumbers, celery, and other vegetables that I routinely pass by on my way to the dessert bar. Some of these vehicles looked mighty impressive, as Mom and Dad had been carving away for the better part of half an hour. "Can we play too?" I asked the game's supervisor. "Sure," she said, "but you only have five minutes left." Quickly I went to work with knife and vegetables, and after working diligently until bell time, I held in my hands a car that my kids were embarrassed to be around. "Daddy, that's a yucky car," Noelle helpfully informed me. Indeed it

was. It was like the Edsel of vegetable cars, and in its first and only heat, it fell off the downhill track and landed unceremoniously on the ship's floor. We were out of the running of what was officially known as the Mickey 200.

Mickey Mouse himself was brought in to hand out the prize for the winning car. After this was done, we were informed by the master of vegetable-car ceremonies that Mickey would be handing out an additional award for "best-looking" car. Well, that excluded us and our vehicle, which pretty much looked like a potato with four slices of cucumber attached to it. Someone special saw things a little differently, however, and after conducting a careful inspection of all the lovingly constructed cars and one Edsel, Mickey gave the nod to the Edsel. I was happy for the children, who for the rest of the cruise wore their medal as if it were Kurt Angle's Olympic gold, but deep inside, I felt a little sad over what may have been the greatest medal travesty since the U.S. basketball team lost to the U.S.S.R. in the '72 Olympics. On our way back to our room, I confessed my secret fear to my wife. "Colette, I think Mickey Mouse cheated."

I happened across that Mickey 200 medal just days ago and asked Dewey if he remembered what he'd won it for. His answer was pretty insightful and definitely accurate. "Because Mickey Mouse knew who you were."

I was exhausted by the time Disneyland was set to close on April 4. We had been at the park for two straight days and had just about seen and done it all. My children had enjoyed themselves immensely on the rides and had their autograph books nearly filled with the Disney characters they had met. They had all the top stars in there—Pluto, Goofy, Donald, Minnie, Pinocchio, Captain Hook, and others too numerous to mention. The brightest star of all, however, was conspicuous by his absence. Mickey was not in the book.

A park employee had arranged for our family to be picked up by a van in the backstage area so as to avoid being bothered by fans. I sat on a bench with my arms around Dewey and Noelle, both of their weary heads resting on my shoulders. Suddenly, from around the corner, I saw him. Mickey! Except it wasn't a him, it was a her, with a huge Mickey mask held under her arm like a tiny football player returning from a grueling practice. She saw us too, and throwing all caution to the wind, she literally dove behind a parked car so as to avoid detection.

I felt terrible. Because of me, this tiny person had thrown herself on the concrete and was now lying behind a beaten-up LeSabre so that my kids wouldn't find out that Mickey wasn't really a mouse after all. The commotion aroused my kids, who had begun to doze, and Noelle asked why Mickey had been walking "with a helmet under his arm." Man, this was all my fault. I decided to check on Mickey.

Physically, she appeared to be fine, even after her brave car dive, but she was emotionally devastated. She was shaking with fear as she asked "if the little ones had seen me?" "No," I lied, "don't worry, I think they were sleeping." Then my thoughts turned selfish. "I'll pay you if you take a picture with my children." A tiny smile appeared on her delicate frightened face. "You don't have to pay me," she said with a shy smile. "Just give me a minute to get my costume on." I walked out from behind the car to see that my children were wide-awake. In truth, I think that the girl needed about five seconds to put the mask on and another fifty-five seconds to regain her composure. When she emerged from behind that car, however, she was no longer a frightened girl, she *was* Mickey, and with her white gloves waving and her huge mouse ears twitching, she spoke volumes to my children without ever saying a word.

Epilogue: February 2001

MORE THAN TEN MONTHS have passed since Mickey Mouse dove for cover in the Disneyland parking lot. A lot of things have changed since then.

"Stone Cold" Steve Austin is back from his injury and is better than ever. The Godfather is now the Goodfather and has renounced his pimping ways. Val Venis is no longer a porn star, either. He too has renounced his ways. And little Joe C. passed away from celiac disease at the age of twenty-four. Joe had an awful lot of friends in the World Wrestling Entertainment, and I miss hearing his raspy little foul mouth, but I smile when I think of him because he got so much out of a life that he knew all along would be a short one. He hung around longer than his doctors thought and managed to become both a rock star and a wrestling personality before his little body gave out on him.

I've started talking to Droz, and feel a lot better for having done so. I even called him up for a quote for this book. There are still a few people I need to get in touch with and am hoping to do so soon.

A lot of people have wondered about my relationship with The Rock, and with good cause, since comments I made about him in *Beyond the Mat* certainly revealed emotional wounds that didn't appear to have healed.

Well, The Rock and I did what we should have done a long time ago—we talked about it. He couldn't quite explain his actions of January 1999 in Anaheim, and I couldn't quite explain why I chose to hold on to my feelings for two years instead of letting them out in a mature manner. Actually, I think I can explain it. I was simply holding on to some hatred for a promo that never happened. Both of us were wrong, but I think maybe I was more wrong. The Rock made a mistake and apologized as soon as he was informed of it. I may have been the victim, but allowing my bitterness to fester for two years was just plain stupid. And make no mistake about it, I was bitter. Even stupider was my logic for holding it all in: I figured that with all of that anger built up I could cut a hell of a promo with him when the time was right.

My kids are doing fine. Noelle is big on leaving notes that tell me and Colette how much she loves us. And Dewey . . . well, I don't know how to say this, but Dewey doesn't really like wrestling anymore. I had always said that I would never push the little guy into sports (real ones), and as it turns out, he didn't need pushing. He just dove right into them, and now no sport or team is safe from his viewing eyes. Brazilian soccer? Watches it. Baseball, football, hockey? Yeah, he loves it all. But basketball seems to be his passion.

A typical day last week saw him play a basketball video game, go outside to shoot baskets, go to a college game with my dad (who has become Dewey's best friend), and came home to watch the Knicks win over the Dallas Mavericks in double OT. He was then considerate enough to wake up his mom to tell her the good news. Which is really nice of him, except that Colette doesn't care at all about basketball, and at this point she really needs all the sleep she can get.

Why? Because in January 2001, the Foley family proudly welcomed Michael Francis Foley Jr. (little Mickey) into the world. For those doing the math, you might deduce that our tremendous Christmas efforts were for naught, but fortunately another herculean attempt (or attempts) in April did the trick! As fate would have it, ovulation coincided with Easter, which coincided with my family visiting, which brought forth a whole new set of completely transparent reasons to retreat to the bedroom. A bedroom in which, I'm proud to say, no pornos were shown, no lingerie was worn, and bad language was kept to a minimum. Which is good, because I've got this strange theory about children who are conceived from lusting, rather than loving, sperm.

I also altered my look just a little following April's *WrestleMania*. Now, this is a tricky subject and I don't want to seem ungrateful to my fans, but damn, all the attention can be a little overwhelming at times. So in June 2000, I decided to become unrecognizable. I celebrated my thirty-fifth birthday at Hershey Park, where, following an advertised appearance that I had traded out for free room and rides, I retreated to my hotel room with a hair clipper. When I exited the room, I was bald. Completely incognito. Unrecognizable. I walked into the lobby of the Hotel Hershey as a new man . . . for about eleven seconds, when I heard the words, "Are you enjoying your stay, Mr. Foley?"

A week later I was flown to World Wrestling Entertainment headquarters, where I was offered the role of World Wrestling Entertainment Commissioner. And so, when I came through the curtain on June 26, 2000, in Worcester, Massachusetts, to the biggest ovation of my career, it was as the new, bald Mick Foley. A Mick Foley whose drastic haircut had made him more recognizable than ever.

I loved the Commissioner role. Not only was it easy and fun, but in many ways it may have been my most important role to date. The company showed great faith in me by allowing me to be a central part of story lines, counting on me to help build other wrestlers' characters and letting me do it while raising the levels of innocent buffoonery in professional wrestling to new highs.

I made a conscious effort when I came back as the Commish to put a happy face on the World Wrestling Entertainment. I will always be proud of my hardcore reputation, but the passage of time has allowed me to be equally proud of my kinder, gentler, goofier side. The side that inspired Triple H to declare me "a human Muppet." I actually visualized a conversation taking place among wrestling fans that spurred me on to be the most ludicrous, nerdy, nincompoopish performer in the history of sports-entertainment.

"You see that guy out there? He used to be the baddest SOB in wrestling."

"Mick Foley?"

"Yeah. Barbed wire, thumbtacks, you have it, he did it all."

"Mick Foley?"

"Yeah."

"Naah."

"Yeah."

"Naah."

I like to think that conversations like that have already begun to sprout. The world is full of nerds. And I would like to be their role model.

Some of the best times of my career have come as World Wrestling Entertainment Commissioner. Cheap pops? I treasure them. And I would rather put my goofy vignettes with Edge & Christian into a time capsule than my ECW interviews that were so full of anger. I show up when I want (never too late), wear what I want, pretty much say what I want, and usually leave when I want. And in return, am given a bigger audience reaction than my active career ever knew.

I'm proud of my short-lived chemistry with Gerald Brisco that saw us somehow manage to steal verbiage from a Bugs Bunny/Elmer Fudd argument and repeat it verbatim on *Raw*. I'm thrilled to have played some small part in Kurt Angle's rapid ascent to superstardom, and have looked on with great interest as other performers slowly make gains in becoming the Rocks, Stone Colds, and Hunters of the future.

Perhaps most of all, I have enjoyed my talks with Stephanie McMahon, and always look forward to her infectious smile, which makes each day seem just a little nicer. Whenever I get mad at her dad (which is quite often), I think of her and marvel at how, despite his ridiculous workload, Vince McMahon somehow found the time to be a good father along the way.

Sometimes I actually feel sorry for Vince. Business is very personal to Vince, and his best friends are also his business partners, which more or less means Vince doesn't have any real friends at all. His smile and affection for his wrestlers are very much genuine, and I believe that he is genuinely hurt when wrestlers he has nurtured, befriended, and made rich jump ship for the sake of a few more dollars. One of the small comforts in my life is knowing that as a wasted-up, broken-down ex-wrestler, I will probably never have to make a move that would hurt Vince McMahon. Because, after all, as Vince has been kind enough to point out on many occasions, billionaires have feelings too.

Often I get the feeling that Vince is his own worst enemy. I find it ironic that the man who revolutionized sports-entertainment, erased the stigma of fakery surrounding it, and paved the way for an honest book like this one to find acceptance is the one guy in the company who feels compelled to become a wrestling character whenever a camera light turns on.

No wonder he didn't like *Beyond the Mat*—he looks like a jerk in it. If Blaustein's camera wasn't on, there's no way he would make Droz throw up in that garbage can. Vince McMahon is a hell of a guy—probably the most unique man I will ever meet in my life. But Vince would rather show the world "Mr. McMahon," and as a World Wrestling Entertainment stockholder, I wish that would change. Because the business world is scared to death of the "Mr. McMahon" that he allows them to see.

With that being said (and hopefully not edited out), I love the World Wrestling Entertainment and in some weird son-who-can't-get-rid-of-his-dad way, I suppose I have some love for Vince too. Which is why I take such offense at criticisms leveled against the company that I feel are overblown and unfair. As if it's not bad enough that the public perceives our leader as some kind of lunatic, they also have been led to believe that our show is some kind of immoral wasteland.

For a long time I think we may have encouraged this perception in order to come off as rebellious and cool, but as Popeye the Sailor once said, "I stands all I can stands, and I can't stands no more." For crying out loud, I even had a very famous adult film star tell me that she didn't let her son watch our show. Just how bad is our show?

I decided to find out. Please feel free to stop reading this book if you have no desire to read what is essentially a whole other book. A book that hopefully debunks myths and educates with facts. Hopefully, it will be educational and kind of fun as well.

When I was in elementary school, "Bubble Yum" was a hot commodity. Every cool kid chewed it, as well as the dorks who were trying to be cool. One day I heard a rumor: Bubble Yum used spider eggs to soften their gum. Actually everyone heard the rumor. And within days, no one was chewing Bubble Yum anymore. The cool kids weren't chewing it. Neither were the dorks who were trying to be cool. Within weeks, I saw a two-page ad in the *New York Times* that read, "Someone has been telling your children very bad things about a very good gum." Sometimes I feel like I work for that company. Because when it comes to the World Wrestling Entertainment, it is my feeling that "someone is saying very bad things about a very good company." So I feel that it is my duty to stand up in defense of the World Wrestling Entertainment.

In Defense of the World Wrestling Entertainment

THE INDIANA UNIVERSITY STUDY

Although I consider myself a loyal World Wrestling Entertainment employee, I have not always been in agreement with World Wrestling Entertainment decisions concerning content. Sometimes I think the envelope has been pushed too far, and often, when it is, I find it has been done so for no other reason than to prove we can push it. It seems to shine a negative light on the product, and invites harsh criticism with no real upside in return.

I think the language is too often too coarse, and I think that the multitude of huge breasts can sometimes be overwhelming. And I'm really at a loss to explain how "suck it" became a part of the cultural landscape.

Nonetheless, I was a little bit taken aback when the results of an Indiana University study concerning the contents of *Raw* started becoming public knowledge in early 1999. I may not have been in total agreement with all of the World Wrestling Entertainment's ideas, but by no means did I consider it to be a filthy show. On the contrary, I considered *Raw* to be a fun, action-packed show that happened to contain a *little* filth. So when the results came out, they were a bit shocking.

In a year's worth of *Raw* episodes, the study, which was commissioned by *Inside Edition*, revealed:

- 157 instances of wrestlers or audience members giving the finger

- 434 instances of the slogan "suck it" being said by wrestlers or appearing on signs in the audience

- 1,658 instances of wrestlers groping or pointing to their crotches

- 128 instances of simulated sexual activity

- 42 instances of simulated drug use

- 47 references to satanic activity

- 609 instances of wrestlers being hit by objects like garbage cans or nightsticks

Wow! This was a little disheartening, to say the least. I had always felt that wrestling and the World Wrestling Entertainment were a positive influence on families, but I certainly had a hard time arguing with this type of evidence to the contrary.

The media had a field day with these statistics. Everywhere I looked, it seemed that these damning figures were staring me in the face. In addition to scores of television stories and magazine articles, I personally read thirty-seven different newspapers that quoted these statistics. Heavy hitters too, including the *New York Times*, the *New York Post*, the *Chicago Sun-Times*, the *Chicago Tribune*, the *Washington Times*, the *Indianapolis Star*, the *Dallas Morning News*, the *Milwaukee Journal Sentinel*, and *USA Today*, to name just a few.

Yes, it seemed, the World Wrestling Entertainment was a miserable dung heap of sex, vulgarity, and violence. Or was it?

Hey, I had been on just about every show, and while I can vividly recall a plethora of "suck-its," crotch chops, middle fingers and blows of various instruments to the head, I really couldn't recall any simulated drug use and only one simulated sex act. Still, even though I began to doubt the validity of the study, I sat back and did nothing for a while.

In July 2000, I began writing this book, and in reliving the moments from December 1998 through April 2000, I studied slightly over twenty videotapes in order to be as accurate as possible. I kept the Indiana University study results in the back of my mind when viewing my tapes, and I couldn't help but think that the IU results seemed a little extreme.

I spoke at length with Linda McMahon about the

study and asked if she would mind if I conducted a study of my own. She was more than happy to give me her blessing. So, over the course of three days and nights, with the aid of my twenty tapes, a television, a VCR, and a remote control, I carried out my study. I tabulated the results and then multiplied them by 2.5 to yield the equivalent of a full year's worth of results. My findings were somewhat different than those of the IU study:

- 34 instances of wrestlers or audience members giving the finger

- 640 instances of wrestlers grabbing or pointing to their crotches

- 0 instances of simulated sexual activity

- 0 instances of simulated drug use

- 0 instances of satanic activity

- 422 instances of wrestlers being hit by objects like garbage cans or nightsticks

Quite a difference, right? How come? Well, first let me state that I never bothered to count the "suck-it" signs or utterances. Partially because I didn't have the time to count signs in the audience, and partially because I can't justify one "suck it," let alone 434. I really don't believe those words are appropriate in any circumstance, unless of course there is a "please" in front of them. Yeah, I know, there are probably a few people who will read this and say "Well, you said it once or twice, Mick." Yes, I did, but it somehow seemed cute when I did it in December '98.

The lack of middle fingers can be directly attributed to the injury and subsequent departure of "Stone Cold" Steve Austin, who was rather proficient with the gesture. I'm not sure where I stand on the whole finger thing. On one hand, Austin's frequent usage has trivialized a once mighty gesture, and by the same token, turning such an ugly expression into a sign of friendship cannot be seen as altogether bad.

The absence of satanic activity can likewise be directly attributed to the injury and departure of the Undertaker. I wasn't a big fan of that particular angle, but that is probably because I hold the classic Undertaker in such high esteem. You know, the guy with the eerie entrance music, the guy who could make the lights go on and off with a simple gesture of his hands, the guy who used to beat the crap out of me on a regular basis. I missed *that* guy.

Still, in the World Wrestling Entertainment, we are clearly labeling ourselves as "entertainment" and have done so for many years. We play good guys and bad guys, and therefore should have as much right to use the ultimate "bad guy" as any other form of entertainment.

The World Wrestling Entertainment is a strange amalgamation of fact and fiction—in my case mostly fact. I am referred to as "Mick Foley"—my real name—and am accurately portrayed as having a wife and kids. Therefore, there are certain things that I wouldn't feel comfortable doing, such as making references to Satan. The Undertaker, however, doesn't have those constraints, so I therefore have no problem with his satanic portrayal.

I would also like to note that while the IU study looked only at episodes of *Raw*, I incorporated both

Raw and *SmackDown!* into my findings. *Smack-Down!* is a slightly tamer show, but apparently not too much tamer, as the Parents Television Council (or PTC, which I will get into later) voted it as the most offensive broadcast show of the year for 2000. Also, the one year tracked by the IU study (February '98 to January '99) is generally considered to be the highwater mark for controversial World Wrestling Entertainment content.

Still, the differences in the two studies' results were shocking, and I became determined to find out why the discrepancy was so large. I looked further into the IU study and was able to procure the phone number of Dr. Walter Ganz, the man who had headed it. By this point I had vilified Ganz in my mind, and so had no qualms about bombarding his office with phone calls several times a day for many days. (Actually, it was only five calls, but I had already used the word "bombardment," so I went with that theme.)

In truth, I never expected a return call, and was only calling so I could write, "I tried several times to call Dr. Ganz, but he was unavailable for comment." Instead, I received a late-night phone call from the professor, the result of which was eye-opening to say the least.

We actually had a very pleasant, very thorough discussion about the study, and I was very thankful (and remain so) for his time. Especially considering the new light it shed on this World Wrestling Entertainment mystery.

I started out by informing Dr. Ganz that I was in the process of writing a follow-up to my towering *New York Times* number one bestseller *Have a Nice*

Day! This was not surprising, since I begin most of my conversations with words of similar effect. I then informed him that I had conducted my own study, which elicited a surprised "Oh" from Dr. Ganz. I thought that maybe I was onto something, so I asked the professor if he knew of anyone else who had conducted a similar study. To the best of his knowledge, he did not. So right away I had a new statistic: number of journalists, correspondents, editors, and writers who bothered to check out their facts before reporting them: 0.

I then asked Dr. Ganz if he had personally viewed all the hours of the *Raw* episodes in question. He replied that he had not, but that all of the students viewing the tapes had been instructed to meet standardized criteria so as to avoid personal interpretation. Fair enough.

I first shared with Dr. Ganz the disparity between the number of times a wrestler was struck with an object on his study and mine. "Dr. Ganz," I asked, "when adding up the number of times that a wrestler was hit with an object, did you include replays of the blows?"

"Yes, I did," he said.

"Okay, would you have included B-roll footage from a previously recorded show?"

"Yes," he said again, "anytime the World Wrestling Entertainment chose to clearly show one of these shots on the screen we counted it."

As I was writing down his quote, the professor spoke again, this time with a question of his own. "Did you?"

"No, Dr. Ganz, I didn't." I was still finishing his quote, so I didn't elaborate on my answer.

"Why not?" the professor asked.

This time I did elaborate. "Well, Dr. Ganz, if someone told me to look at a tape and count how many home runs Mark McGwire hit last year, I don't think I would include videotaped replays." Unquestionably a good point, and one that brought forth my next question. "How about entrance videos? For example, the reason I don't wrestle anymore is I was hit way too many times in the head and face."

"I'm sorry to hear that," the professor interrupted, and I believe he meant it, too.

"But when I walk down to the ring, I can be seen getting hit in the head with chairs on several occasions. Would you count those too?"

"Once again," Dr. Ganz replied, "if there was a conscious effort made to show it, we included it."

Okay, I could live with that explanation.

Next I wanted to ask about the results of wrestlers grabbing or pointing to their crotches, which is commonly referred to as "crotch chopping." I think that labeling it as grabbing or pointing is a little inaccurate, as a "crotch chop" makes an X with the wrists, so that the fingers actually end up pointing away from the penile instrument. I had recorded 640 of these crotch chops, while Dr. Ganz had compiled a whopping 1,658—that's a lot of chopping! Now, out of 640 chops, 530 were recorded by X-Pac, who seemingly had the market cornered on that particular gesture. Don't get me wrong, I like X-Pac, and I think he's one of the most talented guys in the business, but damn, I was getting tired of seeing him chop around his penis for forty hours. He's prouder of that thing than Kurt

Angle is of his Olympic Gold. Still, I made a weak attempt to cover for him.

"Dr. Ganz, over eighty percent of all pointing to the crotch was done by one wrestler."

"Was his name X-Pac?" Dr. Ganz asked.

"Yes, his name was X-Pac. I noticed that X-Pac tends to point to his crotch in quick bursts of four. Would you count that as four small rude gestures, or just one big one?"

The professor laughed before confirming my suspicions. "That would count as four."

"So I take it you would be counting all of the gestures on their entrance video too."

"Yes, we would."

Well, that cleared that one up in a hurry. The D-Generation X entrance video set an indoor record for most guys pointing in the proximity of their genitals repeatedly in rapid succession. I could easily see where the extra 1,200 chops came in, and frankly was surprised it wasn't a whole lot more.

We then spoke briefly about the satanic references and I shared with him my feelings about the subject and how the absence of the Undertaker could explain the discrepancy. Then a thought entered my head that I hadn't considered before I decided to ask the professor about it. "Dr. Ganz, a wrestler named Gangrel spits a red liquid, that I guess is supposed to look like blood. Would that be considered a satanic reference?"

"Yes," the professor said, "anything dealing with the occult was included in the study."

Now it was on to the subjects that I wondered about the most, sex and drugs. Wait, I'm not sure that came out right—let me try again. Now it was on to the subjects that I wondered about the most as they pertained to Professor Walter Ganz's Indiana University study—sex and drugs. That's better.

This whole "simulated sexual activity" had me baffled. I knew that our shows contained considerable sexual innuendo, several double entendres, and an occasional outright crude remark, but I truly couldn't recall any acts of simulated sex. I shared this feeling with Dr. Ganz. His response was not surprising.

"Well, there was a wrestler named Sexual Chocolate, and he was involved in a situation with a—"

I cut him off. "With a transvestite, right?"

Dr. Ganz concurred. Of all the envelope pushing the World Wrestling Entertainment has done, this one pushed the furthest and offered the least upside. In this scenario, Olympic-weight-lifter-turned-wrestler Mark Henry, who had been nicknamed "Sexual Chocolate" due to his smoothness with the ladies, had a very suggestive erotic session ruined when he reached down and was startled to discover that "Oh sweet Jesus, she has a penis." The World Wrestling Entertainment took a much-deserved critical lambasting for the scene, and in a sense created a snowball effect of harsh criticism from the media that has yet to cease, despite the general toning down of the product.

Even Vince McMahon, who had been a defender of the segment, has come to regret the decision, noting in a recent *Playboy* interview that "there was really no need to go there." Mark Henry's career suffered most of all. A few short weeks earlier Henry had been on the verge of major stardom, but instead found his career on a serious downward spiral, that saw him go from smooth ladies' man, to transvestite

B.J. recipient, to sex addict, to boyfriend of seventy-eight-year-old Mae Young (which was at times actually quite sweet), to also-ran in the Ohio Valley Wrestling league. Hey, if we're going to use a transvestite angle, at least do it with The Rock. Sure, it would be tasteless, but at least it would make money.

I spoke with the professor about the angle, and while admitting my negative feelings about it, told him that I couldn't remember another single episode remotely like it, let alone another 127. So I posed a few questions. "Would a situation where a seventy-eight-year-old woman was lying in a bed, smoking a cigar, presumably after sex, be considered an act of simulated sex?" Dr. Ganz informed me that it would not. "What about giving the impression that a sexual act was going to take place, would that be an act of simulated sex?" Again, the doctor's response was negative. At this point I was legitimately confused. "Well, I'm really at a loss to think of another example," I said.

He tried to clear things up for me, and in a sense he did. "Well, a simulated sex act might be for example, a girl rubbing a man's arm."

RUBBING HIS ARM? "Dr. Ganz," I said with my voice rising steadily higher, the way it does in certain surprising situations, "don't you think that is a little misleading?"

"Why would you say that?" he replied with genuine curiosity in his voice.

"Well, because I think what you've described could more accurately be described as 'simulated flirtation.'" At this point Dr. Ganz started to get a little defensive.

"Well, it would have to be more than just rubbing

an arm, it would have to be done . . . provocatively."

PROVOCATIVELY? What the hell? Dr. Ganz had assured me that all the students' findings would meet standardized criteria, but I now found this hard to believe. After all, a word like "provocative" is open to a great variety of interpretation. Still, I didn't press the professor further because he seemed to get a bit flustered over the whole "simulated sex" example. The last thing I wanted was for Dr. Ganz to hang up on me, especially in light of the discovery I had just stumbled upon. I sensed that there would be another valuable discovery in my immediate future. I was correct.

"Dr. Ganz, I was also unable to find a single episode of simulated drug use, and I wanted to ask you about a few possibilities." Dr. Ganz told me to proceed. "We have one wrestler [X-Pac] who will occasionally put his thumb and forefinger together and pretend to inhale it as if it were a marijuana cigarette. Would that be simulated drug use?"

"No," the professor said, "we wouldn't count that."

"Well, we've got another wrestler [The Godfather] who says, 'Roll a fatty for this pimp daddy.' Would that be considered simulated drug use?"

"No, it would not," Dr. Ganz replied.

Once again I was at a loss to think of a single episode of the alleged moral offense, and once again I asked the professor for clarification. His clarification would actually open the door to a great deal more questions—some of which I'm still trying to answer. Questions about ethics, honesty, responsibility, common sense, and the media's ability to bend a great deal of half-truths into one great big lie.

"That would be beer drinking."

BEER DRINKING? Come on, this had to be a joke, right? Nope.

"Yes," Dr. Ganz said, apparently taking notice of my disbelief, "that would fall under the heading of 'simulated drug and alcohol use.'"

"Now, Dr. Ganz, you can't tell me that you don't consider that figure to be misleading. I mean I have done a great deal of research on this, and I have yet to see one mention of 'simulated alcohol use.'"

Dr. Ganz went into full defensive mode. "Our study was very clear on that," he said. "I can't control what reporters say."

No, I guess he can't, but what he could do was clarify some final questions I had, concerning "simulated drug use" in the World Wrestling Entertainment.

"But you didn't see any simulated use of heroin, did you?" I asked.

"No."

"How about cocaine?"

"No."

"Marijuana?"

"No."

"Or any drugs other than alcohol?"

"None that I can recall."

"Thank you."

The next morning, I called my mother and put her to work. "Mom, for the next week, could you please tape every episode of *General Hospital* and *Cheers* for me?" "Well, I guess so," my mom said without a great deal of enthusiasm, "but why?" My answer perked her up immediately. "I'm doing research on this book I'm writing." Five days later I had the tapes. My mom has always been proud of my

wrestling accomplishments, but she clearly is more impressed with my scholarly endeavors. Her help on this book—especially on these last chapters—has been invaluable.

The IU study had opened up my eyes to the possibility of manipulation and deceit in the media. *Raw* had become the media's whipping boy, but I wondered how other shows would fare when put under a microscope and scrutinized as closely. So with great anticipation, I slid in the *General Hospital* tape.

"Can they really do that at three in the afternoon?" I said to my wife, after witnessing an act that put our World Wrestling Entertainment adventures to shame. Call me old-fashioned, but I was a little shocked to see just how seedy these soap operas were. Suffice to say that if a woman was shown pouring and then licking champagne from my lower back on an episode of *Raw*, we'd be besieged with complaints, not to mention the fact that I personally would have to find a new bed to sleep in.

During the course of five one-hour episodes of *General Hospital*, I was witness to twenty-one acts that would fit comfortably inside Dr. Ganz's definition of "simulated sexual activity." Everything from the aforementioned champagne shenanigans to butt grabbing to passionate kissing. Lots and lots of kissing. Deep kissing. Long kissing. Tongue kissing. You name it, I saw it, and all in a week's worth of programming. All, that is, except for provocative arm rubbing, which I guess remains the sole domain of the World Wrestling Entertainment.

I will now call into play the mathematical skills that yielded me a *D* in Gary Eggers's math class during my junior year of high school. Okay—here goes. According to the Indiana study, a year's worth of *Raw* episodes, which adds up to 100 hours, yielded 128 acts of "simulated sexual activity." This adds up to 1.28 acts per hour.

General Hospital yielded twenty-one acts in five hours, for an average of 4.2 acts per hour. Which means that *General Hospital*, a program broadcast over public airwaves at 3 P.M., was over three times trashier than *Raw*, which is a cable television program that airs between 9 and 11 P.M.

Next up was *Cheers*, one of my all-time favorite shows, but one that seemed to lend itself to instances of "simulated drug use," or "beer drinking," as it is more commonly known. In judging the content, I adhered to the same considerations that Dr. Ganz had expressed to me concerning the frequency of wrestlers being hit by objects; "anytime a cocktail was clearly seen being ingested," I counted it.

The results were not all that surprising and more or less supported the thesis that I had developed when I asked my mom to tape the programs. Sixty-nine examples of beer drinking, or "simulated drug use," in two and a half hours of programming for an average of 27.6 *examples per hour*.

Let's compare that to the World Wrestling Entertainment, whose forty-two instances in 100 hours yield a disgusting, immoral *.42* examples per hour. So, the rate of "simulated drug use" on *Cheers* is roughly *sixty times* higher than that of the evil and much-maligned *Raw. SIXTY TIMES.*

Now, some people out there might think that the relatively short test period of one week that I viewed these programs would not be representative of these shows as a whole. To them I say, "Fire up your VCRs and see for yourself." Just make sure to interpret the evidence using the same criteria.

Man, I felt like a scientist, and I loved it. I wanted more. What about satanic activity? Yeah, let's see how the rest of the entertainment industry stacked up to the World Wrestling Entertainment. In beginning my study, I went back to Dr. Ganz's definition of "satanic activity" as being "anything dealing with the occult." I then consulted my *Webster's* dictionary and looked up "occult," where it was defined as "of or relating to or dealing with supernatural influences, agencies, or phenomena." This certainly left the door open to interpretation, and I decided to interpret very liberally as I opened up to the letter *D* in Leonard Maltin's *2000 Movie and Video Guide*, one of the most thorough review books in its field.

Now, I'd be lying if I said I randomly picked the letter *D*, because in truth I made that letter my choice for the words "devil," "demon," and "Dracula" that would fall within its domain. *D* didn't let me down; indeed it brought forth 187 movies that fit the Indiana definition of "anything dealing with the occult." The letter *D* took up eighty-five pages of Maltin's massive 1,600-page tome. I mean, compared to Leonard, Roger Ebert's book looks like *Tuesdays with Morrie*. Using my newly honed math skills, I figured that the entire Maltin book could conceivably contain over 3,000 movies that dealt with the occult. All of a sudden our forty-seven instances for an average of .47 examples of satanic references per hour didn't look so bad.

What about violence? Certainly, Dr. Ganz's discovery of 609 instances of wrestlers being struck by garbage cans and other objects seems very violent. Yeah, it does, with "seems" being the key word there. I wasn't able to itemize Dr. Ganz's incidents of violence, so I instead chose to go with my list of 169 (which was multiplied by 2.5 to give a fifty-week total of 422), which can be itemized as follows:

1. chair—48

2. garbage can or cookie sheet—34

3. title belt—19

4. kendo stick—17

5. mannequin head—11

6. brass knuckles—7

7. broomstick—4

8. table piece—3

9. stairs—11

10. timekeeper's bell—4

11. shovel—2

12. road sign—2

13. acoustic guitar—4

14. coffeemaker—1

15. pipe—1

16. sledgehammer—1

17. turnbuckle—1

As part of my research I went to the video store, where I picked out the PG-rated family favorite *Home Alone* and took inventory of the violence that transpired therein. The results were impressive:

1. shot from one-foot range with pellet gun to testicles

2. shot from one-foot range from pellet gun to head

3. four-foot fall from slip on ice to concrete

4. fall down icy flight of stairs

5. fall on back of head after slip on ice

6. steam iron falling fifteen feet onto victim's face

7. hand on red-hot doorknob

8. nail in foot, followed by a six-foot fall backward onto concrete

9. blowtorch sets head on fire for seven seconds

10. slip on concrete

11. step with bare feet on glass

12. two slips on toys and fall backward on concrete

13. two swinging paint cans, making direct contact with human face after fifteen-foot swing

14. tarantula bite

15. blow to ribs with crowbar

16. fifteen-foot swing directly into brick wall

17. two blows with a snow shovel to the head

While traveling with the World Wrestling Entertainment, I consulted Dr. Robert Quarrels, who is a board-certified family practitioner, with an emphasis on sports medicine. I asked Dr. Quarrels to look at the separate lists of violent acts and to offer his expert explanation of the expected consequences of such acts.

First the wrestling:

1. chair—possible concussion, laceration, contusion

2. garbage can or cookie sheet—possible laceration and contusion

3. title belt—contusion, possible laceration, possible concussion

4. kendo stick—contusion, possible laceration

5. mannequin head—too ridiculous to warrant a medical opinion

I think you get the idea. With the exception of the sledgehammer shot, which was to the knee, and the brass knuckles, which were only used in one match, we're basically talking about cuts, bruises, and possible concussions. Now let's look at the movie.

Home Alone:

1. pellet to testicles—penetrate scrotum, severe contusion of testicle, and could disrupt small vessels that conduct seminal fluids. May result in complete dysfunction of testicle.

2. pellet to head—severe contusion, no probable penetration

3. four-foot fall from slip on ice—concussion, possible vertebral fractures at various levels, bulging or herniated discs. Subdural hematoma, or other forms of cerebral hemorrhage. Possible broken hip or pelvis.

4. fall down stairs—concussion, intracranial bleeding, possible lower external fracture, vertebral fracture, hip fracture

5. fall on head following slip on ice—see #3

6. iron on face—skull fractures, blow-out fracture of orbit, facial nerve disruption, concussion, intracranial bleeds

7. hand on red-hot doorknob—severe second-degree burns

8. nail in foot—puncture wound could disrupt vessels in foot, exposure to tetanus, severe soft-tissue infection

9. blowtorch—third-degree burns, tissue loses all function

10. slip on concrete—see #3

11. bare feet on glass—multiple puncture wounds, risk of tetanus and infection

12. two slips on toys—see #3

13. swinging paint cans—blow-out fracture of orbit, facial fractures, dental fractures, disruption of nasal cartilage, concussion, intracranial bleeding

14. tarantula bite—possible T-toxin infection, possible neurotoxicity

15. crowbar to ribs—rib fracture, possible lung puncture and deflation due to broken rib, possible ruptured spleen

16. swing into wall—multiple fractures

17. snow shovel to head—concussion, laceration, possible skull fracture

I was so impressed with my *Home Alone* results that I decided to investigate the sequel, *Home Alone 2*. I could feel for the director while I watched this one. In some ways, I'm sure he felt the pressure to top the first one, much as I have felt the pressure to top some of the big matches of my past. Here's how they topped it:

1. four bricks to the head, from a height of four stories

2. staple gun to buttocks

3. ten-foot fall backward onto concrete

4. twenty-foot fall face-first onto concrete

5. sixteen-second electrocution

6. blowtorch sets hair on fire for seventeen seconds

7. hundred-pound sandbag drops on head from twenty feet

8. steel object swinging ten feet into faces of two men, followed by simultaneous twenty-five-foot falls onto concrete. Steel object then drops twenty-five feet on top of them.

9. heavy tool cart goes down flight of stairs and sandwiches men into wall

10. two simultaneous thirty-foot falls off a rope onto concrete

I then spoke with Dr. Quarrels about the fate of the two victims. Things were not looking too good for them. Let's take a look.

1. bricks to head—death, skull fracture, intracranial bleeding

2. staple gun to buttocks—puncture wounds

3. ten-foot fall onto concrete—impact fracture where skull caves in, various vertebral fractures, herniated discs, soft-tissue injury, lacerations, contusions, organ contusions

4. twenty-foot face-first fall on concrete—death. High likelihood of multiple skeletal extremity fractures, organ contusions, and possible rup-

tures, intra-abdominal bleeds, cranial injuries and bleeds

5. sixteen-second electrocution—cardiac arrest, possible death

6. blowtorch to head—flames would engulf head, definite third-degree burns, skin meltdown

7. hundred-pound sandbag—skull fracture, vertebral fracture, intracranial bleeds, paralysis, death

8. steel object to face followed by twenty-five-foot fall onto concrete—blow-out fractures of orbit, dental fractures, intracranial bleeds

9. tool cart—possible death, rib fractures, pneumothorax, organ puncture

10. thirty-foot falls—see #1, followed by contusions, facial fractures, broken bones

Pretty devastating stuff, huh? It kind of makes you wonder why Joe Pesci and Daniel Stern, the victims of all this deadly abuse, aren't kicking ass and taking names in the World Wrestling Entertainment. After all, they withstood all of that abuse and were still on their feet at each movie's end. For crying out loud, guys, would you sell the moves a little bit? Even Al Snow would have stayed down after a thirty-foot fall.

I know some of these examples are ridiculous. They're meant to be. But are they really any more ridiculous than the misleading interpretations of Dr. Ganz's study? I don't think so.

Unfortunately, there is a major difference between our two studies. Mine was meant to be fun (with the exception of *General Hospital*, which I really did find shocking), whereas the Indiana University study was accepted as hard facts by a media either too apathetic or too reckless to seek the truth. And in some ways, our (World Wrestling Entertainment) survival, or at least our prosperity, depends on the public being able to differentiate facts from smears and truths from half-truths. For the truth is out there, and like I told you earlier, it's not as bad as we've been led to believe.

I do feel a little sad for Dr. Ganz. After all, he dedicated a great deal of time and energy to this project, while a much easier alternative was so close at hand. I mean, if the professor had really wanted to study vulgar language, obscene gestures, and inappropriate behavior, he could have simply walked down to Assembly Hall, where Indiana coach Bobby Knight (who was still very much employed by the university at the time of the study) would have put the World Wrestling Entertainment's collection of middle-finger givers, crotch choppers, "suck-it" sayers, simulated drug users, simulated sex receivers, and garbage-can hitters all to shame.

THE PTC

I was in Albany, New York, in late 1999 when a pre-taped interview was suddenly halted. "Wait," the producer of the segment said, "let's do it again; there's a Coke machine in the background." So I did the interview and proceeded with the day. On the following afternoon, I noticed our usual supply of Cokes and Diet Cokes had been replaced with Pepsi. It didn't seem like the biggest of deals, but a Tuesday afternoon of *SmackDown!* preparation can be quite a drag, so I decided to do a little investigation. "Hey, what's the deal with all the Pepsis?" I asked one of our cameramen. "Coke pulled their sponsorship," he replied. "Some group has been complaining about our show." The answer was surprising, but not too much so, as the World Wrestling Entertainment periodically experiences sponsor changes, which are considered a normal part of doing business. Besides, Pepsi had been there to snap up the commercial spots, business had never been better, and there seemed to be no end in sight for the World Wrestling Entertainment's fortunes.

Sponsors, however, began departing in greater frequency, including the much-publicized June 2000 withdrawal of MCI WorldCom, which had been a mainstay since *SmackDown!*'s inception. Ten weeks after my April 2, 2000, retirement match, I returned to wrestling as the new World Wrestling Entertainment Commissioner. There was, I sensed, a genuine concern in the air.

A group called the PTC (Parents Television Council), a self-described "conservative media watchdog organization," was taking credit for these withdrawals. The PTC was headed by a man named L. Brent Bozell III, and used veteran entertainer Steve Allen as their honorary national chairperson. The PTC had deemed *SmackDown!* "the sleaziest show on broadcast TV."[1] The PTC had limited its wrath to broadcast television "because broadcasters, which use public airwaves to transmit programs, must be licensed by the federal government,[2] although Bozell has since inexplicably talked of looking into cable as well.

In addition, the PTC was blaming the World

Wrestling Entertainment for the deaths of four children. "Four children have been killed by peers who are emulating wrestling moves they learned by watching programs such as *World Wrestling Entertainment SmackDown!*," said Steve Allen at the MCI WorldCom shareholders' meeting on June 1, 2000.[3] Despite the fact that three of the incidents seemed to point to poor adult supervision, and three of the deaths occurring before *SmackDown!* even premiered (with the fourth death occurring only two days after the show's debut), the accusation seemed to feed the growing paranoia that was becoming prevalent among our sponsors.

Following my analysis of the Indiana University study of 1999, I had reason to doubt the veracity of the PTC's own study, which had found that "*SmackDown!* alone was responsible for more than 11 percent of the sex, cursing and violence in the 1999 study." At that point, with the memory of IU professor Walter Ganz's willingness to cooperate still fresh in my mind, I attempted to contact the PTC to discuss their study. My calls were not returned.

I found the accusations of the PTC study hard to fathom. Unlike the IU study, which had been done at a time when the World Wrestling Entertainment content was at its most risqué, the 2000 version of the World Wrestling Entertainment was somewhat toned down, especially *SmackDown!* It was common knowledge among wrestlers that the rougher language and more offensive gestures should be kept from broadcast television. Personally, I found the 2000 product to be fast-paced, exciting, and with the rise of Kurt Angle, the metamorphosis of Edge & Christian, and the return of Mick Foley, often downright nerdy.

You couldn't have guessed that from the actions of the PTC, which were relentless, and especially from the words of its founder, Mr. Bozell, who said, "It is sickening to me being a father of five, four of them boys, to turn on the television and see an arena filled with youngsters . . . swearing at wrestlers, calling for blood and violence while worked into a frenzy."[4] From my vantage point, which I believe was a great deal more accurate and intimate than Mr. Bozell's, I saw some other things that he perhaps wouldn't take note of. Often I would look at the crowd from behind the curtain, and view families laughing together, high-fiving each other, and on several occasions that always made me smile, dads putting an arm around their sons.

Something, somehow, just didn't add up. It was while sharing my Indiana University findings with Linda McMahon that I found out what that something was, although in retrospect, it was just the tip of the iceberg. I was beginning to realize that the PTC wasn't going to volunteer to me any information on their study, so I wanted to be careful about criticizing it or them without proof. Having just come off my six days in court in May, I was in no hurry to be sued again, so I posed my question to Linda very delicately. "Can I legally say that the paranoia concerning our sponsors reminds me of the hysteria that led to McCarthyism in the fifties?" Linda's eyes lit up, and she smiled as she said, "Mick, Brent Bozell's father was a speechwriter for Joe McCarthy."

I know a lot of people find U.S. history boring, but I think that a certain amount of background is essential in learning to understand Senator Joe

McCarthy, McCarthyism, the Big Lie, and how aspects of all of them are very much alive in the strange case of the World Wrestling Entertainment vs. the PTC and L. Brent Bozell III.

First, a couple of definitions that will be helpful to keep in the back of your mind as we chart our course.

McCarthyism: Kenneth C. Davis's *Don't Know Much About History* defines McCarthyism as "a smear campaign of groundless accusations from which the accused cannot escape, because professions of innocence become admissions of guilt and only confessions are accepted."[5]

The Big Lie: Comedian/actor Richard Belzer's definition in "UFOs, JFK and Elvis" is as good as any I've heard, and a lot simpler to remember. "If you tell a lie that's big enough, and you tell it often enough, people will believe you are telling the truth, even when what you are saying is total crap."[6]

JOE MCCARTHY

Joseph McCarthy was a senator from Wisconsin whose career was floundering—until he played on America's anticommunist fears to become one of the most powerful men in the world in the early 1950s. With communism spreading quickly throughout Europe and Asia following the end of World War II, many Americans feared communist infiltration of the United States. McCarthy fanned the flames of this fear in an infamous speech in Wheeling, West Virginia, in which he claimed to have a list of 205 members of the Communist party who were employed in the U.S. State Department.

Over the next four years, McCarthy's baseless

accusations ruined countless lives. He was finally exposed on Edward R. Murrow's nationally broadcast television show *See It Now*, and in 1954 the televised Army–McCarthy hearings gave the public a chance to witness his crude ways and remorseless destruction of decency.

Following the hearings, McCarthy saw his public support slip away and was censured by the Senate, a combination that sent him into a tailspin. It was during this final, pathetic chapter of his life that Brent Bozell entered the picture. McCarthy eventually drank himself to death and died in 1957.

THE BOZELL–MCCARTHY CONNECTION

Brent Bozell II attended Yale in the 1940s, where he became best friends and political allies with William F. Buckley Jr. Buckley would go on to become the United States' best-known conservative political figure all the way through the 1970s. Together, Buckley and Bozell became a formidable debating team, with Bozell standing out as both the better speaker and the brighter student.[7] Indeed, Mr. Bozell's intellect was so impressive that he had won the National American Legion prize as foremost high school orator in the nation in 1943.[8]

In 1954, Bozell and Buckley published *McCarthy and His Enemies*, which was described as "the first book about McCarthy not written by an enemy or by McCarthy himself."[9] The authors seemed to summarize their feelings on McCarthyism, and their acceptance of his unfair tactics, with the telling sentence, "Justice, we are saying, is not the major objective here."[10]

In the book, the two authors do question

McCarthy's methods but continually excuse these methods and even agreed to "rewrite" several passages that the senator thought were "too stridently" anti-McCarthy.[11]

McCarthy took a liking to Bozell, and brought him aboard his staff following the disastrous Army–McCarthy hearings. At the same time Bozell and Buckley formed the conservative periodical *National Review*. During this time Bozell, by all accounts, wrote tremendous speeches for the censured senator, but unfortunately, they fell on deaf ears, as McCarthy had outlived the public's and the Senate's interest in him.

Following McCarthy's death, Bozell went to work as a speechwriter for Arizona senator Barry Goldwater, who was attempting to bring the conservative movement into the mainstream. He even ghostwrote *Conscience of a Conservative* for Goldwater, which was a bestseller in 1960.[12] According to one report, Goldwater's confidence was such that he never even read Bozell's work before sending it off to the publisher.

About that time some people began questioning Bozell's conscience and his sanity. "He was my first realization that you could look wonderful and be bright and intelligent, clear-eyed and be totally bananas," recalled John Leonard, who had worked with Bozell on the *National Review*. Bozell, you see, was a strong proponent of a preemptive nuclear strike on Moscow, and didn't seem to care a whole lot about the consequence of that action. Said Leonard, "I just had this sense of a red-haired guy who could wipe out a city without really being able to imagine that there were people in the city."[13]

In 1963, Bozell took his family (including future PTC head Brent, who would have been around eight at the time) to Spain, where he became involved in an ultraconservative movement whose primary goal was restoring the Spanish monarchical succession that had been interrupted in the 1830s. Upon returning, he resigned as senior editor of *National Review* in an attempt to forge an identity distinct from Buckley and *National Review*. Despite Bozell's fine reputation as a writer and orator, it was Buckley who had captured most of the public's attention, a fact that troubled Bozell deeply.[14]

Another reason for the split is that Buckley simply wasn't conservative enough for Bozell.[15] Just how conservative was this Bozell guy? Well, as David M. Oshinsky, the man who wrote *A Conspiracy So Immense*, the definitive book on the life of Joe McCarthy, told me, "Brent Bozell was about as far to the right as you could possibly get."[16]

Following the split with Buckley, Bozell attempted to run for Congress on the Republican ticket in Montgomery County, Maryland, but was crushed by the incumbent in a campaign that "was marked by his (Bozell's) looming eccentricity."[17]

Those eccentricities started coming to the forefront in the following years, first when he tried to form his own political party (which was immediately rejected) and then with the formation of his own right-wing Catholic journal, *Triumph*. In his book, *William F. Buckley Jr.: Patron Saint of the Conservatives*, John Judis wrote of *Triumph* that its "politics became theocratic rather than conservative with Bozell denouncing America and its constitutional tradition of religious tolerance."[18] Buckley himself put it as gently as possible when he wrote, "Brent went further than I would do in pressing the demand of our Church in the secular realm."[19] Apparently so.

Mr. Bozell, you see, had a 1970 arrest and conviction when, while swinging a huge wooden cross, he smashed his way into the Student Health Service at George Washington University, which he claimed was counseling abortions. Young Brent III would have been fifteen at the time of his father's criminal activity. Not to be outdone, however, Brent III's mom was arrested for storming the stage at the Catholic University auditorium and attempting to assault feminist speaker Ti-Grace Atkinson.

Oh, there was more, much more, but I'm not attempting to inflict injury on the Bozell name. I'm merely trying to show that L. Brent Bozell III, the man who claims to stand for traditional family values, didn't exactly have Ozzie and Harriet for a mom and dad and he didn't exactly grow up with the most traditional of family values to learn from.

L. BRENT BOZELL III

I would like to point out that the historians I spoke to about L. Brent Bozell III's dad were adamant in telling me that by all accounts the elder Bozell had never anything but the best intentions.[20] He was a true believer in his cause, and in the Catholic Church. I can respect and even admire that, being a person who has found great comfort in the Catholic Church, at one point even seriously contemplating joining the priesthood. Hey, Brent's brother Michael was enough of a believer to become a Benedictine monk, in which capacity, from the tone of his writings, he seems very happy.[21] Great. Another of Brent's brothers, Chris, was enough of a believer to form his own religious group, Los Hiyas de Tormenta, or Sons of Thunder, which Brent's father was leading when he broke into George Washington University. Not so great. But at least he was a believer.

So based on his family's history, who am I to doubt Mr. Bozell's PTC intentions? Maybe he is a true believer. Maybe he truly believes that he is worth the hundreds of thousands of dollars that he pays himself as the head of his charitable organization. Money that is sent in the form of donations from worried parents who he has urged to "clean up TV now."[22] Maybe he *truly believes* his own bullshit. And there certainly is a lot of that to sift through.

I have never met L. Brent Bozell III, nor have we ever spoken. This was not for a lack of effort, however, as I made over a dozen attempts to interview him. I would have been glad to travel anywhere for a face-to-face visit, but unfortunately, as I mentioned earlier, my calls were never returned.

As a result, much of what I know about Mr. Bozell's PTC has come from reading newspaper quotes, which follow a McCarthy-like pattern of exaggeration, half-truths, and lies. I have not been impressed with the little I have seen of him, which is limited to CNN's post–Republican Party convention coverage and his own *The National Campaign to Clean Up TV Now* videocassette. I am told that he is physically a dead ringer for his father,[23] although unfortunately, the vaunted Bozell oratory skills seem to have bypassed the younger Brent. Indeed, Mr. Bozell seems to be engaged in a neck-and-neck struggle with a small soapdish in my shower for charismatic supremacy . . . and I think the soapdish is winning. Mr. Bozell's pattern of speech is so singsongy, his mannerisms so robotic, and his inflection so void of any real human emotion that I find him downright spooky. Even more frightening is the fact that people actually send this guy money, and that they swallow the crap he feeds them.

Maybe, as I mentioned earlier, Mr. Bozell has our best interests at heart. Then again, his dad had our best interests at heart when he advocated initiating a nuclear war, a war that would have killed millions and devastated the entire world.

Until recently, I never quite realized just how extreme Mr. Bozell's views were. Oddly, it was, of all things, his review of my Christmas book, *Mick Foley's Christmas Chaos*, that I read in the December 12 edition of the *Daily Oklahoman* that really opened my eyes. *Chaos* was a source of great pride for me, and its message of a special young boy who puts the spirit of Christmas back into a down-hearted Santa Claus has touched many people.

Jeff Guinn, a respected book critic with the *Fort Worth Star-Telegram* whose reviews are syndicated in dozens of newspapers across the country, voted it as the best children's book of the year.

Mr. Bozell didn't see it that way. He lambasted the book as being "wretched" and wondered what kind of parents would purchase such "garbage." Jeez, don't you think this guy was going a little overboard?

Mr. Bozell didn't stop there. He delved into *Chaos* as if he was looking into the Kennedy conspiracy, making meaningless observations and creating ludicrous theories along the way. He criticized

artist Jerry "The King" Lawler's drawing of The Godfather and X-Pac on the back cover, even though neither person is mentioned in the story. He derided the depiction of a child wearing a "Stone Cold" Steve Austin shirt, and perhaps most shocking of all, hated that a child has on her toy list a

Santa thought all hope was lost, as he opened up the last:
"Let's see how greedy this kid is, who comes from Lawrence, Mass."
Santa quickly turned the page, and when the page was turned,
He saw a photo of the boy, who'd been very badly burned.

DEAR SANTA CLAUS,

I WRITE TO ASK,
PLEASE MAKE MY WISH COME
TRUE.
I DO NOT WANT A TOY THIS
YEAR—ALL I WANT IS YOU!

TO PACK YOUR BAGS AND
SPREAD GOOD CHEER AGAIN ON
CHRISTMAS EVE.
TO GIVE ALL KIDS AROUND THE
WORLD A REASON TO BELIEVE.

"Chyna action figure," because Chyna, you see, had posed for *Playboy*.

Brent, come on, get a grip on yourself, and I don't mean that in the sexually self-gratifying sense. (Wow, is that a scary thought.) I mean, come on, let's inject a little dose of reality into the picture. For crying out loud, Lawler's art depicts a scene in which selfish kids are waiting on a line to see Santa—some brandishing long lists of toys.

The words are meant to convey Santa's growing unhappiness with the commercialization of Christmas.

> I sit inside these shopping malls, while little girls and chaps
> All rattle off long lists of toys, and pee on Santa's lap.
> It used to be so easy, the boys liked choo-choo trains,
> The girls just wanted dollies, or a single candy cane.
> Now the lists are longer, the kids want bigger things—
> CDs, TVs, VCRs and gigantic wrestling rings.[24]

The Chyna action figure is on a list that visibly includes J.R.'s BBQ Sauce, *Al Snow's Greatest Hits* video, and a Kat T-shirt. The Lawler drawing is eight by eleven inches. The words "Chyna action figure" take up exactly one-eighth by one-half of an inch. They are so small as to be almost invisible. So small that Mr. Bozell had to be *looking* for things to criticize. So small that with his criticism, he has brought the art of nitpicking to previously unknown lows. Please, Mr. Bozell, leave the book alone; surely your time could be better served backward-masking old Beatles records in an attempt to find satanic messages or looking for hidden penises in the ice cubes of magazine ads.

Look, *nothing* can come away completely unscathed when it's put under the type of moral micro-scope which *Mick Foley's Christmas Chaos* was viewed through. *Nothing*. I wondered how Mr. Bozell himself would fare when placed under such a microscope? As it turned out, Mr. Bozell didn't fare too well at all. And I didn't even need a microscope. Just a library card. No, indeed, Brent seems quite adept at this type of thing; in fact, as far as I could gather, it's the only thing he really is adept at. Besides raising money for his negative spin campaigns, which he also seems to have a remarkable talent for.

In 1991, when legendary Supreme Court justice Thurgood Marshall retired, George Bush nominated Clarence Thomas for his position. With a history of conservatism, Thomas was sure to appeal to the political right, and as an African-American, it was thought that he could at least divide the civil rights and women's groups that had fought so hard against Judge Robert Bork, whose Supreme Court nomination had been rejected in 1987. The conservatives, however, were taking no chances, and called in the Conservative Victory Committee, whose executive director was . . . gasp! . . . one L. Brent Bozell III.

A week before the important Judiciary Committee hearings began, Bozell previewed a television commercial for the press.[25]

The ad said little about Thomas, but instead leveled harsh personal attacks against the three men that seemed to be his most obvious opposition in the Senate—Joe Biden, Alan Cranston, and especially Ted Kennedy. The ad was vicious in its attack on Kennedy, "dredging up the old embarrassments about his suspension from Harvard for cheating, and his departure from the scene of an accident on Martha's Vineyard where a young woman died in his car."[26]

The ad set new standards for bad taste, and was decried even by several Republicans. Clarence Thomas himself hated the ad, as did President Bush, who personally asked his chief of staff to call Bozell and tell him to pull it. Bozell refused. He loved the controversy, which saw the ad receive increased attention via replays on national network news shows,[27] which had probably been his plan all along. As his Conservative Victory Committee partner Floyd Brown said, regarding the Thomas ad controversy, "We like being attacked, because when we're attacked, our donors like it, they send us more money."[28] And this was all before the Judiciary Committee hearings made "Long Dong Silver" a part of our cultural landscape.

As I mentioned earlier, nothing and no one can withstand a microscope as powerful as the one Mr. Bozell uses to examine his opponents. Nothing. It doesn't take a genius to attack a person's character, just as it doesn't take a genius to cherry-pick a few offensive segments of *SmackDown!* and present them to the public as if they were an accurate representation of the show as a whole. They're not. It's misleading and unfair, and there are a number of comparisons you could make within the political arena that display these unfair tactics.

It's like judging Michael Dukakis's career solely on the Willie Horton debacle rather than on his impressive record as governor of Massachusetts. A governorship that actually saw the crime rate fall in that state. Or judging Ted Kennedy's career solely on his personal problems rather than thirty years of distinguished senatorial service. How about representing John F. Kennedy's whole career as a series of extramarital affairs rather than acknowledging that he rescued our country from the brink of nuclear disaster during the Cuban Missile Crisis of 1962? Or what about judging President George Bush's career on the basis of a shoddy civil rights record during the 1960s,[29] as opposed to recognizing him as a voice of reason during the Gulf War. Should we focus on his son George W. Bush's record as one of endless executions, instead of pointing to all the positive things he accomplished? (Although, off the top of my head, I can't think of any.)

I don't know why Brent Bozell founded the PTC. I really don't. I imagine the real truth lies somewhere at the intersection of making lots of money and doing some good in the world. I can, however, give a good guess as to why he singled out *SmackDown!* as his *cause célèbre*. After all, Mr. Bozell isn't just anti-*SmackDown!*, he's anti just about everything on television. By his own admission, "out of almost 100 series on prime-time broadcast television, there are only about a half dozen left that aren't radioactive for youngsters."[30] Jeez, Brent, that's quite a bit of radioactivity coming out of those television sets. Not quite as much as your dad advocated unleashing on millions of innocent people in Russia, but quite a bit nonetheless.

So why target *SmackDown!*? I mean, why systematically attempt to destroy this one show with millions of charitable dollars, when there is just so damn much radioactive stuff out there? Not to mention cable. Why focus almost the PTC's entire spon-

sor boycott energy on *SmackDown!*? Besides, as Brent said on CNN's post–Republican Party Convention coverage, "I have nothing against wrestling."[31] Which I guess means what—that Brent is an ECW fan, or a student of Japanese wrestling, or maybe women's apartment wrestling? Brent, a quick tip from someone who has addressed a crowd or two . . . when speaking in public, try not to sound so damn ignorant.

Why not target *Ally McBeal* or *Buffy the Vampire Slayer* or *The Drew Carey Show* or *Will and Grace*? I mean they all made the PTC's top-ten list of "worst shows," despite the fact that they are all critically acclaimed. Maybe because if those shows were targeted, the PTC would suffer a media backlash. But what television critic in their right mind is going to come to the defense of *SmackDown!*, a lowly wrestling show? Answer—none. No, nobody's going to come to our defense, and the overall feeling among those in the media is probably that the PTC is doing an honorable thing. What a perfect marriage. All of the media attention meets none of the media criticism.

And surely, no one is going to question your study concerning sex, violence, and foul language. After all no one (save a one-eared *New York Times* #1 bestselling author) questioned the Indiana University study, which I've got to believe had something to do with your targeting *SmackDown!* in the first place.

Yes, indeed, when it comes to lowbrow entertainment like professional wrestling, not only can the media take potshots, but by golly, they don't even have to do their homework in order to do it. Isn't that right, Margaret Carlson? Margaret Carlson is a respected political journalist who on the August 13, 2000, edition of the *Capitol Gang* show on CNN, said of The Rock that he was "a white skinhead hateful wrestling guy."[32] Thataway, Margaret! You go, girl! Except for one little point. Um, Margaret, I don't know how to break this to you, but, um . . . The Rock is black. And I haven't always been in favor of his hairstyles, but he's not a skinhead either.

But hey, why let a little thing like the truth get in the way of Margaret Carlson's opinion? Because a week later she was in the pages of *Time* magazine writing that The Rock was "anti-woman, anti-gay, anti-black, with language so coarse and vulgar that I can't repeat it here."[33]

Shame on you, Margaret Carlson, shame on you! Your destruction of a man's character without any background checking is reprehensible. Your groundless, mean-spirited accusations are a disgrace to your profession.

Could you imagine if she had said that about General Colin Powell? Or Michael Jordan? There would be outrage. And lawsuits. And possibly termination of journalistic duties. But because it was wrestling, Margaret Carlson, to the best of my knowledge, was able to skate away without even a slap on the wrist or a stain on her reputation. But on behalf of The Rock, I would like to say to Margaret Carlson, "KNOW YOUR ROLE AND SHUT YOUR MOUTH."

Now, with that being said, let's look into that study, shall we? My goodness, Mr. Bozell's allegations are strong. After all, according to the PTC study, *SmackDown!* is the worst show on broadcast television and "was responsible for more than 11 percent of the sex, cursing and violence on broadcast TV in the 1999 study." According to Mr. Bozell, the study counted "both visual depictions and verbal allusions to sex and violence [as well as] all offensive uses of language."[34]

Hmm. Considering my talk with Dr. Ganz about his Indiana University study, I would say that Mr. Bozell's comments leave the door fairly wide open for interpretation. I decided to find out.

Unfortunately, as I've previously discussed, the PTC representatives were not quite as accommodating as Professor Ganz had been, and so, with my writing deadline rapidly approaching, I stepped up my calling campaign. In each of my phone calls, I was unfailingly polite, and made sure to mention my name and what my purpose was. The PTC representatives were polite as well, as they continually took messages and directed me to other representatives in a sort of awkward chain of command that I had not experienced since trying to get a decisive answer in my WCW days. Finally, I got a definitive name. Tom Johnson, I was told, was my man. On January 19, 2001, at 5:15 P.M., I dialed Mr. Johnson's number.

"Hello, Mr. Johnson, my name is Mick Foley, and I'm writing a book on professional wrestling. I'm planning on writing a chapter on the PTC, and I was hoping that you could help me clarify the study that your organization did last year concerning sex, violence, and foul language on broadcast television."

"Um, just a second," Mr. Johnson replied.

When he came back, he had a question of his own. "Okay, what did you say your name was?"

"Mick Foley."

"THE Mick Foley?" he said, with his voice noticeably higher.

"Well, I'm *a* Mick Foley," I replied.

"I mean Mankind, are you Mankind?"

"Yeah, that would be me."

"Oh, um, wow. Hold on, I'll be right back."

Oh, um, wow? *Oh, um, wow?* Now look, I can't prove anything from Mr. Johnson's words, but as a wrestler who has met with and spoken with several thousand wrestling fans over the course of a sixteen-year career, I certainly think I know one when I hear one. And in my expert opinion, well, if Mr. Johnson wasn't a wrestling fan, he certainly sounded like one.

Mr. Bozell, I don't want to be a stooge, but have you looked into the backgrounds of your employees for subversive elements? In the name of Senator Joe McCarthy, I urge you to eliminate any wrestling infiltrators from your midst. Bring back the loyalty oaths from the fifties. Better yet, start making groundless accusations. Fire now . . . there will be plenty of time for half-truths, exaggerations, and guilt by association later. For crying out loud, Brent, our children are being dragged down a moral sewer.

In a short while Tom Johnson was back. Not the same Tom Johnson who had fawned over my name like a sixth-grade girl at an 'N Sync concert. No, this Tom Johnson was bolder. Badder. Better. This was a Tom Johnson who got on the phone and blurted out, "We're not allowed to talk to the World Wrestling Entertainment!" *Click.* No, he didn't say "click," that was the sound of the phone hanging up.

Or was it? Yes, I was 99 percent sure that I'd been hung up on by a man who displayed all the emo-

tional maturity of a twelve-year-old breaking up with his first girlfriend, but I had to be sure. I wasn't Margaret Carlson, dammit, I was Mick Foley, a *New York Times* #1 bestselling author. And I needed to be sure. So, while clinging to the hope that some technical error had separated me from Mr. Johnson, I dutifully dialed the phone. To do anything but that might result in a case of premature exaggeration.

"Hello, Parents Television Council."

"Yeah, Tom, it's me, Mick. I think we were somehow disconnected."

Click. Now I was sure.

I hate to make assumptions. Because I read what can happen "when you assume" on the front of a drunk guy's T-shirt one time. But Mr. Bozell and his Parents Television Council really left me no alternative. So, based on the fact that no one would return my calls, based on the fact that I was hung up on by the PTC, and based on my analysis of a similar study (Indiana University), I'm going to make an educated assumption here. I am going to assume that even though Mr. Bozell's PTC is a very *conservative* organization, his interpretations of what constitutes sex, foul language, and violence are very, very *liberal*.

I really wish I had a chance to talk with Mr. Bozell. I had so many questions for him. Like, "Is testicle a verbal allusion to sex, or is it offensive language?" Or is it both? Is it a word so foul that it constitutes a double whammy and winds up on both of these lists? Or "testicular fortitude." Would this rather unusual way of saying "courage," a word that I myself brought into mainstream America, be placed on both of the PTC lists?

Or better yet, I'd like to ask Mr. Bozell about the word "ass," as in the familiar wrestling battle cry, "I'm going to kick your ass." Is this a verbal allusion to sex? After all, the human ass can be a very sexual body part, although even the staunchest wrestling critic could be hard-pressed to find anything sexual about mine. Is it a threat of violence? Or is it foul language? Or is it all three? Is it a phrase so vile, so immoral, and so disgusting that it merits inclusion on all three of the PTC's clinically documented lists? Is it that ultrarare trifecta of filth? Is it a once-in-a-lifetime triple play of such epic "gutteral" proportions that it becomes a putrid potpourri of sex, violence, and foul language all rolled up in one? Or is it simply a phrase that I've heard on *Malcolm in the Middle*?

What about sexual innuendo? Double entendres? Is there a different subcategory if they are done in a clever way, like on *Frasier*? What about a sexy tone of voice? Or, say, a girl rubbing a guy's arm . . . you know, as long as it is done provocatively.

Is all sex bad? Is an act that is more or less responsible for every single person on earth being here automatically vilified? Or does Mr. Bozell and his staff subcategorize sexual material into "good" and "bad"? Or "hot" and "so-so." Or "acceptable to his own tastes" and "not something he's into."

Before delving into the issue of offensive language, I would like to share a fact with all of you. Because *SmackDown!* is taped on a Tuesday and is aired on Thursday, I have had the chance to watch almost every single episode with my children. Sometimes I get slightly embarrassed. Sometimes my children ask questions that need to be answered gently.

But I will say without even a hint of exaggeration that I had less sexual questions to answer after a full year of *SmackDown!* than I did following my daughter's kindergarten visit to a petting zoo.

Language

"Go to a mall and listen to the obscenities," Mr. Bozell tells us on his *National Campaign to Clean Up TV Now* video. "Turn on the television and watch the latest school shooting. Look at the statistics of all the unwed teenage girls who are walking the streets pregnant. Something is going on here. Today's youth is being poisoned." Pretty serious

stuff. Lucky for us that L. Brent Bozell III has the antidote. Just send ol' Brent a few bucks and he'll get that damn *SmackDown!* off the air, and then all of the problems just listed will simply cease to exist.

Is there really any research that supports the idea that television leads to school shootings or teen pregnancy? Or cursing?

I'm not an expert on the effects of television on teenage pregnancy. For all I know, unwed teenage girls get a look at me in my sagging sweatpants and flannel shirt and hop right into the sack. And I will share a few thoughts on school shootings in just a little while. But for now I'd like to take a look at Mr. Bozell's first comment: "Go to a mall and listen to the obscenities."

Hey, I've heard obscenities at shopping malls. But then again I've heard them at ball games and at picnics, in courtrooms and on boats and just about any conceivable place where people speak. And don't quote me on this, but I think some of these people may have learned to curse from a source other than TV.

Professor Robert Thompson, the director of the Center for the Study of Popular Television at Syracuse University, agrees. "Television not only didn't teach us how to swear, it was unbelievable how long it took for television to learn how to swear from everybody else," said Thompson. "It's only recently that television has begun to sound remotely like so many Americans talk."[35]

I was always somewhat confused by the PTC's selection of Steve Allen as its honorary chairperson. I know I'm skating on thin ice here, because Allen was justifiably a legend in the entertainment field and certainly seemed to be a genuinely nice guy. So I'll try to be as nice and respectful to his memory as I can, but I don't think that it would be in bad taste to question some of his words and actions as it pertains to the PTC, the World Wrestling Entertainment, and the issues that stand between them.

As the *Buffalo News* wrote in a November 3, 2000, article about his death, "Allen was an unlikely public face for what was an adjunct of conservative advocate L. Brent Bozell's Washington, D.C.–based Media Research Center. The entertainer had long been an advocate for both liberal politics and culturally daring artists."[36]

Perhaps the best example of this was his personal friendship with and professional admiration for controversial comedian Lenny Bruce, an early pioneer of foulmouthed entertainment. Mr. Allen, however, didn't see this fact as being inconsistent with his recent views on television. "People have said to me, 'If you're against all the four-letter words in comedy, how come you were such a big fan of Lenny?'" Allen said in the *Buffalo News* story. "The answer is simple: Lenny never used four-letter words for a cheap shock laugh."[37]

Okay, does that mean that the PTC scans through every instance of language they find offensive and then crosses the ones that are not done for "a cheap shock laugh" off the list? Or is it simply okay for Steve Allen's friends to use offensive language but not anyone in the World Wrestling Entertainment?

In many ways, I view *SmackDown!* and *Raw* as being like a variety show or a circus. There is a little bit there for everyone. If you don't enjoy the tightrope walker, you'll probably laugh at the thirteen clowns piling out of the Pinto. There's also some T&A, but the backlash against it is disproportionate to its use and importance on the shows. And honestly, I saw as much skin and as many sexy outfits at last summer's Sydney Olympics.

At its best, however, the World Wrestling Entertainment is about suspending our audiences' disbelief, and getting them caught up in the lives of the wrestlers. Sometimes suspending disbelief *does* include rough language, and I defend my right to let such language fly on the appropriate occasions.

For example, in January of 2000, within the context of our World Wrestling Entertainment story line, I had been publicly fired, barred from the arenas, laughed at by my opponents, had my book ridiculed, my wife used as fodder for jokes, and had a Mick Foley impostor portray me as a mentally challenged, bumbling fool. Then, upon my return, I was ganged up on and beaten bloody.

In the words of Bob Thompson, "If you're going to tell a story about an ambiguous, ugly brutal experience, I think one needs to be able to use ambiguous, ugly, brutal language."

So, when I got on the microphone to describe what might lie ahead in my opponent's future, I used language that one might very well be able to make a case for calling offensive.

Still, I'd like to get my hands on that PTC study. As I mentioned earlier, most offensive language is deliberately kept off *SmackDown!* and most of what remains is bleeped out. Does the PTC count these bleeped words as being offensive? Do they count offensive words that might appear on a sign in the crowd? Or do they count offensive words like "asshole" that the crowd may chant at our less likable (or heel) performers? And if, say, 17,000 people were chanting, would they count the word 17,000 times?

I don't know. I tried to ask these questions to the good and moral people at the PTC, but they were unavailable for comment . . . oh, I'm sorry, they *were* available, but they decided to hang up on me instead of talking.

Who knows, maybe someday Mr. Bozell will change his mind and offer me his double secret study. By then, however, the study will be of no use to me, so I would simply roll that study up and tell him where to place it . . . in an ambiguous, ugly, brutal way.

VIOLENCE

That should be easy, right? I'm sure Brent sits down and gives his crack staff pointers on what is violent, and what is not, and then makes them adhere to very strict standardized criteria. All to avoid the possibility of personal interpretation. Or maybe, better yet, he personally supervises *all* of the prime-time action. Or at least *SmackDown!*, his own pet project. After all, if Mr. Bozell's father could write all of Senator Goldwater's book, then I'm sure Brent III could tolerate at least supervising our show for two hours a week.

Let me take you on a fictional journey inside the PTC compound for a hypothetical look at the scientific standardized tests that constitute the PTC study.

"Mr. Bozell, we've got a hardcore match between Al Snow and Test on *SmackDown!*"

"Oh, very good, this should be interesting."

"Um, Mr. Bozell, Test's matches are usually not very interesting."

"I know that, but if they would have only pushed him a little harder after his breakup with Stephanie instead of having him lose to . . . um, never mind. Okay, let's monitor the content."

"Okay, Test is coming down to the ring to this cool entrance music."

"Do you think his ring attire is suggestive?"

"Well, kind of."

"Good, put that on our sex list."

"But, Mr. Bozell, don't you think that—"

"Shut up, look at those sculpted deltoids, look at those chiseled abs . . . he's teasing us! Count it."

"Yes, sir, Mr. Bozell. Here comes Al Snow."

"Look at that mannequin's head he's carrying. Everyone knows that it's just an easy way to get a cheap double-entendre 'head pop.' Count that on the sex list."

"Yes, sir."

"But it also is clearly meant to be a severed head, which as everyone knows is a textbook lesson on spousal abuse. So count it on the violent list also."

"But, Mr. Bozell, we can't put it on two lists at once."

"Dammit, don't mess with me. Do you know who you're dealing with? I kicked Teddy Kennedy's fat ass! I—"

"Mr. Bozell, you just said a bad word."

"No, that was the TV. Count it on the violence list. And the sex list. And the foul-language list. Count it! Count it! Count it!"

Yeah, I know this is a little ridiculous. But what is the standard for judging violence? Mr. Bozell's own words shed a very dubious light on this question. In his own October 31, 2000, *Washington Times* column, Mr. Bozell leveled harsh criticism against the ABC network for fairing poorly in the PTC letter-grading report.

In the column, he wrote that "ABC avoided family oblivion in terms of scripted material last season only by dint of its TGIF comedies *Sabrina* and the now cancelled *Boy Meets World*."[38] Hey, I was on *Boy Meets World* last year; I must be a good person. And I can say that the cast was all extremely nice, and that teen heartthrob Danielle Fishel calls my house once in a while. That should be good for some Bozell brownie points, right? It truly is a great show, and one that I enjoy watching (in reruns) with my family on a regular basis. Even if the January 22, 2001, 4:30 P.M. show on the Disney Channel did have themes of cross-dressing and implied homosexual thoughts. You see, when Shaun dressed up as a girl to cover a story for the school newspaper, Corey couldn't help but feel attracted to him, in an innocent PG kind of way. Should I count it?

Come to think of it, I believe there was some violence on the show I was on. I'll go find the tape!

Okay, I'm back (and I really did just go watch the tape). Unfortunately, the violent content on this PTC tested and approved show was staggeringly high. On this episode, entitled "For Love and Apartments," I tallied:

two knees to the midsection (I did these)

one choke (I did this one too)

one body slam onto a couch (I did the slamming)

one attempted punch to the face (blocked)

one sleeper hold

four slams of the head into a plate of sandwiches

one slam of the head into a wood table

two grabs of the nose (one by me)

one throw into a stair banister

three punches to the upper pectoral region

one throw into the stairs

one kick to the ribs

one pull of the hair, resulting in victim being dragged across the floor

one rear chin lock (submission hold resulting in victory)

two soft-drink cans crushed on the head

one mandible-claw submission hold administered with the aid of a sweatsock (me)

one toss in the air (show went off the air with actor Will Friedle in midair, leaving a frightened nation to contemplate his fate)

Oh, the humanity! Twenty-five despicable acts of violence on a half-hour sitcom—and one that the PTC ranked in their top-ten, no less. No wonder our children are so confused!

A ridiculous example? Certainly. But is it really any more ridiculous than a PTC representative sitting back and counting every act of "violence" on a two-hour episode of *SmackDown!*? I don't think so. Think about it. Depending on whose criteria were used to count the violence, a wrestling-match total would add up quicker than Roger Daltrey's pinball score in the rock opera *Tommy*.

Out of curiosity, I called Bob Tischler, who was the executive producer of *Boy Meets World* and the man responsible for bringing me onto the show. I wanted to find out why he could bring me, the proud possessor of only half a right ear, the veteran of vicious Japanese barbed-wire matches, and recipient of over 325 stitches, onto a show that so many impressionable youngsters were watching? Well, Bob, why?

"We liked your character," Bob said, "and we thought it would be great to have a wrestling thing on the show. And we thought that if we put on a wrestler that everyone knew, that it would really amp it up a lot."

"But, Bob, weren't you worried about any negative feedback for having a guy like me on your show?"

"No," Bob said with a laugh, "not one bit. We knew that our viewers would be into wrestling."

"You did?"

"Yeah, Mick, demographically, we found that the audiences for the two shows were not that different at all."[39]

Gee. I wonder if the PTC tests for things like demographics and crossover audiences? Do they? I don't know, they refused to discuss their findings with me. But I think that Mr. Bozell fails to understand that television shows shouldn't have to fall into categories that he defines. Programs that he finds offensive might be found by others to be intelligent, thought-provoking, and cutting edge. Besides, I think his definitions of "good" and "bad" and "violent" and "nonviolent" could use a little reexamining. And what better time than now?

"What family programming is left on the Disney-owned network [ABC]?" Bozell asked. "*Who Wants to Be a Millionaire* and *Monday Night Football*—but no dramas or sitcoms."[40]

I've caught a few glimpses of *Who Wants to Be a Millionaire?*, but since my name was an answer to one of their questions, I will applaud Mr. Bozell's decision to advocate such a fine and morally upstanding show. But *Monday Night Football*? Is he kidding me? It's not that I have anything against the venerable Monday-night institution, even if it does go head-to-head with our *Raw* show. But how could a man such as Bozell approve of such a violent sport?

Bottom line: Football is a violent game. If you don't believe me, take it from the players.

"I like to think my best hits border on felonious assaults." So said Jack Tatum, the Oakland Raiders' defensive back with the decidedly nonviolent nickname "The Assassin" in his 1979 autobiography, *They Call Me Assassin*.[41]

Conrad Dobler, in his 1988 autobiography, *They Call Me Dirty,* expressed similar sentiments when he said, "I could never find a nonviolent way to hit a guy."[42]

Granted, Tatum had a reputation as a vicious hitter, and Dobler was known as "the dirtiest player in the game." But what about Tim Green, a former all-pro lineman, a respected announcer, and the author of several critically acclaimed novels as well as *The Dark Side of the Game*, which in my opinion is the best book ever written about life in the NFL? And no ghostwriter for Green, either. Unlike Tatum, Dobler, and Arizona senator and 1964 presidential candidate Barry Goldwater, Green actually writes his own books. What did Green have to say about the NFL? Well, he described it as a place where "you hit hard and you hit first, where bashing someone unconscious is a badge of honor, and breaking bones is a treat." Furthermore, he wrote, "You need to be bad on the playing field, vicious and mean, that's part of the game. That is the game."

I spoke with Darren Drozdov, a former World Wrestling Entertainment wrestler (Droz suffered a career-ending injury that was written of earlier) who played two seasons with the Denver Broncos and is best remembered as the guy who threw up on the ball on a *Monday Night Football* broadcast. I asked him to tell me a little about the violence in an NFL game, and he was happy to do so.

"I've always seen football as a sport like boxing where you could get all your frustrations out and not be punished for it. We get to hit someone as hard as we want on every play . . . and the man who beats the other man up worse wins. Bottom line."

"So," I asked, "is the violence in football worse than that in pro wrestling?"

"Yeah," he said without hesitation. "Because you're not pulling hits in football. Whether you want to believe it or not, people are trying to hurt each other on every play."[43]

Let me reiterate, football *is* a violent game. So why is it a show that Mr. Bozell approves of? Does the violence not count if it happens to occur on a program that Mr. Bozell enjoys? Or do his stooges make it a point not to count the "real" violence on television? Therefore the breathtaking quarterback sack that sends Steve Young into a concussion-induced early retirement doesn't count, but a People's Elbow does?

Or maybe in his heart, Mr. Bozell doesn't believe the contact on a football field is violent. Despite the overwhelming consensus of NFL players that football is a violent game, L. Brent Bozell III, a man who doesn't appear capable of whipping cream with an outboard motor, knows better. He always knows better. That's why he's L. Brent Bozell III, dammit!

Mr. Bozell, it seems, would like to blame all of our country's problems on offensive television programs. After all, listen to the narrator on the PTC *National Campaign to Clean Up TV Now* video. (Imagine a very deep, official-sounding voice while you read.)

"By the time our children reach age eighteen, they will witness sixteen thousand murders and over two hundred thousand acts of violence on television . . . the result: an epidemic of teenage sexual disease, 1.5 million unwed teenagers pregnant each year, and an explosion in juvenile crime."

I've already talked a little about the teenage-sex issue, which frankly I'm not an expert on, as I was nineteen and 351/365ths years old when I had my first sexual encounter. But what about violence? Is there really a correlation?

Certainly, there have been many studies to support the theory that watching violent television programs results in more aggressive behavior, but as one reporter asks, do these studies "prove that such shows make people aggressive, or rather that aggressive types are attracted to entertainment matching their temperament?"[44]

These studies also don't explain why the crime rate in Canada is so much lower than in the United States, when their television viewing habits are almost identical.

These studies also don't explain the marked contrast in violence between the United States and Japan. I don't claim to be an expert on deviant behavior (although it was my major as a college freshman), but I do think that fifteen trips to Japan in 1995–97 makes me something of an expert on the Japanese people.

So drawing upon my personal experience, I can tell you that the television that children are exposed to in Japan is far more violent; nudity is allowed on public television, the pornography is far more deviant and degrading to women, and the wrestling can be far more violent. In addition, photos of nude women are featured in many of the respected newsmagazines, and comic strips depicting every imaginable sex act are included in most respected newspapers. These strips contain graphic language as well, which for some reason is printed in English.

Pretty shocking, huh? Even more shocking is the fact that the frequency of violence is extremely low, with the rape of women, especially, being almost unheard of. When there is violence, such as the "sarin nerve-gas attacks" on a Japanese train in 1995, it is a source of major news and embarrassment to the Japanese people. The nerve-gas attacks were committed by a radical religious group, the

Aum Shinrikyo, whose leader Shoko Asahara's past behavior included breaking into a student health center while swinging a large wooden cross and an attempted assault on a feminist speaker. Oh wait, I think I just confused Asahara's radical behavior with that of Mr. Bozell's mom and dad.

"Children watch an average of twenty-eight hours of television a week," the deep-voiced narrator of the *National Campaign to Clean Up TV Now* video tells us.[45] Almost immediately after, celebrity PTC spokesman Dean Jones serves up his own scientifically tested remark by telling us "children watch an average of seven hours of television a day."[46] Um, Dean, I don't know how to tell you this, but if you multiply the number of hours a day that the children in your quote watched TV by the number of days in a week, the result would be forty-nine hours a week. Or almost double the total that your own narrator just told us. Unless, of course, the children that Dean Jones was talking about only watched television on Mondays, Wednesdays, Fridays, and alternating Saturdays and Sundays.

At one point Steve Allen mentions (in a hushed tone) the tragedies of "Paducah, Jonesboro, Columbine High School" and then says, "Today's violent programming does incite the mind of our impressionable youth,"[47] thereby clearly drawing a correlation between television and the aforementioned tragedies.

This is where I start to take things personally. *SmackDown!*, you see, is the show that Mr. Bozell has called "despicable,"[48] and to him it is clearly the most offensive show on broadcast television. So when Steve Allen, the tape's narrator, talks about "poisoning our children" and being led down a "moral sewer," he is clearly indicating that *SmackDown!* is the worst offender.

During the ten-minute (approximately) duration of this tape, no one image or person is seen more than twice. Except for me. My image is seen *eleven* times. Over and over again I am seen being thrown off the top and through the top (two different moves) of a sixteen-foot-high steel-mesh-cage structure. The match in question didn't take place on *SmackDown!* either, but on a June 1998 Pay-Per-View, a full fourteen months before *SmackDown!* premiered.

As possibly the single wildest match in the history of sports-entertainment, it is in no way representative of our show as a whole. It is also the match I hear most about from wrestling fans. Actually, I hear so much about that match that I'm sick of talking about it. Literally thousands of people have asked me questions and offered their opinion of the match. *Never* have I heard it called "offensive" or "sick" or "poison" or "filth."

By deliberately choosing to feature my image *eleven* times, I very strongly feel that he is telling the public that "on that sick show, Mick Foley is the sickest; of all the things that poison our children, Mick Foley is the most poisonous, and of all the filth out there, Mick Foley is the filthiest."

How dare you, Mr. Bozell, how dare you! And how dare you try to turn the tragic losses at Paducah, Jonesboro, and Columbine High School into your own personal gains. Because I guarantee, Mr. Bozell, I'm a hell of a lot closer to the situation at Columbine High School than you are.

I have been friends with Joe and Ann Kechter since April 1999. I met them only a few days after they lost their beloved son Matthew in the senseless tragedy. Friends in the sense that we have exchanged phone calls, sent letters, given presents, and shared our emotions since that horrible day. They have been my guests at the matches on two occasions, and I proudly wear a pin on the lapel of my denim jacket that reads NEVER FORGET, a gift from Ann.

The World Wrestling Entertainment had received a phone call that day from Matthew's uncle, asking if I might be able to call Matthew's brother Adam. I was Adam's favorite wrestler, and a phone call, his uncle hoped, might boost his spirits, which had been understandably crushed.

I wanted the phone call to be special, so for an hour I walked around the arena asking the other wrestlers to say a few words to Adam. As entertainers, I'm not sure that we have an obligation to help, but on that day none of us saw it as an obligation but as an honor. Mrs. Kechter, who had received a phone call from President Clinton, told me that our call had meant more, because she knew it had come from the heart. She was right.

When I met the Kechters in Denver, Ann told me that the family had watched the World Wrestling Entertainment together the night before Matt died. Her last image of her son, she said, was of him wrestling with the family dog during commercials. Then she broke down in tears.

I spoke with her recently, after receiving a wonderful Christmas card from the family.

Mrs. Kechter had told me last year that she would not mind or consider it a breach of our friendship if

I brought her name up in public. I opted not to do this because I thought doing so would be just that, a breach. Our conversation turned to the killings and their aftermath, which are obviously still being felt today. Once again, she told me of her willingness to help, and once again I told her that I wouldn't feel right about it. And then I thought of Mr. Bozell, and his words. And his tape. And his smears. And my image. Eleven times. So I asked her a question.

"Ann, I watched a videotape that kind of placed the blame for the killings on violence seen on television. I was wondering how you felt about that."

Ann Kechter was quick to answer, and the answer came with assertiveness and a bit of anger. "I blame the parents. After seeing the videotapes that those boys had made, and what was going on right under their parents' noses." Only a few of the victims' families had seen the videotapes, and although Mrs. Kechter didn't go into details, she said the tapes showed that the boys had planned the murders out well ahead of time. "I watched the video," Ann repeated, "all the stuff going on in their own home and they had no clue."[49]

Guns in the house. Internet messages of doom. Parents seemingly too busy to notice or care. In the end, aren't children's viewing habits what parental responsibility should be all about? As a youth, I'm sure I watched some shows that my parents weren't aware of. I highly doubt they knew that I set my alarm clock for 1 A.M. when I was fourteen so I could sneak into the living room and watch Jill Clayburgh in *An Unmarried Woman* on HBO. But parents certainly are aware, or at least should be, of viewing patterns. And watching *SmackDown!* from 8 to 10 P.M. every Thursday is a viewing pattern. Many hundreds of discussions with wrestling fans and their parents have shown me that *SmackDown!* is largely a show families watch together. *Smack-Down!* has a PG rating, and it deserves it. Parents should watch the show with their children, and should feel free to change channels when a situation that they feel is inappropriate presents itself. As Ann Kechter told me, "I sat down and watched the shows with my kids, and if something bugged me, we would talk about it."[50]

Unfortunately, some parents use television as an electronic baby-sitter and don't care enough to monitor their children's viewing habits. I happen to support Mr. Bozell's suggestion of removing televisions from children's bedrooms. I also believe that the V chip, which is capable of blocking out shows and is mandatory on all new televisions, is a decent idea, even though the public's disinterest in this device seems to indicate that parents either feel comfortable monitoring their own kids, or that they simply don't care. Parents who feel comfortable monitoring their children really don't need Mr. Bozell's self-righteous sentiments, and parents who don't care have problems far too deep for Mr. Bozell's *National Campaign to Clean Up TV Now* to handle.

I hate to point out the obvious, and I know this is a touchy subject, but doesn't it stand to reason that the U.S. crime rate might be lower, and that the murders in Paducah, Jonesboro, and Columbine might never have happened if guns weren't so goddamned easy to get? Look, I don't want to lose a bunch of my fans here, but could the reason the violent crime rate is so much lower in Canada and almost nil in Japan be maybe, just maybe, because the civilians in those countries aren't armed to the teeth? Doesn't that make just a little sense?

Not all deaths are caused by guns, though. L. Brent Bozell III and his PTC would have us believe that four such deaths were caused by professional wrestling. These deaths are the focus of their video, the focus of their pledge campaign, and the focus of their sponsor boycott.

Nothing displays Mr. Bozell's penchant for distortion more than these four deaths. Nothing illustrates his contempt for facts and his misuse of the media more than these four deaths. And in my opinion, it is his distortion of the facts regarding these four deaths that will in the end expose him as the manipulator I think he is, expose his PTC for the factory of half-truths and exaggerations I think it is, and force Mr. Bozell into a hasty retreat.

THE FOUR DEATHS

Dallas, Texas: On May 27, 1999, a three-year-old boy was killed while playing with his seven-year-old brother. "He said he pushed his brother . . . and said he'd seen it on wrestling on TV," said Dallas police lieutenant Bill Walsh.[51] When the seven-year-old was asked to describe what happened, the boy "backed up about ten feet and ran toward a police detective who was holding up a doll about the same size as the three-year-old."[52] As he neared the doll, he stuck out his arm and knocked the doll down in a clothesline-like maneuver.[53]

But autopsy reports revealed that the head injuries sustained were not consistent with a fall like the one the three-year-old would have suffered from a clothesline, but instead reminded doctors "of something from a severe auto accident."[54] The seven-year-old also claimed to have jumped up and down on his brother after the fall, although that was also inconsistent with autopsy reports.[55] The death was ruled as accidental, and the seven-year-old will not face criminal charges.[56] No charges were brought against the World Wrestling Entertainment.

This didn't stop the PTC from blaming the World Wrestling Entertainment, however, as the incident was used repeatedly in their public smear campaign, which included the words "in the wake of tragedies like the Columbine school shootings, and the killing of children by other children imitating wrestling moves they've seen on TV shows like *World Wrestling Entertainment SmackDown!*" in a PTC solicitation letter.[57]

For the PTC to include this little boy's accidental death in the same sentence as the Columbine massacre is shameful and unforgivable. The injuries sustained by the three-year-old boy make me question both the accidental nature of the incident and whether a clothesline was even used. A seven-year-old boy just does not generate enough power to make a fall on a carpet[58] resemble an injury from a severe auto accident.

Even if the accident was caused by a wrestling move, common sense leads me to believe that blaming the World Wrestling Entertainment is ludicrous. Using the logic of the PTC, the door would be open to blaming untold deaths on something or someone. Children die every year while playing sports. Using Mr. Bozell's logic, the NFL, NBA, NHL, and Major

League Baseball would be held responsible. Auto accidents would be blamed on NASCAR and a golfer hit by a stray ball could put the blame on the PGA, and so on and so on, etc., etc. Assuming that a clothesline was the cause of death, it is simply a very tragic accident. For Mr. Bozell to claim anything else makes him an opportunistic vulture, willing to feed off of a little boy's blood to line the PTC's pockets with charitable donations.

Yakima, Washington: A nineteen-month-old toddler was brutally murdered when his twelve-year-old cousin slammed the infant to the floor as many as eight times[59] on January 16, 1999.

The twelve-year-old, Jason Whala, was upset that he had been forced to baby-sit his cousin, and became further angered when the infant would not stop crying. His anger exploded when the baby got into his videogames, at which point Whala commenced the savage beating, which ended only when the twelve-year-old became tired.[60] At that point he returned to watching *Brady Bunch* reruns on television.[61]

Where exactly does the World Wrestling Entertainment fit into this? Well, it doesn't, because Whala was a WCW fan, but wrestling came into the scenario when the term "jackknife powerbomb" was used to describe what Whala had done to his cousin.[62] But even Whala's own defense attorney said that the wrestling move could not have been the cause of death "because William [the nineteen-month-old] had no severe external injuries that would match Whala's description of how he slammed the toddler repeatedly to the floor."[63]

So how can wrestling be to blame if the guy's own attorney disagreed? Well, I guess that is what negative spin campaigns are all about, and Bozell, as an expert in this disgusting art, has taken a little bit of nothing and once again turned it into a big gain for himself and his PTC. "Killings of children by other children imitating wrestling moves they've seen on TV shows like *World Wrestling Entertainment SmackDown!*" Bullshit. This was murder committed by a cold-hearted human being who never should have been baby-sitting in the first place.

Whala's father had been contacted by school officials who expressed "extreme concern about the boy's behavior" only nine days before the murder.[64] The officials urged the father to take his son to a psychologist for evaluation, but according to Dr. Paul Schneider, who testified at Whala's murder trial, "Greg Whala failed to attend a second meeting to discuss his son's academic and behavior problems at school."[65] The boy did not take part in class lessons, failed to do his homework and had seemed to shut down," said Schneider.[66] Indeed, psychiatric evaluations following the murder showed the boy to have an extremely low IQ and that he suffered from depression and attention-deficit disorder.[67] So why the hell was this person forced, or allowed, to baby-sit a nineteen-month-old baby for up to seventeen hours a week?[68] Perhaps the boy's father is to blame for showing such indifference to his son's problems, but the major blame belongs to Jason Whala for his depraved indifference to human life. The jury agreed and convicted Whala of second-degree murder. Murder that wrestling, which surfaced only as a dubious footnote, cannot be blamed for. No, it cannot, but in Brent Bozell's campaign, it was once again.

Warner Robbins, Georgia: Ramone François King, a fifteen-month-old boy, was killed when he was allegedly struck and kicked off a bed by a four-year-old boy on October 29, 1999. The killing occurred when baby-sitter Earl Rose, twenty-four, who was watching five other children ranging in age from four to nine, left the house for a period of twenty minutes and supposedly put in a World Wrestling Entertainment videotape to occupy the children.[69] In his absence, the four-year-old boy entered the sleeping infant's room and attacked him. The boy later claimed that he was merely trying to kill roaches that were crawling on the infant's body[70] but three of the other children reported seeing him hitting and kicking the child.[71]

Can wrestling or the World Wrestling Entertainment really be blamed for the fifteen-month-old child's death? Not when there is plenty of blame elsewhere. What about Earl Rose, the baby-sitter who stepped out to make a phone call? What kind of a man leaves seven children alone for twenty minutes? Probably the same type of man who was sentenced to five years' probation a year earlier for cocaine possession, driving without a license, and giving false information to police.[72] Probably the same type of guy who went to prison following the infant's death for failing to report to his probation officer, failure to pay a $1,700 fine, failure to attend drug and alcohol counseling, and failure to hold a steady job.[73] What kind of woman would allow a man like Mr. Rose to baby-sit at her home (where three of the children lived)? Probably the same type of woman who would be engaged to him.[74]

Mr. Rose was indicted on and pled guilty to charges of involuntary manslaughter and reckless conduct.

Can the World Wrestling Entertainment possibly be to blame for this child's death, which so clearly was the result of poor parental judgment and reckless behavior on the part of a convicted felon? Mr. Bozell apparently thinks so. "The killings of children by other children imitating wrestling moves they've seen on TV shows like *World Wrestling Entertainment SmackDown!*"

Fort Lauderdale, Florida: This one was L. Brent Bozell and the Parents Television Council's crown jewel, and the one with which they received enormous national media coverage.

Lionel Tate, twelve, killed six-year-old Tiffany Eunick in Tate's home on July 28, 1999, while supposedly imitating professional wrestling moves. According to Tate's attorney, James Lewis, his client was simply "a kid who used poor judgment. He didn't intend to cause any harm. He was playing. He was doing what he had seen on television."[75] Well, I guess if he was just playing, we ought to excuse him for fracturing little Tiffany Eunick's skull, lacerating her kidney, cracking her rib, and causing over thirty bruises all over her body. At least that is what Mr. Lewis and Mr. Bozell would like us to do. Remove the blame from a 170-pound, twelve-year-old boy who beat to death a 48-pound, six-year-old girl and place it squarely on the shoulders of the World Wrestling Entertainment.

On the day of Tiffany's death, she was brought to Tate's town house by Lionel's mother, Florida Highway Patrol trooper Kathleen Grossett-Tate. Mrs. Grossett-Tate fed the two children and then went upstairs to take a nap, leaving Lionel and Tiffany to watch television.[76]

At 10:40 P.M., Mrs. Grossett-Tate was awakened by Lionel, who informed his mother that Tiffany had stopped breathing. Grossett-Tate attempted to revive the girl, but was too late and Tiffany was later pronounced dead at the hospital.[77]

Two days after Tiffany's death, Tiffany's mother, Deweese Eunick-Paul, was informed by police that her daughter had died of multiple blunt traumas instead of choking, as Grossett-Tate had told her.[78] Lionel Tate then changed his story and told detectives that he was playing tag with Tiffany and that she had hit her head on a coffee table while being held by Tate in a bear hug.[79]

In fact, according to prosecuting attorney Ken Padowitz, Lionel never mentioned wrestling until a month after Tiffany's death. In this third rendition of what took place in the Tate home, Lionel claimed that he "wrestled with her and hit her about four times."[80] But when the autopsy revealed the shocking multitude of injuries, Tate's story changed again. This time Lionel claimed that the injuries were caused when he threw Tiffany into the metal banister of a spiral staircase instead of onto the couch that he'd been aiming for. By now, the four punches had turned into thirty-five to forty.[81] Even though the defense's own experts later testified that "Tate's story would not have accounted for all of Tiffany's injuries,"[82] the "wrestling defense," with some generous media assistance from Mr. Bozell, was under way.

Attorney Lewis continually claimed that Tate was just imitating his heroes. He was, said Lewis, "engaged in what appears to be childlike horsing-around activity."[83]

A fractured skull. A lacerated kidney. A cracked rib. Child's play? These were injuries that one prosecution expert said were comparable to falling from a three-story building.[84] Injuries bad enough that Tiffany's screams woke up Mrs. Grossett-Tate. At which point she reportedly opened the bedroom door and yelled, "Stop making that noise or I'm going to spank your butt."[85] When Lionel informed his mother that it was Tiffany who was crying, prosecutors said that Grossett-Tate yelled "get her to stop."[86]

If Mr. Lewis's "wrestling defense" is to be believed, one would think that Lionel Tate would have been overwhelmed by grief following the death of little Tiffany as a result of this "horseplay." Right? Well, Tiffany's mother testified that when she told Lionel that her daughter was dead, "he shrugged and rolled his eyes."[87] She also testified that Lionel asked if he could live with her and have Tiffany's toys.[88] Several experts also testified that Lionel had shown "little or no remorse" since Tiffany's death.[89] Dr. Joel Klass, who was hired by Lewis, claimed Tate had not expressed remorse because he was scared of going to jail.[90] I think it is probably more likely that he simply had no remorse to express.

Mr. Lewis also tried to portray his client as a child so naïve that he couldn't separate truth from fiction, as it pertained to wrestling. But according to psychologists who spoke with Tate, he said that he knew that wrestling was not real, and that he had watched a program that explained how wrestlers made the moves look realistic.[91]

Perhaps most ridiculous of all was Mr. Lewis's contention that it would be a "stretch" to try to prove that one child was physically abusing another when no weapons were involved.[92] I actually had to reread this a few times to make sure I hadn't misunderstood Mr. Lewis's meaning. But I think his meaning is clear. I also think it might be a "stretch" to prove that Lewis's brain was functioning when he made this statement. His thought process on this subject is so nonsensical as to defy logic. Lionel Tate weighed 170 pounds at the time of the killing. Tiffany Eunick weighed 48 pounds. And Mr. Lewis would like us to believe that Tate wasn't physically capable of abusing the little girl because he didn't have a weapon?

I spoke to Sergeant Gary Perna, an eighteen-year veteran of the Stamford, Connecticut, Police Department about Lewis's claim. Sergeant Perna's comment was brief and to the point. "We see domestic abuse all the time that doesn't involve a weapon. In our line of work, that kind of thinking [Lewis's] would be absurd."[93]

A fractured skull. A lacerated kidney. A cracked rib. Over thirty bruises. Horseplay? Or a brutal murder? The PTC contended it was another case of "the killings of children by other children imitating moves they've seen on TV shows like World Wrestling Entertainment SmackDown!"

Unfortunately for Mr. Lewis and Mr. Bozell, the

jury in the trial of Lionel Tate didn't see it that way. After deliberating for only three hours, an incredibly short amount of time for a case with such serious ramifications, they brought in a first-degree-murder verdict. Judge Joel Lazarus made his feelings clear when he sentenced Tate to life in prison stating, "It is inconceivable that such injuries could be caused by roughhousing or horseplay or by replicating wrestling moves." Obviously, Tate should have accepted the very lenient plea bargain that the prosecution had offered.

I firmly believe that James Lewis thought that the "wrestling defense" trial was going to make him a star. In some ways it already had. He'd appeared on national talk shows, had been quoted many times in newspapers around the country, and had even appeared on the PTC videotape claiming that "the finger of blame is pointing directly at the World Wrestling Entertainment." Actually, Mr. Lewis, the finger of blame was pointing directly at your client, who brutally murdered an innocent little girl and then showed no remorse. It was the foundless accusations, half-truths, exaggerations, and lies that were pointing right at the World Wrestling Entertainment. By the way, Mr. Lewis, I've got a special finger for you.

The World Wrestling Entertainment should be completely absolved and Brent Bozell should have to retract all his injurious statements that somehow link the World Wrestling Entertainment to children's deaths. A giant victory for the World Wrestling Entertainment and a crushing defeat for the PTC, right? Well, not really. Why? Because L. Brent Bozell III was largely successful in his larger goal of demeaning the name of the World Wrestling Entertainment and in using his tactics to scare off sponsors and to bring in his charitable donations.

The Lionel Tate case (and the other three cases as well, but to a lesser degree) will forever be linked to professional wrestling and in many people's minds, that link will always carry some implication of guilt no matter what a jury in Florida said on January 25, 2001. And to understand why, I have to go back to the Belzer definition of the Big Lie: "If you tell a lie that's big enough and you tell it often enough, people will believe you are telling the truth even when what you are saying is total crap." Justice by all means *should* be the major objective here, but, unfortunately, justice is often not enough to clear a name.

Although Mr. Bozell comes off to me as a charismatically challenged, lying sack of shit, he didn't become such a leader in the field of negative spin by being stupid. No, he was actually quite intelligent in his attack. Look at the four cases. Three of them had no witnesses, and in the one that did have witnesses, they were young children. Three of the cases involved autopsy reports that were inconsistent with the alleged causes of death. Mr. Bozell should have known that the defense could not possibly prove that wrestling was at fault in any of the cases. But he also had to have known that it would be difficult to prove that wrestling was not at fault either. After all, with literally hundreds of thousands of matches to its credit, the world of professional wrestling has in its existence seen people do just about everything imaginable to each other in its quest to entertain. ANYTHING one human being could do to another in the sense of physical punishment could be interpreted as being professional wrestling.

It was a strategy that has produced marvelous results in the storied history of smear campaigns. No one could possibly prove that they were *not* a witch during the Witch Trials in Salem, Massachusetts. The Jewish people could not prove that they were *not* a cause of economic problems in Germany in the 1930s. Alleged Communists could not possibly prove that they were *not* communists during the McCarthy era of the 1950s. And Bozell probably believes that the World Wrestling Entertainment cannot possibly prove that wrestling did *not* play any part in those four deaths. As Kenneth Davis wrote in *Don't Know Much About History*, "the accused cannot escape because professions of innocence become admissions of guilt and only confessions are accepted."[94]

For the World Wrestling Entertainment full vindication will never be complete and partial vindication has come with a heavy price, the heaviest of which is our loss of sponsors.

According to Mr. Bozell, the process of eliminating World Wrestling Entertainment sponsors is a simple one. He has simply "taken these offensive shows directly to the sponsors, we've explained to the sponsors that they are responsible for this poison. And I tell you, time and time again these sponsors look at this, they don't want anything to do with it, and they pull their ads in a New York minute."[95] According to PTC celebrity spokesman Pat Boone, this is a strategy that "strikes terror into the sponsors' hearts . . . and cash registers."[96] Sounds simple, right? Let's take a look at just how simple the MCI WorldCom situation was.

MCI WorldCom

According to the PTC's own Web site, "Direct Contact," MCI representatives had been contacted concerning *SmackDown!*'s content several times before sending honorary cochairman Steve Allen and Dr. Delores Tucker, the president and founder of the National Congress of Black Women, to the annual MCI WorldCom shareholders' meeting on June 1, 2000, in Mississippi.[97]

After ten months of written correspondence yielded no action from MCI, the PTC began a campaign of telephone inquiries.[98] An early attempt to get MCI WorldCom to withdraw support was thwarted when, according to Steve Allen's own MCI shareholder address, "Ginger Fitzgerald of MCI advertising stated MCI was fully aware of the content of the program and that it was in their opinion perfectly acceptable."[99]

The PTC called again on May 10, 2000, at which time, according to Allen, Claire Hassett of MCI's public-relations department said, "We don't advertise on particular shows or endorse particular shows. We purchase advertising on a network and our goal is to reach a certain target audience. I apologize on behalf of the company if that offends you."[100]

At this point Mr. Bozell and the Parents Television Council stepped up their campaign by declaring on their Web site on May 31, 2000, that Steve Allen and Dr. Tucker were going to the shareholders' meeting "To let MCI know that if it continues to advertise on World Wrestling Entertainment programming the PTC will hold it personally responsible for every child who is injured or killed as a result of wrestling moves."[101]

As Pat Boone said, the PTC "strikes terror into the sponsors' hearts . . . and cash registers."[102] Well, I should say so, Pat, you shameless profiteer and homogenizer of the great soul singers of the fifties. This goes a whole lot further than simply showing a video to a sponsor, this is pretty much threatening to call them "baby killers."

How the hell does the PTC, a supposed moral group, pull off a stunt this low and claim to do it in the name of decency? Even more disturbing is the fact that Bozell seems to have pulled this move directly from Joe McCarthy's playbook.

In 1950, Senator McCarthy was embroiled in a feud with columnist Drew Pearson, who criticized the senator both in his columns and on his radio show. Despite Pearson's reputation as a tough anticommunist, McCarthy insisted that he was a "sugar-coated voice of Russia" and urged people to rise up against "this Moscow-directed character assassin."[103]

He then threatened an economic boycott of the Adam Hat Company, which was Pearson's radio sponsor, if it did not withdraw from his show at once. The Adam Hat Company immediately pulled its support from the show.[104]

In late 1951, McCarthy employed a similar strategy against *Time* magazine for an uncomplimentary story they had published about the senator from Wisconsin.

"As you well know," McCarthy wrote *Time*'s publisher, "I am preparing material on *Time* to furnish all of your advertisers so that they may be fully aware of the type of publication they are supporting."[105] Letters were then sent to the advertisers warning them not to do business with a pro-Communist magazine. *Time*'s editors retreated from their stance, a decision they later regretted.[106]

McCarthy's accusations were baseless, but effective nonetheless. Bozell's accusations are, as a court of law in Fort Lauderdale, Florida, proved, equally baseless, but also effective. Following the PTC's threat and Steve Allen's shareholders' address, MCI WorldCom ceased advertising on *SmackDown!*

Allen began his speech to MCI shareholders by throwing around some financial figures and tossing about words like "disgusting," "negative," and "detrimental."

He then quoted sportscaster Bob Costas, who seemed somewhat less than happy with the current World Wrestling Entertainment product. Which is fine, because everyone is entitled to an opinion, and I won't let Mr. Costas's diminish my ability to enjoy his considerable talents.

Next up was a quote from "Superstar" Billy Graham, a former World Wrestling Entertainment Champion from the seventies who said, "I stopped watching wrestling because they pushed the envelope too far. The shows are very degrading to women, there's foul language and gestures, and there's real strong sexual overtones. I decided I didn't want this stuff coming into my house, my eyes, or my mind. It made me physically ill." Pretty strong words. But this is the same Billy Graham who paid me and Terry Funk to wrestle in a "Texas Death Match" on May 12, 1998, at Lamar University near Houston. This was at a time following Mr. Graham's religious conversion, and in fact the Lamar show was to benefit a religious cause. The show was canceled, but was done so for financial reasons not moral ones.

Mr. Allen then spoke of "at least thirty-five corporations that have pledged to withhold advertising from the show." Funny, he didn't use the word "withdrawn" as the PTC had previously done. Unfortunately for the PTC, "withhold" and "withdraw" do not have the same meaning. You see, out of the nearly forty companies that he claims to have persuaded to pull their ads, twenty-five of those companies have never advertised with the World Wrestling Entertainment.[107] How does a company withdraw something that they've never given to begin with?

Well, it's all about the illusion of power that the PTC presents, which does, in fact, lead to real power. "He, Bozell, inflates the numbers, but he has in fact caused advertisers to not buy World Wrestling Entertainment," said World Wrestling Entertainment attorney Jerry McDevitt. "He creates an atmosphere where he makes advertisers fear continuing to advertise."[108]

For example, according to a Procter & Gamble spokeswoman, the company "is cited by the PTC as having shut out the World Wrestling Entertainment on its recommendation, but has never been a World Wrestling Entertainment advertiser."[109]

I'm also intrigued at the sponsors listed by the PTC. M&M/Mars? The same M&M/Mars that hired me and Stephanie McMahon to entertain and sign autographs at their corporate Halloween party?

Hershey's? The same Hershey's whose arena we wrestle in regularly and whose theme park I appeared at as an advertised attraction?

7 UP? 7 UP, whose slogan includes the phrase "up

yours"? Presumably they dropped sponsorship because the World Wrestling Entertainment with its "suck-it" slogan was too vulgar. If these slogans are to be taken in their literal form, then I feel that 7 UP is guilty of condemning one form of sodomy while advocating another, much more painful (or so I'm guessing) sodomitic act!

Mr. Allen himself dipped into a moral sewer when he brought up the deaths of the four children previously mentioned.

Mr. Allen then offhandedly mentioned that his first job on television was as a wrestling announcer in the 1940s. He conveniently forgot to mention that he was a paid guest at the World Wrestling Entertainment's *WrestleMania VI* before admitting that "a year or so ago I hosted a television documentary about the history of wrestling." He also admitted that he loved the sport, but that he certainly didn't "love its present emphasis on cheap sex, vulgarity, and violence of the most sadistic sort."[110]

Does this not seem just a little bit strange? A guy hosts *The Unreal History of Professional Wrestling* on the A&E network and then tries to bury the very product he claims to love. The A&E special made its debut on April 28, 1998, at a time, as we've mentioned, that the World Wrestling Entertainment was at its most risqué. Does Mr. Allen expect us to believe that he didn't know that? To the contrary, the cheap sex, vulgarity, and violence of the most sadistic sort was on full display as Allen narrated away with the voice of a true wrestling fan.[111]

Maybe what Steve Allen was saying is that it's okay for him to like wrestling, just not anyone else.

Finally, after lobbing a last "cultural sewage" reference toward the World Wrestling Entertainment, Mr. Allen ominously concluded by saying, "If MCI continues to sponsor *World Wrestling Entertainment SmackDown!*, we will make this a national issue by letting our membership, as well as the general public, know that MCI does not care about the damage the World Wrestling Entertainment and it are doing to our children and that MCI's values are the same as those of the obscene, racist, violent and sexually graphic *World Wrestling Entertainment SmackDown!*"[112]

I'm not sure if I can really blame MCI president and CEO, Bernard Ebbers, for folding like a cheap accordion under the PTC's pressure. Maybe he really felt that *SmackDown!* was repulsive. Or maybe he felt like a jury member during John Gotti's first few trials. Or maybe he lacks a certain type of fortitude.

THE SENATORS

Most of the people I talk to are in complete disagreement with Mr. Bozell and his PTC. Granted, most of these people I am in discussion with are wrestling fans, but nonetheless, I feel that their views are valid ones. When I was doing book signings for *Christmas Chaos*, I often made a point to ask parents with young children how they felt about *SmackDown!*'s content. In contrast to the stereotypical view of wrestling fans as uneducated ruffians, the people who lined up for *Chaos* (and *Have a Nice Day!* a year before) were patient, polite, and pretty much regular-looking people. Sure, I got an occasional "Foley is God" yeller, but they were the exception rather than the rule.

The overwhelming majority of the parents of these young children felt that the PTC's perception of our show was greatly exaggerated. Many of them admitted that the show occasionally yielded segments of poor taste, but felt that overall, *SmackDown!* was acceptable family viewing.

A few weeks ago I went to World Wrestling Entertainment headquarters to do the play-by-play for a match with announcer Kevin Kelly for my new videotape and DVD, *Hard Knocks and Cheap Pops*. Our decidedly underhanded objective on that day was to watch the Al Snow–Big Boss Man "Kennel of Hell" match, which was one of the all-time-great stinkers of the industry and announce it like it was an all-time classic. After doing this devious deed (which will no doubt add to my long list of punishing Al Snow verbal knockouts), I sat back and watched some of the other "knocks and pops" segments with Kevin. The tape's director, Steve Cooney, did a wonderful job of weaving some of my favorite moments into a continuous narrative, a narrative that captured the innocent foolishness that is a much-overlooked part of the World Wrestling Entertainment. "How can people say our show is so horrible?" I asked Kevin. "Don't they know that so much of it is harmless comedy?" I think my question was merely rhetorical, as I already had the sneaking suspicion that most of our critics don't have a clue about what is on *SmackDown!*

Senator Sam Brownback of Kansas is a member of the PTC advisory board and, in fact, is a part of their *Campaign to Clean Up TV Now* videotape. He sure seemed to know his stuff when it comes to censoring other people's viewing choices. Or does he? A

May 31, 2000, article in the *Chicago Sun-Times* suggests not.

When the senator claimed that the PTC "quantifies what everybody sees," he was asked what he had personally seen. "I've seen some of the World Wrestling Entertainment," he said. "I've seen clips that we pulled from some [offending] shows." The *Sun-Times* then asked if he could be specific. "I'm not remembering the shows that the clips were out of," he said.[113]

Brownback then mentioned some other non-wrestling shows that he watched with his children, shows that he claimed were "just replete with sexually suggestive content." Unfortunately, the senator couldn't remember the names of those shows either, and was at a loss to explain why he allowed his children to view such offensive material.[114]

So once again the World Wrestling Entertainment falls victim to the dreaded "offensive clips" campaign. For some reason, I don't think that Christian trying to sweat off a pound by wearing a fuzzy chicken outfit, or my impersonating Frank Sinatra singing Britney Spears was seen by Senator Brownback. No, I'm sure the senator simply saw the worst of the worst (whether the clips were actually from *SmackDown!* or from a combination of *SmackDown!*, *Raw*, and Pay-Per-View is a question I would like to have answered) and decided he would take part in Mr. Bozell's campaign.

What about Joe Lieberman? He seems like a nice guy, and damn, he was almost our country's vice-president. And everyone knows that a dummy can't be vice-presi—oops. Dan Quayle just shot down that theory in a pile of burning wreckage. Still, Senator Lieberman is Mr. Bozell's right-hand man. Whenever anyone accuses the PTC of being ultra-conservative, he throws Joe Lieberman in their face. When he was defending his group against "McCarthyite" insinuations, he said, "Tell Joe Lieberman. He's on our advisory board."[115] So, surely knowing that his image means so much to the PTC's credibility, Joe Lieberman would know his stuff when it came to the PTC's number one, and, as far as I can tell, only cause.

When questioned about *SmackDown!*, Joe was ready with some astute social commentary. "There is a case where these kids watch violent acts that are presumably faux and artificial, but they can't distinguish that."[116] They can't? Is Senator Joe Lieberman trying to suggest that kids think wrestling is real? I'm sure that some kids do, but they are pretty much

the same kids who think that Dr. Evil is really trying to take over the world in the Austin Powers movies.

Well, what else did Joe have to say about *Smack-Down!*? "There's only so much I watch myself," he said. When the *Sun-Times* pressed him further, he "didn't sound pleased by the tone of the question." "Forgive me, I'm busy! I flip the dials. I read some of the reports on content."[117]

Reports on content? The same reports that I tried to get a look at? Maybe I can give Joe a call and find out if "testicle" is considered a sexual reference or foul language. In return, I could offer him some reports that I have drawn up on the content of some family favorites. Reports that would tear out the spirit of the shows and leave only ugly carcasses that misrepresent the show as a whole. Or pretty much what the PTC does to our show. Reports that would turn a classic book like *The Wizard of Oz* into a story of witchcraft, death by house dropping, theft, quadruple limb amputation (book version), forty-two decapitations (book), forty neck breakings (book), suggested drug use (poppies), contract killing, kidnapping, and murder by melting.

Or how about a report on "Hansel and Gretel," which would be reduced to child abuse, child abandonment, trespassing, destruction of property, kidnapping, imprisonment, attempted cannibalism, and murder by boiling.

When this book is published, I am going to keep a copy for myself, give one to my mother, and then drive directly to Senator Lieberman's office, where he can feel free to do with it what he wants. But if he is the decent guy that I feel in my heart he is, I hope that he will at least take the time to read it and learn who it is exactly that he's in bed with before he decides to screw around with him any further.

Because Joe Lieberman, your ignorance is Mr. Bozell's bliss, and you deserve better than to be remembered as Brent's lackey. And besides, that kiss that your running mate laid on Tipper at the Democratic Convention was at least as offensive as anything I've seen on *SmackDown!*

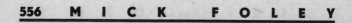

Conclusion

WHEN I LOOK BACK at my sixteen years in wrestling, I very rarely think of the big matches, or the big crowds, or the hoopla that surrounded the World Wrestling Entertainment for the past few years. Maybe as I grow older, I'll watch tapes of who I was and perhaps take my career mementos out of boxes.

But for now, I usually think of little things. Fans who touched my heart with their letters or their words. Joey Greynolds, who I gave my Rock 'n' Sock jacket to when he was at death's door, and who sent me a Christmas card saying that his brain tumor had inexplicably disappeared. Tom Bleasdale from England, to whom a match-worn Mankind shirt was a cause for celebration, and whose mother's kind words caused my wife to break down in tears. Even musician Billy Corgan, who wrote me a long letter telling me that my career had somehow inspired him to make better music.

And I think of Mickey Mouse that day at the theme park. Her frightened face. Her way with my children. Not a week goes by that I don't think of Mickey, diving on concrete so as not to disappoint the fans. Mickey . . . diving on concrete . . . so as not to disappoint the fans. No wonder I think of it so often. In a way I was looking at my own career.

I am a thirty-five-year-old man with a wife and three children who has done his best to entertain for sixteen years through a strange blend of blood, sweat, tears, black ink, and bad jokes. I may not be perfect, and I'm certainly not God, but neither am I the poisoner of minds or the killer of children. I am Mick Foley, and Foley is . . . Good.

Afterword

GEEZ, I MAY HAVE BEEN a little overdramatic at the end there. Actually, I was just being true to my feelings at the time. A year after writing this book, however, I can see that I sound a little overdramatic.

In the introduction to this book, I wrote that I preferred *Foley is Good* to *Have a Nice Day!* Now, I'm not so sure. Actually, I *am* sure . . . sure of the fact that *Have a Nice Day!* is better. Readers' opinions seemed split. Some went out of their way to let me know they enjoyed this book more. A lot of other fans thought 500 pages of *Have a Nice Day!* was enough and decided to pass on another 592.

I could go on forever comparing both of them (and chances are, if you catch me drunk in a bar somewhere a few years from now, I probably will). I think above all else, *Foley is Good* is a wrestling book for its place and time, while *Have a Nice Day!* is a wrestling book for *all* time.

I mean, I'm looking through *Foley is Good* a few days ago and thinking, *Does the world really need an in-depth look at the Mankind-Big Show angle?* The answer I keep coming up with is, "Probably not."

I regret getting so deep into the whole PTC situation. Sure, I think I did some good—and sure, I got a kick out of being an investigative reporter—but damn, those 30,000 words took up seven months of my time. I think that the first two months of little Mickey's life just might have been too high a tab to pay, especially for an effort that I don't feel was ever completely appreciated by the World Wrestling Entertainment.

Don't get me wrong, I'm very proud of this book, and it brought some wonderful opportunities my way. But after September 11, I just can't help feeling that the last year of my career really wasn't quite as important as I thought it was.

But here's an important question: Is that last year of my career worth the $7.99 you spent for this paperback? You better believe it is! "The Boy Who Saved Christmas" and the chapters on Owen Hart and Brian Hildebrand will fill my heart long after all memories of the Mankind-Big Show rivalry have faded. And let's be honest here, "The Legend of the Penis Suplex" alone is worth the price of admission.

But for those of you who already bought the hardcover, making the book a towering *New York Times* No. 1 bestseller, I have another question: Is this bonus chapter *alone* worth the extra $7.99 it will take to own it? Probably not. Why? Because I simply lack the energy and testicular fortitude to throw myself headlong into another hard-hitting, brutally honest, behind-the-scenes exposé. So instead, I'll give you some shallow observations on wrestling, an update on Al Snow, Test and the Mean Street Posse, and I'll shamelessly plug my upcoming first novel, *Antietam Brown*. But above all else, I'll give you "Reflections on Katie." I know you won't want to miss that.

Damn, I just felt a little twinge of guilt. I've got to at least tell you why I left the World Wrestling Entertainment, don't I? Well, here's the *Cliff's Notes* version: When I was beaten, embarrassed, bludgeoned and fired from my position as World Wrestling Entertainment Commissioner in December 2000, I really thought I'd be back in a couple of months. After all, in the world of sports-entertainment, that incident was merely my excuse to take a short paternity leave. I wanted to be there to welcome my son into the world (and also spend ridiculous hours researching and writing my PTC dissertation).

Well, that vacation took longer than I expected. After bowing out of my proposed *WrestleMania* match-up with Mr. McMahon, I found myself still at home until the May release of *Foley is Good*. I returned only to plug the hell out of my book, which skyrocketed to the top of the *New York Times* bestseller list—until *John Adams* pulled me back down and administered a literary ass-kicking the likes of which hadn't been seen since *Have a Nice Day!* did likewise to the Dali Lama in 1999.

I had actually engineered a brilliant plan to use the *Foley* book as the impetus for a titanic McMahon-Foley showdown, but unfortunately the plan pulled up lame coming out of the gate. Instead, I decided to shoot the whole damn scenario in the head and put it out of its misery. In other words, I bailed out again.

I really felt like maybe I had one more good match left in me, but the setup had to be perfect. To be more specific, I felt like I had to be "forced" out of retirement—kind of like Creed did to Balboa in *Rocky II*.

So from this, we can establish two very important truths:

1. It's okay to go back on your real-life word, as long as it makes sense in a fictional storyline.

2. Every wrestling idea I have ever conceived has, in truth, come from the seven *Rocky* movies— at least it seemed like there were seven.

From there, I returned as the only man capable of refereeing the legendary "Bra and Panties" match at *SummerSlam*. Lastly, I returned as a commissioner, but it seemed my sole purpose in that role was to play Hungry Hippos in William Regal's office.

It was during this Hungry Hippos stint that I began writing my novel. In truth, it was the novel, more than anything else, that led to my ultimate departure from the World Wrestling Entertainment.

You see, I love writing. *Antietam Brown* had been in my mind for close to a year. When I finally put pen to paper in October, the whole story kind of came flowing out. *Foley is Good* seemed to indicate to the world that my first book wasn't a fluke. And to my surprise, the very idea of a Foley novel had actually garnered some interest in the literary world. So I asked for a release from the World Wrestling Entertainment to pursue that endeavor, and they agreed.

So there you go. The condensed version. There are far too many details to delve into here.

Now, let's get to some updates.

Mean Street Posse

Damn, talk about poor timing. These guys were gone by the time the book came out and never got to come back. I don't know why. Personally, I got a kick out of them, and I thought they were making great strides as a result of their dedication and hard work. Hopefully, I'll see them on TV. Granted, they may not have been fully polished as performers, but if talent is, indeed, a prerequisite for World Wrestling Entertainment employment, would somebody please explain how the hell Test keeps his job?

Test

Actually, Test has come a long way. Although it hurt me greatly to do it, I even told him so. I even think I told him that . . . God, this is hard . . . he had the look of . . . don't make me say it . . . a main-eventer. Whew, I made it. I saw Test the day before the book's release, and he said, "Hey Mick, good to see you."

"I don't think you'll be saying that tomorrow," I said.

"Oh man, what did you say about me?"

In truth, he took the jokes well. After seeing how my similar treatment of Al Snow had catapulted him all the way to middle-of-the-card status, Test willingly played his role as the guy-who-pretended-to-be-mad about the jokes.

Sure, the Test jokes were juvenile. Sure, I overdid them. But in spite of that, I will always and forever consider my Test joke on page 150 to be one of the greatest accomplishments of my career.

Al Snow

I hate Al.

No, I don't hate him as a person, I just hate him for being so damn good on *Tough Enough*. He was so talented, genuine and even—dare I say it—charismatic that I can't find it in me to make jokes about him anymore. I'll even go out on a limb here and say that the World Wrestling Entertainment missed the boat by not making him a big star on their programs.

So I guess that in much the same way that Linus had to give up his blanket, I have had to give up my Al Snow jokes. But while I have moved on, Al's name will remain firmly entrenched as the most repeated punch line in literary history. Besides, I still close every college lecture I give with "The Legend of the Penis Suplex." (By the way, I'm not sure Linus ever did give up his blanket.)

Senator Joseph Lieberman (Democrat-Connecticut)

Back when I was in my "taking-myself-really-seriously" stage, I claimed that I was going to keep the first copy of *Foley is Good*, give the second to my mother, and then drive to Lieberman's office and present the senator from Connecticut with the third. Did it work out that way? Well, not exactly. I did keep the first. I did give my mother the second. And I did drive directly to Hartford to present the senator with the book. But before I got to Lieberman's office, I stopped at a hotel for the night. I stayed up all night reading Lieberman's book *In Praise of Public Life*. The next morning I headed to a radio station in Hartford, where I proceeded to give the heralded third copy to former Twisted Sister front-man and rising radio personality, Dee Snyder. Which, I guess, is how things should be.

I dropped the fourth copy off at the senator's office. Joe wasn't in, but one of his representatives granted me quite a bit of time to air my grievances and I've remained in touch with his office for several months. Unfortunately, I never got to speak directly to the senator, but I would like to think that my words have affected him in some small way.

In a touching footnote to the Lieberman saga, Dee Snyder and I hit it off instantly and I have been a guest on his show several times since then. He actually lives in the town I grew up in and has become my only famous friend outside of wrestling. While I have met many famous people in my life, Dee Snyder is the only one whose name (with one notable exception) I drop on a regular basis.

My late-night reading of Lieberman's book was by no means an isolated incident. Indeed, my research on the PTC had the odd effect of turning me into something of a political fanatic for the first time in my life. I'd always enjoyed history, but I discovered that it's impossible to appreciate history without knowing about the politics responsible for it.

So it really was a short step from the PTC to McCarthyism, from McCarthyism to the Cold War, from the Cold War to the Civil Rights movement, and on and on. I read partly for enjoyment but also out of necessity. I was hoping that my book would capture the attention of the media, and if it did I would need to be prepared. Personal experience has shown me that much of the media is all too willing to take a cheap shot at a pro wrestler. I figured they would be even more inclined to do so with a wrestler passing himself off as some kind of political expert. I was determined not to let anyone catch me unprepared, so I went about trying to learn as much as I could—in a hurry.

I read everything I could get my hands on, about any subject that I felt was even *remotely* connected to my book. I mentioned Ted Kennedy in one paragraph of my book. One tiny little paragraph. I could just imagine some interviewer calling my bluff on Kennedy. I couldn't let that happen, so I read a 500-page biography.

Was it worth it? No, not at all. The media actually did come, but even the tough questions were based solely on subjects that I'd researched for my book. But, by golly, if someone had wanted to know about Ted Kennedy's actions in the war between Nigeria and Biafra in 1968, I was ready.

Actually, I was asked one question that almost made the whole studying-up thing worth my while. Almost. *ABC World News Tonight* was doing a piece on my book and Don Harris asked me the fairly tough question, "Do you consider the PTC to be a McCarthyist organization?"

This was it, the big one. The moment I'd studied hundreds of hours for. The reason I'd highlighted political tomes. The motivation behind notebooks full of my scrawled notes. A tough political question, and I was ready.

"Well," I said, "consider this: The PTC told our sponsors that the public can't distinguish between the sponsors and the shows that they choose to support. Consider the fact that L. Brent Bozell III was Pat Buchanan's aide during Buchanan's presidential campaign. Consider that Buchanan's autobiography *Right from the Beginning* features a chapter entitled 'As We Remember Joe' in which he speaks reverently about Senator McCarthy. And when you consider that Bozell's father was a speechwriter for McCarthy who wrote a very pro-McCarthy book entitled *McCarthy and His Enemies*, then yes, I don't see how you could consider the PTC to be anything *but* a McCarthyist organization."

Harris looked up at his producer and said, "We're going to need to do a longer piece." Unfortunately, that particular clip never aired. The piece that did air was fairly positive, although I did think that there was an unnecessary—and out of context—clip from *Beyond the Mat* shown, but man, I wish they'd aired the McCarthy stuff.

The Media

I spent quite a bit of time blasting the media in this book. For the most part, I feel justified. In retrospect, perhaps there were a few instances where I was either a little harsh or possibly didn't quite understand how things worked in their world.

Maybe I was a little rough on Margaret Carlson. So she didn't know The Rock is black. Everyone makes mistakes, right? Besides, she seems to be nice, and I find myself agreeing with her most of the time. I'm sure she took the criticism from a professional wrestler mighty hard. Hopefully, these words will pacify her. Besides, I'll give credit where credit is due—she must have a strong stomach to deal with Bob Novak every week.

Of all the media I assailed, I was most vocal about

the *New York Times*. So it was with some surprise, and just a little fear, that I learned that a reporter from the *Times* was coming over to my house to do a story on my book.

"Is this good news?" I asked my publicist Jennifer.

"Mick, trust me, this is the best news you can possibly get," she said. If I'd known how right she was, I probably would have been a little more nervous about the whole thing. But truth be told, I felt pretty good about it and was actually looking forward to our meeting.

What a great meeting it was, too. I swear she felt like an old friend or something, we got along so well. She even told colleagues that it was the most fun she'd ever had doing an interview. She was a kind, intelligent, and fascinating person. And once that article hit the press, man, the phone started ringing.

Suddenly, with the power of the *New York Times* behind my book, the media that I felt had shunned me, suddenly welcomed me—all in rapid succession. *People, Leno, Regis, World News Tonight* and even *The Today Show*. Which leads me to . . .

Reflections on Katie

Sometimes I'm guilty of doing stupid things just to entertain myself. And I'll be brutally honest with you: I didn't really feel like writing this bonus chapter. If it weren't for Katie, I probably wouldn't be doing it at all. But I just kept thinking of the words "Reflections on Katie" and how surreal they would look in a wrestling book. The thought always made me smile. (Actually, it's making me smile now, as I write.) I think that's pretty much Katie's secret—

she has the unbelievable propensity to bring forth human smiles. She is kind of like a real-life Mary Richards; she can "take a nothing day and suddenly make it all seem worthwhile."

I received a call from Jennifer the day the *New York Times* piece came out. Jennifer is so cool, she's always genuinely happy when something good happens to me. On this day, something *really good* was happening.

"*The Today Show* wants you," she said.

"Wow." My distinguished reply.

"And Katie's going to do the interview."

"Cool." Yet another wise retort from the two-time, No. 1 bestselling author.

Jennifer didn't want to burst my bubble, but she also didn't want me to go blindly into the interview. "Katie can be tough," she said.

"Hey, Jenn, I'm not concerned with tough. Tough is okay, I'm just concerned with fair. And Katie's *definitely* fair."

"Yes, she is. So you're cool with doing the show?"

"Definitely. And Jenn, don't worry about me. I'm definitely *not* afraid of Katie Couric."

No, indeed, I wasn't afraid of Katie or her tough questions. That night, I drove into New York City, got a good night's sleep, and awoke feeling fit as a fiddle—ready to take on America's sweetheart. (Actually, I wasn't fit at all, and haven't been for a long time, but I think you know what I'm saying.)

I really felt like I was in the zone while I was waiting in the Green Room. I mentally prepared myself for whatever tough questions might come my way. Sure, Katie might be tough, but I was tougher. I was fine. At least until I got on to the set; the moment I looked at her I fell apart quicker than an Al Snow pay-per-view offering.

She was so beautiful sitting there, and just so . . . so . . . so *Katie*. I momentarily feared falling victim to the Cindy Brady syndrome once that red light turned on. Like a good portion of America, I had watched Katie many mornings over the years, but I never considered myself to be a Katie-aholic. At least not until I sat next to her on the set of *The Today Show*.

The next thing I knew, we were on the air. Katie hit me with, of all things, a tough question about the World Wrestling Entertainment show's controversial content. What the heck? What's with the tough stuff, Katie? Why didn't anyone warn me? Oh, that's right, Jenn had, hadn't she? Well, anyway, I handled the question. It really wasn't all that bad. I'd like to think that I managed it with a certain amount of grace and knowledge. And then, as if by magic, Katie actually laughed at one of my stupid jokes! Rumor has it that at one point she even touched my knee (I think I may have started that rumor).

As the interview drew to a close Katie mentioned that I had also written a children's book and I said, "Yeah, as a matter of fact, I think both our books were on the list at the same time."

Katie smiled, as only she can, and said, "May I say that I was in very good company?"

I officially blushed and said something along the lines of "Ooahuhhh." I think it was truly the goofiest that I have ever looked on television. While I'm at it, I might as well mention that I looked pretty handsome that day. At least by my standards.

When the interview ended, I thanked Katie and she hugged me so tight that it nearly took my breath

away. Okay, so maybe I made up that part. She did thank me for being there and told me that she had really enjoyed my cage matches with Abdullah the Butcher in '92. All right, I made that up, too. But as I opened the door to leave the studio, Katie gave me the biggest compliment of my life. I don't think it was meant for me to hear. I think it was meant for the crew, or Matt or Al. But I heard it. It really meant a great deal to me when she said . . . when she said . . . when she said . . .

Nope, sorry, I'm not going to tell you.

Look, I talk an awful lot about my private life in this book. I've got to keep a little something for myself. Katie's compliment is one of those things. So, sorry, none of Katie's kind words for your $7.99.

A week later, I received another call from Jennifer. "Guess who wants you?" she asked. Her voice was all bubbly, like she had some kind of special secret she was just dying to share.

"Who?"

"*The Today Show.*"

"*The Today Show*?"

"*The Today Show.*"

"But Jenn, I was just on *The Today Show.*"

"I know, but as soon as they found out you had a Halloween book coming out, they booked you for October 31."

Suddenly, I found myself being hurled through the portals of time—sailing back, back, back, all the way to eighth-grade gym class. I said, "Does that mean Katie likes me?"

"Well, Mick, someone must like you," Jennifer laughed, "because they just booked you five months in advance."

I looked forward to that interview for five months. After September 11, I really expected it to be canceled. I would have understood completely if it had been, but as Halloween approached, I was still on the schedule.

A few days before the show Jenn asked me if I would like to read to some kids during my segment. "Definitely," I said. "Oh, and Jenn, could you . . . ?"

"No Mick, I can't request Katie for your interview."

"Damn, how did you know I was going to ask that?"

"Because it's the same question you always ask."

"Damn."

I brought the family with me to New York City in preparation for my big reading. When I spoke with the woman who would be producing my segment, I tried to sound as casual as possible as I popped the big question.

"So, um, do you, uh, know who will be interviewing me?"

"I'm not sure," she said, "but I would assume it will be Katie."

In a flash, I was back in that eighth-grade gymnasium saying, "Really? Do you think so? Really? Why?"

"Well, I heard you two really hit it off last time and—"

The eighth-grader in me interrupted her. "Where'd you hear that? Did Katie say that? Did Katie say it?"

Man, sometimes I wonder how the real world hasn't chewed me up and spit me out yet, because I really am kind of pathetic.

Well, Katie did do the interview and it went very well. But when I think about that day and I think about Katie, it's not the interview that sticks out in my mind.

As I departed the studio I kept my ears open just in case Katie had another compliment ready. But unfortunately she didn't. But on the way out I ran into *Weekend Today* anchor Soledad O'Brien, who asked me if I'd just moved to Northport.

"Yeah, I did, about a year ago," I said.

"My parents are your next-door neighbors," she told me.

Soledad and I chatted amiably about the odd coincidence for a few minutes. I went into the hallway to check on Colette and the kids but was surprised to see my baby absent from his stroller.

"Where's Mickey?" I asked.

"He's with Katie," my wife said, a big smile lighting up her face.

"With Katie? How?"

"She introduced herself during the break and asked if she could hold Mickey."

"Really?" I gushed.

"Yeah, she's going to hold him at the end of the show."

So with my arm around my wife and my eyes glued to the monitor, I beamed as Katie held my baby boy. I watched his little pumpkin cap push down his tiny ear, while America's sweetheart flashed the smile that makes every day seem worthwhile. There it was, the greatest moment of my career: Katie Couric with her arms around my child.

I can almost hear the wrestling fans revolting, saying, "Greatest moment? What about the 'Hell

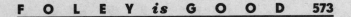

in the Cell'? What about the 'King of the Death-match'?"

Well, for starters, I really need to be conscious to consider a moment great. That alone rules out the "Cell" match. And it's kind of tough to enjoy any match that results in forty-two stitches and second-degree burns—so there goes the "Deathmatch" as well.

So my personal highlight goes to Katie and little Mick.

Watching the tape later, I had another revelation. I kept rewinding and replaying it, rewinding and replaying it. Maybe I was mistaken. But time and again, the visual evidence seemed to support my conclusion. I had to admit that at age thirty-six, with 325 stitches in my body, two missing teeth and one missing ear, I was, nonetheless, pretty damn handsome.

Hey, I'm not kidding. I know I'm the same guy who used to bill himself as "The World's Ugliest Wrestler," but it just wasn't true anymore. No, after all these years, I have come to accept that my name is Mick Foley, and Foley is Good . . . looking.

Thanks a lot everybody for sixteen years of blood, sweat and tears. It's been a wonderful ride!

Sources

Books

Bayley, Edwin R., *Joe McCarthy and the Press*. Madison, Wisconsin: The University of Wisconsin Press, 1981.

Black, Christine M., and Thomas Oliphant, *All by Myself: The Unmaking of a Presidential Campaign*.

Buckley, William F., Jr., *Nearer My God: An Autobiography of Faith*. New York: Doubleday, 1997.

Casden, Sheldon, *The Witch Must Die: How Fairy Tales Shape Our Lives*. New York: Basic Books, 1999.

Clymer, Adam, *Edward M. Kennedy: A Biography*. New York: William Morrow and Company, 1999.

Davis, Kenneth C., *Don't Know Much About History*. New York: Avon Books, 1990.

Dobler, Conrad, and Vic Carucci, *They Call Me Dirty*. New York: G. P. Putnam's Sons, 1988.

Edsall, Thomas Byrne, and Mary D. Edsall, *Chain Reaction: The Impact of Race, Rights, and Taxes on American Politics*. New York: W. W. Norton, 1991.

Foley, Mick, *Have a Nice Day: A Tale of Blood and Sweatsocks*. New York: HarperCollins, 1999.

———, *Mick Foley's Christmas Chaos*. New York: HarperCollins, 2000.

Gitenstein, Mark, *Matters of Principle: An Insider's Account of America's Rejection of Robert Bork's Nomination to the Supreme Court*. New York: Simon & Schuster, 1992.

Green, Tim, *The Dark Side of the Game: My Life in the NFL*. New York: Warner Books, 1996.

Herman, Arthur, *Joseph McCarthy: Re-examining the Life of America's Most Hated Senator*. New York: The Free Press, 2000.

Hersh, Burton, *The Shadow President: Ted Kennedy in Opposition*. South Royalton, Vermont: Steerforth Press, 1997.

Judis, John B., *Grand Illusion: Cities and Champions of the American Century*. Farrar, Straus & Giroux, 1992.

———, *William F. Buckley Jr.: Patron Saint of the Conservatives*. New York: Simon & Schuster, 1988.

Maltin, Leonard, *Leonard Maltin's 2000 Movie and Video Guide*. New York: Penguin, 1999.

Oshinsky, David M., *A Conspiracy So Immense: The World of Joe McCarthy*. New York: The Free Press, 1983.

Phelps, Timothy M., and Helen Winternitz, *Capitol Games: The Inside Story of Clarence Thomas, Anita Hill and a Supreme Court Nomination*. New York: Hyperion, 1992.

Reeves, Thomas C., *The Life and Times of Joe McCarthy: A Biography*. New York: Stein & Day, 1982.

Simon, Paul, *Advice and Consent: Clarence Thomas, Robert Bork, and the Intriguing History of the Supreme Court's Nomination Battles*. Washington, DC: National Press Books, 1992.

Videotapes

World Wrestling Entertainment Raw Is War, January 17, 1999; January 24, 1999; July 24, 1999; August 30, 1999; September 27, 1999; November 18, 1999; June 12, 2000; June 19, 2000; July 10, 2000; July 17, 2000; July 31, 2000; August 4, 2000

World Wrestling Entertainment SmackDown!, January 14, 1999; November 4, 1999; December 8, 1999; January 6, 2000; November 7, 2000; November 14, 2000

World Wrestling Entertainment No Way Out, World Wrestling Entertainment Home Video, 2000

Edward R. Murrow: The McCarthy Years, CBS News, 1992

Hard Knocks & Cheap Pops, World Wrestling Entertainment Home Video, 2001

Point of Order: The Army–McCarthy Hearings, New York Video, 1963

The National Campaign to Clean Up TV Now, Parents Television Council, 2000

The Wonderful, Horrible Life of Leni Riefenstahl, 1993

Home Alone, 1990, 20th Century Fox

Home Alone 2: Lost in New York, 20th Century Fox, 1992

Baby's Day Out, 20th Century Fox, 1994

Beyond the Mat, Universal, 1999

Boy Meets World: "For Love and Apartments," October 1, 1999

Television Programs

The Unreal History of Professional Wrestling, A&E, April 28, 1998

Cheers: five episodes, September 2000

General Hospital: five episodes, September 2000

The O'Reilly Factor, April 28, 2000, Fox News

Weekend Magazine with Stone Phillips, October 30, 1999, MSNBC

The Capitol Gang Show, August 13, 2000, CNN

CNN Post–Republican Party Convention Coverage, August 2000

Magazines, Newsletters, and so on

Time, August 2000

New Republic, "McCarthy and Hitler: A Delusive Parallel," August 23, 1954

Entertainment Weekly, April 14, 2000

Wrestling Observer Newsletter, November 14, 2000
Steve Allen's MCI Stockholders' Address, PTC Web site,
   June 1, 2000
Dr. Delores Tucker's Statement, PTC Web site, June 1, 2000

Newspapers

Milwaukee Journal Sentinel, "Try Try Again," August 23,
   1999, Cue & Jump, p.1
Saint Paul Pioneer Press, August 23, 1999
Indianapolis Star, July 21, 1999
Milwaukee Journal Sentinel, July 7, 1999

IU STUDY
Florida Times-Union, Jacksonville, FL, June 19, 1999
Dallas Morning News, June 16, 1999
State Journal Register, Springfield, IL, June 9, 1999
Indianapolis News, June 7, 1999
Washington Times, June 2, 1999
Arizona Republic, May 30, 1999
New York Post, February 22, 1999; May 30, 1999
State Journal Register, Springfield, IL, May 30, 1999
Chicago Sun-Times, April 4, 1999; May 25, 1999
Indianapolis Star, April 29, 1999; May 17, 1999
Commercial Appeal, Memphis, TN, April 10, 1999
Tulsa World, April 6, 1999
Ottawa Sun, April 4, 1999
Cincinnati Enquirer, March 12, 1999
News and Observer, Raleigh, NC, March 7, 1999
Chicago Tribune, March 1, 1999
New York Times, February 28, 1999
Post and Courier, Charleston, SC, February 28, 1999
Star Tribune, Minneapolis, MN, February 27, 1999
San Francisco Chronicle, February 26, 1999
Tampa Tribune, February 26, 1999
Indianapolis News, February 25, 1999
Buffalo News, February 24, 1999

Columbian, Vancouver, WA, February 24, 1999
Deseret News, Salt Lake City, UT, February 23, 1999
Florida Times-Union, Jacksonville, FL, February 23, 1999
USA Today, February 23, 1999

PTC STUDY
Washington Times, March 31, 2000
Times Union, Albany, NY, August 28, 2000
Dallas Morning News, August 21, 2000
Arkansas Democrat Gazette, April 13, 2000
Chattanooga Times/Chattanooga Free Press, April 7, 2000
Washington Times, March 31, 2000
Tampa Tribune, August 14, 2000
Times Union, Albany, NY, August 3, 2000
National Journal, August 2, 2000
Chicago Sun-Times, May 31, 2000
Milwaukee Journal Sentinel, May 28, 2000
Seattle Post-Intelligencer, May 9, 2000

TATE CASE
Sun-Sentinel, Ft. Lauderdale, April 4, 2000; May 5, 2000;
    May 10, 2000; May 19, 2000; May 27, 2000; June
    28, 2000; June 29, 2000; September 25, 2000
Associated Press, State and Local Wire, April 15, 2000
Miami Herald, October 8, 2000
APBnews.com, April 5, 2000; April 12, 2000

DALLAS, TEXAS, CASE
Calgary Herald, July 2, 1999
Dallas Morning News, July 1, 1999; July 2, 1999; July 3,
    1999

YAKIMA, WASHINGTON, CASE
Yakima (Wash.) *Herald-Republic,* January 18, 1999; Jan-
    uary 20, 1999; January 22, 1999; January 29, 1999;
    February 3, 1999; February 4, 1999; May 1, 1999;

May 4, 1999; May 6, 1999; May 7, 1999; May 11, 1999

Daily Oklahoman, December 12, 2000

Fort Worth Star-Telegram, November 26, 2000

ROBBINS, GEORGIA, WARNER CASE

Associated Press, State and Local Wire, September 1, 1999; September 2, 1999; November 17, 1999;

Macon Telegraph, September 2, 1999; November 17, 1999

Atlanta Journal and Constitution, September 2, 1999; September 3, 1999; November 18, 1999

Deseret News, Salt Lake City, UT, September 2, 1999

Augusta (GA) *Chronicle,* September 4, 1999

Notes

1   *Chattanooga Times/Chattanooga Free Press*, 4/7/00
2   *Dallas Morning News*, 8/31/00
3   Steve Allen's MCI shareholders' address, 6/1/00
4   Bozell quote from Alex Marvez interview
5   Davis, *Don't Know Much About History*, p. 327
6   Belzer, *UFOs, JFK and Elvis: Conspiracies You Don't Have to Be Crazy to Believe*
7   Judis, *William F. Buckley, Jr.: Patron Saint of the Conservatives*
8   Buckley, Jr., *Nearer My God*
9   Ibid., p. 261
10 Oshinsky, *A Conspiracy So Immense*, p. 307
11 Judis, p. 198
12 Ibid.
13 Ibid., p. 318
14 Ibid., p. 320
15 Telephone conversation with David M. Oshinsky
16 Ibid.
17 Judis, p. 318
18 Ibid., p. 319
19 Buckley, Jr., p. 256
20 Conversations with Oshinsky and Sam Tanenhaus
21 Buckley, Jr., p. 256
22 World Wrestling Entertainment press release, 11/9/00
23 Conversation with Oshinsky

24 *Mick Foley's Christmas Chaos*
25 Gitenstein, *Matters of Principle*, p. 336
26 Phelps and Winternitz, *Capitol Games*, p. 142
27 Ibid., p. 143
28 Ibid.
29 Phelps and Winternitz, p. 190
30 *Washington Times*, 10/31/00
31 CNN post–Republican Party coverage
32 CNN *The Capitol Gang*, 8/13/00
33 *Time*
34 *Washington Times*, 3/31/00
35 *Milwaukee Journal Sentinel*, 5/28/00
36 *Buffalo News*, 11/3/00
37 Ibid.
38 *Washington Times*, 10/31/00
39 Telephone conversation with Bob Tischler, 1/24/01
40 *Washington Times*, 10/31/00
41 Tatum, *They Call Me Assassin*
42 Dobler, *They Call Me Dirty*
43 Telephone interview with Darren Drozdov, 1/24/01
44 American Jewish Committee commentary, 12/1/00
45 PTC *National Campaign to Clean Up TV Now* video
46 Ibid.
47 Ibid.
48 Ibid.
49 Telephone interview with Ann Kechter, 1/20/01
50 Ibid.
51 *Calgary Herald*, 7/2/99
52 *Dallas Morning News*, 7/1/99
53 Ibid.
54 *Dallas Morning News*, 7/2/99
55 Ibid.
56 *Calgary Herald*, 7/2/99
57 PTC solicitation letter
58 *Dallas Morning News*, 7/1/99
59 *Yakima Herald-Republic*, 5/7/99

60   Ibid.
61   Ibid.
62   Ibid.
63   Ibid.
64   *Yakima Herald-Republic,* 5/4/99
65   Ibid.
66   Ibid.
67   *Yakima Herald-Republic,* 5/7/99
68   *Yakima Herald-Republic,* 5/4/99
69   Cox News Service, 9/2/99
70   *Augusta Chronicle,* 9/4/99
71   Associated Press, State and Local Wire, 9/1/99
72   *Macon Telegraph,* 11/17/99
73   Ibid.
74   Ibid.
75   Associated Press, State and Local Wire, 4/15/00
76   Ibid.
77   *Sun-Sentinel,* 5/5/00
78   *Sun-Sentinel,* 6/29/00
79   Ibid.
80   *Sun-Sentinel,* 5/5/00
81   Ibid.
82   *Newsday,* 1/26/01
83   *Weekend Magazine with Stone Phillips,* 10/30/99
84   *Newsday,* 1/26/01
85   APBnews.com, 4/5/00
86   Ibid.
87   *New York Times,* 1/26/01
88   Ibid.
89   *Sun-Sentinel,* 9/25/99
90   Ibid.
91   *Sun-Sentinel,* 4/4/00
92   *Sun-Sentinel,* 5/5/00
93   Telephone conversation with Gary Perna, 1/26/01
94   Davis, p. 327
95   PTC *National Campaign to Clean Up TV Now*
      video

96   Ibid.
97   PTC Direct Contact, 5/31/00
98   Dr. Delores Tucker's statement at MCI WorldCom shareholders' meeting, 6/1/00
99   Steve Allen's MCI shareholders' address, 6/1/00
100 Ibid.
101 PTC Direct Contact, 5/31/00
102 PTC *National Campaign to Clean Up TV Now* video
103 Oshinsky, p. 181
104 Ibid.
105 Ibid., p. 185
106 Ibid.
107 Ibid.
108 Cahner's Business Information, 11/13/00
109 Ibid.
110 Steve Allen's MCI shareholders' address
111 *The Unreal History of Professional Wrestling,* A&E, 4/20/98
112 Steve Allen's MCI shareholders' address
113 *Chicago Sun-Times,* 5/31/00
114 Ibid.
115 *Boston Globe,* 12/7/00
116 *Chicago Sun-Times,* 5/31/00
117 Ibid.

Acknowledgments

THIS BOOK WOULD NOT have been possible without the help, wisdom and kindness of many people. I would first like to thank Judith Regan for her faith in me as a writer and for convincing me to get rid of a whole lot of the Epilogue. Adam Hopkins and John Porco for allowing me access to hundreds of newspapers and magazines. Beth Zazza for her energy and attention to all my concerns. Betsy Brown and Sue Slabicki for deciphering my handwriting and turning my notebook paper into a book. Jerry McDevitt for his legal expertise. My publicist, Jennifer Suitor, for always going way above and beyond the call of duty to help me out. My editor, Dana Albarella, for her advice and for being on my side when things got ugly. My manager, Barry Bloom, for his guidance. Dave Meltzer for his facts, figures and dates. The librarians at my library who were always willing to help a computer-illiterate author access information. Dr. Walter Ganz for discussing his study with me. Historians/authors David Oshinsky and Sam Tanenhaus for taking a wrestler/author seriously. Colette for tolerating my writing obsession. Noelle and Dewey for putting up with all the hassles that come with having me for a dad. Baby Mickey for allowing me to write about my attempts to create him. And most important, to God for all the blessings in life.

Photograph Captions and Credits

34   Noelle offers me a Skittle while a doctor stitches
        my head following the "I Quit" match. © 2001
        World Wrestling Entertainment, Inc. All rights
        reserved. Photograph by David McLain
        1/24/99.

46   Hanging out at Yankee Stadium with Mayor
        Giuliani on the night Mike Piazza was beaned.
        Courtesy of the author's collection.

52   I lie unconscious as The Undertaker looks down
        from above. "Hell in a Cell." © 2001 World
        Wrestling Entertainment, Inc. All rights reserved.
        Photograph by Tom Buchanan 6/28/98.

81   The Rock and I battle in an empty arena during
        the "Halftime Heat" match, January 1999.
        © 2001 World Wrestling Entertainment, Inc. All
        rights reserved. Photograph by Tom Buchanan
        1/25/99.

82   The most ridiculous camera shot in sports-
        entertainment history, January 1999. © 2001
        World Wrestling Entertainment, Inc. All rights
        reserved. Photograph by Tom Buchanan
        1/26/99.

94   The Iron Sheik, Bob Backlund, and Dominic
        DeNucci lend a hand before my "Last Man Stand-
        ing" match in February 1999. © 2001 World
        Wrestling Entertainment, Inc. All rights reserved.
        Photograph by David McLain 2/14/99.

99   This one hurt a lot. "Last Man Standing,"
        February 1999. © 2001 World Wrestling Enter-
        tainment, Inc. All rights reserved. Photograph by
        Tom Buchanan 2/14/99.

100   The *Rocky II* finish at "Last Man Standing."
        © 2001 World Wrestling Entertainment, Inc. All

rights reserved. Photograph by Tom Buchanan 2/14/99.

107   Pimpin' ain't easy. Do you recognize the girl on the right? © 2001 World Wrestling Entertainment, Inc. All rights reserved. Photograph by Rich Freeda 1/25/99.

115   The Rock is probably talking about a guy's ass here. © 2001 World Wrestling Entertainment, Inc. All rights reserved. Photograph by Tom Buchanan 2/14/00.

124   *WrestleMania 1999* was not a career highlight for me. © 2001 World Wrestling Entertainment, Inc. All rights reserved. Photograph by Rich Freeda 3/28/99.

135   Tazz couldn't guarantee Jerry Seinfeld nothin'. © 2001 World Wrestling Entertainment, Inc. All rights reserved. Photograph by Tom Buchanan 1/23/00.

147   With Kane and Uncle Paul around the time of the Scranton situation. © 2001 World Wrestling Entertainment, Inc. All rights reserved. Photograph by David McLain 7/13/98.

160   Cactus Jack is back, for one night against Mideon, May 1999. © 2001 World Wrestling Entertainment, Inc. All rights reserved. Photograph by Rich Freeda 5/10/99.

164   With my dad at the Suffolk County Sports Hall of Fame. © 2001 World Wrestling Entertainment, Inc. All rights reserved. Photograph by John Giamundo 4/22/99.

174   One of my favorite photographs with Owen and Terry Funk in 1998. Courtesy of the author's collection.

250 Pete Gas, Rodney, and Joey Abs—the Posse.
Photograph by Rich Freeda 7/26/99.

267 Rock 'n' Sock mania was running wild following our first tag team title in August 1999. Photograph by Rich Freeda 8/30/99.

276 Rock—this is your life, September 1999. Photograph by Craig Melvin 9/27/99.

282 My first book signing, October 1999, New York City. Photograph by Rich Freeda 10/21/99.

289 The world's largest reading. My book had just hit the *New York Times* bestseller list. Photograph by Tom Buchanan 10/26/99.

306 Cheering up my buddy Al Snow after another humiliating loss, October 1999. Photograph by Tom Buchanan 11/15/99.

312 Reaching for Mr. Socko, October 1999. Photograph by Rich Freeda 10/17/00.

316 Enjoying some family time. Courtesy of the author's collection.

329 Al Snow in the "Kennel from Hell"—an all-time stinker in the wrestling industry. Photograph by Tom Buchanan 9/26/99.

336   Bob Holly, my conspirator in "The Legend of the Penis Suplex," November 1999. Photograph by Rich Freeda 4/2/00.

375   I used this photo as a visual aid for an Al Snow joke. Courtesy of the author's collection.

386   Test. Yes, I did print the goofiest photograph of him I could find. Photograph by Tom Buchanan 8/9/99.

392   My going-away present for the younger guys. Courtesy of the author's collection.

395   Hanging out with Bogus Mankind, Dennis Knight, at Universal Studios, January 2000. Photograph by Rich Freeda 1/4/00.

399   Bloodied but not beaten. Photograph by Tom Buchanan 1/10/00.

404   Pulling out all the stops at the *Royal Rumble*, January 2000. Photograph by Rich Freeda 1/23/00.

407   I lost the match but the *Royal Rumble* was a huge moral victory. Photograph by Rich Freeda 1/23/00.

418   Mr. McMahon and I have had our verbal confrontations in and out of the ring. Photograph by Vinny Pugliese 6/1/98.

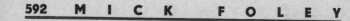